Race to the Finish

Race to the Finish

The Life and Times of
FRED ARCHER

AMANDA MURRAY

ROBSON
BOOKS

First published in Great Britain in 2003 by Robson Books,
The Chrysalis Building, Bramley Road, London W10 6SP

An imprint of Chrysalis Books Group plc

British Library Cataloguing in Publication Data
A catalogue record for this title is available from the British Library.

ISBN 1 86105 611 7

Typeset by SX Composing DTP, Rayleigh, Essex
Printed by Creative Print & Design (Wales), Ebbw Vale

Contents

Acknowledgements   vii

Preface   ix

Introduction   xi

1   The Formative Years   1

2   From Apprentice to First Jockey   19

3   The Owner, The Trainer and The Jockey   48

4   Age and Experience   76

5   Behind the Image   91

6   Fred and Helen Rose   124

7   Mixed Fortune   140

8   The Progress of a Champion Jockey   160

9   The Final Furlong   183

Epilogue   191

Fred Archer's Winners, 1869–86   205

Bibliography   267

Acknowledgements

My thanks go to all those people without whose assistance, enthusiasm and, above all, patience, this book would not have been possible. They have not only contributed to this project, but also to my understanding of the history of horseracing for which I shall always be grateful. My special thanks go first to Mr Eric Dunning of the Local History Society in Newmarket who kept in constant touch and brought me up to date with the latest articles detailing Fred's life; and second to the staff of the Humanities and Reference Section of Liverpool Central Library who made sure the microfiche and Internet were always available when I needed them and who must have got sick of the sight of me going in so often to use them!

In addition my thanks go to the staff of the Newspaper Library attached to the British Library; David Boyd in Berkshire; the Jockey Club; Christopher Jakes, Senior Librarian at Cambridge City Library; Judith Curthoys, Assistant Archivist at Christ Church College, Oxford University; National Archives, Dublin; Gloucestershire Record Office; Anthony Goodsell at Cambridge Central Library; John Gallimore, Company Secretary (now retired) of Weatherbys; Gill Gough, Assistant Archivist at Berkshire Record Office; Mrs P Hatfield, College Archivist at Eton College, Berkshire; Mr Troke and Stephen Ellison, Archivists at the House of Lords Record Office; Chris Hammond, Birmingham; Lord John Oaksey; Jeremy Richardson of the Injured Jockeys Fund; Maghull Public Library; Graham Snelling, Curator of the

National Horseracing Museum; Public Record Office, London; Doug Marks in Lambourn; John Penfold, Lambourn Archivist; Pamela Clark, Deputy Registrar at the Royal Archives, Windsor Castle; R E and G B Way in Newmarket; York Racing Museum and Library.

My thanks go to Fred Archer's descendants – in particular his great-grandson, Alex Tosetti, who provided me with a detailed account of his family background as well as unstinting support and enthusiasm, and who, at the eleventh hour, was able to provide the Preface which opens this book. I would also like to thank all my friends, past and present, who have worked with me at Dale Street and Tithebarn House for their interest and encouragement, and in particular Bill Parker who said that since I was such a good writer I could write his work performance review. In addition, my thanks go to my editor, Jennifer Lansbury, to Melanie Letts and my publisher, Jeremy Robson.

Last, but not least to all of my family – in both England and Israel – who provided me with the encouragement to see this through.

Amanda Murray

Preface

It is a great pleasure to write this preface for Amanda Murray. My great-grandfather, Fred Archer, was arguably one of Britain's very first sporting heroes. A remarkable jockey of the late nineteenth century, he averaged one win in every three rides during a short seventeen-year career – an unparalleled achievement. He won thirteen jockey Championships, rode 2,748 winners and amassed 21 Classic races including the Derby five times. Fred was an exceptional professional, but being tall he suffered constant physical wasting to keep his weight down, and endured a racing schedule of unbelievable pressure. He never had the benefit of the variety of transport options to get to race meetings that jockeys enjoy today. Fred had such a ruthless and burning ambition to win that he exceeded 200 winners each season for half of his career.

Every time I go racing the hairs stand up on the back of my neck as I try to recall what the crowd murmurings would have been some 120 years ago. 'The Tinman has arrived. Look, Archer's up,' the crowd would roar. He was idolised and public expectations would have been immense, as he rode for the Prince of Wales, Lord Falmouth, Lord and Lady Hastings, the Duchess of Montrose and the Duke of Westminster, to name but a few.

It is sad to contemplate the particular pressure on these rare few, such as Archer, whose achievement and sporting heroism in such glamorous Victorian times became public property to the point of fatal persecution. It was a tragic twist that shook the racing world when Fred Archer shot himself at his home in Newmarket in a fit of delirium during a sudden illness. He was 29 and at the peak of his career. The public dismay that greeted his suicide by all accounts must have been similar to the reaction to the news of the sudden death of Princess Diana in 1997. *The Times* observed that 'hardly anything could cause a more widespread and painful sensation . . . The news of his death has come with a sense of shock and almost personal loss to millions.'

Fred had a harrowing personal life, which he kept very private and which undoubtedly contributed to his depression in those latter years. He adored his wife, Helen Rose, the niece of his trainer, Mathew Dawson. She died giving birth to their daughter, Nellie Rose, some two years before Fred's suicide. Their child, orphaned so young, was brought up by her Dawson grandparents; she eventually married a 'Tosetti' and never continued the racing instinct.

My great-grandfather was a legend and should be remembered for his formidable achievements set against tragic personal circumstances. On behalf of the family, I welcome this biography.

Alex Tosetti
March 2003

Introduction

On the cold, wet Friday of 12 November 1886, the horseracing centre of Newmarket in Suffolk was literally shut down as the residents prepared for what was probably the saddest event for thirteen years in the town and certainly the most public. Shops were closed and blinds were drawn out of respect, and the local populace lined the streets. There were also visitors from different parts of the country comprising representatives of Royalty, members of the aristocracy, sportsmen and journalists, as well as just ordinary people who wanted to pay a final tribute to a young widower called Frederick James Archer.

Known by everybody, rich and poor, simply as Fred, he had been a quiet, unassuming man whose suicide on 8 November had been met, at first, with disbelief. 'The rumour was discredited,' the *Newmarket Journal* recorded, 'but when enquiry had proved it to be only [too] true . . . the news spread like wildfire and furnished an absorbing topic for discussion and comment on all sides.'

Fred Archer had not been a member of the aristocracy, nor a politician. He had not been a soldier, nor a celebrated explorer or a great writer. He had not, indeed, been destined for any of these things and had come from a humble background, yet the top national newspapers of the day, as well as local newspapers, paid tribute to him in a way usually reserved for those of a higher status.

He had not even been born in Newmarket but the people there considered him as one of their own. To them, he was a local hero; to the country as a whole, he was a national hero and, given his achievements abroad and the fact that his name was well known in Europe and America, he had also acquired international status, even if he had not altogether achieved international respect. He was one of England's most talented sportsmen, a jockey who took the sport of horseracing and pushed it beyond its limits, creating a higher standard and achieving records that would remain unbroken for decades after his death; but what people saw on Friday 12 November 1886, was the funeral of a young man who had achieved fame and fortune, but had suffered great personal tragedy and was now dead at the age of 29.

For some of his family and friends his death was too much to bear. Fred's father, William Archer, himself a former jockey, could not attend the funeral service, being unable to face the burial of a second son in eight years. He remained behind at Fred's home – Falmouth House. A former close friend of Fred, a Captain Machell, was too wracked with guilt to attend, having disowned him just days before the jockey's death. But Newmarket played host to virtually everyone else who had been closely associated with the young man and shared in their mutual grief. 'A great incubus of sorrow seemed to overshadow the place,' reported the *Newmarket Journal*.

By the early afternoon the general public lined the route from Falmouth House to Newmarket Cemetery and no-one was put off by the bad weather which threatened rain. They waited patiently for the procession to start and just before 2 p.m. a bell tolled in All Saints' Church, signalling that the service was about to begin and the mourners gathering along the route became quiet.

At Falmouth House the invited mourners and family members prepared themselves. Fred's coffin had been placed inside the waiting hearse, which was already filled to capacity with flowers, almost hiding the coffin from view. So great were the numbers of flowers that several carriages had to be laid on.

Fred's only surviving brother, Charlie, travelled in the first private carriage with an uncle and his nephew, Frederick Charles Pratt, a young boy who had lived with Fred and his wife for two years until 1884. Fred's father-in-law, John Dawson and two brothers-in-law then followed behind; and behind them came other mourners, including Fred's closest friend – Captain Bowling. Even more distinguished mourners included Lord Grosvenor, who represented his father the Duke of Westminster. He travelled with Lord Alington who presented the wreath from the Prince of Wales but who also came as a personal friend. Fred's first retainer and friend, Viscount Falmouth was represented by his son and a Mr Evans represented one of Fred's greatest female admirers – the Duchess of Montrose. According to the *Newmarket Journal*, others were prevented from going through illness: Captain Machell, the jockey Tom Cannon and the trainer Robert Peck. There were, quite literally, hundreds of mourners (each one listed in the *Newmarket Journal* in its reports of the funeral) and it became obvious that there was no room inside the church for all of them, so they overflowed into the churchyard.

The burial service was conducted by the Reverend E H Littlewood, Vicar of All Saints', Newmarket, and he was assisted by Fred's childhood friend, the Reverend Bagshot de la Bere (now of Brighton, the *Newmarket Journal* noted, but formerly the Vicar of Prestbury, the place where Fred spent much of his childhood).

When the service was over, Fred's coffin was taken from the church to the cemetery where his wife and infant son were buried. He was laid to rest beside them and the *Newmarket Journal*, determined to pinpoint every single detail of the scene, described the grave for many of its readers: '9ft deep, bricked up for a distance of 2ft, from the bottom with white bricks, 8ft long and 3ft wide; the sides were lined with evergreens and decorated with white chrysanthemums, so that the earth was entirely hidden from view.'

People began filing past. As the *Newmarket Journal* noted on Sunday 14 November, it was an event unique in the history of Newmarket and in the lives of all those who had known Fred and had followed his career, and its like would not be witnessed again. 'Several hundreds of persons visited the cemetery, attracted by a sight such as they may possibly never have an opportunity of seeing again.'

The importance of Fred's position was emphasised by the fact that 'the wreath sent by the Prince of Wales was judiciously placed where it could be seen and admired by all' – proof that although Fred was employed by the highest personages in the land, he had also earned their respect; but the most poignant tribute came from someone closer to home – a large bunch of violets, sent on behalf of his daughter, Nellie Rose, with the inscription: 'With baby's fondest love to her father.'

The elaborately Victorian funeral sermon (quoted in full in the *Newmarket Journal*) was read out to a small gathering of mourners in the chapel – family members, the Falmouth House household and also the Duke of Rutland – and begged the question: 'What combination of circumstances have gathered themselves together against thee and carried thee to an early grave?' It then added a warning message – one which seemed to answer the question direct: 'Even the youthful student, in the ardour of his aspirations, may overtax his immature strength, and ere yet his vessel has set sail make shipwreck of the possibilities of life . . . there is needed on all sides a lesson of prudence and caution.'

The 'lesson of prudence and caution' was one that Fred Archer was unable to understand and his life, filled with complexity, was that of a man trying to balance the demands of ambition against the trials and tribulations of success. He was liked, admired and loved, yet also feared, even hated. He could be gracious, brilliant, a perfect gentleman and the most generous of friends, but he also had a ruthless streak and could be reckless. He was a man of honesty and integrity, yet he came under scrutiny and was sometimes regarded with suspicion. He was uneducated, yet he was a man known for his superior intelligence who could outwit, outmanoeuvre and generally outclass anyone or anything.

Women adored Fred and he caught the attention of a duchess, but he loved only one woman. He had friends in high places. On his death the Prince of Wales (the future Edward VII) wanted as much information as possible about his final days, and a member of the aristocracy, the Honourable George Lambton – one of England's finest trainers – would devote part of his autobiography *Men and Horses I Have Known* (1924), to the young jockey's career. 'I was in Liverpool when the news came,' he wrote. 'It was a terrible blow to me . . . He certainly was the most attractive figure that I have ever come across on the racecourse.'

Loved by the press and public, everything Fred Archer did was followed with interest by all the national and local newspapers of the day. During his career lasting just seventeen years from 1869 to 1886, he rode over 8,000 races and won almost 3,000. He was Champion Jockey for twelve years and became a partner of one of the most prestigious stables in the country. He amassed a personal fortune and, although being a gambler, was shrewd with money, earning himself the nickname 'The Tinman'. He approached horseracing as if it were a science, won races against impossible odds and broke records. He even helped the Americans to snatch the coveted Blue Riband in English racing by winning the Derby on an American-owned horse.

He was, in his day, almost unbeatable, but if he was ruthless with others, he was also ruthless with himself and placed so much pressure on his mind and body that in the end his final illness proved too much. He had already suffered a double tragedy in his life in the space of two years. Although he was a close family man, his daughter, almost from the moment of her birth, was cared for by her maternal grandparents.

Fred Archer was a man of contradictions, unable to relax with the adulation his success inspired. He tried to remain true to himself, but people saw different sides to him, different personas and, in turn, many approached him with respect, wonder, disbelief, exasperation, intolerance and hero worship.

This book is a study of a man who pushed himself beyond limits and took horseracing to new heights only to find that he was in a race against the one thing he could not beat – himself. Fred Archer was a great celebrity in his day and I have attempted to do justice to the wealth of written information which exists. By piecing together all the races in which he took part between 1869 and 1886, I was able to gain a much wider perspective on his career as a jockey, the highs and the lows, and how his life affected his work. As well as consulting the many books and archive records listed on pages 267–9 of this book, I have also studied the vast range of national and local newspapers that followed his career from his first days as a jockey to the aftermath of his death and which even today still examine his life and times. These have been invaluable in providing first-hand accounts, contemporary viewpoints and analysis as well as giving a colourful picture of horseracing in the nineteenth century.

Complementing these are the autobiographies of the people who knew Fred Archer personally, which either confirm or dispute the newspaper articles about him. Harry Custance, the Duke of Portland, Sir John Astley, Sir George Chetwynd and the Honourable George Lambton left invaluable records. These have provided individual perceptions of Fred as a jockey, friend and associate. I have also used more recent biographies in my research, in particular, Edith M Humphris' *The Life of Fred Archer* (1923), an account which depends in part upon the memories and recollections of many of Fred's relations, friends and colleagues. In the course of her investigations into Fred's life, she met a great number of them, but in particular she knew his sister, Mrs Alice Pratt, who provided many fascinating details about Fred as a child and what he was like as an adult. My thanks also go to the writer of the most comprehensive account of Fred's career – John Welcome who wrote *Fred Archer: A Complete Study* in 1967.

I have tried to achieve a balance between Fred the man and Fred the jockey – not an easy task since he could not separate his private life from his work, but I hope I have gone some way to contributing a greater understanding of the sportsman and the era in which he lived.

The Formative Years

Fred did not have the most auspicious of beginnings, nor did he come from a long line of jockeys and trainers like some of his acquaintances. He was the fourth child and second son of a steeplechase jockey, William Archer, and his wife Emma. Fred was born on 11 January 1857 at St George's Cottages, St George's Place in Cheltenham[1] – the family home since the days of his paternal grandfather, another William Archer. But the Archers were not there for very long, moving to Cintra House in nearby Prestbury where the baby was christened Frederick James on 12 April.

Even residence here was short-lived. Before his second birthday Fred and his family were back at St George's, only to return again to Prestbury in 1860! This time the family settled there permanently, although Fred would remain only for the next nine years growing up with his siblings: Emily (born around 1850 or 1851); William Hayward (born 1853); Alice Elizabeth (born 1856); and Charles Edward (born 22 December 1858).[2]

From the very start horseracing played an active part in Fred's life and he was surrounded by people who talked of nothing but racing both past and present. He had a specific role model in his father, who had known success many times in the 22 years or so that he had been a steeplechase jockey, although by the time Fred was three years old, William Archer had almost retired from racing.

William, born on 1 January 1826, had left home at the age of eleven to pursue his ambition as a jockey. Until the age of seventeen, he rode in steeplechases in various parts of the country, initially at Elmstone Hardwicke, near Cheltenham, then on to the Midlands, Warwickshire and Staffordshire.[3] In May 1843, he was offered a unique change in career for one so young and the seventeen-year-old jockey, accompanied by a hundred thoroughbreds, found himself travelling to St Petersburg, Russia to manage the stud of Tsar Nicholas I.[4] This was actually located just outside St Petersburg, at the Imperial residence, Tsarskoe Selo (Tsar's Village). William would perhaps have remained in the Tsar's service for several years had it not been for Russia's notorious winters. The temperatures, which could fall from $-20°$ to $-40°$,[5] got the better of him and in the autumn of 1844 he returned to England, arriving at St Catherine's Dock in Gravesend and bringing with him some very valuable knowledge of riding, which he was anxious to put into practice. He quickly re-established old contacts and made new ones, so that over the next few years he rode for personages such as the Earl of Strathmore and Prince Baratsky.[6]

William Archer rode well, worked hard and built up a favourable reputation once more as a steeplechase jockey. In 1847 he returned to his home in Cheltenham and came second in the Grand Annual Steeplechase there.[7] Five years later, on 12 April 1852, he rode Tipperary Boy to victory in the Grand Midland Steeplechase. Then on 6 March 1858 he rode Little Charley in Aintree's Grand National, reputed even then to be the most dangerous race in the world, but that year it was fraught with additional danger in the form of high winds, blizzards and temperatures below freezing.[8] This made the course almost impossible and merely completing it would have been a feat in itself. So bad were the conditions that many of the runners were withdrawn, including some of the favourites, so that there were only sixteen runners left – William Archer and Little Charley among them standing at 100 to 1.[9] If he returned to his young family a hero, it was because he had not only negotiated the course but survived it, and he is remembered for it today even if the horse he rode did drift into obscurity.

The Grand National was the last significant event of a career lasting 21 years, and, although William Archer would continue to ride until 1862, his first priority was now his small family and providing for them. Racing had been good to him financially and they were comfortable, but he could not race forever and the Archer family needed something more secure.

William had first met Fred's mother sometime between 1847 and 1848. Emma Hayward was the beautiful, aristocratic-looking daughter of William Hayward – the landlord of the King's Arms in Prestbury[10] and the churchwarden of the local church. Emma was not only beautiful but also educated – a complete contrast to her husband who, at times, took pride in not having had much schooling and was, in addition, rough and ready in his demeanour. According to their younger daughter, Alice, Emma was tall and dark with an almost oriental type of beauty. A sketch of her, which was in the possession of Alice's daughter Emmie, revealed a refinement and gentility about her.[11]

William and Emma were married on 13 February 1849 but did not really settle down until 1860. Emma's father died and her husband became the landlord of the King's Arms in Prestbury. Far more spacious than St George's Cottages, the King's Arms was ideal for bringing up five growing children. Fred and Charlie, aged three and two respectively, were too young to remember their first home in Cheltenham. The King's Arms was quietly situated not far from the church and, being over 400 years old at the time when the Archers moved in, remained one of the landmarks of Prestbury. Fred's mother had been born there, growing up in the village and attending school nearby, so for her, especially, it must have felt like returning home. Fred's sister, Alice, who retained a fondness for the place well into old age, told her brother's biographer, Edith M Humphris, how the King's Arms, a beautiful building with white walls and black oak beams, had an old-world appearance as though it were trapped in time. She described it as being old-fashioned, but hinted at it being untouched and unspoilt, expressing disappointment at the fact that the village as a whole had succumbed to the noise and clamour of modern transport in the decades since she and her family had lived there.[12]

The King's Arms was the centre of village life and had a smoke room which was the equivalent of a club with all the existing social strictures, catering solely for the squire, the parson, the doctor, the lawyer and tradesmen. The smoke room was the exclusive domain of the gentry at the time and everyone else had to make do with the tap room downstairs. However, one regular – a former jockey by the name of John Cheswas – used to annoy William Archer by sitting in the smoke room instead of mingling with his own class downstairs. There was nothing William could actually do about it, despite having plenty to say, and John Cheswas, ignoring all conventions, did not take himself downstairs where he belonged and continued to mix with his betters in the smoke room upstairs.[13]

What appears to be such a trivial detail actually contributes to a much wider social picture, revealing the status of jockeys at that time and, more interestingly, William Archer's attitude to that status and his annoyance at John's crossing of boundaries and getting above himself, particularly in the presence of other more 'professional figures' with 'standing', even in a small village like Prestbury. It would perhaps have been one of the first indications to Fred of the social differences between 'the professional', 'the gentry' and 'the sportsman' and of how society regarded each. Certainly it was a difference that would dominate his own life and career, but he would also have been aware of the esteem in which sportsmen – and jockeys in particular – were held. They were classed as heroes of a sort. Some of these tough, hardened characters had seen battle during the Napoleonic Wars[14] or come from such poverty that sheer will and determination had driven them on to succeed. These would have been the men Fred would have been encouraged to aspire to and one such character, by the name of Tom Olliver, used to visit the King's Arms.

He was an old friend of William Archer and had been his best man at his wedding. A three-times winner of the Aintree Grand National, in his retirement he turned his hand to training, both in horseracing and boxing.[15] A true genius in his field, he was renowned for being able to ride anything over anything. He was also known for constantly getting into fights, owing money, ending up in gaol and not remembering how his own surname was spelt.[16] However, his was the kind of success story that William Archer understood and one that would serve as an example to Fred of how to get on in life with nothing but sheer talent and will power. Tom Olliver was an example of someone who could fly in the face of convention, live and fight as he pleased, and return home his own master with his own income and only himself to answer to.

Unfortunately this was only on the surface. Such tough, rough and ready, yet talented jockeys as Tom Olliver and William Archer were seen as servants by those people – the professional, the gentry, the aristocracy and Royalty – for whom they rode and upon whose patronage they depended.[17] No amount of success could alter that, particularly when, despite their own personal popularity, jockeys were for the most part identified only by the colours adopted by those patrons. But whatever the reality, William Archer, Fred and his brothers entered a world which was totally removed from any other open to them – one which provided excitement, entertainment and a certain standing in life which, unless you were highborn, could seldom be achieved elsewhere. The children were captivated by such prospects and certainly the boys, who sought to emulate their father and Tom Olliver almost as soon as they could walk, were encouraged by their father to ride. Nor were they afraid to try, especially Fred who, from an early age, was very much at ease around horses and displayed a flair for sportsmanship which his father was anxious to develop.

The Archers were well-known and popular members of the community.[18] The children in particular were very well known around the village of Prestbury. Fred's sister, Alice, remembered how all five of them would wander about with a donkey in tow.[19]

William and Emma Archer ran the King's Arms between them. William took care of the day-to-day running of the place and Emma dealt with the paperwork and wrote her husband's letters. They were not a demonstrative couple, but William was genuinely fond of his wife, despite their vastly different temperaments. He was hot-tempered; she was placid. He was rugged and down to earth; she was gracious and genteel. She was also the apple of her husband's eye and he was inordinately proud of her.[20]

Neither seem to have been very strict parents, given that the mid-nineteenth century was renowned for encouraging parental discipline in the home. Fred Archer's early home life appears to have been supremely happy. Encouraged to ride, he and his brothers were also urged to box which was one of the great national sports of its day. One famed boxer, John Gully, had become a Member of Parliament and Jockey Club Steward, a clear example of how far one could get in sport – even in the nineteenth century. Alice remembered the sparring matches between the two younger boys, Fred and Charlie, which took place in the club room of the King's Arms, to the delight of the rest of the neighbourhood which used to come and watch. According to Alice, the two boys would box according to the rules until they lost their tempers – and, to all intents and purposes, forgot fair play which would have been an added bonus to the spectators.[21]

Fred, who was by no means pugnacious, was showing signs of competitiveness which would dominate his life, but at such a young age he did not like to lose and neither, it seems, did his younger brother Charlie, who could certainly hold his own against Fred when he had to. Being just under two years apart in age, Fred and Charlie perhaps had more in common with each other than with their older brother William.

Known as Billy to friends and family, he was gentler and perhaps less competitive than his two brothers, although he may not have wished to compete against two boys who were respectively four and five years younger than he was. The local residents remembered him as being kind-hearted and generous, but although Alice described both Charles and Fred to Edith M Humphris, she had very little to say about brother William.[22] Even so, the Archer children were extremely close and it was a unity which brought out the best in young Fred who would always remain close and at ease with his family to whom he was naturally affectionate.

Fred was what people of today would call 'bubbly'; a pleasant, outgoing little boy who was described by an old acquaintance as something of a chatterbox. He loved his home village and was at ease with the people who lived there. In fact, despite a certain degree of shyness, he was used to having people about him, particularly adults. Nor did he mind the presence of an audience when he was involved in boxing matches with Charlie – even if the competitiveness was taken a bit too far and the two boys had to be prised apart. It was well known how fascinated Fred was by horses, and the villagers indulged him and his energetic enthusiasm for wanting to learn to ride. If he was not using his mother's brother as an impromptu horse,[23] he was persuading his father's acquaintances to let him ride their horses, often clambering on to their backs regardless of safety. Having a natural affinity with them, like his father and two brothers, it was an interest which seemed to increase as he grew older. His father's confidence had certainly rubbed off on to him and William Archer was quite happy to allow his young son to develop what skills he had while at the same time enjoying his childhood.

Fred was happy, confident and possessed a charm which people would remember for years afterwards. In fact he seemed to be all things to all members of his family – a promising horseman in his father's eyes; gentle and pleasant like his elder brother Billy; he had the potential of being a hero in the eyes of his sisters; and could easily stand up to his brother Charlie in fights. Of the whole family, he was the most emotional, very sensitive and, as will be seen later, insecure – particularly without his family around him; but surrounded by the fascinating personalities who visited his father and talked about nothing but racing, he never had any trouble in making friends or persuading people to bend to his wishes. He was sometimes seen heading off in the direction of Bushcombe Hill where his father's coachman, Wilcox, lived.[24] There, Wilcox could always be persuaded by the little boy to set up the jumps so that he could practise going over them.

By the age of seven Fred was already quite accomplished and if a career in racing was what he wanted, then his father was only too happy to oblige him. William may have retired from racing, but he had never lost his own ambition which was now concentrated in all of his sons, especially Fred. When it came to the boy's education, it was a different matter altogether and it was just as difficult getting him to go to school as it was to get him out of the saddle.

Unaware at the time of any problems he could be creating for himself in the future, Fred's education – or lack of it – was perhaps the one aspect of his life about which his parents disagreed and one which would overshadow his progress later. Ironically it was the one person who encouraged him the most, his father, who was to blame for his lack of interest in school, particularly since William himself used to boast to his family and friends alike that he had had only two days' learning in his entire life.[25] His daughter Alice thought that was something of an exaggeration, but what was true was that he had very little time for education in general, so the importance of being able to read and write was not, in those early years, understood by Fred.

His father was so blasé about schooling as a whole that it would have been very difficult for the little boy, with horses on his mind, to take it seriously either, despite his mother's concerns. She was genuinely concerned that not going to school would do Fred more harm than good and she constantly argued the point with her husband that opportunities were being wasted. Being educated herself and having a greater insight into the importance of learning, she found it almost impossible to convince her husband of the benefits Fred could acquire in later life, but William understood the world more than he understood books. From what Alice told Edith M Humphris, it seems that her mother had problems trying to persuade her father of the possible harm that could result from Fred not being properly educated.[26]

William in turn became increasingly annoyed over the matter and told his wife to leave the boy alone – an indication that perhaps she not only argued with her husband, but also scolded her son for not attending school – pointing out that he would make more money through being a jockey than as a scholar. His argument stemmed from the fact that racing had been his only interest all his life and revealed a short-sightedness that he could not see his wife's point of view on the matter. Friends of the Archers, however, saw what an opportunity had been missed – even in the case of William, who was always judged as a shrewd and astute individual.

A friend of William, a Mr Edwards and his son (who later took the name De La Bere) in particular enjoyed talking to him and the Edwards boy became great friends with Fred and his brothers. It was Mr Edwards who declared that, had William had a decent education and not become a jockey, he would have been a great man in some field or other,[27] but Archer felt that he had acquired enough personal fame and prosperity over the years to enable him and his family to live comfortably. Security had been his prime concern; his chosen career had provided that and it amused him to think that he had done it all without any formal learning, pointing out a word or phrase (usually about racing) in a newspaper which his wife, for all her education, could not understand. He followed racing avidly in *Bell's Life*, which appeared in Prestbury once a week costing sixpence. He would shut himself up for hours with his paper before allowing the rest of the neighbourhood to read it. He would then cut out the most interesting racing articles and preserve them, but by the time Alice disclosed this to her brother's biographer, over fifty years later, the collection had long since been destroyed, having been left in a damp kitchen to turn into pulp and become illegible.[28]

Having an instinct for racing and all the technicalities associated with it, William did not see how education could benefit his three boys when all of them could become equally successful, if not more so, as jockeys. He believed that Billy, Fred and Charlie could manage well enough without books, but Emma was shrewd enough to see the wider picture.

Fred was naturally intelligent. His expertise at riding pointed to the fact that he was not only a quick learner, but was capable of teaching himself. He had a mental energy which, if channelled in other directions, could take him further than a racecourse. He could focus, directing his attention on to anything that took his interest, and he liked the challenge of learning. Racing might lead to fame and fortune, but it was not the most secure direction in life. William Archer had had to start from scratch and work his way up, relying upon the patronage of others, whereas education would give his son a head start in life and he would be his own man. A jockey had no true status in society; education could open doors. Education meant security for the long-term future. William had retired from racing at the age of 36 and although he had his own enterprises and the King's Arms, within a few short years he and his family would not be quite so well off.

Despite all her arguments Emma could not persuade William that Fred needed more in life than an ability to ride, but even though the idea of education as a backup was not taken too seriously either, William did finally, perhaps under increasing pressure from his wife, send all his children to school. Alice and her older sister Emily attended the same establishment their mother had attended when she was a girl. Fred, for a while, was at Mr Cox's school in Cheltenham, then at Hygeia House which stood opposite the King's Arms. Charlie attended with him, but as riding and boxing became more of a priority in their lives, so academic lessons began to taper off – especially in the case of Fred who, although quite bright and intelligent, lacked the interest and the motivation to continue his lessons. At one point, he was only attending school two days a week, so that his reading and writing skills suffered as a result. This was something he would always regret in adulthood, when it appears that although, according to Alice, he could write reasonably well when he had to, he usually asked other people to write letters on his behalf.

As a child Fred appears to have thought very little of playing truant from school. Since his father tended to jump to his defence whenever his mother expressed her concerns, he seemed quite happy to spend every available minute in the saddle, particularly as he had proved that he could win races and it was now taken for granted that he would be a jockey.[29]

He had already ridden his first race at the age of eight in Prestbury. As proof of his dedication to ride well, he had dressed smartly for the occasion and, for his age, professionally, with new breeches and colours with a top coat.[30] It was a precocious attitude but one for which he would always be remembered. All the best jockeys of the past had dressed well – Frank Buckle and Jem Mason included[31] – and for his part Fred was learning early on that appearance, the idea of making a first favourable impression, was important although of course it did not help you to win as he found out. Despite his best efforts, he lost on a course which was twice round an orchard at the back of an inn, The Plough, and twice over a small brook.[32] Fred was reported to have ridden well on his pony, but the donkey he was riding against won by a neck.

Ironically, his first win was in a donkey race with three runners – Fred on Southern Lass and two others on Penarth and Peter Simple. It was run in a small paddock and the prize was a new bridle. Charlie recalled the race, years after his brother's death, to a friend and recounted that his father William had a wager of a fiver – a real show of confidence in his son's ability if ever there was one. It was a half-mile race, ending by the donkey's stable door and Fred won it with his father, ever convinced that his son had the makings of a jockey, walking away with his winnings.[33]

It seems that Fred's confidence was gaining by the day. Developing into a competent horseman, he had no qualms about riding against men on hunters, and he frequently rode with the hounds over the Cotswold Hills. When William Archer had first taken over the King's Arms, he had come out hunting on a cob with Fred and Charlie on ponies, so as time passed Fred's potential had been acknowledged and recognised then, even if it was just locally. His modest career was temporarily cut short when he suffered an accident and broke his leg.

Even this physical injury did not put him off and he resumed his riding as if nothing had happened, happily taking part in a country meeting near Naunton Inn.[34] It was an episode in his life which characterised his devotion to his chosen sport and one which was hardening his resolve to do better. It also reveals William Archer's attitude – he had no intention of wrapping his son up in cotton wool and the accident may have served as proof to him that Fred was serious about becoming a jockey. In fact accidents which could have killed the boy only made him more determined and, despite his mother's arguments over his lack of education, his father did not hesitate to encourage his son's talent,[35] knowing that he had the stamina to take the knocks the sport would inevitably throw at him in later years. In order to give his son as much practice as possible, he bought Fred a dun-coloured pony, known as Moss Rose.[36]

Fred was now ten years old, a bright, good-looking boy, dark like his mother, with large inquisitive eyes. Edith M Humphris was told that his eyes were grey, but portraits painted of him in later years suggest that they may have been blue. His top teeth protruded very slightly and, rather than detracting from his looks, they gave him a gentle charm. He had long, angular features and if the resemblance with his mother continued into adulthood, he would be a very tall young man. His appearance as a gentle and shy little boy belied the fact that he was extremely tough, but in a quiet, unobtrusive way. He was not like his father – in fact they were like chalk and cheese and horses were all that they had in common.

Fred was delighted with his new pony and the two became inseparable. Standing at just over 12 hands, Moss Rose proved to be at her best when running to hounds, but she was not always the most reliable of animals, particularly in races when she had a tendency to jump the rails, taking Fred with her.[37] However, Fred had the measure of her, turned the pony about and, jumping the rails, continued on the course – again as if nothing had happened. His dogged determination, lack of fear and faith in his own skill had a lot to do with his father's teaching methods.

Biographers would stress how much William depended on Fred's generosity in later years and how his son was always sending cheques home to pay for bills, but the foundation of Fred's success had been formed, partly, by his father's own experience. William had gone as far as he could go in his own career – if his sons could go further, he would see to it that they had the chance. If they had the talent, he was not going to let them waste it. Once he recognised that Fred had a gift for horsemanship above and beyond anything he had ever known in his own career, he resolved to teach his son what he knew, tapping into Fred's innate ability and being intent upon pushing the young, impressionable boy to the limit and beyond if necessary. There was far more for him to learn than just how to ride in a race.

William Archer was never quick to praise his son's efforts. In his whole life he would only ever speak his mind, whether for good or bad, and if his son needed a measure of bullying, then so be it. Racing was a harsh life and the sooner Fred realised this, the better. If the ambition was there, it had to be instilled into him until it became second nature and in teaching his son, William Archer found it almost necessary to reinvent him.

The boy had to be prepared for a world that, if he remained soft-hearted, would not tolerate him. William Archer probably understood his son better than anyone and it was clearly evident that Fred needed toughening up, both physically and emotionally. He needed to learn how to control the horse. He needed total confidence, to know how to fight back and boxing matches were ideal for this. As well as being an excellent character builder, they would also ensure the strengthening of the muscles and reflexes needed to control a horse.

William also taught Fred about the rigours of competition, not friendly competition as he was used to at home, but real competition against jockeys who had been riding for twenty or thirty years. William made it clear from the very beginning that the last thing Fred needed to fear was staying on the horse.

These lessons attracted the attention of the local villagers who would watch as William put Fred through his paces. Various acquaintances of the Archers recalled how hard William could be on his son, telling Edith M Humphris how he would grab all the grass and turf he could lay his hands on and, by way of encouragement, fling the lot at his son – meanwhile turning the air blue with his language.[38] Nor was he concerned about the presence of others, watching fascinated on the sidelines, but the spectators must have felt sorry for Fred, despite knowing that if anything was capable of putting the fear of God into him, it was certainly not going to be the pony he was riding.

It may have been harsh treatment, but William was providing his son with a glimpse of what horseracing could really be like. He himself had had to adjust to a sport which was unruly, often corrupt and dangerous.[39] Now, years later, the sport, while being more disciplined, could still be corrupt and certainly dangerous,[40] so Fred had to be both competitive and competent enough to be able to cope with danger and the fear of it. He had to be able to control his emotions and not allow them to influence his work. Riding was one thing, but competing in races for the highest stakes was altogether different.

William wanted his son to be in control of his mount's every move and to ride the animal as if he had literally been born in the saddle. Relying, therefore, on his own extensive knowledge and experience, he continued to instruct Fred, being at his worst so that his son could be at his best when confronted by some of the toughest personalities on the turf. He forced him to concentrate on the movements of his horse and to improve his ability to handle those movements. Fred learnt control and how to rise above distractions until riding was not just a case of getting into the saddle and hoping for the best, but second nature – going out to races knowing that he could win. This is what his father wanted. It says a great deal about William Archer that, from an early age, he had been prepared to travel anywhere in the country to establish his reputation – another lesson that Fred had to learn. Though he might receive help from some quarters, he would always be responsible for his own success, how he achieved it and how far he wanted it to go.

From the garden of the King's Arms, lessons moved on to Prestbury Park racecourse where the same regime continued to the extent where Fred did not relish defeat. When he lost his first race, he returned home in tears,[41] although whether through losing or fear of what his father would say is not certain, but he made sure that he won his next race and from then onwards and in fact throughout his career, it was clear that he would not tolerate losing.

William Archer was a role model first by example and then in practice who succeeded, to a certain extent, in knocking some of the sensitivity out of his son and replacing it with a more emboldened spirit. Certainly Fred possessed the motivation to win and wanted to be the best. He had unlimited energy and although his mother still objected, she did not directly interfere with William teaching their son.

Cross-country riding also provided him with invaluable experience and, with his two brothers, he rode in the district meets of the Cotswold Hounds. He would later be described as being one of the worst riders to hounds ever seen,[42] but it would not be through lack of experience. In fact hunting from such an early age would have provided Fred and his brothers with the preparation needed for racing, both on the flat and in steeple-chases. They would also have been in the company of boys of their own age, who would have provided Fred and his brothers with the peer pressure needed to encourage their sense of competition. While Fred was toughening up and proving his worth, his sensitivity remained despite his father's attempts to work it out of him. Fred learnt, at an early age, to mask it.

By the late 1860s the Archer family had fallen into financial difficulties. Alice remembered that whereas her father was a competent business man, he had never seen the need for savings and neither had his wife.[43] William had made a lot of money, consistently, throughout his career as a jockey, but once that was over, he lost the security money had afforded him and his family. Now he found himself in a financial dilemma – 'under the weather' was how Alice described it – and their situation seemed to justify Emma Archer's fears for Fred's lack of education. Having both lived comfortably for the best part of their lives, neither of them were happy to find that their finances were at such a low ebb. They would have to adjust, but they were also very proud, particularly William. When it was suggested that because of his former career as a jockey *Bell's Life* set up a subscription, a financial appeal, for him, he refused.[44] Instead Alice had to leave school early (her sister had already completed her education) and so from the age of eleven she missed out on some of her education which was a terrible disappointment for her.

Trade began to fall at the King's Arms and William became hard-pressed. It was at this time that his sons began leaving home to become apprentice jockeys. Young Billy was a steeplechase jockey like his father; Charlie was sent to William Reed's stable; and Fred was recommended elsewhere after an acquaintance of his father, Dick La Terriere, met him with his father by chance one day and asked if he was serious about racing. On being told that he was, La Terriere contacted a Newmarket trainer called Mathew Dawson. Within a few days Dawson had responded, agreeing to take the boy as an apprentice. With no time to feel nervous about leaving home, Fred accompanied his father to Newmarket.[45]

Notes

1. Humphris, Edith M, *The Life of Fred Archer*, p.2
2. Details courtesy of Alex Tosetti
3. Humphris, *The Life of Fred Archer*, p.22
4. Massie, Suzanne, *The Beauty of Old Russia: Land of the Firebird*, pp.123–48, 337
5. Harthausen, August von, ed., *Studies on the Interior of Russia*, p.224
6. Humphris, *The Life of Fred Archer*, p.23
7. *Bell's Life*, 18 April 1852
8. *Bell's Life*, 7 March 1858
9. Green, Reg, *The History of the Grand National*, pp.51–2
10. Humphris, *The Life of Fred Archer*, p.25
11. Ibid, p.30
12. Ibid, p.34
13. Ibid, p.36
14–16. Longrigg, Roger, *The History of Horseracing*, p.161
17. Lambton, The Honourable George, *Men and Horses I Have Known*, p.74
18. Humphris, *The Life of Fred Archer*, p.40
19. Ryder, T A, *A Portrait of Gloucestershire*, pp.119–20
20. Humphris, *The Life of Fred Archer*, p.38
21. Ibid, p.39

22–3.   Ibid, p.40
24–5.   Ibid, p.42
26.   Ibid, pp.25–6
27.   Ibid, p.39
28–9.   Ibid, p.41
30.   Welcome, John, *Fred Archer: A Complete Study*, p.13
31.   Tanner, Michael & Cranham, Gerry, *Great Jockeys of the Flat: A Celebration of Two Centuries of Jockeyship*, pp.14 & 15
32.   Humphris, *The Life of Fred Archer*, p.43
33.   *The Times*, 8 November 1933
34.   Welcome, *Fred Archer: A Complete Study*, p.13
35.   Humphris, *The Life of Fred Archer*, p.43
36.   Welcome, *Fred Archer: A Complete Study*, p.13
37.   Ibid, p.14
38.   Humphris, *The Life of Fred Archer*, p.42
39.   Longrigg, Roger, *The History of Horseracing*, pp.116–17
40.   Oaksey, Lord John & Rodney, Bob, *A Racing Companion*, pp.387–94
41.   Welcome, *Fred Archer: A Complete Study*, p.13
42.   Portland, 6th Duke of, *Memories of Racing and Hunting*, p.227
43–4.   Humphris, *The Life of Fred Archer*, p.40
45.   Ibid, p.46

From Apprentice to
First Jockey

Fred's destination was Heath House, the residence of the trainer, Mathew Dawson. It was a pleasing red brick mansion, situated just outside Newmarket with direct access to the town's High Street. It lay between 'The Severals', which was surrounded by other training establishments and included a cricket ground, and the Gallops.[1] Heath House was a two-storey building standing in beautiful grounds with an imposing driveway, trees, shrubs and flower beds. It had large windows which dominated the front, overlooking the driveway and overshadowed by trees which were taller than the two big chimney stacks at either end of the house. Heath House stables adjoined the property and were a fairly substantial addition.[2]

For Fred, coming from a small village, Heath House must have seemed very imposing. To suddenly find himself at this establishment, despite his knowing of course that he was to be apprenticed there and that this was an opportunity he could not possibly miss, must have nevertheless come as a shock to the eleven-year-old as he stood nervously before Dawson on that cold February day in 1868.

Although Dawson had not been in Newmarket long, having taken up residence in 1866,[3] he already had a formidable reputation and had trained horses for some of the wealthiest people in the land. It was understood that he did not normally take on new apprentices on verbal recommendation alone, but he had taken La Terriere at his word and sent for Fred quite quickly in order to give him a trial. This meant additional pressure on the boy to do well and to justify Dawson's decision to send for him. Fred also found himself for the first time in his life in a strange environment. Since the day his father had taken over the King's Arms, he had never lived away from home and was now faced with the prospect of not seeing his family for a long time and of having to adjust to a totally different way of life. Somewhat overwhelmed therefore at the speed of events and naturally sensitive and shy, it could not have helped Fred to realise that he was to receive his apprenticeship in one of the most formidable testing grounds in the country.

Newmarket, considered the foundation of modern horse-racing[4] and the principal location for horseracing and training for some two hundred years, had expanded considerably throughout the first half of the nineteenth century and was by then the centre of a highly organised sport, thanks to the power and influence of the Jockey Club which had established its headquarters there. Founded around 1750 by wealthy racing and horsebreeding gentlemen who met in the coffee houses of St James's, London, the Jockey Club decided to base itself at Newmarket and built the Coffee Room as its headquarters – where the present-day premises now stand. The Club's members included members of the royal family and the aristocracy (the saying went that you had to be related to God to be a member), and no-one was above its authority – not even Royalty as George IV, as Prince of Wales, discovered when he was held to account in 1791 for the bad performance of his horse Escape.[5]

The Rules of Racing, which had been laid down specifically for Newmarket in 1836, now applied to the whole country and would soon be influencing the progress of the sport overseas too. To break these rules was to place the sport into disrepute: 'To be warned off Newmarket Heath,' Julian Bedford wrote in his *World Atlas of Horseracing* (1989), 'is the final sanction in the racing world and still prevents one from visiting any racecourse.'[6]

Taking just a brief look at how the sport stood back then, one can understand why William Archer was so ruthless with his son. It was essentially a game of survival. Crime and corruption were two of the biggest problems the Jockey Club was trying to eradicate and it seemed that as the organisation and rules surrounding horseracing became more strict, so the crimes themselves became more sophisticated.[7] Over the years there were reports of horses being poisoned, of horses being pulled up in races (where jockeys restrained their horses to prevent them from taking the lead), or of even being swapped with other horses. Fights on the racecourses were commonplace and pickpockets were rife, but fraud was one of the biggest problems and sometimes it took the law courts to sort this out.

Fred could hardly have chosen a more turbulent career upon which to embark, but it also brought with it the potential of material wealth, although this would not change his and other jockeys' social status as Fred's future friend and twentieth-century trainer, the Honourable George Lambton stipulated in his autobiography, *Men and Horses I Have Known* (1924). Jockeys were servants, he noted – highly paid ones, it had to be said, but servants[8] – and never more so than in Fred Archer's day. Lambton's observations, in fact, would have been much closer to the truth when Fred began his apprenticeship in 1868, for he was not simply being trained as a jockey for his own benefit as such, but for his potential 'owners' whose 'colours' he would ride and promote.

However, there were plenty of role models for Fred to emulate even if they were hard-bitten characters, standing no nonsense from each other, anyone else or their horses. Until the Jockey Club began to institute measures to discipline racing, the racecourse was a veritable battleground, attracting battle-worn men who fought as much in the saddle as they did out of it.[9] At least during the enlightened years of the mid-nineteenth century the spectators themselves did not make things worse by beating up the winning jockey for having the audacity to come in ahead of the favourite, a practice which was very common in the preceding century – that and actually stopping the leader from reaching the post.

In fact by the time Fred Archer arrived at Newmarket everything about racing – from the discipline of the jockeys to the men who trained them – was being reformed in an effort to make the sport more respectable. This was the aim of the Jockey Club's top administrators, or 'Dictators of the Turf'. The first 'Dictator', Sir Charles Bunbury, a Jockey Club Steward from 1768, had reformed flat racing by introducing shorter races with lighter weights for young horses, placing the emphasis on speed and timing. He had also succeeded in increasing the authority of the Jockey Club and extending such authority beyond the bounds of Newmarket. (The five Classics were also founded during his time – the Derby, the Oaks, St Leger and the One and Two Thousand Guineas.) The second 'Dictator' was Lord George Bentinck, who in the 1840s sought to tackle crime by introducing order and discipline where there was fraud and corruption. His successor, the third and final 'Dictator of the Turf',[10] who would be evident throughout the first half of Fred Archer's career, was Admiral Henry John Rous.

As well as overhauling the system of handicapping horses, Rous, in particular, had no qualms about putting trainers in their place, sometimes at his own cost. In his book *The Laws and Practice of Horseracing* (1850), Rous had outlined everything that was wrong with the sport and what was needed to put it right. The book was updated in 1866 and included 'On the State of the English Turf, On the State of the Law, On the Rules of Racing, On Starting–Riding Races–Jockeys and on the Rules of Betting'.[11] Rous thought that young jockeys, in particular, rode the worst and cited the example of an unnamed, but celebrated rider who effectively threw away three important races because of impatience. Rous noted that young jockeys tended to take matters into their own hands, ignoring instructions, and were intent upon winning at all costs, bolting from the start before being overtaken by a more astute jockey and being beaten by a head. He was also quick to note that the treatment of the horses themselves needed to be improved. While so many races were won by persuasion, others were lost by the whip and spur – an abusive method.[12]

To a certain extent Rous had a lot of respect for jockeys, but like the rest of Britain's aristocracy, he did not treat them as social equals, although as far as the image of racing was concerned, anyone, from the top of the social ladder to the very bottom, was answerable to Rous. He felt that jockeys received too much money which was liable to turn their heads and warned that vanity could breed arrogance – they would no longer listen to the advice of others. A certain standard, therefore, had to be achieved and maintained and to this end trainers, as well as jockeys, came under Rous' scrutiny and if they did not toe the line, their careers could be ruined.

Newmarket, therefore, as far as racing was concerned, was the ultimate authority. If anyone mentioned the term 'head-quarters', they meant Newmarket, but despite this and the fact that some of the country's most popular fixtures – the One Thousand and Two Thousand Guineas, the Cambridgeshire and the Cesarewitch – were (and still are) held at Newmarket, racing here during the 1860s and through to the 1870s, did not appear to be at its best. The Jockey Club Steward, Sir George Chetwynd (a close associate of Fred Archer and one who would write extensively on the jockey in his autobiography *Racing Reminiscences and Experience of the Turf*) noted that the best way to view the races was on horseback since the refreshment facilities were very poor: 'one small stand comprising a luncheon room with a balcony outside, and a room below for sheltering from the rain . . .'[13]

Unfortunately very little would improve over the coming years, prompting a barrage of complaints from the press, but

Newmarket was still acknowledged as the authority in horseracing, both for training and administration. It was seen as an honour to be summoned there – especially if the trainer happened to be the Scots-born Mathew Dawson.

Despite La Terriere's recommendation, Dawson still needed to be absolutely sure of Fred's capabilities. For the first week he was put through his paces with his father watching in the background, leading some to speculate that Dawson knew William Archer personally[14] as well as by professional reputation and that this was another reason why Fred had been sent for so quickly. At the end of the first week, with William watching on the sidelines, the trainer had assessed the potential apprentice and was satisfied that he could do something with the boy. Fred's formal indentures were then set up and, on 10 February 1868, the trainer, apprentice jockey and the apprentice jockey's father, all signed his indentures, a legally binding document which outlined Fred's responsibilities as an apprentice to a training 'master' over the next five years. Fred became, officially, an apprentice of Heath House Stables. His father then took leave of his son and returned to Prestbury.

The overall message which the document conveyed was that of dedication to duty. Given the way jockeys tended to behave, nothing was being left to chance and the indentures emphasised Fred's moral as well as practical welfare. His behaviour had to be beyond reproach. During the five years, the document stipulated, he could not fornicate, marry, gamble or buy and sell. Nor could he 'haunt' taverns or playhouses. In short he could not do anything that would inconvenience his trainer or bring his training establishment into disrepute. In fact Fred was not allowed to leave the establishment without the knowledge and permission of his training 'master', although he tended to break this rule. By the same token, Dawson had a duty of care towards Fred and the document outlined how much the apprentice was to be paid: seven guineas for the first year; nine guineas for the second;

eleven guineas for the third; and thirteen guineas for the fourth and fifth. William Archer was instructed to provide his son with clothing and washing necessities.[15]

Fred found it extremely difficult at first to settle down in his new home, particularly since he knew that he would not be returning to his old one for over twelve months. The sudden move from Prestbury, the break from family and friends and the move to a strange environment where no one knew him only served to compound his feelings of homesickness. He was also looked down on by Mathew Dawson's niece, Jean Neale, who was staying at Heath House at the time. She found him ignorant and took it upon herself to help with his lessons,[16] although given that he grew up with only the most basic writing skills, she could not have had much success. Nor did she treat him with any degree of friendliness, which could not have done a great deal for his morale. Add to this nerves and the knowledge that when he grew up he would probably be too tall to be a jockey anyway, he was soon begging his mother to allow him to return home – even at the danger of incurring his father's wrath.

His shyness also made him a victim of bullying; he was not tough enough to be a true jockey, it seemed, despite his father's unorthodox tuition, so from the beginning more seemed to be against him than for him. Despite having proved at home that he had the makings of a good jockey, Fred had not really gained much in confidence, at least not social confidence. This, however, did not perturb Dawson. As time went on Dawson began to notice that the eleven-year-old had a certain confidence in his ability to ride and seemed at home in the saddle.[17] It was this particular self-assurance that Dawson sought to develop. Fred was lonely, unsure of himself and constantly sending letters home, but he was in the stable yard with the other lads each morning,[18] albeit reluctantly, and, in his spare time, studied the form book, a publication containing details of all the races run in a season. He had the motivation and the ambition to continue. It was Dawson's job to channel those qualities and turn Fred, the rider, into Fred Archer the jockey.

In truth he could not have been in better hands, since Dawson was a top-class trainer whose reputation was as solid as that of his family which had, quite literally, preceded him. The training of horses ran in Mathew Dawson's family and his brothers, Tom, Joseph and John, all had their own establishments.

Mathew, born on 9 January 1820, was one of seventeen children and the third son of George and Jean Dawson. All the children bar the eldest, Tom, who was born at Bogside, in Irvine, Ayrshire in 1809, were born at Stamford Hall, Guillane – the so-called 'Malton of Scotland'[19]. Mathew was very much like his father who was described as an upright, skilful and industrious trainer. George was also very strict, particularly about his sons' education, wanting them all to be able to write in a legible hand.[20]

The eldest son, Tom, left home with his younger brother John to set up as trainers first at Belleish in Scotland, then moving south to Tupgill, Middleham in Yorkshire. Here they worked together for nine years. In due course, after being apprenticed to his father, Mathew joined Tom in 1838, at the age of eighteen. Mathew was a man of direct words, never heaping praise where it was not justified, and he would always maintain that Tom was the best of his day. Nevertheless he wanted to become a trainer in his own right and, leaving his brother in Yorkshire, returned to Scotland. In 1840 Mathew had his first runner in the Derby, Pathfinder, belonging to Lord Kelburn, but it ran unplaced; and, indeed, during these years Mathew found the acquisition of success a struggle.

He moved to Russley, near Lambourn in Berkshire where he began training in 1857, for one James Merry, originally a Scottish ironmaster who would become Member of Parliament for the Falkirk Burghs. Merry, despite his surname, was a difficult personality to deal with, as Dawson discovered, but their working relationship was nevertheless a successful one and between them they won some significant races. In 1858 Dawson trained the winner of the St Leger, Sunbeam and two years later trained Thormanby who secured the Derby – one of the earliest examples of Dawson's consistent ability to pick out winners from the least promising horses. It is also indicative of Merry's apparent lack of faith in his judgement.

Thormanby was a colt which no-one seemed interested in, but Dawson was sufficiently impressed to buy him for 350 sovereigns for James Merry, who loudly expressed his reservations and, it is said, insisted that his trainer take care of him out of his own pocket.[21] Dawson did so and, as a two-year-old, Thormanby went on to win nine out of fourteen races. Merry, having now seen the proof, backed his trainer's plans to train the horse for the Derby and the preparations began. He was entered as the second favourite, his jockey was Harry Custance (a future friend of Fred Archer) and they won by a length and a half, earning James Merry 6,000 sovereigns in winning stakes, in addition to the 70,000 sovereigns he won in bets. Dawson received 1,000 sovereigns for his trouble and Custance walked away with 100 sovereigns. A party was thrown for the villagers in Russley.[22]

Dawson remained with Merry for just six years after this and, in July 1866, decided to move to Newmarket. His brother Joseph was the first to set up as a trainer at Newmarket after moving from Isley in Berkshire. He rented stables near Heath House, before taking over the place in its entirety, although he still lived at Bedford Lodge nearby. Mathew was living in a house opposite St Mary's Rectory and when Joseph decided to leave, he took over Heath House. From here he began training for the young and rather impetuous Dukes of Hamilton and Newcastle who, being inexperienced in the administrative side of horseracing, very often bought poor quality horses without seeking Dawson's advice. Newcastle was also a heavy gambler and, as the losses began to outweigh the successes, it became evident that neither Hamilton nor Newcastle could manage the expense of keeping horses, and in 1869 they and Mathew Dawson parted company. Dawson's brother John lived nearby at Warren House, with his small family – among them a son called John and a daughter, Helen Rose. By 1868 Mathew Dawson had a sound professional reputation at Newmarket and, given the patronage of some of England's nobility, his stables would eventually become known as 'The Aristocratic Stables'.[23]

Dawson was an elegantly dressed gentleman with complete awareness of everything about him. Constantly on the move and never still, he was always ready to add an opinion or two. In many photographs taken of him, his eyes reveal a very sharp intelligence marked with a forthright appreciation of everything about him. He was a tough character, but his facial expression as a whole could portray sincerity and joviality, but above all fearlessness.

He belonged to a long tradition of trainers who treated their horses and apprentices fairly, with firmness and judgement. He did not treat his apprentice jockeys (or any jockey for that matter) as anything special for it was, ultimately, in their best interests for him not to. He wanted them to remain true to their skill and keep their heads out of the clouds. He had a responsibility not only to them, but the rich owners for whom they would eventually ride. The nation's press was gaining almost on the scale of racing and its readership was widening, leaving the world of horseracing in general much more open to public scrutiny and criticism. The responsibility upon trainers like Dawson was immense and where he played the piper, his young apprentices and stable jockeys had to follow the tune.

His niece, Jean Neale, claimed that her uncle was something of an autocrat,[24] but whereas he could be strict with his apprentices and stable boys, he was genuinely concerned for their welfare, as was his wife. Mrs Dawson set up an evening school and a schoolmaster was employed to help the boys with their reading and writing during the week while she gave them morning and evening lessons on a Sunday – with her husband sometimes preaching a sermon. As the boys left their Sunday lessons, they were handed slices of cake – a ploy to ensure that they attended the next Sunday lesson which, apparently, was not compulsory. Being possessed of a very sweet tooth, Fred is reputed to have gone for the largest slice of cake and, from what Jean Neale told the biographer Edith M Humphris, would do so even if it was effectively put out of his reach. Even as late as 1914 a fellow jockey and friend of Fred's recalled his penchant for sweet things – jam as well as cakes. Jean Neale also had Fred running errands for her and would have no-one else. It seems that he knew his crochet cottons too – as Jean Neale told Humphris.[25] I suspect that Jean Neale had quite a soft spot for Fred.

Life at Heath House became more tolerable and Fred began to make friends – two in particular, Fred Webb, who joined the stables in 1869, and Harry Morgan, whom Dawson referred to as 'Morgie' and who, in later years, would provide Edith M Humphris with details of Fred's life at Heath House.[26] Fred Webb was closest to Archer and it is a measure of his loyalty that he remained Fred Webb's friend to the end of his life, even though they competed against each other many times.

Fred was also quite popular with all the Dawson family, but with Mathew Dawson in particular. He could tell from Fred's earliest days at Heath House that he was going to go far and it was through his influence that Fred's confidence gradually began to increase. He certainly learnt to set aside his own fears and to concentrate on what he was good at. As time went by his fellow apprentices, who had formerly bullied him, began to respect his willingness to take on some of the most difficult of horses – his father's bullying tuition paying off. In fact he became renowned for handling horses in the most difficult of conditions, particularly on icy ground, and was not put off by the fact that one boy had been killed. His control of the horse was almost instinctive by now and he earned the nickname 'the little cat', given to him by Mrs Dawson.[27]

Mathew Dawson was impressed by Fred's handling power, but would never tell him. Occasionally he would single him out for the attention of visitors, to show them how he was progressing, but there was no favouritism and Fred had to learn to trust his own judgement without praise from others.

In this respect all the apprentices were treated the same. If they did wrong, they were told, but there was no praise and so everyone knew exactly where they and their fellow jockeys stood. They were expected to maintain a certain level of decorum even when they were not riding. Discipline was maintained at all times and not just within the confines of Heath House Stables. They had to conduct themselves accordingly no matter where they were and woe betide anyone who brought disgrace to the stables. The routine was strict and a wire fence placed around the house and stables ensured that the apprentices could not wander off whenever the fancy took them,[28] but Fred was becoming devious as he got older and he and his fellow apprentices always knew of ways of getting out of the grounds, proof that although Dawson was a disciplinarian, Fred was at least sufficiently comfortable with his regime to get up to a little mischief sometimes. In fact, despite being temperamental and 'autocratic' as Jean Neale described her uncle, Dawson was more like a father figure to his apprentices.[29]

Like his fellow trainer John Scott, he was changing people's perceptions of the role and importance of the trainer and the standard of jockeys and horses alike reflected this. Trainers were becoming much more 'well-conducted', honest and well-educated. They were seen to treat their stable lads well and these, in consequence, were happy. Certainly in the case of Heath House, Dawson's methods instilled confidence, perseverance and discipline in his jockeys and within fifteen months of arriving Fred had got over his homesickness and settled into the routine of Heath House.[30] Religion was important as the Dawsons themselves stressed; and in the case of another trainer, John Day (of the famous racing and training Day Clan of the early nineteenth century), church services were extended to include Bible readings.[31] The boys were well fed and clothed – if they rode for Royalty, they wore livery – a reminder of the fact that, although fortunate to represent such personages, they were still servants. With the power of the Jockey Club Stewards being extended in 1863, jockeys could be suspended or expelled if they stepped out of line. The attitude and professionalism of a jockey and apprentice jockeys therefore had to be beyond reproach, reflecting in turn the stable which trained them. If Dawson did appear autocratic at times, it was because he was concerned about his horses, his lads and whether or not things were going well.

His much more placid wife kept him on an even keel and assisted him where she could, but it was understood that he ruled Heath House. He even had a room there which he called the 'Sanctum'.[32] According to his niece, no-one was allowed in that room unless they were invited. Another room, the so-called 'Inner Sanctum', was only accessible to Dawson and his wife. With family, stable lads, apprentice jockeys and clients constantly passing through, it was probably the only room where Dawson could be left in peace.

In addition to decorum and good manners, self-discipline and dignity were also extended to the horses and Fred was taught to treat them with respect. This was paramount since many had in the past been abused to the point of complete breakdown and such cruelty had started to make the newspapers. Heath House had a strict policy where the horses were concerned and it was a golden rule that all were to be treated with respect and not ill-treated in any way.[33] Jockeys could get the best out of their horses without resorting to measures which could amount to cruelty, a message which Fred, throughout his early career, would sometimes forget as his hero and mentor, Tom French, often did in practice.

Tom French, the very best of his generation, but unsparing with the whip, was Dawson's First Jockey at Heath House and had been there since 1868, the year Fred Archer joined the stables. Like Fred, he was quiet and reserved and yet he was possessed of the same mettle which characterised Archer's efforts. He was also tall, which was a further boost to Fred. As First Jockey he had already proved himself to be the best,[34] so that Dawson believed that determination and hard work outweighed whatever disadvantages may exist.

French was born in Liverpool in 1844[35] and grew up at a time when racing was still trying to establish itself as a seriously organised sport. Travelling south to Newmarket, he became apprenticed to James Godding at Palace Stables. His success rate was somewhat slow off the mark. He was deemed ready enough to ride The Greek in the 1859 Lincolnshire Handicap, but he had no wins until 1861 when he secured the Great Metropolitan followed by the Chester Cup on a horse called St Albans owned by Lord Allensbury.[36]

He won the Great Metropolitan again on Planet four years later and by that time was proving to be one of the most skilful jockeys of his generation with an ability to get the very best out of the horses he rode. He came second in a Derby on Christmas Carol, the winner being the French horse, Gladiateur, and this, in itself, ensured that he was in a class of his own. By sheer example, he had everything to teach the young, impressionable Fred Archer who, being unhappy and homesick initially, felt he had so much to prove to himself and to Heath House. There were certainly many superior jockeys he had to look up to, but French would, for him, remain the epitome of excellence, particularly when Fred himself was called upon to prove his skills.

Fred's first public ride since starting his apprenticeship took place in the Newmarket Town Plate, during the Second October Meeting, on Honoria, but he finished last and was furious, revealing an impatient streak which would flare up intermittently throughout his career. Dawson, however, seeing the wider picture, only saw Fred's performance as a further test, and stressed the importance of keeping a balance between winning and losing. Fred was setting high standards of achievement for himself very often without relying upon practical judgement, so that, when he lost, he took it badly and became angry with himself. His friend Harry Morgan told Edith M Humphris that Fred sometimes argued with the other apprentices[37] but it is interesting to note that when he lost the Newmarket Town Plate that year, he did not begrudge the fact that his other close friend, Fred Webb, did win it. In fact Webb had been the real focus of attention in that race – riding Viscount Falmouth's Stromboli – further proof that there was no favouritism at Heath House, and that Fred Archer had to take the rough with the smooth along with all the other jockeys, but he was angry with himself and this served to sharpen his competitive edge.

However, Dawson had no intention of placing too much responsibility on Fred too soon, but he did win a race later in 1869 although not on the flat, but in a steeplechase. His mount was a pony called Maid of Trent and the race was the Bangor Steeplechase. She belonged to one Mrs Willins of Rugby[38] who, in looking for a lightweight jockey to ride her horse, had approved William Archer's recommendation that his son should ride. She therefore sought Dawson's permission to use Fred and the trainer, perhaps seeing the race as valuable experience for the boy, duly gave his consent. The twelve-year-old, fresh-faced, neatly attired and anxious to have his chance, won the race, an achievement he was particularly proud of, but for Dawson it was just a stepping stone and one which served to test Fred's ability. He was no longer riding for himself – he was riding in public as an apprentice of Heath House, even if on this occasion he was riding for Mrs Willins, and these two factors were responsibility enough. The sooner he learnt to place both success and failure into perspective, the sooner he would be able to settle into the life of a jockey. Small races at this stage were merely the foundation to that life. Unfortunately

Fred did not see it that way and he had a tendency to expect too much too soon.

Time moved on and Archer had sixteen races in 1870.[39] It was a quiet year for him – an exercise in building confidence, but sometimes his efforts fell short of expectation, and he made very little impression. When he did, it was occasionally for the wrong reasons as on 7 October when he was disqualified from the Edinburgh Handicap on the appropriately named Irregularity. Irregularity had come in second, but he was disqualified because he passed the winning post on the wrong side of the rail, so the money for second place went to Bobby and his jockey who had come in third.[40] Still, out of his sixteen rides, Fred secured two wins to his credit that year. The first, taking place almost a year after Honoria, was at Chesterfield on 28 September. He had hoped to repeat his success the following day when he rode Athol Daisy in the Hartington Plate, but this time he came in second, much to his chagrin. There was no doubt that he was in the hard school now, and one which did not allow for age. Other, older, more experienced jockeys were beginning to take notice of him and if they perceived a desire to win on his part as a touch of arrogance, they had every intention of knocking it right out of him. Soon after the Hartington Plate he rode in another race, which provided him with some taste of the scorn of other jockeys, particularly when Jim Snowden, who was also in the race, told Fred in no uncertain terms what he thought of his performance and that he could not ride for nuts![41]

It had always been made clear to Fred that this was the type of treatment he should expect and from his father's tuition to the early days of Heath House he had never been wrapped in cotton wool. In fact he had toughened up considerably over the past couple of years and, taking whatever verbal abuse was hurled at him by other jockeys, concentrated all his energies in his work and increased his motivation. He continued to study the form book, determined to perfect his knowledge and became more punctual in his preparation for a race, preferring to be two minutes early than two minutes late.

On 14 October 1870, he started favourite on Lincoln Lass in the Tay Handicap, during the Caledonian Hunt Meeting, and won. He was learning to place failure in perspective so that he could appreciate success. It was all made that bit easier of course by the fact that he did not have to worry about his weight at this stage. He certainly did not have to consider wasting – taking purgatives or restricting his diet, often almost to the point of starvation – something which a great many older jockeys were forced to do in order to meet the required weights. (While some jockeys were hardy enough to have a career in racing and live full lives during their retirement, others found their health was permanently damaged from wasting.) Fred was able to maintain a minimum of 5st 7lb from 1871 to 1872.[42] Mathew Dawson's nephew, John Dawson, later told Edith M Humphris about Fred's life at Heath House – a life which was like that of any other lad who lived and worked near stables – but Fred was exceptional, John Dawson noted, by the fact that he learnt fast and acquired his skills as a jockey earlier than others.[43]

He had learnt much, but still had a long way to go before he could measure his own performance against that of other jockeys who had been riding since before he was born. Two, in particular, George Fordham and Charles Maidment, fought to secure first place in the race for Champion Jockey in 1871. It was a dead heat. Fred Archer on the other hand had only three wins to his credit that year: one on the unnamed horse belonging to Mr R C Naylor at the start of the season on 13 April; the second on Skiff in the Kelston Claiming Plate on 16 May; and the third on Gravelthorpe in a Selling Race on 14 August.[44] Nor was patience a great virtue at this stage and on one occasion misconduct at the post awarded Fred a fortnight's ban. Immediately aware of how important it was to make the right impression, he never repeated that mistake again, but by the same token was very much aware that his successes and failures were hit and miss. He could begin well, but could not sustain the momentum needed to win races on a regular basis.

Again, as in 1870, Fred was making very little impression and he must have been acutely aware of this, particularly when he compared his performance with that of Fred Webb who, according to the Racing Calendar for 1871, seemed a more promising jockey than Archer – securing more rides in the big races, particularly at Epsom, and more wins than his friend.[45] This may have been another reason why Fred was so determined to do well as Webb's success provided the impetus he needed to improve. At least things were beginning to look up as 1872 marked a turning point, not a great one, but one which provided him with greater motivation and brought him more to the attention of prospective retainers.

He achieved a total of 27 wins in 1872, although the first on 9 April was a dead heat, but his progress from then on was proof that his hard work had paid off. He was beginning to show a measure of consistency, success was beginning to outweigh failure and the number of races increased considerably. They were more consistent and steady, with the momentum being sustained right through the season. On 30 April he won the May Stakes on Sydmonton. On 1 May he won a Handicap Plate on Invader and the following day won another Handicap, again on Invader. His races between 2 May and 19 June were sporadic, but on 19 June he won a Handicap on Chorister and, on the same day, another Handicap on Nadel. On 26 July he won the Westmoreland Plate and the Milton Stakes; then there was nothing until 29 August when he won the Berkshire Stakes and the Thames Valley.

October and November proved to be particularly successful and, in fact, set a pattern for his career – in that he seemed to ride especially well in autumn and at the start of winter.[46] On 7 October he won the Free Handicap on Black Stocking and on the following day he won what was his principal win for the year, the Cesarewitch on Salvanos at 11 to 2.[47] He was entered at a weight (minimum) of 5st 7lb and, possibly because of this, Salvanos proved to be a difficult horse to handle, being so heavy. Still, Fred came recommended and was running a good enough race, not only to attract the notice of prospective retainers, but the newspapers as well. According to *The Sporting Life* he possessed the 'coolness and steadiness of a veteran . . . altogether free from the "flashiness" of the modern school of "feathers" who have come to such utter grief before they are well out of their teens . . .'[48]

This was not the first time he had come to the attention of *The Sporting Life*. Dawson had pointed him out to John Corlett, the owner and editor, when Fred was in the first years of his apprenticeship and even then Corlett's impressions were favourable – at least favourable enough to recall years later how Fred had demonstrated his riding skills by jumping a fence.[49] Now, in 1872, the praise Fred received from *The Sporting Life* was indicative of how much he had learnt since 1869. He no longer allowed impatience to get the better of him and was mature beyond his years in a profession which could make or break the most talented or ambitious. He was also modest in his achievements and, in short, showed future promise. It was a clear message to anyone who would back him that he would go far.

The owner of Salvanos, Mr Radcliffe, was equally delighted at this win – not only because the horse had bolted on a previous occasion, but because many of his losses had been temporarily reversed.[50] Fred had controlled a potentially difficult horse, but, as proof that he still had much to learn, he rode Salvanos in another race and ran unplaced.

Undaunted he secured other wins. Two days after the Cesarewitch, he rode Strathtay to victory in a Handicap Sweepstakes on 10 October. He was still on a roll in the following month when he won the Liverpool Nursery Stakes on Sioux on 6 November. On the next day he won the Palatine

Nursery on Cingalina and on 16 November the Innkeeper Plate on L'Orient – one of his final wins for 1872.[51]

The majority of these rides (there were 136 with some 27 wins) may have been minor compared to other, more significant races, since he was still not getting the rides in big meetings, but they indicate that Fred was becoming a more popular jockey to commission. He was showing an increasing ability to get the best out of the horses he rode, as in the case of Invader. He was making a promising name for himself and was becoming a worthy competitor against older jockeys. Compared to 1870 and 1871 his number of rides and wins increased almost thirty fold.

He was still able to maintain his weight at the beginning of 1873, but his friend Fred Webb was unable to do so. Archer's apprenticeship came to an end at Christmas 1872 and he replaced Fred Webb as the lightweight jockey for Heath House in the New Year. He also rode as a freelance jockey.

The start of the season was promising, giving every indication of his tremendous improvement over the last two years. On 26 and 27 March Fred won the Aintree Handicap and a Handicap Plate on Woodcut before taking the Nottingham Spring Handicap on Sybarite four days later. From there, he went to Northampton to ride in the Delapre Free Handicap, followed by the Lincoln Meeting. But after 5 April there was a significant slowdown in the number of races that he was winning – as if he had run out of steam. This continued until 7 May when he won the Chesterfield Flying Stakes on Bassoon and began to pick up the pace again which continued throughout May.[52]

Fred was very much in demand and, in learning the art of analysis, was able to tell owners and trainers precisely how a race was won or lost – showing a perceptiveness which was not lost on those owners and trainers who were following his progress with a keen eye.[53] They were struck, in particular, by his acute sense of observation – acute because for one so young and just out of his apprenticeship, he was showing a maturity of style and an ability to look at the wider picture which could only continue to improve, and his use of analysis was a trait that was fast becoming second nature. It was one which would be of benefit both to him and the people he rode for. Even at this stage in his career he was not only taking into account the key elements of a given race – the pace at which the course was run and the distance – but also comparing his own performance with that of his competitors; this would help to set him aside from other jockeys as it gave him a broader picture of a race in progress and allowed him to assess critically his own perform-ance and how to improve it. This and his knowledge of the form book went a long way towards perfecting his professional scope and judgement.

Among his admirers were Prince Batthyany (originally from Hungary but who now lived in England and was one of the best respected 'turfites' of his generation) and the Earls of Rosebery and Bradford. Through their interest and that of other potential retainers, Fred's rides increased and his wins began to show the same level of consistency that they had shown the year before, so long as he could remember to maintain the pace. From 21 May the number of wins increased significantly and on that date he won the Londesborough Cup on Bohemian. Two days later he had two wins to his credit: the Salisbury Cup on Sir John and the South Western Railway Handicap on the favourite. He also secured the Bentinck Plate on Blackstone on 28 May and rode Woodcut to victory again in the City Handicap Plate on 4 June, but from then his efforts became sporadic again until the beginning of July when he seemed to have a splurge of energy and was virtually unstoppable until the end of October.[54] On 17 July he had four wins: the Stewards Handicap on Chloris (he had won the Selling Handicap on Chloris the day before); the Worcester Stakes on Bassoon; the Severn Stakes on Mystery; and the Croome Nursery on Genevieve. He rode Mystery again the next day and won the Ladies' Plate. He maintained the pace throughout the next

month, winning the Town Selling Stakes on 14 August once
again on Mystery. On 29 August he gained three wins: the
Innkeeper's Plate on Maud; the Whitley Stakes on Decoration;
and the Thames Valley on Early Morn. Having spent the first
few weeks of the season getting into his stride, he had built up
his self-confidence and had also maintained the confidence of
the owners who commissioned his services, so that by 29
August 1873, at the age of sixteen, he was fast developing a
favourable reputation.[55] He did not win any Classic races that
year, but by the end of the season, with over a hundred wins, he
would be competing against top jockey Harry Constable for
first place in the winning jockeys' table.

On Saturday 30 August the First Jockey of Heath House, and
Fred's mentor, Tom French died.[56] The announcement was
made in the national papers on Monday 1 September.[57] Fred
could not fail to have been aware of the tragedy which had
overtaken the racing world and the changes which would come
about at Heath House and which would affect his life forever.

Due to his efforts to keep his weight down and despite his
many successes, Tom French developed tuberculosis and his
doctors ordered him to go abroad for the winter of 1872 to
1873. He went to Egypt where the climate was more favourable, but instead of resting, he rode in Khadive's Grand Prize
on Sir George Chetwynd's Falerio. By the time he returned
home, his health had deteriorated badly and the tuberculosis
was rendered irreversible. Attending the Brighton races but too
ill to ride, being ever active, he played cricket instead. His
health became worse towards the end of August, but then he
seemed to rally and it was even hoped that he would ride
Viscount Falmouth's Andred in the St Leger. He suffered a
relapse on the following Friday and never recovered, dying the
following day.[58]

He was described by *The Times* as elegant and he was
certainly acknowledged as accomplished with a high level of
personal integrity – important attributes for any aspiring jockey.

In fact the overall view was that he had brought professionalism and dignity to the sport. His influence, the paper noted, would be greatly missed – not least by Fred himself.[59]

Tom French's funeral took place in Newmarket, at noon, on the Thursday after his death and was covered by the *Cambridge Independent Press*. In acknowledging the importance of Tom French as a sportsman, people from all walks of life attended the funeral despite the horrendous weather that day and respect for him was so great that many shops in Newmarket had closed for the day. It was an admiration which was heartfelt 'by all classes towards the esteemed jockey, who is everywhere spoken of as the model of his profession'.[60]

His death marked another turning point in Fred Archer's life. Tom French had been so unique in his talents that replacing him at Heath House as First Jockey was not going to be easy and, indeed, he would not be replaced at all until the following year. The *Biographical Encyclopaedia of British Flat Racing* (1978) describes him as a flamboyant rider,[61] suggesting that his confidence lay in his skill as a jockey. His influence on Fred Archer was profound and there is no doubt that the young jockey was inspired by him – not least because of his ambition, but also because of his strength of will which was capable of pushing him to even greater success on the racecourse. He was, very much, a hard act to follow – an acclaimed figure, both personally and professionally. If there were some who felt that he could not be matched, Dawson, at least, could see that he would have a worthy successor. In the case of Fred Archer, he was not yet absolutely sure. Fred still had a lot to learn, but his efforts succeeded in bringing him to the attention of Tom French's retainer – Viscount Falmouth.

In fact closer attention was now paid to Fred all round, especially since he had come second to Constable's first in the winning tables, and throughout 1874 he began to ride more for Falmouth in the Viscount's magpie colours of black and white. His weight was not a problem, remaining at a steady 6st 1lb.

On 25 March 1874, at the start of the season, he had one of his most popular wins to date on Tomahawk (owned by Fred Swindell) in the Lincolnshire Handicap during the Lincoln Spring Meeting. Tomahawk had been a favourite for some time and *The Times* noted that while other horses were backed from 20 to 1 to 66 to 1, Tomahawk was quoted at 14 to 1, so confidence was especially high. The fact that Fred was chosen to ride him gives some impression of the confidence placed in him by Dawson to see how he measured up as Heath House's First Jockey.[62]

The race had been beset by two or three false starts but finally got away to an even start, according to *The Times* with Cora, Shylocks, Oxford Mixture, Salvanos and the Infanto colt dominating the field, along with others who kept up the middle and forward positions. Fred kept Tomahawk well back to begin with, reserving the horse's energy and speed until within a quarter of a mile of the post when many began to fall back and Tomahawk came through with such speed that he overtook Shylocks and Oxford Mixture and went on to win by three lengths – a comparatively easy victory, the press noted.

It was an example of Archer's advantageous and efficient use of speed and timing – in sharp contrast to the race which had opened the Lincoln Spring Meeting, the Scurry Handicap Plate in which he rode Prince Batthyany's Nightstar, pushing the horse forward too soon at the start of the race while the rest followed, only to be overtaken and come in fourth.[63]

At times he could be spot on in striking the balance between distance and pace and at others miss it completely, but at least throughout April and early May he did well.[64] He was learning from his wins as well as his mistakes and from spring to early summer won several minor races, in one of which he rode Viscount Falmouth's Ladylove on 5 May. He still had to prove himself in the Classics and on 6 May he was given what would prove to be Dawson's biggest test to date – Falmouth's Atlantic in the Two Thousand Guineas.[65]

Fred had already received something of a test in the shape of Falmouth's Andred, a temperamental four-year-old by the equally temperamental Blair Athol.[66] Even some of the most skilled of jockeys had found Andred difficult, but Fred successfully rode the horse to victory in the Great Cheshire Stakes on 15 May. The Ditch Mile Handicap, however, proved to be a different story altogether and Fred, disappointed and blaming himself, lost the race, but at least it proved to Dawson and Falmouth that he could work a horse and get the best out of him, so they gave him Atlantic.

Atlantic was a chestnut colt owned by Viscount Falmouth. He was by Thormanby out of Hurricane[67] and had not been the best of horses to train,[68] so from the start he was a challenge and confidence in him was very low at Heath House, particularly as Atlantic was fairly lazy by nature. The favourite for the Two Thousand Guineas was M. Lefevre's Ecossais, a horse popular with both the public and the newspapers (although *The Times* was not wholly impressed by his legs)[69] and whose jockey would be George Fordham – the former Champion Jockey who was destined to be Fred's racing nemesis.

Fred, still managing to keep his weight down without too much effort, was carrying three stone dead weight on a horse which was started at 10 to 1. From the beginning Atlantic led the race, achieving a dominant position and maintaining it despite changes among those in the rear which did not impede his own progress.[70]

It seemed that once this horse began to run, it was necessary to keep him on the move. Although at one point Ecossais did threaten Atlantic's lead, he was soon beaten back, so that any other challengers were quickly seen off too. Reverberation tried to overtake, but Atlantic's dominance remained unopposed to the last, even though he only won by a neck. Reverberation quickly caught up and came second. Ecossais finished a bad third. His jockey, George Fordham would not forget Fred Archer in a hurry. It was a defeat which *The Sporting Life* reported as creating 'a degree of sensation such as not often witnessed'.[71]

Despite the fact that the horse had lost, *The Sporting Life* devoted a great deal of space to describing Ecossais before assessing Atlantic. The Two Thousand Guineas winner had good speed, the paper acknowledged, but being lazy, needed constant riding.[72] Nevertheless it was a popular and dramatic win and Viscount Falmouth was cheered on the return to the Weighing Room after the race. Confidence in the horse's abilities had now reached such a level that the general impression seemed to be that Atlantic was capable of proving himself in the forthcoming Derby, although he still had much to achieve before the event.

Fred Archer received quite a good write up in *The Sporting Life* – not just for winning the Two Thousand Guineas, his first Classic, but for what it called his 'repeated successes', making it clear that he had been followed with interest over recent years and was gaining not only in potential, but also in public popularity. His success was a measure and justification of Dawson's judgement too and while newspapers pinpointed Fred as unique, so too was Dawson in his method. His confidence in Fred was not lost on the newspapers – as one correspondent noted, it was rare for featherweight riders to be placed at all weights and yet that was exactly what Dawson did. *The Times* described the effort on Fred's part as 'clever'[73] and felt that had the distance been greater, Fred would still have been able to match it and win by half a length. In fact the race remained one of his most popular.

A Steward of the Jockey Club, Sir George Chetwynd, who later became well acquainted with Fred throughout his career, wrote, 'This was a great triumph for so light a jockey . . . he justified Lord Falmouth's confidence in him by riding a patient race.'[74]

Even writers of today, over a hundred years after Fred's death, pay homage to his first Classic victory. John Welcome, Fred's future biographer, described it as a 'copybook race',[75] perfectly timed with a determined effort towards the finish.

Atlantic was another significant turning point – not only in Archer's career, but in how he would be viewed in the future. He was not only gaining the confidence of future owners and experts like Chetwynd, but the newspaper coverage of his work would increase and, as readership was also widening, he would come more to the attention of a larger public. The light was now on him, but Dawson, despite such encouraging publicity, did not allow him to get in over his head since there was still a great deal of work to be done. Fred would not be riding Atlantic in the Derby or St Leger. He rode King of Tyre in the Derby, but finished unplaced. Still the Two Thousand Guineas win seemed to set the seal on the relationship between Archer, Falmouth and Dawson and the win rubbed off on another race which took place later on the same day. Here, on 6 May Fred rode Vintage in the Welter Selling Stakes, taking the lead within the distance and securing a four-length victory.

On the racecourse Fred was becoming more of a force to be reckoned with, showing greater strength. Between March and the end of May 1874 he had increased his wins gradually and consistently, proof that he was becoming more relaxed in his work and more confident in his ability. The month of September was his best to date with almost thirty wins and then there was a steady downturn towards the end of the season[76] – his final win being in late November.

He competed ferociously, whether it was against older jockeys or Fred Webb or even his brother Charlie, who was riding for a different stable. The years 1873 and 1874 show Fred and Charlie literally vying for position and revealing the level of competitiveness which had characterised their childhood and which was now extended into adulthood. Fred thought nothing of knocking his brother into second or third place or out of the running altogether. Indeed, although Charlie had many races as a jockey, his wins, compared to his brother's, tended to be more sporadic. Both of them, however, were adapting remarkably to the demands of their work – so much so that Fred's position at Heath House was about to become more defined. Becoming Champion Jockey at the end of 1874, he ended the season certain that he would begin the next as Tom French's successor as First Jockey at Heath House with Viscount Falmouth as his principal retainer – at just £100.

Notes

1.   Map of Newmarket (courtesy of Suffolk Record Office)
2.   Picture of Heath House (courtesy of Eric Dunning)
3.   Humphris, Edith M, *The Life of Mathew Dawson*, p.84
4.   Bedford, Julian, *The World Atlas of Horseracing*, pp.12 & 13
5.   Tyrrel, John, *Running Racing: The Jockey Club Years Since 1750*, p.13
6.   Bedford, pp.11 & 12
7.   Longrigg, Roger, *The History of Horseracing*, pp.99, 115 & 116
8.   Lambton, The Honourable George, *Men and Horses I Have Known*, p.74
9.   Longrigg
10.   Mortimer, Roger, Onslow, Richard & Willet, Peter, *The Biographical Encyclopaedia of British Flat Racing*, pp.55–8, 90–1, 523 & 524
11.   Tyrrel, pp.39–49
12.   Mortimer, Onslow & Willet, p.523
13.   Chetwynd, Sir George, *Racing Reminiscences and Experience of the Turf*, p.7
14.   Welcome, John, *Fred Archer: A Complete Study*, p.14
15.   Indentures as shown in *The Times*, 1 November 1933
16–17.   Humphris, *The Life of Mathew Dawson*, pp.85–6
18.   Humphris, *The Life of Fred Archer*, p.64
19.   Humphris, *The Life of Mathew Dawson*, p.27
20.   Mortimer, Onslow & Willet, pp.157–9
21.   Humphris, *The Life of Mathew Dawson*, pp.74–83
22.   Mortimer, Onslow & Willet, pp.382–3
23.   Humphris, *The Life of Fred Archer*, p.59
24.   Humphris, *The Life of Mathew Dawson*, p.115
25.   Ibid, pp.85 & 86
26–7.   Humphris, *The Life of Fred Archer*, p.101
28.   Humphris, *The Life of Mathew Dawson*, pp.85 & 86
29.   Welcome, John, *Fred Archer: A Complete Study*, p.17
30.   Humphris, *The Life of Mathew Dawson*, pp.115 & 116
31.   Welcome, John, *Fred Archer: A Complete Study*, p.65
32.   Mortimer, Onslow & Willet, pp.161–3
33.   Humphris, *The Life of Mathew Dawson*, p.89

34. Humphris, *The Life of Fred Archer*, p.64
35. Tanner, Michael & Cranham, Gerry, *Great Jockeys of the Flat: A Celebration of Two Centuries of Jockeyship*, pp.71 & 84
36. *The Times*, 6 September 1873
37. Mortimer, Onslow & Willet, *The Biographical Encyclopaedia of British Flat Racing*, p.223
38. Humphris, *The Life of Fred Archer*, p.100
39. Welcome, John, *Fred Archer: A Complete Study* pp.68 & 69
40–1. Weatherby, J E & J P, *The Racing Calendar for the Year 1870*
42. Tanner & Cranham, p.84
43. Humphris, *The Life of Fred Archer*, pp.74–5
44–5. Weatherby, J E & J P, *The Racing Calendar for the Year 1871*
46–7. Weatherby, J E & J P, *The Racing Calendar for the Year 1872*
48–9. *The Sporting Life*, 9 October 1872
50. Humphris, *The Life of Fred Archer*, p.66
51. Weatherby, J E & J P, *The Racing Calendar for the Year 1872*
52–5. Weatherby, J E & J P, *The Racing Calendar for the Year 1873*
56. *Cambridge Independent Press*, 6 September 1873
57–9. *The Times*, 1 September 1873
60. *Cambridge Independent Press*, 6 September 1873
61. Mortimer, Onslow & Willet, p.223
62–3. *The Times*, 26 March 1874
64. Weatherby, J E & J P, *The Racing Calendar for the Year 1874*
65. Lane, Charles, *Harry Hall's Classic Winners*, pp.900–1
66. Welcome, John, *Fred Archer: A Complete Study*, pp.25–6
67. Mortimer, Onslow & Willet, p.32
68. Lane, pp.90–1
69. *The Times*, 7 May 1874
70–2. *The Sporting Life*, 9 May 1874
73. *The Times*, 7 April 1874
74. Chetwynd, pp.99–100
75. Welcome, John, *Fred Archer: A Complete Study*, p.26
76. Weatherby, J E & J P, *The Racing Calendar for the Year 1874*

The Owner, The Trainer and
The Jockey

There were few partnerships in nineteenth-century racing which were destined to have such an impact on the sport as the one that developed between Falmouth, Dawson and Archer. Completely different in character, they nevertheless complemented one another enough to take horseracing to new heights in an age where superiority, excellence and wealth were everything.

Viscount Falmouth, who raced under the pseudonym Mr T Valentine[1] (no-one is altogether sure of the origin of this name), belonged to the elite, but had it not been for a distant relative, he might not have inherited a title – and from there, might not have become involved in racing and Dawson, not to mention Archer.[2]

Born Evelyn Boscawen in 1819 at Wootton, he was the first son of John Evelyn Boscawen. Records in the Eton College Library show that he began attending school there in the summer of 1832, stayed until 1838[3] and then went up to Christ Church, Oxford as a commoner, matriculating on 5 December 1838. According to notes held on term tests (which were conducted orally) he studied classical texts, theology and mathematics[4] but he could not have been very successful or dedicated because he went down at the close of the summer term in 1840.

Opting for a legal career he became a barrister and entered the Middle Temple in 1846, but he had no sooner been called to the bar than his cousin, the 5th Viscount Falmouth, died and young Boscawen became the 6th Viscount. That signalled the end of his career in the law and he took his place among the privileged aristocracy. He then married the Countess Despencer (a countess in her own right) whose own lands and property, including Mereworth Castle in Kent, substantially added to his own.

In appearance Falmouth was of sturdy build with heavy-set features and the side whiskers typical of gentlemen in mid-Victorian England. A picture in Edith M Humphris's book shows his expression to be both shrewd and passive – the whole demeanour quiet, but observant. An image in *Vanity Fair*, entitled 'Never Bets', portrays his shrewdness (as well as a rather portly stature).

Before sending his horses to Heath House, Falmouth had been sending them to the quiet, unassuming but superb trainer, John Scott of Malton[5] in Yorkshire. He developed a stud to equal many of his aristocratic contemporaries and believed that it was far better to breed horses from the mare rather than the sire – a technique that was to hold him in good stead for years.[6] Unlike his aristocratic contemporaries, he did not gamble, earning himself the nickname 'Never Bets'. He had done so only once – for sixpence – and had lost graciously to John Scott's wife, to whom he gave the coin as a brooch set in diamonds. On Scott's death on 4 October 1871, Falmouth decided to move his horses to Newmarket; Dawson had been recommended to him, so he sent his horses to Heath House. Dawson had trained for Falmouth before – most notably his horse Kingcraft, who Tom French had ridden to victory in the 1870 Derby.[7] Falmouth was appreciative of Dawson's approach and trusted his judgement, although his character was the complete opposite of John Scott's.

Falmouth was never associated with racing for the gambling, and was the scourge of bookmakers and journalists who relied in part upon the impressions and betting of the owners in order to assess the chances of their horses. Although not directly involved in the cause of improving racing at home, Falmouth was, nevertheless, concerned with its fate abroad, particularly in France, proposing that foreign-bred animals should be excluded from English races.

Concerned with technique, discipline and reputation, he and Mathew Dawson were alike in their aims and understanding of the sport, but at times had disputes over the capabilities of specific horses.[8]

In the main their relationship was one of mutual respect, but in November 1870 this very nearly ended before it had a chance to begin. Falmouth issued instructions to Tom French before he rode in the Newmarket Derby and went over Mathew Dawson's head in doing so as the trainer had already issued instructions of his own. French rode to Falmouth's specifications and Dawson was left thinking that he had been deliberately disobeyed by the jockey but when he learnt the truth, he wrote to Falmouth and asked him to remove his horses from the Heath House stables forthwith. The *Sporting Magazine* for November picked up on the story and felt that Dawson had acted hastily, but the incident was to have no effect on what would prove to be a highly successful working relationship.[9]

Dawson admired Viscount Falmouth and in later years would often attribute Fred's overall success to the fact that he began his career riding the Viscount's horses.[10] Dawson also approved of how the horses were bred and could pinpoint some of the best examples – the Two Thousand Guineas winner, Atlantic, being one of them – but he never paid lip service to Falmouth, (although he called him a good 'master') or to anyone else for that matter.

For the benefit of anyone, but especially the horse owners, Mathew Dawson made it clear that what you saw was what you got. Those who sent their horses to him had to learn very quickly where they themselves stood, including Viscount Falmouth.

Dawson was well aware that he was training horses for some of the richest and most powerful people in the world (people who could, at a stroke, ruin him or others without a second thought). At the same time Dawson believed that he was being employed to do a job for which he had years of experience and he was not going to allow anyone, even those from the highest ranks of the aristocracy,[11] to browbeat him or instruct him in his work – work which entailed method, preparation and execution on a vast scale and which required total professionalism. Owners could make suggestions as to how a horse should be trained, but if Dawson did not think such suggestions practical, he would tell them so and it was, therefore, well known that if any owner was dissatisfied with his work, they could take their horses elsewhere.[12] Some did (such as the Dukes of Hamilton and Newcastle; see page 27), but – knowing how disciplined and professional he was, and the fact that he came from a family of professional trainers – his other prestigious clients knew better than to try and tell him his job and never took offence if he criticised – if rather undiplomatically – their opinions on horse management. In fact he was always remembered with deep affection, particularly by the Duke of Portland who saw him as a unique character and one who was true to himself.[13]

He was certainly possessed of a dry wit – one which, in being direct and honest, was always appreciated. When people insisted upon spelling his Christian name as 'Matthew' instead of 'Mathew' he responded, 'Why will they persist in giving me so much Tea (T)? I hate the dom'd stuff.'[14] He had turned the lapse of others into a joke and had such a good sense of irony that he must have kept his clients constantly amused, but in his case it was a humour which was never merely indulged – he was always taken seriously.

Many owners, the Duke of Portland included, did not always call him by his surname, which would have been how owners would have addressed an employee or servant. Dawson was very often just 'Mat' which meant that they thought so highly of him that he was a man very much in their confidence. It was also an acknowledgement that he was one of the few men of his profession who could stand up to many of those 'owners' who considered the deference of others as their God-given right. He could be extremely critical and, perhaps because of his approach and that of others like him, a new respect for the role of trainers began to emerge.

Portland especially found his services invaluable from the start. When he inherited the dukedom, he bought three yearlings at the Doncaster Sale. The one he was particularly proud of was Greensleeves. He was especially pleased because of her pedigree, descending from Thormanby, and, feeling very proud, the young Duke took himself off to Mat Dawson and informed him of his purchase, making it clear why he had bought Greensleeves. But Dawson was his own best judge. He never took the word of an owner when assessing the potential of a horse. He inspected all three yearlings, eyed them critically and then completely burst the Duke's bubble by remarking that they, and Greensleeves in particular, were no good.[15] He did not doubt that she came from a good breed, but noted that she was a 'damned bad specimen' of it. He then turned to the suitably deflated Duke and added, 'If you want a specimen of that breed or any other, you should buy a better looking one.'[16]

Portland, young though he was and anxious to make his mark, could have told Mathew Dawson not to be so impudent, but he took on board what the trainer said and remembered the incident well over fifty years later.

The Honourable George Lambton said in his autobiography years later, 'In spite of his [Dawson's] strong, fearless character, which would brook no interference from any man in what he thought the duties of his profession, he was the most courteous of men, both to his employers and to those who worked for him, and I never met anyone in any rank of life who had not the greatest respect for him, while those who knew him well loved him.'[17]

Dawson had a reputation for being a perfectionist and, in pinpointing his sound business sense, Lambton noted that Dawson had no time for horses and men that did not come up to scratch. Horses cost money to look after and train.[18] The owners could buy them at prices often running into thousands, but it was Dawson who had to make them pay and if they did not measure up, there was no point in wasting time or money on them, hence his blunt attitude towards Portland's purchase of the three yearlings. If the horses were successful, there was no harm, however, in enjoying the wealth they generated.[19] The one extravagance he did not indulge in was gambling and he was constantly warning Lambton against betting beyond his means as some aristocrats were prone to do – like Henry Weysford Charles Plantagenet Rawdon-Hastings, the Marquess of Hastings, who gambled away every single penny of his inheritance and was dead by the age of 26.[20] Dawson was not a penny-pincher and, according to Lambton, liked to do things on a grand scale when the occasion demanded. He lived well: 'and the principle of "look after the pennies and the pounds will look after themselves" found no favour with him,' Lambton wrote.[21]

Many photographs show Dawson standing alongside his clients and sometimes it is difficult to tell who is the member of the aristocracy and who is not. Steady, straightforward and no nonsense, but possessed of a barbed wit, always impeccably dressed with perfect, gracious manners to match, he did have a fondness for Scotch. Portland recalled this in his memoirs, while at the same time revealing Dawson's clever diplomacy when dealing with suggestions on how to treat a horse. Responding to Portland's recommendation that they give his horse Atlanta whisky which, in those days, was allowed, Dawson responded by humouring him, but at the same time said no. ' "By all means, Your Grace, if you like," said old Mat, "but I can't help thinking it would do me more good than the mare, so may I share it with her?" He was clearly no believer in infusing Dutch (or even Scotch!) courage into racehorses.'[22]

Dawson was very exacting. He never missed anything, being absolute in his methods of training. Together with Falmouth, he provided Fred with the security the young man needed to cope with the rigours of being on the turf. Both the owner and trainer treated the jockey like a son, particularly during these early years. They advised and guided him. Appreciating his need to learn, they gave him the space to develop, to form his own style, but at the same time succeeded in keeping his head out of the clouds. Being practical and business-minded both Dawson and Falmouth maintained a detachment from Fred's fame – and the idea of fame in general – so that, by example, they showed him that he could not rest on his laurels. Racing required not only total professionalism, but total commitment. In the case of Falmouth he saw it as a developing science – it was not just a sport – and Dawson brought a respect and direct honesty to it which he instilled into Fred; two factors which, in later years, people would always appreciate in him.

During these years, Dawson, for his part, still treated Fred like an apprentice and reminded him who was boss and the First Jockey at Heath House still had to follow the same routine there as he had always done since his first day in 1868. Falmouth, who could have had his pick of any jockey – some far superior to Fred – took it upon himself to advise him about money. He understood the value of money because, unlike his peers, he had set out in life with the intention of earning his own living, whereas his titled contemporaries, born to their privilege and riches, were brought up not to worry about such matters. It was bad taste to be constantly wondering about one's bank balance[23] particularly if one was a gentleman, and it was considered a mark of the true aristocrat not to care about it. But the unconventional Falmouth was one gentleman who was never frivolous about money and wanted to instil into Fred a certain discipline where his earnings were concerned.

Here both he and Dawson assisted where Fred's family could not. His sister Alice recalled how Fred regularly sent home cheques to help pay for their parents' expenses.[24] This was commendable in the immediate sense, but it was necessary for Fred to provide for his own future too, and not go the way of some jockeys who squandered their earnings on dissolute living. Dawson and Falmouth were only too aware of the reputation some jockeys acquired and how they could become ruined through drink or gambling or both, their talents wasted and their lives wrecked. But Fred was not only an investment; it is fair to say that Dawson and Falmouth brought him up and were certainly the most important influence in his life after he left home. To his own family, back in Prestbury, he was a hero and they were delighted with and proud of him.

Quiet and unpretentious, he still enjoyed, when he was not preparing for his next race, peaceful pursuits and he and Fred Webb were often seen playing billiards in the Rutland Arms in Newmarket.[25]

In discussing the two friends with Edith M Humphris in 1914, their fellow jockey at Heath House, Harry 'Morgie' Morgan, described how quiet the two boys were, even though they were rivals on the racecourse, and told her how Fred Webb was often invited to stay at Archer's parents' home, first in Prestbury and then after the family moved in Andoversford. In fact while Archer was away, 'Morgie' had his rooms at Heath House – rooms which were always well kept with photographs pinned up here and there. He also remembered young Fred Archer's temper, which was likely to surface when he lost races as he could not stand losing; according to 'Morgie' he had to be first always. Fred continued to study the form book constantly in an effort to understand, precisely, what his work entailed. As time passed, he would learn that success could never be taken for granted.[26]

Both Falmouth and Dawson were forward-thinking and shrewd enough to see that British horseracing needed to change and develop if it was to become the best in the world and the most respected. To this end, there was constant communication between these two and Fred, creating a joint understanding of their work. It was a relationship that allowed Fred to develop his skills to the very best of his ability and certainly with each successive season he did just that.

Falmouth was not his only retainer, but he was his first retainer – and at only 100 sovereigns, a figure which would never change even when others would pay far more. Over the next few years Fred would include, among his other retainers, the Duke of Portland, the Duke of Westminster, Lord Hastings and Lord Alington; from them Fred would earn the best part of 10,000 sovereigns a year. He would also ride for many others such as Sir George Chetwynd, Sir John Astley (another Steward of the Jockey Club) and Lord Wilton, but Viscount Falmouth would always have first claim.

Fred's first year as Champion Jockey and First Jockey, 1875, began well enough although through the winter of 1874 to 1875 he had put on weight and was beginning to find it difficult to keep it off, only getting down to 6st 12lb without resorting to drastic measures[27] – that is, considerable wasting. However, as time went on, his weight became a matter of concern to him and he began a starvation diet which, for the remainder of his life, would be the norm.[28] In a single day he would have a tablespoon of hot castor oil and half an orange, and later a single sardine washed down with a small glass of champagne. (Champagne was believed to be a good way to control weight, or at least keep appetite at bay, and aristocratic women would drink it for breakfast.) The effects of such a diet did not impede his progress, however, and the number of rides he secured between March and the end of April were consistent with the year before, except that this year his success rate was slightly higher.[29]

Even so the start of the season was not without its disappointments and having ridden Camballo to third place in the Northamptonshire Cup on 30 March, Fred missed the opportunity of riding him in the Two Thousand Guineas, scheduled for 28 April. He also missed the chance of repeating his 1874 success in the race as he rode unplaced on Falmouth's Garterley Bell. He had better luck with the One Thousand Guineas which took place two days later and rode Falmouth's Spinaway to victory.[30]

In fact 1875 is remembered for Fred's association with Spinaway and her stable companion[31] Ladylove – also owned by Viscount Falmouth. Neither Falmouth nor Dawson could make up their minds which was the best of the two. They even caused a measure of confusion when both horses were entered for the Oaks on 28 May, as Sir George Chetwynd recalled when Spinaway was set to run alongside Ladylove. 'Just before the race,' Chetwynd wrote in his autobiography years later, 'Lord Falmouth told me he and Mat Dawson disagreed about the merits of the two animals; hence his letting each take her chance.'

The Oaks was moderate compared to other years with the field being small and the quality unexceptional, apart from Spinaway and Ladylove and their prime contender La Santeuse. Of the three, Ladylove was being seen as the favourite. She possessed more style and had a readiness about her which was hard to miss, according to one newspaper which felt that she had more power than her stable companion.

The Sporting Life, however, felt that both Spinaway and Ladylove were of equal merit, particularly once the race was over, since the two effectively had the run of the finish between them.[32] Ladylove may have been judged superior, but Spinaway had the measure of her and *The Times*, although noting the perfect condition of each, was effusive in its praise of Spinaway – she looked the more physically dominant of the two.[33]

The betting was not made easier by the fact that Falmouth himself was not revealing which of the two stood the greater chance of winning, but then again he never did – in any race. Nor could he agree with Dawson over who was superior of the two; as a result both Ladylove and Spinaway went to the starting post virtual co-favourites with an equal chance of coming in ahead of the competition.[34]

Falmouth's reticence in making a declaration may also have had something to do with the Jockey Club's wariness of two horses, from the same stable, riding in the same race. Had Falmouth declared one or the other to win, then the other horse may have been seen as the pacemaker.[35] This was a practice that the Jockey Club was trying to stop, since the members and stewards believed that it was either encouraging jockeys to deliberately stall or 'pull up' their horses in favour of others or else led to accusations of malpractice on the part of the owners themselves. It could cause confusion and resentment, but was never abolished because to do so would have been an infringement of the rights of the owners who, it was acknowledged, were deemed the best judges of their horses and how they were run. Falmouth, along with Dawson was always considered a good judge, but in the case of the race with Ladylove and Spinaway, he was giving nothing away, so the press could only speculate on their chances. *The Times*, taking note of the fact that Archer was Spinaway's jockey, believed this could be an advantage in the betting, particularly in the wake of their One Thousand Guineas success some weeks before.[36]

At the start of the race Sister to Musket took the lead with Merry Maid a short distance behind, then came Fairminster, Spinaway, Ladylove, La Santeuse and Hazeldean, keeping their positions steady for a quarter of a mile before Fairminster overtook Merry Maid. Before reaching Tattenham Corner Ladylove and La Santeuse were ahead with Spinaway a close third, but as they rounded Tattenham Corner, Spinaway, being ridden particularly hard by Fred, immediately took control of the race. She headed Sister to Musket off and, being joined by Ladylove, ran the remaining distance before she pulled away easily, almost without effort, from Ladylove and won the race in a canter by three lengths at 2 minutes and 50 seconds. Many had braved the damp conditions to view these two horses.

The race had, indeed, belonged to them.[37] 'The finish gave the backers of Spinaway a severe fright,' Sir George Chetwynd recalled.[38]

Later in the year, on 14 October, when Fred rode Spinaway in the Newmarket Oaks, Ladylove also ran, but this time in definite opposition to her stable companion, so that there was no confusion in the betting and everyone knew where they stood.[39] Ladylove dominated the field, but, being well aware of the merits of both horses, Fred overtook her and secured another win by a length. He would also have secured the Ascot Derby on Spinaway (for which she was quoted as favourite) on 9 June had it not been for the appearance of George Fordham on Gilbert who trounced him in the final few lengths, coming first to Fred's second, but he did secure the Epsom Cup on the favourite, Modena, on 28 May, the same day that he won the Oaks, despite the fact that he was held back for much of the distance by Genuine before finally overtaking her and winning by a neck.[40]

Throughout the first half of the 1875 season, Fred was gaining credence, but still lacked the sophistication that placed other, more experienced jockeys ahead of him. He lacked the flair, ingenuity and style of riders like Fordham and Tom Cannon, and was too impatient, too impulsive. There were too many rough edges and at one point during the year he had thirteen losers and one winner – Ladylove – during the Three-Year-Old Triennial.[41]

In June Fred crossed the channel to France to take part in the Grand Prix de Paris on Camballo. Napoleon had established racing in France and successive rulers had built it up, but even by 1875, when Fred first rode there, the standard was not to be compared with the English.[42] Very few Frenchmen were qualified to ride, so many of the jockeys were English and, although the French fared better at training, the methods employed were essentially Newmarket-based. Fred never took to France and likewise the French never took to him, particularly later on in his career, but on this, his first French visit, he ran unplaced in the Grand Prix on 6 June, so he did not appear to be that much of a threat. However, he did not go away empty-handed, having won a race called the Prix des Pavillons by a canter on a horse called Paradoxe earlier in the day.[43]

His stamina was unmatched and, particularly throughout the summer, he was riding between six and nine races a day before moving on to the next race meeting in another part of the country.[44] There were no aeroplanes to whisk him off to his next engagement. He had to do all his travelling by train and was, more often than not, required to ride almost the moment he arrived.

He set a significant standard in 1875 which would remain consistent for the next decade and ended the season Champion Jockey for the second year running, having secured 172 wins out of 605 rides. Having begun the season in a strong position, he had maintained this throughout the summer, resulting in an equally strong finish in the autumn and winter.[45] He had more confidence in his ability to handle the horse and, in acquiring knowledge of the racecourses, was gaining greater awareness of what was needed and expected in order to negotiate those courses. Possessing tremendous energy and willpower, he went beyond expectation and more than justified Dawson's decision to make him First Jockey of Heath House.

Unfortunately the 1876 season did not begin on an auspicious note when he ran unplaced on Modena in the Batthyany Stakes Handicap on 20 March, but he did improve on Caesarion in the Tathwell Stakes when he came second.[46] From then on the start of the season was an immense improvement on the year before, with Fred winning 21 races.[47] On 25 April he won his first City and Suburban on Thunder, owned by a Mr Vyner and acknowledged by *The Times* as a formidable runner, even against Murrumbidgee – a three-year-old owned by a Mr Quartermaine-East and trained by Mathew Dawson. In fact

Dawson's stable was expected to dominate throughout, but Thunder had had a particularly good season, although opinion over his potential for the City and Suburban had been split. Many had predicted that he would win, but others paid him very little attention. On the day itself 23 horses were to run against Thunder in the City and Suburban and he stood at 22 to 1.

The fractious behaviour of Sweet Thought caused a delay of several minutes at the start. Because the horse broke away twice and took off into a valley, this may have been enough to unsettle the others and the race did not begin until 3.36 p.m. This time the start was trouble-free and, from the moment the flag fell, Fred kept Thunder back until they were at the distance. Vittoria had kept the lead, followed by Halifax and Hesper, Brigg Boy, Little Harry and Woodlands. Thunder headed a group behind them and all positions were maintained until Brigg Boy tried to take the lead and succeeded in building up the overall pace. Positions shifted as a result and the pace was such that Brigg Boy began to encounter difficulties. Archer, biding his time until the bell, guided Thunder through and, as in previous races, his judgement of speed and timing paid off and Thunder, overtaking steadily, won the race by three lengths.[48] '[S]o I need only say,' *The Sporting Life* recorded, 'that Thunder far eclipsed the performances of Knight of the Garter and Cremorne . . . and, with Archer sitting still, sailed in a winner.'[49]

Many, of course, were disappointed that they had not anticipated his success sooner, particularly since it had been predicted at the Lincoln Meeting; and *The Times* paid tribute to his performance, but the greater tribute was paid to Fred who, the papers noted, had exercised judgement and patience and had bided his time sufficiently to steer Thunder, labelled a heavyweight, through all the others to win comfortably.[50]

Thunder was a fairly consistent horse who seemed to know what was required of him and *The Times* was impressed with his performance in a trial in preparation for the Two Thousand

Guineas. In fact, unlike Atlantic two years earlier, Thunder did not have to be urged to run and his pace was so good that Fred rode him to victory by four lengths when the race took place on 2 May, proving, not for the first time, that he was at his best when riding in the big races. The season, for Fred, had got off to a flying start and that year he rode 602 races, with 218 wins.[51]

Archer's success continued when, in the same meeting as the Two Thousand Guineas he rode Domiduca, belonging to a Mr Gretton, in the Selling Stakes, and, from the beginning, dominated the race, winning in a canter by three lengths. At the end of the month came Epsom. Once again Fred rode Thunder in the Craven Stakes at 9 to 2 on and he proved himself competent for the occasion, carrying 10st 12lb and making all the running. By this stage both horse and jockey had a good enough reputation to see off any challenges and the race was theirs for the taking, with few contenders able to catch them, so that Thunder won by half a length. They also took the Great Cheshire Stakes on 12 May.

Throughout the summer Fred was very much in demand,[52] although Falmouth still had first claim on him. During the summer months the wins were based mainly on quantity rather than quality and while he achieved some significant victories – the Gold Vase on 13 June, the St James Palace Stakes (walked over) two days later and the Prince of Wales Stakes on 27 July – he failed to win others which he could have won. For instance, he ran unplaced in the Epsom Cup on 1 June – a race he had secured the previous year on Modena. He also ran unplaced in the Ascot Stakes on 13 June,[53] but his consistent ability to judge form never failed to impress and in October he was approached by two brothers, James and Sydney Smith, who owned a horse called Rosebery.

Rosebery, by Speculum out of Ladylike, was not the most remarkable of horses, but he was a stayer and the two brothers were impressed enough to believe that he was a better handicapper than Salvanos – Fred's 1872 Cesarewitch winner and a horse he had ridden on numerous occasions since then. The Smith brothers entered Rosebery for the 1876 Cesarewitch which was due to take place on 10 October and the Cambridgeshire, scheduled for a fortnight later, before approaching Fred and requesting that he ride Rosebery in the first of the two races. For the Cambridgeshire they approached Harry Constable. Fred agreed, but, given that the horse had never won a race in its life, Admiral Rous, the country's foremost handicapper, who literally wrote the rules on handicapping, was in a quandary as to how to handicap this particular horse.[54] He gave him 5st 13lb only to change his mind later when others persuaded him that the horse had great potential and he gave him 7st 3lb instead.

Fred, wasting very hard to meet the weights, was placed under considerable pressure to reveal his knowledge of Rosebery's capabilities since his riding a maiden four-year-old in a long distance handicap was considered somewhat out of the ordinary. The fact that the horse was also being backed down from its starting price of 50 to 1 increased speculation.[55] Rosebery began in front, held off the competition and won by four lengths. Sir George Chetwynd was there and remembered the jubilation which followed. The financial gain of the Smith brothers, no doubt enormous, was never made public, but Fred's gift payment of a thousand sovereigns was a huge reward for a nineteen-year-old. Nor was the Cesarewitch a one-off for Rosebery. Several days later, on Tuesday 24 October, he won the Cambridgeshire, with Constable up and with 14lb on his back and a short price.

For Fred, 1876 was even better than the previous year and he was becoming much more established, literally sweeping the board – achieving 207 winners, and ending the season, once again, as Champion Jockey. Harry Constable came second and achieved just 74. The winter closed in and Fred returned to hunting, not necessarily to break away from racing until the beginning of the next season, but to prepare for it. At the start of the 1877 season he was back at Heath House preparing for what would prove to be a significantly triumphant year.[56] It got off to a very good start and he relaxed into the process straightaway, not experiencing the same start-of-season jitters which had marked other years. He was more focused and secured early wins,[57] and from that point he never looked back, achieving more than twenty wins over the first five weeks of the season alone.

The Heath House stables dominated the turf between 1877 and 1879 and, according to Fred's biographers, Lord Rosebery arranged for a large number of congratulatory cards to be printed off, perhaps in anticipation of future wins. The first half of 1877 was spent preparing Falmouth's Silvio – a bay by Blair Athol out of Silverhair – for the Classics. The horse held great promise and, winning the Ham Stakes at Goodwood on his first appearance, went on to win three other events at Newmarket. However, 'I may mention,' wrote Chetwynd, 'the defeat of . . . Silvio in the Biennial at the Craven Week, owing to a blinding storm right in the face of the horses. The winner was Grey Friar . . .'[58]

Fred blamed the weather too, but he could not use the same excuse in the Two Thousand Guineas, when Silvio finished an unsatisfactory third to Chamant, and Heath House was left to wonder if the bay would be ready for the Derby in May. For his jockey, though, success continued to follow him and, before the Derby was due to take place, he was taking part in the City and Suburban again on 24 April. This time his mount was Julius Caesar.[59] It was a fine day which enhanced the City and Suburban's reputation as one of the great races of the year, with many favourites to choose from, making it unpredictable but exciting.

Deciding the possible winner had been difficult in recent weeks since the standard was so high and Julius Caesar had only entered the running a fortnight before. But, despite having a firm position, there was still a problem. Just before the race was due to start, someone tried to have him excluded by sending a telegram containing instructions to withdraw him from the race; it was proved to be a false telegram, and once the fraud was uncovered, the race was allowed to go ahead.[60] A number of the lightweights refused to settle at first, but once everyone was in order, the flag fell and Julius Caesar took the lead straightaway. He held it for a dozen paces before being pulled back – another example of Archer reserving his horse's energy. He maintained a steady pace before regaining the lead at the distance; and, as the others began to fall away, won the race in a canter by six lengths.[61]

Fred was being studied with increasing interest and, as proof of his individual approach to races, did not adopt the same tactics twice. Everything depended upon the type of race, the course and the mount. During the same Epsom Spring Meeting he rode in the Maiden Plate on Birdie who quickly took the lead and kept it. As *The Times* noted, the race was hardly worth reporting since Archer and Birdie's chances of winning were hardly in dispute and indeed they won, in a canter, by four lengths.

If jockeys could be distinguished by particular trademarks (with George Fordham it was the element of surprise), with Fred Archer it was the judgement of speed and distance, and reporters and public alike were beginning to recognise the aspects of his method which secured victory; how he maintained a set position and speed from the start, waiting until the very last second before giving the horse its head and running clear of the rest of the field to win by two, three or four lengths.

His ability to exercise control over a horse and judge its staying power at set distances was becoming expert, making his progress in a race appear almost leisurely. In the Derby, on 30 May he kept Silvio at what was described as a moderate distance, allowing Glen Arthur to secure a lead.[62] This remained the state of play until all seventeen Derby runners came down the hill, and as they started their approach to home they began to catch up with one another, signifying that at this point the real competition began. The pace increased to such an extent that Glen Arthur, having kept the lead unopposed, now found himself challenged by Silvio, so that as they reached the distance, they were sufficiently close for Silvio to take the lead and win by half a length.

Fred's parents, watching the whole event, were inordinately proud of their son. Mrs Archer, who appeared to have overcome her fears that Fred's life would be wasted without the benefit of an education and even enjoyed the odd bet herself, cried as the crowds cheered her son while her husband stood by with a huge smile on his face.

'. . . F. Archer may undoubtedly claim to have thus early in his career surpassed . . . the feats of all other jockeys,' *The Sporting Life* noted afterwards. 'F. Archer commands so great a following . . . that every victory . . . achieved by him is more generally welcomed than perhaps that of any other jockey . . .'[63]

The victory had been a triumph, but six seconds had been added to the 1876 time. Fred had completed the race in 2 minutes 50 seconds, against the previous year's 2 minutes 44 seconds.[64]

After the Derby, Silvio was ridden in the St Leger, again by Fred, alongside his stable companion, Lady Golightly, who had come fourth in the Oaks. Unfortunately Silvio was not on top form – 'shaky' was the opinion of *The Times* and despite his popularity and Falmouth's and Dawson's confidence in his ability to beat Lady Golightly, the public was prepared to back the mare because of her success at York. To add to Fred's troubles, the ground was heavy, due to a recent downpour, but this had not affected attendance and many people turned up at Doncaster.[65] 'It was rumoured,' noted *The Sporting Life* on 15 September, 'that Archer had declared his wish to ride the mare instead of the Derby hero.'[66]

The Times also picked up on this, noting that Archer had in the end decided to go along with whatever Falmouth wanted. As for the public, they continued to back Lady Golightly and with both her and Fred as favourites, many quipped that Falmouth (owner of the horse and retainer of the jockey) would be first and second.[67] Expectation, therefore, was high, justifying Dawson's and Falmouth's confidence, especially when Lady Golightly's 3 to 1 went back a point, and the race itself seemed to go in Silvio's favour.

In the event, however, Lady Golightly would prove to be a formidable opponent. Sheldrake took the lead, followed by Plunger and Manoeuvre. Silvio and Hidalgo, with Fontainebleau, came next with Lady Golightly and these positions were maintained to the foot of the hill where Plunger rushed forward to take the lead. After this some of the horses had difficulty keeping the pace up and Sheldrake gave way, along with Plunger. The lead was held by Manoeuvre until the straight when Silvio, being pushed to the limit by Fred, increased his speed, gained an advantage over Manoeuvre and continued on steadily towards the distance with Manoeuvre and Lady Golightly taking up second and third places. But then Lady Golightly, after a hectic run, overtook Manoeuvre to take second place as Silvio won by three lengths, the time standing at 2 minutes 20 seconds. It was a popular win, but the shakiness in Silvio which seemed evident, would become more characteristic later on. *The Sporting Life*, however, expressed disappointment at the pace, commenting that although it was a good race, it was rather slow.[68]

By 1878 Silvio's successes were moderate compared with the previous year. He won two races at Newmarket in the spring, with Archer up, but he did not take the Ascot Gold Cup. Verneuil had that privilege. Silvio came second in the Champion Stakes on 10 October while his stable companion Jannette (as ridden by Fred) came first. He did not do too badly here, however, because, following on behind were Petrarch,

Glen Arthur and Verneuil. He later won the Jockey Club Cup, but failed to win any race as a five-year-old.[69]

Having ended 1877 as Champion Jockey yet again, with a total of 218 wins, Fred outclassed all jockeys on the turf by securing five wins in as many days at the very start of the 1878 season. In fact this year showed him going from strength to strength, riding 619 races, with 229 wins, but at a cost. He was still struggling to meet the required weights and this year he began using a powerful laxative concoction, the contents of which remain a mystery, but which served its purpose for anyone who had the nerve to try it (see the chapter 'Behind the Image'). Fred's stamina and energy amazed everyone and as he continued to increase his rides, he took the year by storm.

1879 was a below-average year for Fred, with just 197 wins.[70] But he did secure the City and Suburban on 22 April on a horse, owned by the American Mr P Lorillard, named Parole, an animal which Sir John Astley (a close friend and associate of Fred) recalled in his memoirs, *Fifty Years of My Life in the World of Sport at Home and Abroad* (1893). He was not very impressed when he first set eyes on him in 1879, referring to Parole as having a 'shaggy and rough coat'.[71] 'An American sportsman, Mr Robins,' he wrote, 'wanted me to back him for the Newmarket Handicap, which was run that week, to win 20,000 sovereigns.'

Robins was well acquainted with Parole's owner – to the point where he managed all his horses and had travelled over from America with Parole. He was, therefore, in a position to know the horse's potential and to know what he was talking about, but Astley thought otherwise.

'I suggested,' he wrote afterwards, 'that he should . . . state what money he was game to lose, and that I would do the best I could for him; moreover, I should get a better price than most, because I was going to back my own horse Drumhead, for a monkey for the same race; the result was that I agreed to back Parole for a monkey. He carried 8st 4lb and mine 7st 2lb and to look at the two horses, it was good odds that mine ought to beat the other at even weights.'[72]

Parole won the Newmarket Handicap.

'You can't go by looks, that's for certain, ain't it? . . . like a fool,' continued Astley, 'I never had a bob on the Yankee. Nevertheless I saw him win very cleverly, a long way in front of my sleek old gee.'

The Sporting Life was not impressed either initially. 'Light-necked, rough-coated, leggy and curby-hocked' was the description given. The newspaper also believed that had no-one known who he was, many would have backed against him on sight. However, when he 'cleverly' won the City and Suburban in April, *The Sporting Life* acknowledged that the Americans had the measure of the British when it came to horseracing, and that the British could do worse than learn from their overseas counterparts – a message which would be reiterated in later years.[73]

Fred rode Parole again on 8 May in the Great Cheshire Handicap Stakes[74] and won by three lengths with Sir John Astley's Drumhead coming fifth. Parole won the Epsom Gold Cup on 30 May, this time with Morbey up. He then ran unplaced in the Ascot Stakes on 10 June,[75] but there was no denying that Parole was an exceptional horse, just as Fred was an exceptional jockey.

Fred's favourite horse for this year was Jannette, another of Viscount Falmouth's string and who had been foaled in 1875. She was a bay filly by Lord Clifden out of Chevisaunce. From the beginning, she showed immense promise securing such races as the Richmond, Clearwell and Criterion Stakes, among others in 1877, before taking the Oaks, the St Leger, the Park Hill and Champion Stakes, as well as the Newmarket and Yorkshire Oaks in 1878. Each time Fred had been her jockey. She also came second in the One Thousand Guineas.[76]

At the start of the 1879 season Silvio, Jannette and their two stable companions, Wheel of Fortune and Charibert, appeared to be the finest of the Heath House collection and Dawson took pleasure in showing them off to Falmouth, their owner, during trials held on the Rowley Mile start at Newmarket.[77] But later successive races revealed that Silvio was losing his enthusiasm, possibly, it has been suggested, because he was being used too much for trials in which he was the pacemaker – in particular for Jannette and Wheel of Fortune. He had also gone up in the weights and no longer seemed to have the energy or the inclination for running. Whatever the reason, he began losing races, such as the Hardwicke Stakes against Fordham's Chippendale and then the Ascot Gold Vase to the up-and-coming star of the turf Isonomy on 10 June. The question was: who was the best of the two stayers, Isonomy or Silvio?

Sir George Chetwynd remembered Isonomy's performance from the year before: 'Isonomy showed us that he was a good horse by winning the Cambridgeshire by two lengths from Touchet and La Merveille . . . Porter never could have known that the winner was the great horse he demonstrated himself to be afterwards, or he never would have started at 40 to 1.[78]

So Isonomy was a horse with a certain level of power and although small, achieving a maximum height of 15.2 hands, he was sturdy enough and able to hold his own against larger yearlings. '[A]nd thus earned his nickname,' writes the sports writer, Richard Onslow, in his *Royal Ascot*, 'the definition of "Isonomy" being "the equal distribution of rights and privileges."'[79]

At the start of the race Archer, on Silvio, brought up the rear and all the riders maintained their positions until they rounded the top turn, but on the descent Castlereagh gathered pace and led by half a dozen lengths with Isonomy second.[80] He maintained his lead into the straight before Isonomy sought to challenge the leader and then Silvio began to gather pace and the race was between these two with Castlereagh falling back into third place before Isonomy won by half a length. *The Times* expressed the view that Tom Cannon had seemed uneasy on

Isonomy and that Archer had looked the more likely winner, but Silvio, *The Times* commented, had a weakness about him, possibly inherited, and he lacked staying power as a result. Isonomy, therefore, wore him down and had no problems winning the race.

After that Silvio never quite reached the levels of fitness that he had formerly shown and his progress in the future led Falmouth to consider retiring him to stud. He came second in the Bunbury Stakes at the Newmarket July Meeting, being beaten by a head by the French horse Phenix,[81] but it was due to Archer's skill and ability to keep him going that he managed to finish at all. So Silvio was retired to stud and later exported to France, earning his owner 7,000 sovereigns. France seemed to suit him and he became champion sire.[82]

Wheel of Fortune was a mare of formidable standing and if any horse could be identified with the unique partnership that was Falmouth, Dawson and Archer, then it was her. By Adventurer out of Queen Bertha (the latter another favourite of Falmouth and winner of the 1865 Derby), she was possessed of tremendous speed, staying power and a big appetite – particularly oranges, nuts and, on one occasion, meat pies. She was a pleasure to watch and a favourite of press and public alike.[83]

On 2 May 1879, Fred rode her in the One Thousand Guineas at Newmarket, after it had been rumoured that she was not on her best form, although the truth was that no-one was really sure what her condition was.[84] The press declared that even if she was not on form, given her previous performances, she would still be extremely difficult to beat. There was a respect for Wheel of Fortune which was never misplaced, particularly since she was further testimony to Fred's ability to judge speed and timing. She began some lengths behind the leaders and, using a formula which was now quite familiar, Archer tapped into her speed and applied it accordingly by, first, keeping her back – reserving her speed in the first quarter of a mile before allowing her to gradually increase her pace and overtake her rivals to win by a canter – four lengths ahead of Mr T Jennings' Abaye, maintaining her popularity and strengthening her reputation.[85]

Her presence at the Oaks during the Epsom Summer Meeting drew large crowds and Wheel of Fortune was already a legend in her own time. She had, as yet, remained unbeaten and Fred acknowledged her as the best horse he had ever ridden. Dawson too admitted that she was exceptional, even though he always claimed that another mare, Catherine Hayes, was the best he ever trained. Wheel of Fortune's performance in the Oaks on 30 May, therefore, was met with spirited confidence, although some wondered about her staying qualities; perhaps some felt that her success was a bubble waiting to burst, but Heath House had total confidence and, once again, Fred was to ride her.

As the race started, Fred held her back at a steady pace until they were halfway, then denounced all her critics by taking Wheel of Fortune to the front and from there taking the race – winning in a canter by three lengths. A popular win, but for Fred not as perfect as the Oaks of 1878. In terms of speed he had not improved on the previous year, completing the course in 3 minutes 2 seconds, whereas in 1878 he had won the Oaks in 2 minutes 54 seconds.[86] This, however, did not detract from the general enthusiasm felt by all.

Yet the health of Wheel of Fortune always seemed to be a source of great interest to the media of the time. The day after the Oaks, The Times reported once more that she had a clean bill of health and she was now heralded as Viscount Falmouth's 'Grand Mare'.[87] It was more or less accepted that Wheel of Fortune would follow her stable companion, Jannette, to the St Leger at Doncaster in September. However, as The Times reported in a final note, Doncaster required stayers even if Epsom did not, so Falmouth's colours would not perhaps be quite so lucky.

At that stage, however, there was no reason to suppose that Wheel of Fortune could not win the race, but, unfortunately, the words of The Times were to prove prophetic and she would never reach the St Leger. She had won all, bar one, of her races, but broke down during the Great Yorkshire Stakes. It was afterwards discovered that there was an enlargement in one of her forelegs. As a result she had to be taken out of the running for the St Leger and Fred would ride Visconti in her stead. Withdrawing her from racing, Viscount Falmouth sold her to the 5th Duke of Portland (who would die that December) and Wheel of Fortune became a brood mare, although not a very good one.[88]

The unique partnership that was Falmouth, Dawson and Archer was so renowned by now that the racing public was confused by Charibert's entry for the Two Thousand Guineas on 30 April at 25 to 1.[89] As there seemed to be no other horse capable of matching Charibert, no-one knew where to put their money. Since Falmouth never placed bets on any horse, including his own, the bookmakers were not happy either. Charibert, with Archer up, won by a length and a half. Two days later Wheel of Fortune won the One Thousand Guineas[90] and Falmouth achieved a double, albeit with two different horses. But for some time Charibert had been a cause for concern which was probably why he was allowed to start at 25 to 1. He had developed wind trouble that affected his breathing and became progressively worse as time went on, so much so that Falmouth was forced to sell him, at a loss, to a Mr Clare Vyner.

That left the last of the four, Jannette – Fred's favourite in 1878 but no longer on form the following year. Trained for the Ascot Gold Cup, she was literally floored by Isonomy.[91] She was also beaten in the Queen's Plate at Doncaster. Isonomy was in this race too and in fact was proving to be the shining light of 1879, but in the race for the Gold Cup Archer ensured that Jannette ran at her best and for a while the two seemed neck and neck. In the end though, Isonomy, with Tom Cannon up, won the race. Jannette did go on to win the Jockey Club Cup on 24 October, but it was to be her last victory and Fred did not ride her again.

Having secured 197 wins this year, Fred maintained his status as Champion Jockey. He was ending the decade on a particularly high note and the approach of a new one signalled hope for the future. Except for one element which was becoming a continual source of aggravation – George Fordham.

Notes

1.   Mortimer, Roger, Onslow, Richard & Willet, Peter, *The Biographical Encyclopaedia of British Flat Racing*, pp.206–7
2.   Lane, Charles, *Harry Hall's Classic Winners*, p.96
3.   Correspondence from P Hatfield, College Archivist of Eton College
4.   Correspondence from Judith Courtheys, Assistant Archivist of Christ Church, Oxford University
5.   Mortimer, Onslow & Willet, pp.206–7
6.   *The Times*, 10 November 1889
7.   Tanner, Michael & Cranham, Gerry, *Great Jockeys of the Flat: A Celebration of Two Centuries of Jockeyship*, p.63
8.   Chetwynd, Sir George, *Racing Reminiscences and Experience of the Turf*, pp.136–7
9.   Humphris, Edith M, *The Life of Mathew Dawson*, pp.95–6
10.   Ibid, p.95
11.   Portland, 6th Duke of, *Memories of Racing and Hunting*, pp.23–4
12.   Humphris, *The Life of Mathew Dawson*, p.103
13.   Portland, pp.23–4
14.   Ibid, p.28
15–16. Ibid, p.14
17–19. Lambton, The Honourable George, *Men and Horses I Have Known*, p.38
20.   Mortimer, Onslow & Willet, p.264
21.   Lambton, p.38
22.   Portland, p.24
23.   Welcome, John, *Fred Archer: A Complete Study*, p.32
24.   Humphris, *The Life of Fred Archer*, p.71
25.   Ibid, p.100
26.   Ibid, p.101
27–8.   Welcome, John, *Fred Archer: A Complete Study*, p.29
29–30. Weatherby, J E & J P, *The Racing Calendar for the Year 1875*
31.   *The Times*, 29 May 1875
32.   *The Sporting Life*, 28 May 1875
33–4.   *The Times*, 29 May 1875
35.   Lane, p.92

36–7.   *The Times*, 29 May 1875
38.   Chetwynd, pp.136–7
39.   *The Times*, 15 October 1875
40.   *The Sporting Life*, 15 October 1875
41.   Weatherby, J E & J P, *The Racing Calendar for the Year 1875*
42.   Longrigg, Roger, *The History of Horseracing*, p.175
43–5.   Weatherby, J E & J P, *The Racing Calendar for the Year 1875 (Continental Races)*
46–7.   Weatherby, J E & J P, *The Racing Calendar for the Year 1876*
48.   *The Times*, 26 April 1876
49.   *The Sporting Life*, 26 April 1876
50.   *The Times*, 20 April 1876
51–3.   Weatherby, J E & J P *The Racing Calendar for the Year 1876*
54–5.   Welcome, John, *Fred Archer: A Complete Study*, pp.37–9
56–7.   Weatherby, J E & J P, *The Racing Calendar for the Year 1877*
58.   Chetwynd, p.154
59.   Welcome, John, *Fred Archer: A Complete Study*, p.53
60.   Chetwynd, p.154
61.   *The Times*, 24 April 1877
62.   *The Times*, 31 May 1877
63–4.   *The Sporting Life*, 31 May 1877
65.   *The Times*, 15 September 1877
66.   *The Sporting Life*, 15 September 1877
67.   *The Times*, 15 September 1877
68.   *The Sporting Life*, 15 September 1877
69.   Weatherby, J E & J P, *The Racing Calendar for the Year 1878*
70.   Weatherby, J E & J P, *The Racing Calendar for the Year 1879*
71–2.   Astley, Sir John Dugdale, *Fifty Years of My Life in the World of Sport at Home and Abroad*, pp.300–8
73.   *The Sporting Life*, 23 April 1879
74–5.   Weatherby, J E & J P, *The Racing Calendar for the Year 1879*
76.   Mortimer, Onslow, & Willet, p.300
77.   Welcome, John, *Fred Archer: A Complete Study*, p.50
78.   Chetwynd, pp.179–80
79.   Onslow, Richard, *Royal Ascot*, p.54
80.   *The Times*, 11 June 1879
81.   Lane, p.98
82.   Mortimer, Onslow & Willet, p.562
83.   Ibid, p.100
84–5.   *The Times*, 3 May 1879
86–7.   *The Times*, 31 May 1879
88.   Mortimer, Onslow & Willet, p.654
89.   Welcome, John, *Fred Archer: A Complete Study*, p.52
90–1.   Mortimer, Onslow & Willet, p.654

Age and Experience

A rather classic clash of personalities existed between Fred Archer and his arch rival, George Fordham, a jockey twenty years his senior. Archer was acknowledged as an excellent horseman and jockey, perhaps one of the finest of his generation, who was able to give above and beyond expectation, but it was George Fordham who was regarded by many as the true genius – one whose skill seemed to be effortless. 'Fordham was, without doubt, one of the greatest jockeys who ever rode,' remembered Portland for whom Fordham rode on several occasions. 'Some people thought he was even better than Archer – especially at Newmarket.'[1]

In fact Portland expressed the view most people shared – even Archer, himself, admitted that he could never quite fathom Fordham out and that his riding skills, unlike those of other jockeys, were to say the least, sometimes beyond his comprehension. Nor could Archer find it within himself to admire him for it, at least not openly.

In order to understand the relationship between Fred and George, it is necessary to look at Fred's relationships with other jockeys. Despite the high level of competitiveness which existed in the racing world, Fred could count some of the most professional jockeys – Tom Cannon and others – as his friends. He respected them and admired them all; and if he was ever beaten by them in races, he gave them full credit. There was a mutual respect in a highly competitive sport and the respect was extended off the course, but with George Fordham it was a different matter and it frustrated Archer to think that he was one of the few jockeys he could not beat.

From the moment Fred began racing for Heath House, he was riding against George Fordham, but their most significant meeting happened on 6 May 1874 when Fred won the Two Thousand Guineas on Atlantic and Fordham, riding the favourite Ecossais, came in a poor third. They had been battling it out ever since, although it was not until Fred had really become successful that their rivalry began to take hold and, as their little battles on the racecourse became more well known, so the public never failed to be entertained by them.

George Fordham had very little time for Fred Archer. Born in Cambridge on 24 September 1837, he had had his first winner in 1851, six years before Fred was born, and he secured the Cambridgeshire in 1852. He was Champion Jockey between 1855 and 1863, then again in 1865, 1867, 1868 and 1869, and joint Champion Jockey with Charles Maidment in 1871,[2] when Fred was nothing more than a willing apprentice and was being told by other jockeys that he could not ride for nuts. Fordham's reputation was therefore already firmly established long before Fred put his stamp on the turf – certainly long before he was in the running for First Jockey at Heath House.

Although Fordham secured the Oaks in 1859, 1868 and 1870, the One Thousand Guineas in 1859, 1861, 1865, 1868 and 1869, and the Two Thousand Guineas in 1867 and 1868,[3] two races – the Derby and the St Leger – always eluded him. Not that he was unduly put out by this. He was self-assured enough to know that he had nothing to prove to 'Mr Archer', as he rather sarcastically called him as if making a mockery of what he supposed was Fred's inflated ego. In fact Fordham had nothing to prove to anyone and had reached a stage in his life where he could take horseracing in his stride as he invariably did.

George Fordham was an extremely accomplished and able rider. *The Times* noted that he rode with his head as well as his hands and his skill resembled that of the modern jockey.[4] He rode with short leathers, in the manner of today's jockeys. Since the method, known as the 'monkey on a stick method', became popular only in the early twentieth century, thanks to the American jockey Tod Sloan, who adopted it, it is fair to say that Fordham was some thirty or forty years ahead of his time.[5] Add to this a gentle, but guiding control of his horse without resorting to the use of a whip, plus an ability to keep the animal perfectly balanced right to the end of a race, it is little wonder that so many admired him, but Fred Archer, impatient for success and thwarted at every turn by Fordham, found him very difficult to tolerate.

'He was the most unassuming and, perhaps, honest man I ever met,' wrote Harry Custance of George Fordham in his autobiography, *Riding Recollections and Turf Stories* (1894).[6] Custance knew both George and Fred very well during their careers and was someone in whom they could both confide. He in his turn had plenty of scope to observe their contrasting personalities and riding methods and was apt to place the two of them in perspective:

> Many strong arguments still take place regarding which was the better horseman. They were two men totally different both in build and seat. Fordham was very short, and rode short, while Archer was very tall, and rode extra long. Neither of them had the graceful seat of Tom Cannon, who was a happy medium, but still, they were both fine horsemen. Archer had nerves of iron, beautiful hands, a good head, and an extraordinary eye for seeing what other horses were doing in a race.[7]

Custance, who often rode against both Archer and Fordham, believed that Archer was one of the best behaved jockeys at the starting post 'although I know it is not generally thought so,' he continued. 'I don't mean to say that he would not take an advantage if the chance offered . . . but I don't believe he ever went down with a premeditated idea of getting three or four lengths' start.'[8]

Custance, however, was closer to Fordham personally, being nearer to him in age and having been best man at his wedding. He was also his son's godfather. In fact their friendship was so close that many mistook one for the other which Custance always found incredible. 'There was not the slightest resemblance . . . I was very much taller and bigger.'[9]

The artists of *Vanity Fair*, perhaps more generous to Fordham than to Archer, characterised a small, but sturdy individual with side whiskers. Archer's likeness was done when Fred was at the height of his powers, but reveals a character under a great deal of strain. Fordham's appears quite calm and unruffled and this extreme contrast seemed to be the hallmark, not only of their differing characters, but of their whole relationship. Had Fred, in particular, been able to step back more often and view his rival objectively, he may have seen what Custance already knew.

Of their riding skills, Custance believed that whereas Fred's strength lay at the starting post, George Fordham's lay at the finish. Custance wrote:

Fordham sat back in the saddle and, as it were, drove his horse from him, never having loosed his head, both acting together. One peculiarity about horses which Fordham rode was, they always finished straight, and seldom changed their legs. Now, with Archer riding long, he invariably got up the horse's neck, very often finishing with a loose rein, consequently his mounts frequently changed their legs a time or two.[10]

This, he decided, shortened the horse's stride and slowed him down by a neck or more, so Fordham's technique was more advantageous.

In fact Custance seemed to understand Fordham's approach to races far better than Fordham did himself, as did Sir George Chetwynd, who wrote:

> I went down the course about 200 yards from the winning post, and as Fordham passed me, he was sitting like a monkey on Trombone's neck. I conclude to ease the horse's back for a moment from the weight, and I could see his little hands and fingers gripping the single rein in a vice of iron as the old horse struggled for his head. 'Not yet, old man! Not yet!' you could almost swear Fordham was saying encouragingly to his mount till within ten strides of the post, when he let him have his head inch by inch, and won all out, three quarters of a length from Hermitage, who beat Cat's Eye by a neck.'[11]

Cat's Eye was Archer's mount and the race was the Bushes Handicap in the Craven Meeting in 1875. Chetwynd hinted at Fordham's timing, measure of pace by inches and his absolute control of the horse as well as the finish of the race itself, not allowing the horse its head until the very last moment. Precision was pinpoint and these were skills which had been evident when he won the Cambridgeshire as far back as 1871 on Sabinus. Custance remarked on the fact that the race was 'beautifully timed and resolutely finished'.[12] This was characteristic of Fordham's ability, but once that particular race, or any other for that matter, was over, he had no idea how to explain his tactics or the progress of the race to his waiting employers, being unable to give them a straight answer. It was as if the horse had done all the thinking and he had just gone along for the ride.[13] Unlike Archer, who prided himself on being able to analyse a race before, during and after, Fordham just rode instinctively and subconsciously. He was able to adapt both himself and his horse to the racecourse and the conditions so that their timing was perfect and, more to the point, effortless – as if Fordham's entire race had required no skill at all.

Here was the essential difference between Fordham and Archer. Fordham had been racing for so long that his performance was almost automatic. He did not have to think about how he got his horse from A to B, so that, once the race was over, he did find it difficult to explain to others just how he managed to negotiate the course in order to win it. In fact he appeared indifferent and his rather mundane answers and lack of detail are well known. The answer may lie in the fact that while the race was in progress, he was constantly aware of everything around him and what he had to do to reach the winning post ahead of the other jockeys, but once it was over, he switched off mentally, which Fred could not do. The race was done, finished with – it had been won and that was that. As writers have noted, the actual theory and technicalities[14] of horseracing as a whole held no interest for him.

In fact he was bored by them, but he did know good horses from bad and was not afraid of making his opinions known. He once advised one of the Rothschilds not to buy the winner of a race, only to be ignored and have his judgement justified later when Rothschild discovered that the horse was no good. What is interesting is that, in riding for some very famous and wealthy people, Fordham did not feel himself answerable to them and they, in turn, did not feel inclined to probe into his methods. They had become used to his manner (it became something of a trademark) and his rather off-hand approach to racing only added to his popularity and they still sought him out to ride their horses.

Such an attitude of indifference to a profession which was life and blood to someone as dedicated as Fred would, perhaps, be another reason for the antagonism which existed between the two jockeys. Archer saw his work as a continuing learning process and gave chapter and verse on his own and his horse's performances in a race (not to mention everybody else's performances), but Fordham could only tell his paymasters which position he was holding when he reached the winning post. In fact Fordham may have found Archer's enthusiasm for tactical analysis rather annoying, not to mention precocious, and used his own hidden skills to show that no amount of reasoning and studying could replace years of experience – which is what the older jockey had against the younger.

Fordham was too old and experienced to be swayed by the precocity of another and, having the measure of Archer almost from the very beginning, found it necessary to keep the younger jockey firmly in his place, treating him as if he were nothing more than an apprentice. He enjoyed reminding Fred that victory was not exclusively his, that he could not ride the turf as if he owned it, and was apt to keep the younger jockey on edge whenever he got the chance.

Fordham would allow him the run of a race before challenging in the final few yards, saying 'cluck cluck' to his own horse to let Fred know that he was there, knowing that it would incense Archer. Many wrote of how Fred was often incensed and exasperated by Fordham's tendency to 'cluck cluck' at his horse, not knowing where the 'old man' (as he sometimes called Fordham, among other things) was and being too terrified to look round.[15] This irritating habit of Fordham conditioned Archer into feeling unnerved, so that every time he heard it, it put him off his stride and he would find himself overtaken. Fordham may also have used it to trivialise Archer's efforts – as if to say that it took just a little verbal encouragement to make the horse move faster. Whatever the reason, he would go on to win – pipping Fred to the post in an aggravating 'almost, but not quite – try again next time' fashion. Fred's confidence, on a high with victory in his grasp, would then come crashing down as Fordham overtook him. Coming so close and then being beaten maddened Archer still further and on one occasion he was seen throwing his saddle across the weighing room in rage. Fordham was not only beating him, he was stalling him in his pursuit of success.

What possibly made the situation worse, of course, was how this rivalry looked to others. Since racing was a great public spectacle and reported widely in the newspapers, Fordham and Archer were constantly on show, as were their contemporaries. They themselves were a constant source of interest and, no matter how much the public admired Archer, it also delighted them when Fordham got the better of him and took him by surprise – or rather when Fordham knocked him off his pedestal and presented their rivalry as a source of entertainment.

The irony was that Fordham acknowledged Archer's appeal with the public – he was after all the current Champion Jockey – and this was perhaps another incentive on his part to bring him down a peg or two, to focus the public's attention on the fact that the young jockey, as Champion Jockey, was vulnerable. His title could be taken away from him at any time. Archer was not infallible, he was not the greatest of riders. He was not the hero the public perceived him to be. Even so, seeking the downfall of Fred Archer was not a priority with Fordham – he may have been coming between Fred and his adoring multitude, but not enough to ridicule him outright. At the end of the day the older jockey allowed the younger his stage, so the rivalry, while intense on the racecourse, was not an obsession.

Nor was it with Fred – off the course. He could rant and rave, call Fordham every name under the sun and throw saddles across weighing room floors, but he was as much in awe of the older jockey as anyone else, primarily because Fordham was a master of deception, a man who could ride a horse to victory and not know how he had done it – a man who could take in the progress of a race at a glance and win it with very little effort. It was this, above all else, which unnerved Archer and he never felt at ease while racing against Fordham. He could never tell what Fordham might do, where he might come from. Fordham seemed to have the luck of the devil and by turns he became known as 'The Demon' and 'The Kid'. To Archer, when he was in a generous mood, he was 'The Old Man' or 'The Old Gentleman', but when he was up against him, he was 'The Demon'. The absolute extreme was 'a kidding bastard'.[16]

The only racecourse where Fred seemed to have the upper-hand over Fordham was Epsom. Fordham hated the place, never feeling comfortable with the air of grand superiority which occasions like the Epsom meetings seemed to inspire and in which Fred revelled. Nor did Fordham particularly like the actual course, although in that respect he was not alone; many jockeys thought that it was too dangerous – especially Tattenham Corner with its unpredictable bend – so here at least Fred could say that he was the master.

Standing back, observing them, was Custance who enjoyed the company of both of them. 'Fordham and myself were always the greatest of friends,' Custance remembered[17] which points to another interesting fact in relation to Archer and Fordham: neither jockey drew others into this rivalry of theirs. They had mutual friends all over, in particular Custance, but their mutual disrespect for each other appears to have been concentrated only on the racecourse and was purely professional, not personal.

After all, Fordham had other interests, such as hunting, shooting and cricket. Straightforward, plain speaking, with a no-nonsense 'take me as you find me' attitude, his only weakness appears to have been a fondness for drink. This did not seem to impede his performance in races, unlike the jockey Jem Snowden who went on a drinking binge and turned up at a particular racecourse to take part in a race only to be told that he was a week late. He was left standing trying to figure out where he had been for the last seven days. In Fordham's case alcohol was not a hindrance and when another fellow jockey suggested that the horse he was to ride could benefit from a drop of port, Fordham decided it would be of greater benefit to himself than the horse. He went on to finish the bottle before climbing into the saddle and, ever the accomplished and experienced jockey, rode the race totally drunk and won.[18]

Nor was racing itself necessarily a priority in his life. Despite his evident genius there were aspects of the sport that he had very little time for. He loathed the gambling side of it and it is understood that he would not allow his son to become involved in horseracing.[19] Fordham had proved that he could ride and win races and had been Champion Jockey, so that now, in his later years, he considered racing merely to give him financial security until he could retire – a means to an end.[20] He had every intention of retiring one day (he did so twice) and therefore approached racing in a much more relaxed, if not laid back frame of mind than Archer did or ever could.

Fordham did, however, at one point in his career, have something of a superstitious streak and in this respect it was Tom French, Archer's Heath House mentor, who may have been the only one who could get the better of him. The story goes that French, picking up a horseshoe just minutes before the race, told Fordham that he, French, was going to win. Rattled, Fordham rode the race and subsequently lost it.[21] But now Tom French was dead and no-one had been able to rattle him since.

Some people believed that Fordham had very little trouble with his weight, and that he never had to waste like other jockeys – especially Archer, whose life was becoming regulated by wasting regimes. 'It is a curious fact with regard to Fordham,' Chetwynd noted, 'that although he never wasted and took little exercise, he never seemed to blow.'[22] This is not necessarily the full story. By middle age he was having problems with his weight and had to waste hard to keep it down. Custance, in whom he confided, recalled how he would not play cricket (another sport he was good at) until he had eaten because he had been wasting.[23] Archer seemed, at the moment, to be able to cope with his wasting techniques, but Fordham's would begin to affect his lungs, prompting him to retire for the second time, but this time for good, in 1883.

His first retirement had been several years earlier when, sometime in 1876, Fordham decided he wanted to give up racing and returned to his home in Slough, leaving Fred to dominate the racing scene and maintain his position as winning jockey. As time went on and the season progressed, those who were loyal to Fordham and many of Archer's northern rivals, believed that Archer was becoming overconfident. John Osborne, who was the leading light of the north, noted an arrogance about him which he felt needed to be knocked out of him.[24] As far as Osborne was concerned, no-one believed in Archer more than Archer and something had to be done about it, although Fred was still eagerly sought after – even if it was just for his opinion on the potential of a race or a horse. Even Sir George Chetwynd, the Jockey Club Steward, who did not normally consult jockeys being highly knowledgeable himself,[25] made an exception in his case. Many owners, however, were wary of the fact that Falmouth continued to have first claim on Fred, so that it was difficult for others to secure his services, as Chetwynd discovered. It was this arrangement which prompted him to go off in search of Fordham in the winter of 1877 to 1878 and effect a comeback.[26]

This was easier said than done. Chetwynd found Fordham in a pitiable state. Having lost the bulk of his savings through the machinations of a bad financier, the jockey had taken refuge in drink and was in no mood to listen to any of Chetwynd's plans. The Jockey Club Steward was not to be put off and setting the wheels in motion, he tried to help Fordham get back on form, with the jockey protesting that if he sat on a horse, he would probably fall off! Even so, he returned to Newmarket and, once he began working again, was soon back to something of his old self. He had the support of his old friends, including Harry Custance, but he still needed to build up his confidence. Having been away for so long and still recovering from his 'illness', he allowed his nerves to get the better of him.

'We went down the course together to the Ditch Mile starting-post,' Custance wrote. Fordham must have been walking alongside his horse, for Custance says, 'he got into the saddle about halfway down [the course]. He seemed all right at first, but just before we got to the post, his spirits failed him, and he said to me, "Cus, I wish I hadn't got up."' Harry asked him why and the reason was the appearance of all the young jockeys he was to ride against. Archer was among them – and he was the eldest. Fordham told Harry that he did not know any of the younger ones, meaning that he had been away so long that there were no familiar faces – except Archer.

Custance felt obliged to boost his friend's morale: 'I said "My dear George, don't you trouble about that; they will soon know you when you get up side of them, especially at the finish."'[27]

But Archer beat Fordham by three lengths. A disappointment – or so Custance believed when the race was over, and one which he felt could be explained by Fordham's weak state after such a long absence – but then Fordham said to him, 'You don't think I was going to let him . . . beat me by a neck the first time I rode.'[28]

To all intents and purposes, Fordham, in knowing that he was going to lose, had at the same time rediscovered his sense of rivalry against Archer and had *given* him the three lengths, but was this really the case? Had he kidded Archer or was he kidding himself? If he was trying to convince himself and Custance that he had allowed his young rival to win, then Archer had nothing to worry about, but as it turned out, the opposite was true. Fordham had skilfully provided the Champion Jockey with a false sense of security and Archer, falling for it, was beaten by Fordham the next time they competed.

Fordham could still aggravate the Champion Jockey in the same old manner and of all jockeys, he was the only one who could outwit Archer and throw him off his stride with all the old deviousness that had characterised their former clashes. For as long as the two of them lived, it would always remain so. If Fordham had rediscovered his antagonism towards him, Archer had rediscovered his fear of Fordham. Portland wrote, 'It was really amusing to watch his face almost of agony when he was pitted against Fordham in a match at Newmarket. "That old devil always terrifies me in matches at Newmarket. Nobody knows what he's up to. They're about right when they call him the 'Old Demon'."'[29]

Fordham did at least recognise in Archer a worthy rival and held him in contempt for it and for Archer, Fordham, being the complete opposite of the late Tom French, was still a significant influence in his life, if a rather disagreeable one.

John Osborne saw the Hardwicke Stakes of 1879 as Fordham putting Archer, yet again, firmly back in his place, recalling a race in which Fordham dominated the pace and Fred fought to get clear of him.[30] This was the voice of hard-headed experience, treating Archer like a petulant child and teaching him a lesson. Fred, however, was gaining enough experience himself not to be kept down for long, and he could be as analytical about his rival's performance as with his own, knowing when the 'demon' was making a mistake or when he had tricks up his sleeve. He could watch Fordham with an objectivity he could seldom muster when riding against him and, in watching his performance in one race, he told Lambton that Fordham was 'kidding'. By kidding, Fordham lost the race – threw it away was how Archer put it.[31]

It is curious to note that whereas Archer was quite capable of clinically analysing Fordham[32] and could read his performance as well as he could his own, when they competed against one another he could not foresee or anticipate Fordham's actions at all. He was so used to being able to analyse horses, jockeys and races and to formulate his own methods accordingly to overcome them, that it infuriated him that he could not apply the same technique to Fordham who was, effectively, his Achilles heel. George Fordham of course never had any specific method, plan or trait which Archer could pinpoint and use to his own advantage. He was only consistent in his superb handling of the horse, his ability to surprise and 'kid' other jockeys; no matter how hard he tried, Archer could not put any distance between them. And this was the case from the very beginning and would continue for many years, but it is astonishing to consider how many similarities there were to weigh up against their contrasts.

Both were accomplished riders, both were Champion Jockeys, both made racing look effortless, and both used ingenuity as well as a knowledge of form to win, although in Fordham's case it was almost subconscious. They were ruthless opponents and could use other jockeys' tactics to their own advantage. In this respect they could use psychology in their approach and give other jockeys a false sense of security – Fordham had perfected this in his approach to Archer. Both could get the absolute best out of their horses and both were respected and admired off the course. They had total faith in their individual abilities and could rise to any challenge – frequently creating the challenges for themselves and each other; but whatever problems the younger jockey experienced with the older jockey, there may be one final, curious twist.

In 1883 a journalist from *The World* publication visited the newly married Fred Archer in his new home and in one of the rooms, the journalist noted, there were two photographs standing at either end of the mantelpiece: one of Fred himself and the other of 'Fordham'. Although the journalist did not stipulate the Christian name of this 'Fordham' since Fred knew two – George, and Charlie, the long-suffering stable lad of a horse called St Simon – I am inclined to believe that the picture was of George Fordham and that perhaps Archer had a sneaking admiration for his rival. Add to this the fact that 1883 was the year when Fordham finally retired and was no longer a threat – maybe the two of them had agreed to differ at last and bury the hatchet. Whatever the reason, Fred himself may have felt that although he had achieved success and wealth early in his life, he had not done so without extreme difficulty – difficulty which was often provided by George Fordham himself.

Notes

1. Portland, 6th Duke of, *Memories of Racing and Hunting*, p.77
2. Mortimer, Roger, Onslow, Richard & Willet, Peter, *The Biographical Encyclopaedia of British Flat Racing*, pp.218–20
3. Tanner, Michael & Cranham, Gerry, *Great Jockeys of the Flat: A Celebration of Two Centuries of Jockeyship*, pp.58–71
4. Mortimer, Onslow & Willet, pp.567–8
5. Ibid, pp.218–20
6. Custance, Henry, *Riding Recollections and Turf Stories*, p.112
7. Ibid, p.122
8. Ibid, p.123
9. Ibid, p.117
10. Ibid, pp.123–4
11. Chetwynd, Sir George, *Racing Reminiscences and Experience of the Turf*, p.97
12. Custance, p.114
13–14. Mortimer, Onslow & Willet, pp.218–20
15. Humphris, Edith M, *The Life of Fred Archer*, p.70
16. Welcome, John, *Fred Archer: A Complete Study*, p.31
17. Custance, p.117
18–19. Mortimer, Onslow & Willet, pp.218–20
20–1. Tanner & Cranham, pp.58–71
22. Chetwynd, p.97
23. Custance, p.120
24. Laird, Dorothy, *Royal Ascot: A History of Royal Ascot From Its Founding by Queen Anne to the Present Time*, pp.143–6
25. Chetwynd, p.97
26. Tanner & Cranham, pp.58–71
27. Custance, p.114
28. Ibid, pp.114–18
29. Portland, p.93
30. Laird, pp.143–6
31. Lambton, The Honourable George, *Men and Horses I Have Known*, p.232
32. Humphris, *The Life of Fred Archer*, p.210

Behind the Image

The sport of horseracing was now entering its Golden Era, particularly between 1880 and 1890, as remembered by George Lambton. To him these years were the most memorable when the standard of racing was at its greatest. He acknowledged the sportsmen as the highest in their class and racing now had a dignity about it which made it almost unrecognisable from, say, fifty or sixty years before. The horseowners, trainers and jockeys personified the high standard which gave British racing its international reputation for excellence and the sport now had unofficial ambassadors in the shape of Fred Archer, Tom Cannon and others.[1]

At home the jockeys were fast developing celebrity status and Fred would always be identified with this particular era. The distinction he helped to bring to the sport and his own success meant that the public had a perception of him which was further enhanced by the newspapers. Many of his admirers and followers expected him to have the same, apparent devil-may-care personality which they saw on the racecourse – the same air of confidence which made him a master of the sport, but their perception of him had nothing to do with the real Fred Archer.

George Lambton first saw Fred at St Pancras station in the company of the Duke of Hamilton, one day in 1879.[2] Like many who came across the young jockey for the first time, Lambton found it difficult to equate the personality portrayed in the newspapers with the person who appeared before him.

He was immediately struck by Fred's appearance and described
him as pale and quiet-looking. He was dressed in a dark suit,
with a black tie and the only indication that he was a person of
some standing was the fact that there was a large pearl pin in
the tie.[3] Lambton asked the Duke who he was and his
companion replied, with a small measure of surprise, 'Why,
that is Archer.' So famous was this 22-year-old that he was
already a household name, but, as Lambton wrote many years
later, he was surprised by the Duke of Hamilton's revelation,
for Archer was not how he had imagined him to be.

Even so the image of the quiet and sombrely dressed young
man was one which had been evolving since the end of his
apprenticeship in 1873 and, six years down the line, Lambton
noted the first signs that life as a jockey, bringing with it the
pressure of fame, was beginning to take its toll on Fred. 'There
was, even at that time,' observed Lambton of that first sighting
in 1879, 'the shadow of melancholy in his face which indicated
a side to his nature never far absent in his brightest days.'[4]

Lambton had hit on something much deeper and was not
the first to be caught off guard by the distinction between
the public persona and the reality.[5] The word 'melancholy'
suggests a kind of withdrawal, his quiet, unassuming
appearance a need to hide within himself. There was far more
to Fred Archer than met the eye. Tragedy had already marked
his life in the untimely death of his brother Billy in March 1878
in a riding accident.[6] This may be why Fred was wearing black,
out of respect for his brother, when Lambton first saw him.

The day before his accident, on 21 March, 25-year-old Billy
Archer had been a witness to a fatal accident outside the
Andoversford Arms where a man had fallen from his horse.
Billy was so shocked that he took it to be an omen and at first
refused to ride in a selling hurdle race which was due to take
place the next day, but William Archer, who clearly had no time
for such sentiments, eventually persuaded his son to ride.[7] Billy
did so, the horse (called Salvanie) took a tumble and, as he was

thrown, his mount landed heavily on top of him, severely injuring him. Billy never regained consciousness and died the following day, 23 March. The inquest, held two days later, concluded that the death had been accidental,[8] but for those who believe in bad omens this would have been a classic case. The Victorians were superstitious in the extreme, seeing the death outside the public house as a warning not only to Billy, but the rest of the family too.

Pride, in the acquisition of success, comes before a fall; but, according to Edith M Humphris, Billy was like Fred himself, nervous and highly strung.[9] Modern psychologists would probably concur that the accident outside the Andoversford Arms would have shocked Billy enough to make him considerably wary of his own race the next day. Had he been of his father's mettle, he would probably have dismissed the event as an unfortunate accident. Had he possessed the same measure of ambition as his younger brother, Fred, he would have seen it as even more of a reason to ride the race and win.

Certainly Billy's death highlights the expectations surrounding racing and also the strength of Fred's ambition. At no time did he ever see his brother's death as a warning to himself or seek to review his own technique in running a race. Racing was not safe, as he knew, and he adjusted accordingly – seeing each obstacle or danger as a challenge to be overcome. In fact within days of his brother's death he was back in the saddle, winning four races on 28 and 29 March.[10]

He was skilled, unbeaten and disciplined in his preparation and execution of a race to the point where his perception was so acute that he could view the whole picture while homing in on details few others would have considered. Portland noted his nerve,[11] but Fred also had an unpredictability about him which, for years, would continue to amaze. In each race he always sought new tactics, new ways of negotiating a course and of handling a horse which would never be matched and which would catch everybody unawares.

Fred was, deep down, something of a showman and part of the discipline which went into his work applied to his appearance as a jockey. His colours and silks were immaculate and would have served to boost his confidence. As Fred Archer the jockey, he had an acute sense of the dramatic. He loved the spectacle and atmosphere which surrounded a race meeting and probably derived much of his inspiration, as well as motivation, from it.

Liked and respected by all classes of society, he was lauded by the press and the public alike. In an age which revered heroes, he was especially admired by women. Where George Lambton and others found him quiet and pale-looking, Fred's female followers found him irresistible. He seemed to fit the criteria of tall, dark and handsome, a young man who was always impeccably dressed. Standing at 5ft 10in tall (in his socks) he was the tallest jockey in racing – not short and stocky like the majority, so he was attractive in that respect because it was unusual for an expert jockey to be above average height. Nor was he rough and ready like others of his profession and, in fact, his whole demeanour spoke of someone who was unassuming, yet held a natural charm.

He was not an overpowering character, yet he could command respect and he had it – from the highest to the lowest in society. To all these women who followed his every move, he was a romantic hero and many women were hysterical over him – idolising him, just as women today idolise film stars and pop stars. Fred was, in that respect, a novelty for women – and Victorian High Society women, in particular, loved novelty until something more interesting came along. Fred knew this and knew that the aristocracy was fickle. His novelty and popularity would only last while he continued to win races and remained Champion Jockey. Since no-one knew the true Fred, this admiration was only superficial but it caught the attention of Fred's family and friends. He took very little notice of it and his sister Alice was bemused by the seemingly hysterical reaction of some of these women to whom he appeared indifferent.[12] This indifference appeared as shallow rejection, but instead of putting his admirers off, it intrigued them all the more and many took to writing indiscreetly to him. Alice remembered how she found one such letter from a married lady who demanded to know why Fred was taking no notice of her.[13]

Such obsessive outpourings could have made these high-class admirers vulnerable to blackmail, but Fred was wise enough to exercise some discretion. He found his sister Alice with the letter and told her not to reveal the name of the lady, so she never did. Even decades later Alice refused to reveal the names of those who wrote to her brother. For himself he remained indifferent, but his friends were sufficiently amused by the whole thing to pull him up over it. Alice told Edith M Humphris how he tried to shrug it off, but there was one woman he could not ignore and that was Caroline, Duchess of Montrose.

Born in 1818, and so 39 years Fred's senior, Caroline Beresford had married the Duke of Montrose at the age of seventeen,[14] but by the time she was in her late fifties she was widowed and on the lookout for her second husband, who turned out to be William Stewart Stirling-Crawfurd, a very wealthy man who owned his own stud and was a member of the Jockey Club although he was seldom there.[15] Despite her second marriage and the fact she was officially no longer a duchess, Caroline was only ever referred to as 'the Duchess of Montrose' and the strength of her personality seemed to add to the title. Similarly, a certain Emilie Charlotte Le Breton made her married name of Lillie Langtry famous, even though she divorced her husband, Edward Langtry, remarried and officially became Lady de Bathe.

Portland described the former, or Dowager, Duchess as a great character[16] which for the nineteenth century was indeed unusual, particularly since women, and upper class women at that, were not encouraged to have anything to do with the management side of horseracing. They were not even allowed inside the Jockey Club. The one exception was Lillie Langtry, years later, when her horse won the Cesarewitch and even then she was invited only on the say so of Edward VII.[17] Caroline, even as a young bride of the Duke of Montrose (who was indifferent to racing), studied the form book, involved herself as much as possible in every aspect of the sport, and in addition had to use the force of a particularly dominant personality to override Victorian male prejudice – and Fred Archer unwittingly became a part of this.

Not content with controlling her own stud, Caroline controlled her second husband's too and Stirling-Crawfurd, being very affable and easy-going, let her get on with it.[18] She appears to have been the only woman of her class to know as much, if not more, about racing as her male contemporaries. She was renowned for always having her own way, terrifying her trainers and demanding that they obey her every instruction. She was determined to be taken seriously in what was, essentially, a male domain, and she wanted control, not to be controlled.

Most did as they were told and the only trainer, and in all probability the only person, who could stand up to her was Alec Taylor, who was even prepared to ignore her instructions if he thought them outlandish. He was also capable of giving as good as he got, responding with 'Damned to hell if I know, Your Grace,'[19] when she demanded to know his opinion on something. She too could swear like a trooper and could be particularly foul-mouthed when the occasion demanded, but she could also be very vain about herself. Having originally been dubbed 'Carrie Red' because of her red hair, she dyed it a distinctive gold colour when she got older in order to complement her very heavy make-up.

She was not the typical Victorian hostess, in fact she was the antithesis and while most women of her class spent a fortune on beautiful clothes, hers have been described as masculine. She was beyond the conventional and seemed to live up to this –

adopting masculine characteristics in order to be accepted by the men who ruled horseracing. At the same time she provoked personality clashes – the most famous being the long-standing snub against another of Fred Archer's friends, Captain James Octavius Machell (1837–1902). An army man turned horse manager, he owned property not far from hers. Once after he had upset her, she accused him of deliberately running over her dog to spite her.[20] It was a classic personality clash between the two, since Machell – a moody, cold, suspicious and often vindictive individual who suffered from acute depression and gout – was not the type of person to accept such treatment from a domineering woman, particularly over a dog. He was capable of being charming, gracious and generous, but he could not tolerate Caroline and they were frequently engaged in arguments or at other times ignored each other completely.

She also decided that another man, who scowled all the time, must have murdered his mother and when he politely informed her that his mother, to whom he was devoted, was alive and well and living in Wales, she did not apologise and made it clear that if he did not look the way he did, she would not have to find fault and be forced to make such remarks![21]

She even threatened to have a vicar sacked from his parish because he had prayed for weather which would go against her horses in a coming race meeting.[22] For all that, most people felt inclined to indulge her, forgetting her rather brash side, perhaps passing it off as eccentricity, and preferring to concentrate on the more feminine side of her nature. Lambton, for instance, sought to pay tribute, remarking on her soft and charming voice and the fact that she was the best company in the world.[23] That was of course when things were going right, an indication that if they were not, she was not the best company in the world and she made everyone aware of it.

So where did the young Fred Archer come into all this? It is known that the Duchess had a particular fondness for him;[24] some believed that she was besotted with him and her fascination was picked up by many of her acquaintances. Speculation often led to rumour – salacious gossip which Fred would have been anxious to avoid – and it was even suggested, as Portland mentioned in his memoirs, that Fred himself had wondered whether or not it was possible for him to marry a Duchess. Portland put it on record that he did not believe a word of it and that Fred would not have said such a thing.[25]

Since gossip and rumour were the order of the day in Victorian High Society, and Fred was a popular public figure, the Duchess' pursuit of him – at least her motives for pursuing him – may have been exaggerated, although she was very fond of him and remained so until the day he died.

She was ferociously ambitious and the running and controlling of her stud, as well as the sport of horseracing itself, were her life. Portland noted that hers was a very fine stud, and in making a success of it and earning the respect and recognition of a male peer she had already breached many of the barriers that would have prevented women with less fortitude from getting so close to the control of the sport.[26] However, to have England's Champion Jockey in her control, to have first claim on him would make her dominance complete and place her above the rest. It was even more of a challenge because Fred was not so easily taken in. She could not push and dominate him the way she pushed and dominated others and he was not swayed by her presents and flattery. Such acts of generosity and her tendency to follow him to race meetings whenever she could, must have looked ridiculous in the eyes of her contemporaries who still saw jockeys as members of the serving classes.

Caroline, however, was undaunted. She wanted a majority claim on Fred Archer and she was determined to get it. When her second, most dominated husband shuffled off his mortal coil in 1883, it is understood that Caroline approached Fred again and this time offered him a blank cheque to secure a majority claim. He accepted, but the sum was never disclosed.

Nor did it matter. She had achieved her aim. After her second husband died she took over his scarlet colours and his horses – with his trainer, Alec Taylor, completing the package – and announced that she would race her horses under the pseudonym 'Mr Manton', acquiescing to the male hierarchy which would not allow women to race under their own names. Another to do so, once again, was Lillie Langtry, who raced her own horses under the name Mr Jersey – her place of birth.

Women were fascinated by Fred, but this expert horseman who was capable of breaking women's hearts downplayed his popular image and did not wish to be idolised, so that when admirers were introduced to him for the first time as just plain Fred Archer, the shock was more palpable.

For Lambton, who had his first glimpse of Fred in 1879, it would be another year before he got the chance to speak to him in person, on the day of the Manchester Cup. Fred was not riding that day, so Lambton asked him whom he should back instead. Fred had hopes of The Abbot wining, but did not want to place his new-found acquaintance in the position of being obliged to back the horse on his say so; instead he advised him to back the best horse and the best jockey – in this case Isonomy and Tom Cannon.[27] Fred had been observing Isonomy for some time and knew what the horse was capable of – outstripping everything in sight, so it was no surprise to him when his advice to George Lambton paid off. Isonomy, with Tom Cannon up, won by a neck.[28]

Lambton used the incident to demonstrate that this conversation began their friendship which would last until Fred's death. There was just three years' difference in their ages (Lambton had just turned twenty in 1880) and, although young George Lambton considered himself fairly knowledgeable about horses and racing, he could not match Archer's understanding of the sport. In describing how they met, Lambton gave a brief insight into one of Fred's simpler methods of studying form.[29]

Like Portland, Lambton credited Fred's nerve, his confidence and the fact that both attributes were entirely without conceit. Many of Fred's rivals would not have entirely agreed with this, since he was often seen as being very conceited and over confident. George Fordham recognised a precocity in Fred which he tried to knock out of the younger jockey, but it is fair to say that a great deal of the arrogance which had marked Fred's earlier years had been tempered.

Fred now viewed his work with an objectivity which had not been there when he first started out. He pinpointed strengths and weaknesses in his own performance as well as that of the horse he was riding and was self-critical enough to know when he was doing well and when and how he needed to improve. He no longer flew off the handle when he failed to win, but considered why he lost from different perspectives, using those lessons to improve his performance in the next race. Lambton described his intuitive sense, an observation repeated by *Baily's Magazine* after Fred's death, and his almost scientific approach to a race – where he missed nothing, and if he lost a race, he would go into the whys and wherefores.

Clinical in his observations and attention to detail, Fred understood that his own methods could still benefit from the experience of others. No matter how arrogant he may have appeared to his fellow jockeys, he still had a deep respect for them and their achievements – achievements which helped to put his own into perspective, although Fordham always got the better of him.

There was also a strong rivalry between Fred and the north country jockey Jem Snowden. Snowden was an habitual drunk who lost huge amounts of money and the patronage of the Duke of Westminster as a result of his drinking. But he was also one of the most talented jockeys this country had ever produced; riding in races seemed instinctive to him and his judgement of pace was unequalled.[30] Fred admitted to Lambton that he found him difficult to beat. He believed

Tom Cannon to be the most elegant of jockeys, his friend Fred Webb one of the strongest and Charles Wood an excellent judge of pace.[31]

As Fred's own technique matured, so did his knowledge and understanding of horses, but he still had a slight air of impatience about him which, rather unwittingly, contributed towards his achieving an even greater understanding and tolerance. For instance, at the start of his career he only knew how to ride horses. By the 1880s he was so familiar with their personalities and quirks that some horses refused to be ridden by anyone else. This was not altogether a gradual process of learning and understanding and an incident in 1880 had effectively woken him up to the fact that he could not treat horses how he liked. He discovered that they were only prepared to put up with so much from him. Falmouth's Muley Edris was a case in point.

Fred seemed to have had very little patience with this horse, whom he had ridden occasionally since the late 1870s,[32] and very often took him to task by whipping him. This kind of treatment was by no means unusual in the nineteenth century, although attitudes were changing, but in the case of Muley Edris Fred went too far and, far from merely chastising the animal, succeeded in turning him into a savage one.

Muley Edris decided to give the celebrated jockey a taste of his own medicine and, in snatching his arm between his teeth, dragged him to the ground, before losing his footing and letting go.[33] Finding his feet once more, the horse took off down the course and was retrieved later[34] while Fred was left with a severely injured arm and the knowledge that horses, like elephants, have long memories and do not forgive easily. Mathew Dawson tried later to explain, rather than excuse, Fred's original treatment of Muley Edris by saying that he had found the horse 'cunning' and had needed to punish him.[35] Whatever the reason Fred learnt the lesson and he never so much as raised a finger to any horse ever again.

Ironically enough, it was the incident with Muley Edris that brought about one of Fred's greatest personal and professional victories. At the time when Muley Edris was trying to make mincemeat of Fred's arm on 1 May 1880, the jockey himself was preparing for the Derby, due to take place in just under four weeks' time. He was expected to ride the Duke of Westminster's placid, but powerful chestnut colt Bend Or, by Doncaster out of Rouge Rose. His arm, however, refused to respond to treatment and it was touch and go whether he would be able to ride or not.

Eventually Fred was packed off to see a London physician, Sir James Paget, who, after close examination, told the jockey that he should be all right in two to three weeks' time. Fred asked if he would be fit enough for the Derby. The doctor said he did not see why he could not go. Fred asked if he would be fit enough to ride. The doctor told him to drive to the course. Fred looked at him and then told the eminent physician that he was unaware of whom he was addressing. The physician checked his notes, but even after clarifying that he had a Mr Archer seated before him, was still none the wiser as to who Mr Archer actually was. Fred now found himself having to explain why it was so important for him to ride on 26 May. The doctor asked him how much he stood to lose if he did not ride and Fred replied the best part of 2,000 sovereigns. The doctor said he wished his work was as profitable and Fred took himself back to Newmarket with his newly bound arm.[36]

His arm began to mend, but slowly and, to add insult to injury, Bend Or was having trouble with his shins which, likewise, were not responding to treatment. On top of this Fred had gained weight and was in something of a depressed state, particularly since he only had a matter of days to get his weight down sufficiently to be able to ride in the Derby. The fact that he accomplished this says a great deal about his stamina and determination. It is characteristic of jockeys both past and present who take injuries in their stride and carry on. But in the case of Fred Archer he had taken such a savaging that riding so soon could have caused permanent, irreparable damage and also points to a recklessness on his part in deciding to throw all caution to the winds and continue the preparations for the race. Such is the measure of ambition.

Come Derby Day, his arm was still not 100 per cent and had to be supported by a metal bar. Although Bend Or's shins had recovered sufficiently for him to run, he too was not totally fit, but *The Times* noted that he had gained in muscle and appeared to show the benefits of a good preparation.[37] He was such a placid and gentle animal that he took everything in his stride which is more than can be said for his jockey who, being a nervous wreck and in the foulest of moods, was swearing and shouting at every other jockey within range as the race progressed – yelling dire warnings to anyone who did not give him room.

Sir George Chetwynd recalled the race vividly since it involved Bend Or's rival, Robert the Devil, owned by one Charles Brewer. 'Robert the Devil,' Chetwynd wrote, 'held such a commanding lead at the bell that it looked long odds on him, but Archer was creeping up on Bend Or, and an exciting struggle took place.'[38]

Portland was also present that day. 'It gave me one of the most thrilling sights in the way of a horse race that I have ever viewed,' he wrote and he was not the only one to find it 'thrilling' as the riders approached Tattenham Corner, the most dangerous part of the course with its unforgiving bend.[39] Fred was riding so close to the rails that he was forced to pull his leg up and keep it close to Bend Or's withers for fear it would be broken. It was an act which became the stuff of legend, recalled by generations who saw it as typical of Fred Archer's daring.[40]

As Archer continued to gain steadily, Rossiter, the jockey riding Robert the Devil, appeared powerless, becoming level just before the post.

Not everyone, however, thought that Archer had won. 'I was up in the gallery of our stand,' Chetwynd recalled, 'and underneath, sitting on the rails, I saw Charles Brewer confidently pointing to his horse, which he thought was winning . . . Even after the pair had passed the post he fancied that his . . . had won.'[41]

But Bend Or had it and, considering the odds set against him and Fred in recent weeks, it was a remarkable victory – not to mention a relief. Fred continued to ride for a couple of days until 28 May, perhaps viewing this time as make or break, but it was clear that his arm had not yet recovered and he pulled out of racing for a short while to rest, safe in the knowledge that he had won the Derby.[42] Unfortunately, within weeks of it taking place, the result was brought into question.

At the time of the race Charles Brewer did not object to the win, but the result obviously played on his mind and, a month later, he approached Sir George Chetwynd. 'Just before the July week,' Chetwynd wrote, 'he informed me that he was going to object to Bend Or . . . believing him to be Tadcaster [Tadcaster also belonged to the Duke of Westminster], his conviction being that the two colts had been mistaken when they were sent as yearlings to the training stable.'[43]

The information, Brewer explained, had come from a stud groom previously employed in the Duke of Westminster's service. Brewer had gone to Chester to meet him and had been left in no doubt that the real winner was Tadcaster. Chetwynd told Brewer that he should have approached the Duke about his suspicions and Brewer, stunned by this suggestion, remarked, 'Me go up to the Duke of Westminster's front door, ring the bell and ask to see him!'[44]

So Chetwynd told him that the normal procedure was to lodge a formal complaint with the Jockey Club and Brewer did so at the Newmarket July meeting. Sir George could not assist the other Stewards in reaching a decision on the matter because he had backed Bend Or in the Derby and so was an interested party. Lord Calthorpe, on Sir George's request, acted in his place and the Stewards, after considering the evidence, published their decision on 24 July, declaring that the 1880 Derby winner was Bend Or and was by Doncaster out of Rouge Rose. The objection put forward by Brewer and his co-complainant, Blanton, who co-owned Robert the Devil, was therefore 'overruled'.[45] Nothing underhand was at play, it was argued, just that there may have been an accidental switch since the two were physically alike.

'So that was that,' noted Portland, who had also written about the event,[46] and Chetwynd, too, was adamant that the Stewards had reached the correct conclusion, putting down the stud groom's admission as being nothing more than bitterness at having been dismissed from the Duke's service. But the man stuck to his story until his dying day.

Brewer's horse, Robert the Devil went on to win the Grand Prix and, later in the year, for his owner at least, there appeared to be a certain element of poetic justice at work in the fortunes of this horse as he and Bend Or met again in the St Leger at Doncaster on 15 September. This time Robert the Devil won by three lengths, leaving Bend Or (with Archer up) to finish sixth and *The Times* to note, with disappointment, that the horse was not a stayer.[47] However, he turned the tables around again in 1881 when, competing once more against Robert the Devil, this time for the Epsom Gold Cup and with Archer up, Bend Or won it by a neck. But controversy never seemed to be far away from this horse as in the same year he was the subject of a libel case brought in June 1881 by a veterinary surgeon, Mr G Barrow, against the printer and publisher of the *Morning Post*, who had claimed he had not taken good enough care of Bend Or. Barrow had lost customers as a result, and the whole story ended up in court with Barrow winning damages of £1,750.[48]

In 1880 Fred was all set to have another momentous year and was back on form once his arm had recovered. In fact from July onwards his efforts revealed a need to pick up where he left off and make up for lost time, but his success rate overall was moderate and he achieved only 122 wins.[49]

In the days during the run up to the Derby and Oaks of 1881 he won the Craven Stakes on Captain Machell's Valour (the rival of Sir John Astley's Peter in the Manchester Cup), the Woodcote Stakes on Dunmore and the Epsom Stakes Handicap on the Duke of Beaufort's Petronel; the Epsom Manor Stakes on Newhaven and he also came second on Der Wucherer in the Ashtead Stakes. But the highlight of this Epsom week was the Derby and Fred's ride on Iroquois, owned by the American Lorillard who also owned Parole.[50]

'The public would not yet believe in American horses,' wrote Sir George Chetwynd as he recalled Iroquois' performance in the 1881 Two Thousand Guineas[51] and, as if to reflect this, the horse was started at 50 to 1. The British public had been mistaken before in the case of Parole and, in the case of Iroquois, possibly made the greatest error of judgement that year. He may only have come second in the Two Thousand Guineas, but his performance was further proof that foreign horses were more than a match for the English courses; and, as if to add insult to injury, Don Fulano, another American horse, came third. Not surprisingly the American newspapers were enormously proud of Iroquois and kept a close eye on his progress, since if he could win the Derby, he would be securing the Blue Riband of the Turf from the British.[52]

Epsom had never looked so crowded and *The Times* noted that the attendance rate was the highest for years with people crowding the Downs, the stands and the hillside.[53] The atmosphere was also complemented by good weather and there was a large Royal presence too, with the principal guests including the Prince and Princess of Wales, the Duke and Duchess of Connaught (the Prince of Wales' brother and sister-in-law), the Marchioness of Lorne (the Prince of Wales' sister), the Duke of Cambridge, Prince Christian and Prince

Edward of Saxe-Weimar – the cream of European Royalty and society.

As *The Times* noted, the centre of attraction was not Iroquois, but the Two Thousand Guineas winner, Peregrine, who was deemed to be in perfect condition, despite the opinions of some judges. People had no qualms in placing their bets on him, although bookmakers were in a quandary over the favourite. The papers could not fault Peregrine's stamina, but, given Iroquois' training regime, Peregrine would have to pull out all the stops to meet the kind of speed and pace that the American horse was capable of.[54]

In an attempt to remain unbiased *The Times'* opinion of Iroquois was also favourable. Many thought that he had been trained too hard and appeared overstrained as a result, but being of Lorillard's stable he would have been put through the same rigorous training programme as Parole and so would have had an edge over his rivals even before the starting post. Certainly he looked well, as *The Times* clearly recorded and Iroquois and Archer together drew quite a following. The combination of one of England's finest jockeys and one of America's finest horses must have seemed formidable. Should Archer win the Derby, he would receive international acclaim, but all hopes were pinned on Peregrine, the nation's darling, who, it was noted, had sufficient stamina to dominate, if not win, the race.

Some fifteen minutes after the appointed time the race for the 1881 Derby got underway. Iroquois wasted no time in taking the lead on the inside, but in the first furlong Archer saw fit to hold him back and the remainder of the field moved forward, while the American became one of the last three alongside Geologist and Scobell. The positions remained unchanged and Archer found that he could not achieve the position he wanted at the rails, so Iroquois remained where he was with Peregrine looking certain to win. The field approached the City and Suburban post, but as the horses continued on towards the straight, the order began to shift and Iroquois began to gain steadily, taking third place, but Archer increased the pace.[55]

He passed between Town Moor and Peregrine and won by half a length with Peregrine second. Two seconds, however, had been added to the previous year's time – Iroquois had secured this year's in 2 minutes 50 seconds. The time for 1880 stood at 2 minutes 48 seconds. Had Archer been able to secure the best positions possible during the race, they may have beaten the record, but Iroquois' win had been a comfortable one – proof that Lorillard's severe training methods had paid off – and, more important, Iroquois and Archer had made history. The Blue Riband of racing, the Derby, had at last gone to America.

Horseracing in England would never again be so exclusively European; as *The Times* noted in conclusion, the Derby was now no longer national, but international. Barriers had been broken and the impact on Fred was enormous. He was to become just as popular abroad as at home. *The Sporting Life* was much more effusive and, while congratulating Lorillard, Iroquois and Archer, decided that the combination of Archer and America was formidable.[56] The newspaper also repeated the same declaration used after Parole's win in April 1879, that the British had a great deal to learn from their American counterparts.[57]

The Americans were slowly beginning to dominate horseracing and would, eventually, even alter the way races were run. The American papers could not have agreed more with the enthusiasm shown by *The New York Times* which had been avidly following the horse's and Lorillard's every move. Fred and Iroquois repeated their successes throughout the year: the Prince of Wales Stakes on 14 June; the St James' Palace Stakes on 16 June; and the St Leger on 14 September.[58] Theirs was an indomitable partnership and for the Americans at least Fred could do no wrong, but in the eyes of the British he could.

Even so he had discovered that working with horses did not just mean getting them to run faster. Experience was teaching him that they had to adapt to their surroundings as a whole and not just the racecourses themselves. The more stubborn and temperamental they were, the greater the challenge and Fred found that he had to tap into their personalities as well as their speed and stamina to get anything out of them. He could turn unpredictable traits into assets even when others believed that the horse was hopelessly unreliable,[59] and Fred Archer was one of the first jockeys to use a psychological approach to get a horse to run a race, much less win it.

The most famous example is Peter, who was owned by Jockey Club Steward Sir John Astley. He was one of the most difficult of horses to manage and if any horse alive had a mind of its own, Peter did. In the beginning he was the apple of Astley's eye. Sir John had had his hopes of buying the horse for five years and finally acquired him in 1879. He had originally belonged to one General Peel, but Peel died (making Peter's entry for the 1879 Derby void) and the horse was bought for 6,000 guineas by a Mr Gee, who had no intention of racing him and offered him to Astley. It took Sir John two years to raise the required sum and had his horse, Windsor, not won the 1881 Chester Cup, winning him 5,000 sovereigns, he might have lost Peter forever, but by the Saturday following the race he had his horse.[60]

'On that Saturday morning,' he wrote in his memoirs twelve years after the event, 'I caught Archer on the Bury Hills, and he opened his eyes wide when I told him I had bought Peter, as he imagined that one or two men whose income was more per week, than mine was per year, would buy the horse. I chided him for thinking they would be so rash.'[61]

Fred agreed to ride Peter in the Hunt Cup at Ascot on 15 June and the horse was subsequently put through his paces, giving such an impressive performance that Astley decided to put him in for the Manchester Cup, due to take place on 9 June, at one and three quarter miles.[62] 'Now comes (to my mind) the most extraordinary bad luck I ever heard of,' Astley continued.

A mutual acquaintance of Fred and Sir John, the moody and temperamental Captain Machell, who owned stables in Newmarket, approached Fred and asked if he would ride his horse Valour in the Manchester Cup. Before making any decision, Fred returned to Sir John and told him that, if he so wished, he would ride Peter instead. Adhering to an unwritten law that owners should not take off the jockey of the stable, Astley turned down Archer's offer and kept Charlie Wood, for whom he was retainer and to whom he had already given instructions to ride. He told Fred to ride Valour if he wanted to, but as far as he was concerned, Peter had performed so well recently that nothing and no-one could beat him – not even a top-class jockey like Fred Archer.[63]

'Well!' he wrote, 'it came to pass that my doing the proper thing was the cause of great disaster to me, for in the race, Valour beat Peter a neck, which made a difference to me of over 12,000 sovereigns.'[64]

Astley had also lost the chance of buying another horse called Barcaldine which he was none too pleased about. He always felt that the Manchester Cup was his greatest misfortune, but also Archer's finest race.[65] In a bid to recoup his ever mounting losses, Sir John put his faith in his selling plater called Costa, but the horse was disqualified after he won the race because his jockey, Wood, had not met the sufficient weights. All in all, it was not a very good day. Even in his memoirs years later, he believed that day to be his worst in horseracing and referred to his two losses as 'fiascos'. In hindsight he felt that he should have made a match with Captain Machell, but even at the time he was aware of Peter's unpredictable nature, noting that the horse could not be relied upon, stopping and starting in a race at will. Astley refers to his horse as 'sometimes naughty Peter' and this 'sometimes naughty Peter' clearly had a mind of his own.

Arriving at Ascot he was entered for the Queen's Vase and lived up to his nature by pulling and kicking. As Peter took himself off back to the paddock while the other horses were still running the race, it did not bode well for the Hunt Cup, which was to take place 24 hours later on 15 June, but to Astley's surprise Peter was placed favourite! Archer had to be warned to ride Peter gently – to coax him if necessary, but as an extra precaution (or, perhaps, it could be seen as a desperate measure) Astley sent a jockey by the name of Giles (nicknamed 'Farmer' Giles) to the post with a hunting whip,[66] 'being afraid that Peter might run back and try what the iron gates were made of, at the start of the new mile,' he wrote.[67]

At the start of the race Peter began to kick and struggle, but through determined effort Archer kept him in the field. For a while he was last, but then he suddenly decided to run. He overtook the field and won, proving the maxim that the more unpredictable the horse, the more of a challenge Fred found it, and he exercised great patience in coaxing Peter to perform with the desired result.[68]

Astley was understandably delighted, Fred was confident, 'Farmer' Giles was amazed and everyone began to look forward to the Hardwicke Stakes on 17 June. It was then that Fred used Peter's tendency to struggle to his own advantage as Astley discovered when the jockey approached him and put forward his idea for getting Peter to run more effectively in the next race.

'You know, the start of the mile and a half we run today is just below the spot where Peter stopped to kick on Tuesday,' he reputedly said to Astley, 'and it is very likely, if I canter up past it with other horses, he may take it into his head to repeat this Tuesday's performance. If you will hack canter him round the reverse way of the course, and arrive at the starting post just as the other horses fall in, he may jump off and go kindly.'[69]

Astley thought it an excellent idea, but given his run of misfortune in recent times, decided not to place a penny on the horse until Peter was settled in the race. He was not disappointed and Peter won easily by eight lengths.

'Peter was a rattling good horse that Ascot,' Astley later recalled with rather generous hindsight, but the horse disgraced himself again in the Goodwood Cup, kicking and generally acting true to form. It seems that Fred was the only jockey he ever felt comfortable with, but at least he was able to win again for Astley and Sir John always remained fond of the horse despite his unpredictable temperament.[70]

The year 1881 had turned out to be an exceptional one for Fred. The need to recover the ground lost in 1880 led to one of his best starts to date. He was very much back on form and his success rate between March and July reveals a need to exceed his wins of previous years. The only drawback in maintaining this was his weight and it became increasingly difficult to keep this down, which was reflected in his performance from August onwards when the wins dropped from almost 35 in July to 20. The need to get back on form was still evident, but recovery was slow throughout September and he only achieved the level he wanted in October – a standard he was able to maintain until the end of the season in November. His final win out of a staggering total of 223 was on King of Scotland in a Welter Handicap Plate on 26 November. It was an incredible accomplishment, both physically and professionally. The year 1881 also marked a turning point both for him and horseracing as a whole.[71] But the following year would see the dark side of his fame.

1882 began well enough for him, although as in 1881, he would not ride as many races as he had in the late 1870s. Even so his performance between May and July was the most consistent ever seen with wins averaging 29 per month before the maximum for the whole year rocketed to almost 40 in August. There was a gradual wind down through to November, but there was no doubt that Fred was at the peak of his success.

The last twelve months had been dominated by the fillies – most notably Shotover, owned by the Duke of Westminster,[72] Geheimniss, owned by Lord Stamford and Dutch Oven, owned by Falmouth. Dutch Oven had done well the previous year, winning nine races, but she fell short of expectation in 1882 and was withdrawn from the One Thousand Guineas and the Oaks. Shotover was delicate and it was considered that there was room for improvement, but Geheimniss was unbeaten as a two-year-old and had the potential to go far. For the 1882 Derby, Dutch Oven, with Archer up, was competing against, among others, Shotover, with Tom Cannon up.[73]

The morning of the race on 24 May, also Queen Victoria's birthday, did not begin well. Rain threatened and the winds were such that the roads became dusty. When the rain began, there were such heavy squalls that they were likened to a hurricane, but it did not put people off. Even Royalty made an appearance – the Prince and Princess of Wales, the Duke and Duchess of Edinburgh and the Grand Duke of Mecklenburg-Strelitz – and eventually the bad weather petered out to be replaced by calmer conditions. In all the atmosphere was a sharp contrast to that of Derby Day 1881 and speculation too was not as it had been then, with many thinking that Bruce, owned by a Mr H Rymill, would walk it.[74]

Bruce, carrying 8st 10lb, was considered the favourite. Shotover had not done very well as a two-year-old, but over the season had improved somewhat, doing well in the Two Thousand Guineas as George Lambton recalled, but it was touch and go whether she would do well in this year's Derby. *The Times* recorded there was great interest in her because of her Two Thousand Guineas performance, but still reserved judgement on her potential for the Derby, remarking that it was a question that required a great deal of thought and consideration. Dutch Oven, on the other hand, was something of a mystery at present due to her having been withdrawn from some earlier engagements.[75]

The start was delayed by Pierre Lorillard's Gerald who refused to join the other horses, but once the race got going, it proved to be a good start with Bruce and Dutch Oven on the inside. As the field jockeyed for position, Shotover stayed clear of the last with Satrap. The order changed again beyond the City and Suburban post – Dutch Oven continued steadily, but

Shotover was still bringing up the rear although Cannon was gradually increasing the pace. On the approach to the straight Bruce took the advantage, but as the others began to fall away, encountered difficulty himself and was challenged by Quicklime who then headed Pursebearer. They were a quarter of a mile from home when Shotover appeared, gained a lead of three lengths and secured the Derby – Cannon's first. Dutch Oven finished seventh and the favourite, Bruce came fourth.[76]

Heath House was disappointed and more was to follow. Some months later, on 22 August, Fred rode Dutch Oven in the Yorkshire Oaks alongside two other competitors – Confusion and Actress, but confidence was such that many believed that the Oaks would be decided by Dutch Oven and Actress alone. Even so Confusion gave them both a run for their money and succeeded in getting ahead of Dutch Oven. It was only when they reached the distance that Confusion fell back, leaving the rest of the field to Dutch Oven and Actress. Dutch Oven increased the pace within fifty yards of the post and then won by three lengths. It was a good win, but when she ran third in the Great Yorkshire Stakes two days later, she was classed as a non-stayer, a judgement which would not go very much in her favour later. Describing Dutch Oven as a 'roarer', *The Times* noted that she had breathing difficulties and could not stay the course.[77]

Falmouth stated that she was not effective on heavy ground and when she was given 40 to 1 against for the upcoming St Leger, he considered the option of releasing Archer from the ride so that he could ride Westminster's Shotover instead, but Dawson advised him against it and so Archer was kept. Geheimniss turned out to be the undisputed favourite for the Leger[78] – no-one really believed that Dutch Oven was capable of making much of an impression. During the St Leger on 13 September, Fred kept her steady, allowing Actress to take the lead, and he did not push Dutch Oven forward until they were less than half a mile from the finish. Here many of the other horses had pulled back, so the race was left to Dutch Oven, Shotover and Geheimniss.[79]

Dutch Oven won and her victory was met by a stony silence. All of a sudden, in the past week, as *The Times* put it, her performance had been miraculously brought back to life[80] and her race-going public was left stunned – 'paralysed' was how *The Sporting Life* described the reaction. 'I distinctly saw one man,' the correspondent wrote, 'walk away into a remote corner, and stick a pin into his leg to make sure that he was alive.'[81] Then he checked his race card to make sure that he had the right race. In short – disbelief. Nor was the great race-going public prepared to accept such a win. Bemused, annoyed, it was left to ponder on what had just happened, particularly since the majority would have wagered their very last penny on Geheimniss winning. 'Poooof!' the correspondent for *The Sporting Life* continued, 'it wants thinking about!'

Acknowledging that it was a remarkable recovery of form on Dutch Oven's part, *The Sporting Life* still believed that she had been the last on everyone's minds to win and the question surfaced. How could a filly, classed as a non-stayer and one which had failed in the Derby and the Great Yorkshire Stakes secure the St Leger? Rumours abounded and many were ready to believe that Fred had been pulling her up and was, in effect, guilty of foul riding, an accusation which would remain with him, and would, especially, be brought sharply into focus the following year. Once again the newspapers drove home the opinion that Dutch Oven was a non-stayer.[82]

Even after the Leger, success was mixed. With Archer up she won a race on 27 September and later ran third in the Newmarket Derby. Suspicion may have lingered on Fred, but he ended the season Champion Jockey once more with 211 wins. He was developing an uncanny knack for spotting opportunities most people would never see in a lifetime of studying the form book. 'I must tell you another trait of Archer's extraordinary forethought and keenness to ride a winner,' wrote

Astley and goes on to describe Archer's superb timing in recognising a winner at the right time and in the right place.

Astley had bought a three-year-old called Edensor, but he had been sadly disappointed at the horse's poor performance since he had only won one race at Goodwood and one at Newmarket. It had reached a stage where Astley, in contemplating the Welter Handicap, had decided that he was not worth running when Archer approached him and asked if Edensor was to run. 'On my saying "No, he could have no chance," he replied, "You ought to run him, and if you will let me ride him he will win, and you must back him."'

Astley was dumbfounded, but knowing Fred of old, trusted his judgement. So he gave Edensor to the jockey, took 1000 to 100 out on him and watched as the horse ran favourite at 5 to 2 and won. Astley, always amazed by Fred's insight, expressed total faith in him and years later still maintained the belief that Fred 'knew something' about Edensor's potential to win that race – 'and what is more, the horse never won again.'[83]

People were impressed by Fred's skill and knowledge, but there was another side to him, a more introspective side which very few people, except those closest to him, ever saw or would ever appreciate. Not until much later would anyone fully understand that to be the type of jockey that he was and to reach the level of excellence which was demanded of him, Fred had to struggle very hard.

'He lived in quite a small way, in a single room,' recalled Portland of this particular period in Fred's life. 'Every evening he attended at our stable inspection, and Mat insisted upon his standing strictly to attention like any other boy when anybody spoke to him.'[84]

At this time Dawson was still the dominant figure. 'I well remember one evening,' Portland continued, 'when some friends and I were leaving the stable yard. Archer was talking to someone else and, for that reason, did not hurry to open the gate for us as usual, whereupon Mat indignantly asked,

"Archer, mon, where are your manners? Are you no' going to open the gate?" Archer ran to do so at once. He must have been earning eight to ten thousand sovereigns a year; but old Mat stood no nonsense from him or anyone else.'[85]

To this end, Archer did not seek the adulation he so liberally received from the public and, in doing so, lived up to a comment made in *The Sporting Life* at the start of his career that he would never allow success to go to his head as it had with other jockeys. While enjoying and living up to the spectacle of a big race, he was equally adept at 'switching off' once it was over.[86]

This attitude was, in part, the influence of Mathew Dawson, who insisted upon dignity and decorum both on and off the course, but it was also Fred's attempt to distance himself from the euphoria which his fame was generating. He was not a naturally gregarious character and did not seek to ingratiate himself with people. What friends he had, he kept close and remained loyal to;[87] and he invariably enjoyed the company of his family. In fact he never lost sight of where he came from and was always very family-orientated – having as much patience with the younger as with the older members, maintaining his responsibility towards his parents and helping them financially. He was very close to his brother Charlie, who was by no means cowed by Fred's success, and in July 1882 his newborn nephew – Frederick Charles Archer – was named after him.

Outside his immediate family Fred was closest to Falmouth and Dawson who allowed him a certain independence in his approach to his work. They did not dictate or instruct, but watched as Fred applied innovation and technique to a sport which was fast becoming a science. He still lacked a certain measure of confidence, particularly where his education was concerned, but he was intelligent and knew how to channel his energies into the one thing he knew he was expert at – racing. To this end he was turning into a perfectionist and the sadness which Lambton observed when he first saw him, so early in his career, was the craving for excellence which was beginning to take its toll. His approach to his work – in particular the physical wasting – was extreme.[88]

Portland remembered Dawson gently chiding Fred over his weight, just prior to a race and Fred promised that he would be 8st 10lb by 3 p.m. – the time of the race. 'You see, my medicine hasn't acted yet,' he said, 'and I shall sit in my Turkish bath and no doubt elsewhere until it's time to go to the races.' He was as good as his word, and so took off more than three pounds in weight in as many hours.

Dawson had had Turkish baths installed at Heath House – for the horses no less, so that weight could be sweated out of them, but his equine residents suddenly found themselves sharing these facilities with Fred. Dawson, according to Portland, did not agree with this method of weight loss for the horses as such, but had no qualms about his jockeys using it. 'Fred finds it a'fully useful,' he told Portland, 'and if the others are oerstoot I send them in too.'[89]

Archer did not run, like other jockeys, to lose weight. He found it quicker to starve himself, relying upon the most meagre of morsels and, to ensure that he was able to lose weight in the shortest time possible, he partook of what was one of the quickest methods of losing weight – a laxative mixture, pre-pared for him by his Newmarket doctor, Dr Wright.[90] Most jockeys, if they could bear to touch the stuff at all, took it by the spoonful. Fred took it by the glassful and from then on it was always known as 'Archer's Mixture' – when it was not being referred to as 'dynamite'. His weight preoccupied him incessantly and with constantly keeping it down and possessing a tall frame he developed a slight stoop which *Vanity Fair* used to caricature him. The caricature also made him look frail – certainly too light to ride a horse – to the point where even his silks did not look right on him.

Although the caricature was not meant to be taken seriously or personally, it pinpointed Archer's character at its most extreme and the message was clear.[91] He was taking far greater physical risks than his counterparts. His father and brother had retired from being jockeys because of their weight,[92] but Fred wanted to remain one for as long as he could because, at the end of the day, it was all he knew and all he had known since the age of eleven. He was setting himself impossible standards in order to maintain the excellence he was achieving, but at the same time was attempting to bury a deep sense of insecurity, both personal and financial.

There seemed to be two personalities at work within Fred Archer. When Lambton first encountered him, he was dressed almost as soberly as a clerk or a curate and many were quick to note an image which seemed to be totally at odds with that displayed on the course. Once off the course he dressed so as not to be noticed, as someone who could disappear in a crowd. 'No-one seeing him for the first time,' wrote Lambton, 'would have put him down as a jockey, or suspected that such tremendous energy lurked in that frail body.'[93]

So his image contradicted every perception. About the only consistent thing about him was his enjoyment of taking risks – and not just on the course. Gambling provided another incentive, but more for the competition than the money. He gambled only on horseracing – nothing else, nor did he gamble the high stakes his brother Charlie gambled. He was also known to ride against his own money, so that he would not let his owners down. Through his attitude to gambling and his finances in general, he was nicknamed the 'Tinman' and was affectionately referred to by Dawson as a tin-scraping devil. If anyone was of the opinion that it was only the two Archer brothers who gambled, they were very much mistaken. Their father never gambled, Alice recalled, nor was he a card player, but he never stopped his wife Emma from having the occasional flutter. In fact he allowed her to do exactly as she pleased and, according to her daughter, she loved card playing – with son Fred covering her debts.[94]

Throughout his life Fred enjoyed all sports – from racing to boxing and billiards. He also enjoyed hunting and, in fact, had hunted for far longer than he had been a jockey, but where many of Fred's contemporaries thought he rode well to hounds, others thought he was hopeless.

'[O]ne of the worst riders to hounds I ever saw,' wrote Portland, 'had no idea of putting a horse at a fence, but simply went hard at it.'[95]

Riding in the Cottesmore Hunt on one of Lord Wilton's horses, he rode so hard at one gap in a fence that he inadvertently collided with one of the other riders, who went head over heels and later complained about Fred's behaviour to the man who put Fred in the hunt in the first place – Colonel Forrester. Forrester admonished Fred, who was apologetic and begged that Cussy should not be told.[96]

'Cussy' was Harry Custance (to Fordham he was simply 'Cus') and he always had a dim view of jockeys who did not toe the line when hunting since it put horsemanship, but particularly horseracing, in a bad light altogether; 'and if they could not do better,' wrote Portland, 'they should stay at home.'[97]

Harry Custance knew exactly what Fred was like and, while acknowledging that his friend was an excellent horseman, saw in him a kind of devil-may-care attitude when it came to riding cross-country. He disagreed with Portland over his general performance, saying that 'he was a really good man over a country.'[98]

But Archer did, as Portland noted, go hard at the fences and made tactless manoeuvres which, to the amusement of Custance, had other horsemen, some of whom did not know who Fred was, talking to him 'as if he were a schoolboy' and 'remonstrating with Fred about jumping so close to anyone'.

Fred was obviously still in jockey, rather than hunting, mode and was causing mayhem wherever he went. 'Archer came to stop with me at Manton on the Saturday after,' Custance wrote, 'and, in the course of conversation on the Sunday, we found that he had had four days' hunting, five falls, knocked two people over and was fined a sovereign and costs for riding on the footpath.'

Custance was so impressed, or rather flummoxed, that he, whether seriously or not, suggested that Fred's 'adventures' should be printed, but that was not the end of it. On the Monday, Custance's wife was in Melton and, to her surprise, met Fred, 'laughing all over his face,' Custance recalled. Fred said to Mrs Custance, 'Tell the governor [meaning Harry], I finished up well: I killed a horse yesterday.'[99]

This was true. Fred had ridden an old horse in a particularly gruelling hunt and the animal later died of exhaustion. Again in jockey mode, he had taken a horse, not perhaps as fit as the racehorses he generally rode, and ridden it as if he were in a race – only to have the animal die as a consequence. Fred was not a cruel sportsman, nor a shallow one, for he had genuine respect for the horses he rode and a tolerant indulgence of their characters and quirks – particularly if they could be used to his advantage as in the case of Astley's horse, Peter. But Champion Jockey or no Champion Jockey, he was still capable of getting it wrong, even on the racecourse, and at one point upset Tom Cannon. Writing of the Doncaster Cup in 1879, Portland noted that Fred's spurs could be lethal and went on to describe how, during the race Isonomy, with Tom Cannon up, almost had his shoulder ripped to bits when he came between Fred (riding Jannette) and the rails. Cannon was livid, but Archer excused himself by blaming his feet which, he said, were flat, and his ankles, which, he said, were weak, so that his heels had a way of turning.[100]

Once again Fred was apologetic and always seemed to have an answer for everything, but had something like this occurred fifty years later, as Portland noted, it might have been a different story altogether and Fred would not, perhaps, have got away with it so lightly. It is clear that he knew the extent of his popularity to the point where he had developed a sheepish charm, so that some were willing to forgive him anything.[101]

Fred was not averse to taking risks, even with his own personal safety and, according to John Dawson, used to ride so close to the rails that he could almost ride over them and often came away with ripped boots.[102]

Even his family was not immune and it was well known that he would sooner see his brother over the rails than allow him to win. This was the more aggressive Archer coming into play, the one which belied the softly spoken, quietly dressed character off the course. Although he could swear like a trooper with the best of them during a race, many believed that his use of such language, particularly off the course, was greatly exaggerated. He could switch off the aggressiveness and even the competitiveness and be himself off the course.

Notes

1.   Lambton, The Honourable George, *Men and Horses I Have Known*, p.36
2–3.   Ibid, p.40
4–5.   Ibid, pp.40–1
6.   *Newmarket Journal*, 13 November 1886, containing a Biographical Notice of Frederick James Archer with details of his brother William's life and death
7.   Humphris, Edith M, *The Life of Fred Archer*, pp.122–3
8.   *Newmarket Journal*, 13 November 1886
9.   Humphris, *The Life of Fred Archer*, p.123
10.   Weatherby, J E & J P, *The Racing Calendar for the Year 1878*
11.   Portland, 6th Duke of, *Memories of Racing and Hunting*, p.93
12–13   Humphris, *The Life of Fred Archer*, p.72
14.   Mortimer, Onslow & Willet, pp.391–2
15.   Ibid, p.590
16.   Portland, p.129
17.   Beatty, Laura, *Lillie Langtry: Manners, Masks & Morals*, p.286
18.   Mortimer, Onslow & Willet, pp.391–2
19.   Lambton, p.121
20–3.   Ibid, p.128
24.   Welcome, John, *Fred Archer: A Complete Study*, pp.71–2
25–6.   Portland, p.129
27–8.   Lambton, p.37
29–31. Ibid, p.42
32–4.   Humphris, *The Life of Fred Archer*, p.145
35.   Humphris, *The Life of Mathew Dawson*, p.114

36. Humphris, *The Life of Fred Archer*, pp.146–7
37. *The Times*, 27 May 1880
38. Chetwynd, Sir George, *Racing Reminiscences and Experience of the Turf*, pp.192–3
39. Portland, p.77
40. Humphris, *The Life of Fred Archer*, p.186
41. Chetwynd, pp.192–3
42. Weatherby, J E & J P, *The Racing Calendar for the Year 1880*
43–5. Chetwynd, pp.193–4
46. Portland, p.77
47. *The Times*, 16/17 September 1880
48. *The Times*, 29 June 1881
49. Weatherby, J E & J P, *The Racing Calendar for the Year 1880*
50. Weatherby, J E & J P, *The Racing Calendar for the Year 1881*
51. Chetwynd, p.198
52. *The Sporting Life*, 2 June 1881
53–5. *The Times*, 2 June 1881
56–7. *The Sporting Life*, 2 June 1881
58. Weatherby, J E & J P, *The Racing Calendar for the Year 1881*
59–70. Astley, Sir John Dugdale, *Fifty Years of My Life in the World of Sport at Home and Abroad*, pp.212–18
71. Weatherby, J E & J P, *The Racing Calendar for the Year 1881*
72. Huxley, Gervais, *Victorian Duke: The Life of Hugh Lupus Grosvenor, First Duke of Westminster*, pp.113–19
73. Mortimer, Onslow & Willet, pp.186, 187 & 558
74–6. *The Times*, 25 May 1882
77. *The Times*, 23/24 August 1882
78–80. *The Times*, 14 September 1882
81–2. *The Sporting Life*, 14 September 1882
83. Astley, pp.221–3
84–5. Portland, p.87
86. *The Sporting Life*, 9 October 1873
87. Lambton, pp.92–3
88–9. Portland, p.97
90. Welcome, John, *Fred Archer: A Complete Study*, p.46
91. 'The Tinman' (courtesy of Vanity Fair Press)
92. Mortimer, Onslow & Willet, p.20
93. Lambton, p.41
94. Humphris, *The Life of Fred Archer*, pp.45, 73 & 174
95. Portland, p.227
96. Ibid, p.228
97. Custance, Henry, *Riding Recollections and Turf Stories*, pp.124–7
98–9. Ibid, pp.127–8
100. Portland, pp.4 & 5
101–2. Humphris, *The Life of Fred Archer*, p.186

Fred and Helen Rose

Fred was the most eligible bachelor in the country. Rich, popular, successful and a particular favourite with the women – especially the ageing and dictatorial Duchess of Montrose who was infatuated with him, but he was shrewd enough to see that such infatuations were just that – mingled with hysterical hero worship – and it is probably another reason why he maintained such a low profile off the racecourse.

Since racing was his life and as his family and companions belonged exclusively to the world of racing, it is no wonder that the woman he chose to be his wife not only knew and understood racing, but was a part of the Dawson clan. Helen Rose Dawson, known as Nellie in the family and born around 1861 (exact date unknown), was the daughter of Mathew's brother, John.[1]

Fred had known her since his apprenticeship and had often been charged with the responsibility of seeing her and her brother John safely home if they had been out for the day, so, in truth Nellie and Fred had practically grown up together. He began to court her during the winter of 1880, visiting her at her home, Warren House, before he proposed in 1882. She was pretty, fair and as slim as a sixteen-year-old, according to Fred's sister Alice, and, being of medium height, only came as far as Fred's shoulder. He called her the 'little woman'. From the start she was well liked by Fred's family, in particular his sister Alice.[2]

The engagement was announced to both the Archer and Dawson families, the many and varied members of which all approved of the match and a date for the wedding was set for

31 January 1883, just after Fred's 26th birthday and two
months before the start of the racing season. But, despite the
fact that Fred was to be a welcome addition to the family, the
Dawsons did come in for some criticism.

An acquaintance of Helen Rose's mother expressed surprise at
the idea of a young lady marrying a mere jockey. Mrs Dawson,
shocked by this level of social prejudice and hypocrisy, sought to
defend her future son-in-law from the outset by stating
categorically that Fred was good enough to marry a Princess and
that, it seems, was the end of it. Whatever other criticisms there
might have been were quickly silenced, but the incident did
underline an uncomfortable truth that Fred, rich and successful
though he was, was regarded by some as being on a lower social
scale than his future wife. He was accepted so long as he kept his
place within society, but now that he had aspired to marry his
employer's niece, he was getting above himself and, worse, with
Helen Rose accepting him, she was in danger of marrying
beneath herself. Few, however, realised the true state of things.
Fred was no longer just Mathew Dawson's First Jockey at Heath
House. He was now his partner and had been since the early
months of 1881, so the criticism counted for nothing.[3]

For some time, Dawson had grown used to relying on Fred
and his expertise, seeking his First Jockey's opinion as much as
everyone else. It had reached the stage where, if someone
approached Mat for advice, his reply would invariably be, 'Ask
Archer.'[4] Eventually Fred's role at Heath House became so
invaluable that Dawson decided to invite him to become a
partner. An announcement to that effect appeared in *The
Sportsman* on 29 November 1880[5] and at the start of the 1881
season Fred was officially made Dawson's partner and the two
began running the establishment between them, although the
old man still treated Fred as he had always done and the young
jockey still lived at Heath House.

That, however, was about to change. Fred was quite a wealthy
young man and, aside from the new leap in responsibility, owned

his own racehorses, shares and was earning on average between 8,000 and 10,000 sovereigns a year.[6] Given that, at the start of his apprenticeship just thirteen years before, he was earning just seven guineas a year and was now accumulating over a thousand times that, he could afford to begin married life comfortably and ensure that Helen Rose wanted for nothing, providing her with the type of lifestyle to which she had become accustomed. He had plans which, he hoped, would extend from his work at Heath House. He needed both a home and a working establishment. Once their engagement had been announced, Fred set about putting his plans into effect and arranged for the construction of a mansion which he would eventually name Falmouth House, after Viscount Falmouth, who would assist in both the financial and structural planning.

Falmouth House was to be situated north of the town of Newmarket, surrounded by heath and woodland, with the estate overlooking the Snailwell Road. Being just one mile from the railway station its proximity to Newmarket was close – in fact it was surrounded, first, by the Marquess of Zetland's property, then Mathew Dawson's and then the Woodland Stud while facing, on the other side of Snailwell Road, spacious training grounds and the area known as 'The Severals'.[7] It was a gentleman's establishment in almost every respect, but on what would later be described as a 'moderate'[8] scale, given the palatial grandeur of the residences of Britain's landed aristocracy at that time. Even so, no cost had been spared in the building of the house itself or the arrangement of the grounds; and it was set up to accommodate comfort, practicality and a working environment.

The grounds were spacious with stables, a lodge and cottages on the estate. The stud premises contained 25 boxes with yards and forage houses with a cottage for the stud groom. There were several paddocks, extending over almost 52 acres. The stud premises themselves were very extensive: two stallion boxes with accompanying yards, eleven brood mare boxes with five yards, a barn, forage and corn house. There were also a cart shed and a well; and to cap it all a double cottage. The off-stud premises consisted of twelve boxes, six enclosed yards and a well.[9]

The house was built with a completely modern and tasteful appearance. An advertisement for the property in 1887 described it as 'handsome' with ornamental red brick and carved stone.

Special exterior features included four chimney stacks – the pots of two of the stacks were created with a woven design, and one of the stacks with three pots dominated the side of the house, towering, rather precariously, above a beautifully constructed conservatory. Other features included the windows and doors which were stained internally, and limestone decoration.[10]

It was, perhaps, one of the most exclusive and individual properties to be built at that time and everything about the place denoted space, light and colour alongside beauty and elegance. The drawing room contained exquisitely designed marble and enamel mantelpieces which Edith M Humphris had the chance to see when she was researching her book. There was also a lofty dining room and a morning room.[11]

On the first floor there were four principal bedrooms, a bathroom with WC and three servants' rooms. The plumbing was completely up to date and there was particular attention to detail, not just in the construction of the house, but also in its decoration. The conservatory, which overlooked the gardens, and gave access to the principal rooms on the ground floor, had what the advertisement described as 'painted' glass and a tessellated pavement.[12]

The grounds immediately in front of the house were equally impressive and covered some three acres with many shrubs and trees lining the perimeter and driveway of the house. A 'highly ornamental' fountain and grotto in the grounds had been built at a cost of 500 sovereigns, an enormous sum in those days, but a feature without which the estate would have been incomplete since no respectable residence in Victorian Britain would have been seen without one. Given how they looked on a map produced in 1887, they were large enough to add a touch of opulence to the estate as a whole. There was also a summer house and a walled kitchen garden with a greenhouse, forcing house and potting house.[13]

The house also had other purposes. The basement housed complete beer and wine cellars suggesting, along with the whole layout of the estate that it was not just a working property, but one designed to entertain guests – suggestive of Fred's confidence in his success and happiness. Falmouth House demonstrated his ambition and was moderate – to a point – since it was a complete reflection of how he viewed his future work and progress.

The house was only just completed in time for Fred and Helen Rose's wedding on 31 January 1883. This was an event in Newmarket which was to be treated almost as a royal occasion – an event which the whole town would be involved in, Newmarket's own public holiday. The local newspaper, the *Newmarket Journal* gave the wedding full coverage – from the preparations, to the wedding ceremony itself and the celebrations after the church service. It is indicative of the esteem in which Fred was held by the townspeople.[14]

The wedding was a major public event and also a measure of how proud the town was of the young jockey. The detail in the account of his wedding in the *Newmarket Journal* reveals that it was not just a story of local human interest. The focus was on the fact that Newmarket was witnessing the nuptials of perhaps England's most talented sportsman. The whole town came to a standstill for this event and the level of respect was extended beyond Newmarket as people from different parts of the country descended upon the place to witness an event unique in the town's history. The *Newmarket Journal*, appealing to a readership beyond racegoers, was determined to ensure that its account was as visual as possible, with a step-by-step approach which shows just how commercial Fred and his new bride were.

The level of interest in their popularity was not unlike the write-ups in celebrity magazines of today and, like the readers of today, readers back then would have been given an idea of the wealth enjoyed by their celebrities.[15]

An entire column[16] in the *Newmarket Journal* was devoted to the wedding presents received. Apart from all the jewellery presented to Helen Rose (she received a diamond brooch from Fred in the shape of a horseshoe) there was a 'gold and silver fruit and flower epergne' from her father, 'linen and a family Bible' from her mother. Her brother George gave her paintings on china and her other brother, John, gave her a 'shield, with representation in silver of "Paradise Lost" mounted in velvet'. Her sister Annie gave her a large oil painting of Christchurch, near Winchester. Fred's father also gave an oil painting – of himself on a horse called Thorgenti. Fred's sister Emily, now Mrs Emily Archer Coleman,[17] presented a bronzed pen and ink stand, complete with decorative medallions. Charlie and his wife gave a china breakfast and tea service and Mathew Dawson a silver salver – 'very ancient piece of plate'. His wife gave a 'toilet service, two satin handkerchief sachets, a pair of Dresden china ornaments and ornaments for writing table'. Viscount Falmouth gave a silver dinner service; Countess Baltazzi gave Helen Rose a fan, with a mother-of-pearl handle and the initials "NA" and "A" on the back and front; and Prince Batthyany gave the bride the gold bracelet with a pearl and diamond cluster which she wore going into church. Other presents, given by family and friends, are too numerous to mention here, but are listed in full in the *Newmarket Journal*, which in order to inject a certain measure of humour, described other offerings of not so luxurious a nature.

One of Fred's retainers, Lord George Hastings of Melton Constable in Leicestershire, on deciding to add his contribution, took it upon himself to send a prize bullock to Newmarket on the Friday before the wedding, so that it could be slaughtered and cooked on the day of the ceremony for the benefit of the local townsfolk who would be doing most of their celebrating out on 'The Severals'. Once delivered, the bullock promptly took off and was later recaptured as it strolled nonchalantly out on the Heath – taking 'a constitutional' was how the *Newmarket Journal* put it. It was then taken unceremoniously back to the town, where it was delivered to the Wagon and Horses Hotel to be shot on the Saturday afternoon and hoisted on to its spit by the locals on the Monday.[18]

Tuesday, 30 January, was market day and Hastings' prize, but very dead bullock, found itself on view to a public which was looking forward as much to eating the animal as seeing the wedding for which it had been slaughtered.[19]

'Meanwhile,' noted the *Newmarket Journal*, 'preparations had been going on upon "The Severals" for an unexampled . . . cooking feat. Mr R Kent had raised a brick wall of some 6ft in height with side walls of the same material, and in front of this . . . erected his fireplace and cooking apparatus.'[20]

The newspaper also gave details of the preparations being organised by the locals. 'The Severals' was destined to be busier than it had ever been. One John Lancaster, of the Black Bear Hotel, applied for a temporary licence to serve alcohol there during the wedding celebrations and this was granted by those in charge of Newmarket's Petty Sessions. The celebrations promised to make the wedding an occasion to be long remembered. The days immediately before the wedding saw the whole town and 'The Severals' being prepared not only with food but also a fairground, turning the event into a public holiday, even though the unsettled conditions of Tuesday threatened to place a dampener on the whole proceedings. Still, Wednesday 31 January shone bright and, despite the chill of a frosty day, was seen as 'Queen's Weather'.[21]

People began arriving in the town from early on in the morning and seemed to come from far and wide. The *Newmarket Journal* recorded how they came from the neighbouring towns and villages of Peterborough, Lynn, Wisbech and Cambridge and from northern areas such as Bury and Doncaster, not to mention the capital itself.[22] People were making the most of this wedding and believed that they would never see its like again, adding a kind of magical fervour to the proceedings with the *Newmarket Journal* anxious to add a kind of romanticism to them.

The number of people who would be anxious to have a seat in the church was anticipated and entry to All Saints' Church was ticket-based.

'Half-past eleven was the appointed hour for the ceremonial,' the *Newmarket Journal* reported, 'but eager groups of ticket-holders besieged the gates.'[23]

Other wellwishers crowded the area outside and it was noted that every pew, ledge and window was taken advantage of, so that spectators could see the groom and then the bride arrive. The appearance of so many people, particularly at the church, became a safety issue and a police presence prevented a storming of the church itself. So great was the crowd that the church doors had to be opened at 10 a.m. and within half an hour the church was almost full.[24]

Not surprisingly the families of the bride and groom opted to arrive later and, until their appearance, their guests took the opportunity to look about them in the church. The correspondent for the *Newmarket Journal*, who, it seems, managed to gain entry, noted how the interior of the church was still adorned with decorations left over from Christmas, which seemed to add to the occasion. The newspaper described how the organist and choirmaster, Mr T J Moaksom, and his pupil, Mr Bertie Martin 'whiled away the interval' playing Haydn's Symphonies No.2 and No.3.[25]

The officiating clergy then appeared and the guests took that as a sign that the families were on their way. Minutes later, the immediate family and close relatives of the bridal couple arrived. The correspondent for the *Newmarket Journal* was quick to note who came in first. Mathew Dawson and his wife entered, he wrote, with Fred's brother Charlie who was accompanying his mother, and William Archer – 'Mr Archer Snr' – arrived presently. Then all the others followed, reading like a *Who's Who* of Newmarket's elite – from prestigious family members to friends. Even the appearance of these people alone aroused much interest and many became disorderly in their attempts to get a look at the family and close friends of the famous Fred Archer.

The only member of the family who could not attend was Fred's sister, Alice, who was expecting a baby at the time.[26]

As the guests settled themselves, the crowd outside became aware of Fred's carriage as it made its way through Newmarket, along a route which was lined by a multitude of people. Fred and his best man, noted in the *Newmarket Journal* as 'Mr T Jennings Jnr', arrived at the church to the sound of huge cheers which, no doubt, could be heard inside the church itself. Delighted, Fred alighted from the vehicle, living up to the image of popular hero, and graciously acknowledged his public's approval before moving on to meet his five groomsmen – two of whom were Nellie's two brothers, George and John Dawson – who were all waiting for him to enter the church. Many think it curious that his brother Charlie, being his only surviving brother, was not best man or a groomsman. Fred spent a few minutes in the vestry with the vicar and his curate before making his way to the altar, aware that the atmosphere inside the church had changed to one of heightened expectation.[27]

It was now just a matter of moments before the bride, accompanied by her bridesmaids, would arrive. At least that is what everyone thought, but the minutes went by and she did not appear, causing a great deal of agitation among the ticket-holders inside the church and a moment of drama for the *Newmarket Journal*'s correspondent to add to his account for his readers.[28]

Finally, and cutting it very fine, Helen Rose arrived with her father John Dawson Senior, followed by her bridesmaids. As with all weddings, the bride's dress was of particular interest, being described in detail by the *Newmarket Journal*:

> The bridal dress was of a lovely satin blondinaide, looped with rich old Venetian lace, blended with orange blossoms and sprays. The gupe, handsomely trimmed with point lace, consisted of a rich Surate silk. The beauty of the bridal wreath lay in its simplicity. The veil, a rich piece of fine art worl, executed by nuns in Belgium, gave a charming effect to the tout ensemble.[29]

It had been designed by Harry Tilbury and her entire bridal trousseau had been put together by Messrs Worth and Co under his supervision. Helen Rose was also wearing the jewel-encrusted bracelet, given to her by Prince Batthyany, and the diamond horseshoe brooch, a gift from her future husband.[30]

The bridesmaids numbered six: Helen Rose's sister, Annie Bland Dawson; two cousins – Lillie Dawson and Florrie Bates; Miss Rose Saunders; Miss Aggie Saunders; and Miss Harriet Briggs. They wore 'coral silk gowns and diamond and pearl bracelets given them by the groom'.[31]

With everyone present the service could now begin without further delay and the service, as the *Newmarket Journal* noted, was impressive. As Mendelssohn's 'Wedding March' was played Mr and Mrs Frederick J Archer moved to the vestry to sign the register, accompanied by Annie Bland Dawson, Messrs Thomas S Dawson and Mr T Jennings.[32] Minutes later they emerged, walked down the aisle and out of the church to the people waiting outside who cheered and threw rice. The bells of All Saints', accompanied by those of St Mary's, would ring for the remainder of the day. As Fred and Helen Rose made their way back to Warren House for the wedding breakfast,[33] the toastmaster on 'The Severals' had barely finished his congratulatory toast when everybody made a rush for the food and the demand was so great that it was difficult to keep everyone happy.

Scuffles resulted which slightly overshadowed the general atmosphere of celebration and goodwill.[34] Another source of disappointment was the shape and form of the bullock Lord Hastings had seen fit to donate to the feast. After the trouble it had caused upon its arrival, people found cause to complain now that it was dead. Fred's friend and colleague, Harry Morgan, told Edith M Humphris that, although he did not eat it, he had it on good authority that it had not been cooked properly – neither cooked nor raw, he told her.[35]

Even so people bickered over their share of the animal and it was laid down in the *Newmarket Journal* as one of the highlights of 'The Severals' celebrations – 'bullock on the brain' was the unfortunate expression. It was also understood that Fred himself had requested possession of the hooves and skin which were later sent to the local taxidermist, W Howlett, to be turned into snuff boxes, inkstands and other souvenirs.[36]

The celebrations also included balloons and a firework display: 'brilliant in design and execution . . . to the enjoyment of an immense crowd of sightseers . . . Innumerable rockets, an endless variety of blue and green lights, and two splendid set pieces, a very life-like pyrotechnic illustration of "Archer Up" and the final piece . . . "May they be happy".'[37]

That evening, while the general populace amused itself as best it could on 'The Severals', Mrs John Dawson, Nellie's mother, gave a ball at the Rutland Arms and 80 stable lads employed by Mathew Dawson and Charles Archer were entertained in the long room at the Wagon and Horses Hotel. Fred and Helen Rose had, by this time, left Newmarket, by train, to begin their honeymoon, but even at this point they were not allowed to slip away quietly.[38] 'Special trains were run from outlying villages to bring admirers to the scene. Newmarket was packed with excited throngs who cheered the bride and groom all the way to the station where a special carriage awaited them on the siding.'[39]

After being given such a brilliant send off, the young couple were just as warmly welcomed as they passed through

Cambridge and, in fact, the whole day had been turned into an event that people were determined to remember long after it was over. Soon after his wedding, commemorative photographs of Fred Archer were sold in Newmarket.[40] Alongside photographs of the troublesome bullock!

The honeymoon was spent in Torquay, where they became the subject of local history interest over fifty years later when a Reverend J E Boggis of St John's Vicarage in Torquay sent a letter to *The Times* on 27 October 1933, describing how Fred refused to stay in the church because his wife was not allowed to sit with him.[41] The Archers were not in Torquay for very long and they soon returned to Newmarket to take up residence at Falmouth House. While they were away, there had been a spate of burglaries in and around the Newmarket area. On being told of this, Fred located a gun which had been given to him by a Mr Thomas Roughton as a reward after winning the Liverpool Cup. Fred placed the revolver in the pedestal beside his bed, so that it would be on hand should the house be burgled – which it wasn't – but from then on Fred always kept the gun nearby.[42]

Mr and Mrs Frederick James Archer seemed to complement one another perfectly and from the outset Helen Rose seemed very well able to deal with her husband's fame and popularity. The wedding had been clear proof of the fact that Fred was public property and that not only his, but her life would be watched with interest, particularly in the earliest stages, but Fred had chosen a young girl who understood perfectly the highs and lows of racing life.

Being the daughter of one of England's most popular trainers and a member of a large family devoted to horseracing, she knew exactly what lay in store for her as Fred's wife and would have had no trouble in adjusting to her new role. In fact a photograph of herself and Fred, taken shortly after their marriage shows just how very much at ease she was. Fred stands, smiling shyly at the camera, while Helen Rose leans, casually, against a mock fence in the photographer's studio. Of the two she seems more relaxed and, by virtue of her temperament alone, made Fred's life complete.

Before marrying Helen Rose, Fred's life had been one of chaos. He was no sooner coming to the end of one racing season than he was preparing for the next. He was constantly in demand by trainers, retainers and family and he had no real home of his own. With his marriage all that changed. Within a chaotic existence Helen Rose provided him with an atmosphere of calm and space within an environment that was, essentially, their own.

Being possessed of a gentle, loving nature, she was very much family-orientated and had a particular fondness for Fred's family – the ever increasing clan – going out of her way to accommodate them. The one incident which stayed with her sister-in-law Alice and clearly demonstrates Helen Rose's character took place when Alice visited Falmouth House with her eldest son, six-year-old Frederick Charles Pratt (a man in his thirties when Alice told Edith M Humphris about this incident, she referred to him as 'Little Fred or Freddy'), who was to stay with his uncle and aunt for a few days. The elder Fred apparently told Alice to leave the boy with him.[43]

Alice protested, saying that the boy only had a few clothes with him, but her brother waved this aside and said that extra belongings would be sent for. He asked Freddy himself if he would like to stay and he said yes.[44] In hindsight the decision seemed practical since the Pratts were constantly on the move and young Freddy was developing a talent for horsemanship which could benefit from his uncle's influence.

A visit of a few days turned into two years. Alice seldom saw her son except when he came home to visit, but what greatly impressed her was Helen Rose's care and attention of her young Freddy, particularly since she could have objected to his presence at the house so soon after her wedding. Above all, Alice remembered Helen Rose's lack of selfishness.[45]

Helen Rose also wanted to ensure that Freddy made friends, particularly since he did not have the company of his own brothers and sisters, all of whom were close in age. She arranged for children of his own age and background to come to Falmouth House and organised children's parties for him.[46] She even worried about him – as on one occasion when he became lost on his way home from school. She created a relaxed family atmosphere at Falmouth House, the first her husband could enjoy in his own home since the Prestbury days. It is true that he was more secure now than he had been in recent years. He too enjoyed having young Freddy Pratt about the place and sometimes teased him, as a friend of the boy, one Wyndham Mills (whose father was a friend of the older Fred) remembered years later. Mills recalled a fishing trip when he and Freddy Pratt managed to catch a trout, but when they showed it to Archer he jokingly refused to believe they had caught it.[47]

Wyndham Mills also remembered the children's games which Fred used to enjoy taking part in – in particular a spelling game. It seems that Fred was quite proficient in this, justifying the beliefs of many that he could have followed a professional career, but his nephews – and especially young Freddy Pratt – saw him as a sporting hero; and the huge influence which Fred Archer had on their lives would ensure that they themselves followed careers first as jockeys, then as trainers.[48]

Now that the great Fred Archer was married, the press wanted to see how he lived – a kind of Mr and Mrs Archer at home. In September 1883, when Fred and Helen Rose were settled in their new home, they were visited by a journalist, from *The World* paper, who wrote an article about the young couple, Falmouth House and its contents. This was later published in Edith M Humphris' book and describes Fred at his most contented.[49]

The reporter was shown around the entire property. It seems that Fred regretted the extent of the place, from a security point of view. It was too lavish and, given the burglaries which had been taking place in Newmarket of late, too exposed, but it was, whether he liked it or not, a reflection of his new status and, as

the journalist was shown around, he found that the whole estate
had Fred Archer's mark well and truly stamped on it.

The dining room, being the first room on the left of the main
entrance, he found tastefully furnished and in the morning or
breakfast room (the journalist was not entirely sure what name the
room was given), he was led on to two other rooms (their doors
hidden behind a curtain), which comprised the Turkish baths
described by the reporters as very luxurious – proof that Falmouth
House was a working establishment as well as a home.[50]

Fred and his wife, after showing their guest the interior of the
house, took him on a tour of the grounds and he was shown the
kitchen garden and stables where, in addition to seeing horses
and ponies owned by both Fred and Helen Rose and the
carriages and pony traps, the journalist was shown the Archers'
dogs: Fred's St Bernard – called Bernard, a mastiff called
Sultan; and Helen Rose's pet – a fox terrier.[51] After a wander
around the paddock everyone went back to the house and the
journalist was treated to a peach and a glass of sherry before
John Dawson, Helen Rose's brother, arrived to talk to Fred.

If proof was ever wanted of Fred's need for security and
familiarity, it was the huge art collection which defined him
almost as much as it defined Falmouth House. The rooms and
hallways were full of pictures and portraits of horses and Fred's
family, friends and associates. In the dining room, the journalist
identified pictures of Petronel, Atlantic, Silvio, Archer himself
and his father.[52] The art gallery also extended to the front
entrance with paintings of Parole and members of the Jockey
Club. Paintings of Silvio and Beauminet by artists Hall and
Arnull respectively hung on the left of the entrance hall while
Spinaway adorned the opposite wall, alongside Mat Dawson. In
the morning room were portraits of Fred's parents and photographs of Fred and other jockeys, one of which, most intriguing
of all, may have been of George Fordham (see page 89).

The room which impressed the reporter the most was the
drawing room, partly because there were no pictures of horses

in it, and because it had a tribute from the Prince of Wales. There was also a print of the formidable Admiral Rous, the third 'Dictator of the Turf' who had reformed racing.[53]

Everything about Falmouth House, from its layout, structure and design to the personal details within the house itself was an extension of Fred's life in racing. It was not a place where he could switch off from his life as a jockey, although he might detach himself from the adulation his career inspired. It was solid proof that he was successful in his life and that he had received recognition. Falmouth House was his security for the future – his ambition was embodied in the place and was supported by his wife who made it a home for him. It was a scene of perfect domesticity which would have appealed to the public and would have provided them with a very private view of the life of a man who spent most of his time on public show – and in the year 1883 more than ever, for good and bad.

Notes

1.   Humphris, Edith M, *The Life of Fred Archer*, p.195
2.   Ibid, pp.194–5
3–4.   Welcome, John, *Fred Archer: A Complete Study*, p.87
5.   *The Sportsman*, 29 November 1880
6.   Portland, 6th Duke of, *Memories of Racing and Hunting*, p.87
7.   Map of Newmarket (courtesy of Suffolk Record Office)
8–9.   Falmouth House, Advertisement 1887 (Ref. 6F 506/10/9, Suffolk Record Office)
10.   *Newmarket Journal*, 16 April 1970
11–13. Falmouth House, Advertisement 1887
14–25. *Newmarket Journal*, 3 February 1883
26.   Humphris, *The Life of Fred Archer*, p.194
27–34. *Newmarket Journal*, 3 February 1883
35.   Humphris, *The Life of Fred Archer*, p.102
36–40. *Newmarket Journal*, 3 February 1883
41.   *The Times*, 27 October 1933
42.   Humphris, *The Life of Fred Archer*, p.285
43–8.   Ibid, pp.194–5
49–53. Ibid, pp. 207–13

Mixed Fortune

The years 1883 and 1884 were a time of mixed fortune for Fred. He would see many of his close associates either die or retire from the racing scene; he would see his reputation held in doubt and he would see personal happiness turn to personal tragedy.

The scene was set at the start of the 1883 season which began well enough with Fred winning the Craven Stakes on Grandmaster on 12 April and several days later the Westminster Stakes on Kincaidine.[1] Then on 25 April he rode Galliard, son of the Derby winner Galopin, in the Two Thousand Guineas. Galopin had belonged to Prince Batthyany and, although Galliard was owned by Falmouth, the Prince nevertheless took an interest in his progress, as he did with all of Galopin's offspring and had a special pride in the horse. He was, therefore, especially keen to watch Galliard in the Two Thousand Guineas, particularly since Fred was riding him.[2] Unfortunately it was not meant to be.

Prince Batthyany was on his way back to the Jockey Club Luncheon Room with the Duke of Portland and Lord Charles Beresford in attendance. He had just reached a small flight of steps when, without warning, he fell to the ground. Stunned, Portland and Beresford immediately went to his aid and, lifting him, found that he was dead. Portland, in recounting the shocking event in his memoirs, always believed that Batthyany was dead before he hit the ground.[3] Obviously the excitement had been too much for Batthyany; he had been suffering from heart trouble for some time.

140

The Prince's death served to overshadow the whole day with all the racegoers becoming hushed and subdued, but at least Galliard justified Batthyany's hopes and came in the winner. Fred did not hear of the Prince's death until he came off the course and was very much saddened by it. Batthyany would also have been proud of the fact that Galliard and Fred went on to secure other wins this year.

After coming third in the Derby on 23 May, they came in first in the Prince of Wales Stakes on 5 June, secured the St James' Stakes two days later and the Triennial Stakes the day after that,[4] so out of tragedy came triumph. It would not be the last time that Fred would be successful with Batthyany's horses. The Prince's racing engagements were declared void immediately after his death and it was later announced that his stud would be sold – a particularly significant event in Fred's fortunes.

Another death to occur this year was that of W S Stirling-Crawfurd, the second husband of the 67-year-old Duchess of Montrose. The Duchess, still very much enamoured of Fred Archer who was young enough to be her son, declared that she would still run her late husband's stud, but that the horses would be leased to Sir Frederick Johnstone for twelve months. This was out of respect for her late husband's memory and for that length of time they would run under Johnstone's name. She herself was intent upon running her horses under the pseudonym 'Mr Manton' (see page 99). 'Mr Manton' At around this time she secured Fred's services for an undisclosed figure, but riding for 'Mr Manton' was going to have unfortunate consequences for him much later in the future.[5]

Despite the problems associated with Dutch Oven in 1882 Fred continued to have moderate success with her in 1883 and also rode Shotover and Geheimniss. He proved to have greater success on Geheimniss though – coming first in the Trial Stakes on 5 June, first in the Bunbury handicap on 3 July, first in the Kempton Park Cambridge Trial Handicap on 5 October and first in the Trial for 20 sovereigns on 22 October. Showing great promise as a four-year-old, Geheimniss, with Fred up, went on to secure further victories in 1884, but not before Fred had once again suffered the overshadowing of disappointment.[6]

One horse of 1883 which was approached first with disappointment, but proved to be a winner only to end up as an opportunity lost was a champion two-year-old called Barcaldine, by Solon out of Ballyroe. He was owned by the Scotsman, George Low who, rather than wishing to develop Barcaldine's potential, wanted only to exploit it. This was a great tragedy since the potential of this horse was huge and he had remained undefeated throughout his early career in Ireland, but he was never considered for any of the Classics in either England or Ireland.[7]

He had been entered for the 1880 Manchester Cup and then promptly withdrawn when Low decided to enter him instead for the Northumberland Plate, known then as the 'Pitman's Derby'. Low needed money and when he saw that Barcaldine had been set at 7 to 2, realised that his profit would be very low.[8] He then offered Sir John Astley 1,000 sovereigns to strike out his horse (that is, to remove him from the engagement) and, failing that, was prepared to sell Barcaldine to Astley for 12,000 sovereigns. Astley was disgusted and reported Low to the Jockey Club. The Scotsman was promptly disqualified, for the Club's rules stated that suscription and entries could not be struck out once entries for the race were closed, and in addition Low had effectively tried to bribe Astley. The tragedy was that inevitably Barcaldine was also barred from a number of races, and was eventually auctioned off.[9]

He was brought over to England from Ireland as a two-year-old, and described by Portland as magnificent. The Duke wanted to buy him, but was beaten to it by a Robert Peck and Barcaldine was stabled with a Mr Golding. The loss of Barcaldine, in disappointing Portland, also disappointed Dawson and at one race meeting soon afterwards, Portland remembered seeing someone catching sight of Dawson and running as fast as possible

Fred Archer, and (inset) in his silks, c. 1880

(main · Hulton Archive; inset · Hulton Archive)

Opposite: *Fred wearing hunting clothes,*
posing in his conservatory at Falmouth House
(National Horseracing Museum)

Above: *Newmarket's Wedding of the Year*
(Note Mathew Dawson, second from the right
wearing a top hat)
(National Horseracing Museum)

Above: *Fred with his daughter, Nellie Rose*

(National Horseracing Museum)

Right: *Fred riding Iroquois, the winner of the 1881 Derby*

(Getty Images)

Right: *Ormonde*

(courtesy of Elizabeth Ross)

Left: *St Simon*

(courtesy of Elizabeth Ross)

Below: *Bend Or racing against Robert the Devil*

(Hulton Archive)

Above: *Sir John Astley*
(Mary Evans Picture Library)

Right: *Viscount Falmouth*
(Getty Images)

Below: *The Honourable George Lambton*
(National Portrait Gallery)

Tom Cannon

(Vanity Fair)

Left: *Fred Webb*
(Vanity Fair)

Above: *George Fordham*
(Mary Evans Picture Library)

Below: *Charles Wood*
(National Portrait Gallery)

in the opposite direction.[10] Obviously the man was aware of Dawson's displeasure and wished to avoid him – sharpish. Portland saw fit to remark upon the fact. 'Why, Mat,' he said to Dawson, 'that man seems a bit afraid of you.' Mat replied, 'Well, Your Grace, I don't wonder at that, for he is the damned old fool who prevented our buying Barcaldine.'[11]

Robert Peck was also presented with the rather dubious honour of training him. Barcaldine was in a very poor state and, when Archer saw him, he did not rate him at all and he told Robert Peck so. The trainer did not then feel inclined to back the horse,[12] but sometimes Fred's assessment could fall short even when others were enthusiastic. As it was, Barcaldine went on to win the Epsom Stakes, with Archer up, on 2 May. Two days later he won the Westminster Cup and Archer was won over, going back on his previous lack of faith. Together they won the Orange Cup at Ascot on 6 June.

Encouraged, Peck entered him for the Northumberland Plate, scheduled for 27 June. It was the race denied to Barcaldine three years earlier, but, although successfully completing his trials, he almost broke down on the eve of the race.[13] Desperate situations call for desperate measures and Barcaldine was made to stand with his foot in a bucket of ice, which fortunately did the trick and Fred rode him to victory. Believing that everything was fine, Barcaldine was then entered for the Cambridgeshire later in the year, but it was during his training for this event that he broke down completely. It was the end of a horse which could have been classed as one of the greats.

Fred had been wrong about Barcaldine at the start and later had cause to celebrate, but it was not the first time that his predictions had been proved wrong and people who trusted, not to mention gambled upon, his opinions and judgements, sometimes found themselves suffering for it later. This would happen again with much more tragic consequences, but then there were times when he would make a valid judgement and be ignored – as in the case of Lord Ellesmere's Highland Chief in the one race which subsequently overshadowed the whole year's racing season and would forever be associated with Fred's career and that of his brother Charlie.

The Derby was due to be run on 23 May 1883 and Fred's brother Charlie, who was Highland Chief's trainer, wanted him to ride him.[14] Portland did not rate the horse, and Lambton felt the need to provide a visual impression which would leave one in no doubt of the horse's lack of merit; 'a great, leggy, split up, longstriding horse by Hampton,' he wrote.[15]

Fred had ridden Highland Chief in races before. They had come second in the Houghton Stakes on 27 October 1882[16] and Fred had had little to do with the horse since, but he knew his form well enough and disagreed with Charlie's opinion of the horse's potential, telling his brother so. From the very beginning therefore Highland Chief did not inspire confidence, but Charlie took no notice and, according to Lambton, backed Highland Chief all the way, expecting the horse to secure not only a victory, but a fortune along with it – something in the region of 30,000 sovereigns.[17]

It seems that once Charlie Archer had an idea in his head, nothing could shift it. His confidence came from the fact that his brother Fred, having ridden Highland Chief in a previous race, therefore knew the horse and what he was capable of and, having ridden the Derby, knew the course and therefore would have no trouble negotiating Highland Chief around it. To his mind, Fred was clearly the only choice to secure a Derby victory, but he had forgotten that Viscount Falmouth, being Fred's principal retainer, had prior claim to his services.[18] At the very last before the race was due to start, Falmouth secured Fred to ride Galliard, promptly scuppering Charlie's plans.

Charlie was not happy and if the Duke of Portland remembered anything of that day, it was his reaction. 'This made Charlie,' continued Portland, 'who was by no means a saint in temper, lose whatever temper he had; and when [his replacement jockey] Webb asked him as he mounted the horse how he was to ride it, all Charlie Archer replied was, "Ride him to the devil, if you like!" Not very polite or explicit orders!'[19]

With Fred Archer on Falmouth's Galliard, the Two Thousand Guineas winner, and Fred Webb on Highland Chief, Charles Wood was to ride St Blaise – owned by Lord Alington (another of Fred's retainers) and Sir Frederick Johnstone (who had control of the late Stirling-Crawfurd's horses), trained by John Porter and described by George Lambton as 'a nice handy horse'.[20]

All three horses had ridden against each other in the Two Thousand Guineas, with Highland Chief coming fifth and St Blaise fourth. Porter, St Blaise's trainer, had been working him hard, bringing him up to a new level of fitness, but it was Galliard, who was favourite.[21] Unfortunately, Galliard, being of a highly strung temperament like his sire Galopin, was very skittish and Dawson managed to get permission for him to be saddled at the start, thereby foregoing the preliminary walk about.[22]

The race for the Derby got underway and, watching from the Ladies' Stand, Lambton observed how close the race was as St Blaise, with Galliard behind and Highland Chief third, came round Tattenham Corner. Then Fred Webb spurred Highland Chief (inspired by new energy) onwards and, as Lambton recalled, many thought that he had won – sentiments echoed by the *Manchester Guardian* on 24 May, but, as the paper explained, Highland Chief 'only succeeded, however, in over-hauling Galliard, whom Archer had evidently pumped out'.[23]

The performance of Charles Wood on the actual winner, St Blaise, was described by Sir George Chetwynd as 'fearless': 'hugging the rails and stealing several lengths'.[24]

Once it was announced that St Blaise, with Charles Wood, had secured the Derby, there were ecstatic shouts of 'Bravo, Charlie' and Sir Frederick Johnstone, having backed St Blaise for 10,000 sovereigns, led his winner to the Royal box with a big smile on his face and with rumours abounding that a certain 'distinguished personage', although the *Manchester Guardian* does not specify whom, had an interest in the horse.[25] Lord Alington was equally delighted at the win and looked, according to the correspondent for *The Sporting Life* 'as though he had got all his rents paid a year in advance'.[26]

Lord Ellesmere was in shock and left the course in a dazed state.[27] Not that he ever held the result against Charlie Archer who continued to train for him for many years.

Brother Fred, however, was criticised for riding a bad race or, at least, for not riding with his customary enthusiasm. Sir George Chetwynd believed that he could not have ridden Galliard any better but was not convinced that Fred could have made Galliard win. 'I had more on Galliard than I ever had on a horse in the Derby before,' he wrote, 'and I am quite satisfied that, owing to his heavy shoulders, Galliard would not act down hill, and lost too much ground ever to make it up. The winner, a white-legged chestnut son of Hermit, had, as usual with nearly all that great horse's stock, faultless shoulders.'[28]

Even so, such a criticism contributed towards a change in mood. Within minutes of the race ending, the atmosphere turned as people began to question Archer's overall performance and even that of Fred Webb whose timing, they believed, had been off, but then Webb himself felt that he had ridden a bad race and said so. Archer, however, was not allowed to get off so lightly. Since the racegoing public could still remember the furore over Dutch Oven in 1882, he was accused of throwing this race despite the fact that the majority of people had always judged him to be an honourable sportsman and that it would be totally against his practice to throw any race. He was even known to ride against his own money and had made it clear that it was the interests of his employers which came first, but many were prepared to believe the worst and, in addition, believed that he had had the blessing of his brother, whose copybook with the Jockey Club was not without its blots.[29]

People were ready to acknowledge the rumour that Fred had pulled Galliard in favour of Highland Chief and that if the latter had won, Charlie would have collected an immense fortune, but Highland Chief came second and the fortune was lost. The rumours may also have been compounded by the fact that, on the same day, Fred rode Herald in the Headley Stakes and came first, prompting many to say that he could win if and when he wanted to. Archer was very upset by the lies and allegations and no doubt Charlie was furious. Although the allegations of race fixing were refuted, the two brothers would always be associated with Highland Chief and Galliard, in particular Charlie, and, for the present, neither seemed able to avert suspicion. At least Fred had been proven right in his judgement over Highland Chief's form and George Lambton reiterated Fred's misgivings about Highland Chief before the Derby.[30]

For brother Charlie, the Highland Chief incident would dog him for the rest of his life. It did not totally damage his career but dented it enough to be remembered for decades afterwards. Charlie is still remembered in racing books of today primarily as the trainer of Highland Chief, despite his long career and varied successes throughout the 1880s and 1890s.[31]

It may also be (although there is some argument) that the events of the 1883 Derby affected Fred's relationship with Falmouth. Viscount Falmouth had been considering retiring from the turf for a long time, but, despite the belief that the Highland Chief incident was what tipped the scales, his decision was not confirmed until December 1883. Many people were left stunned that the racing partnership of Falmouth, Dawson and Archer, which had reigned supreme since 1875, was coming to an end. Portland summarised it precisely when he said that they 'farmed' the Classics – that their success had been such that it had become predictable, achieved, as Portland wrote, like 'clockwork'.[32]

The break up was a blow for Fred, whose career had had its very foundations with Falmouth's horses and patronage. He had a lot more to thank him for besides, but, possibly as proof that there were no hard feelings, Falmouth would not disappear entirely once he retired and Fred would still ride for him.

But back in June 1883, within days of the Derby, Fred crossed the Channel to ride in the Grand Prix de Paris,[33] this time on St Blaise. Unfortunately they were beaten by Frontin and many criticised St Blaise's owner for running him again so soon after the Derby. Add to this the fact that he was running in three consecutive races, one after the other, he was literally worn out; and despite riding him several times over the coming months, Fred could not get a winner out of him. In the end, St Blaise was sold off, spending his final days in America before sadly being burnt to death in a stable fire at the age of 29.[34]

In July 1883, the sale of the late Prince Batthyany's horses took place and one in particular was of great interest to Mathew Dawson and his brother John, who had trained for the Prince. The horse was St Simon, a bay by Galopin out of St Angela.

St Angela had never produced a foal of any great merit before and was sixteen when St Simon was born in 1881.[35] He was not expected to have any great potential either – many overlooking the fact that he may have inherited his sire's highly strung nature,[36] as had Galliard. Consequently, as he grew older, he was not recommended for any of the Classics; nor was he recommended for the 1883 Derby, but that mattered little when Batthyany died and all his commitments were declared void. When St Simon came up in the sale, however, he was recommended to Sir George Chetwynd. Someone at least saw potential in the horse. 'Someone told me that St Simon was a flyer,' he wrote, also noting that he had been let into a little secret about the horse: 'that he had had his leg dressed to "look like a blister" and that I must secure him.'[37]

St Simon's hocks had been painted white, possibly by John Dawson who had also expressed an interest in buying him and was anxious to put off any other bidders. Having been approached by another personage (Chetwynd did not say who) to buy one of Batthyany's horses for a thousand sovereigns, Chetwynd considered St Simon and, not having time to discuss this option with his associates, 'went to a relative of his' – again, Chetwynd did not reveal who this 'relative' was – 'and we agreed to go beyond that price'.[38]

Chetwynd discovered that Mathew Dawson was also a bidder, acting on behalf of the Duke of Portland, who was there with his trainer the day before the sale and recalled how he seemed enthusiastic about St Simon. Portland himself was not entirely enthused, but nor was he disappointed.

'This is quite a likely-looking animal,' he said and asked if the 'white substance' on St Simon's hock was indicative of a curb or blister. Mat examined the dressing on St Simon's leg, decided that it had a smell of paint about it and made a note to speak to his brother John. Word got about that Dawson had licked the dressing to see what it was made of.[39] 'If this was so,' wrote Chetwynd, 'all praise to him, and be it understood that I accuse no-one of having been a party to any deception about the horse. I give the story as it reached my ears.'[40]

Dawson was unable to speak to his brother that day, but spoke to him on the day of the sale itself after having made the bid and securing St Simon for 1,600 guineas, a price which John Dawson told his brother Mat was fair. Even so, John, according to Portland, had not been able to determine the horse's true potential. He had tried him against another horse called Rout, but because Rout had met with an accident, the trial had been inconclusive. Dawson, however, was not to be put off, congratulated the Duke on his choice of horse and St Simon was duly placed in his horse box and delivered to Heath House stables.[41] Sir George Chetwynd's bid of 1,000 sovereigns had come second.

The Duke arrived to inspect his prize the next day, full of expectation and reality set in with a thud as the horse was led out. Portland was less than impressed. 'He was not in anything like condition,' he wrote, 'in fact, he was as fat as a bull. Mat sent him for a canter for our inspection, and we were both perfectly disgusted with his action. He appeared to move more like a rabbit than a horse.'[42]

Wondering what he had let himself in for, the Duke could not imagine how the horse would improve and word got about that he was beginning to regret his purchase. Robert Peck duly stepped forward and suggested buying St Simon for 2,000 guineas. The Duke could have said yes and profited by 400 guineas, but he soon reasoned that there had to be something good about the horse for Peck to make such an offer. Despite his original reservations therefore, Portland kept St Simon and, with work, the horse began to improve; so much so in fact that he was earmarked for Goodwood which was in four weeks' time. It is fair to say that Heath House never looked back where this horse was concerned.[43]

On 31 July, with Archer up, he came first in the Halnaker Stakes. The following day they secured the Maiden Stakes. A month after that, on 1 September, they took the Devonshire Nursery Plate. Their success continued, winning the Prince of Wales Nursery Plate on 14 September and the Bretby Stakes Course on 24 October.[44]

Fred decided that St Simon was one of the best horses he had ever ridden and Dawson thought him one of the best he had ever trained. St Simon, even without being extended, possessed amazing speed and energy which Fred was able to tap into; and his finishes, sometimes up towards twenty lengths, left the remainder of the field standing.[45] He was a particular favourite of Fred because his unpredictable and wayward nature was a challenge in itself and was one which few people could or wished to handle. He may have been one of the very best to train, but he was very difficult.

Extremely bad-tempered, St Simon could not be groomed unless he was muzzled. Some stable lads who ran the risk of being bitten or kicked out of his stable preferred to resign rather than have to tackle him. In fact the only stable lad St Simon could tolerate was Charlie Fordham. He, it seems, had the magic touch and was the only one who was prepared to put up with St Simon's cantankerous and wilful personality which, to cap it all, was also highly strung. He was classed as one of the best of his day and was certainly a most elegant-looking horse, standing at 15.3 hands. The temperament, which left much to be desired, did not overshadow his success. But for one that had no equal on the turf, possessed such power and speed and seemed to be afraid of nothing and no-one, St Simon had one abiding fear which left the Duke of Portland speechless with astonishment when he first saw it: open umbrellas.[46] Open one in the horse's presence and he would become skittish. Another fear, which also became a great inconvenience, was of horse boxes. He refused to walk into them head first and usually had to be led into them backwards. Even so, there was no doubting the sharpness of his intelligence.

A photograph taken of him when he was at the peak of his powers speaks volumes.[47] He is standing with one of his stable lads who, looking at him warily, holds him at length with a loose rein, ready to bolt in case his charge becomes nasty. St Simon, himself, does not seem too concerned about his companion and, standing tall and straight in front of him, has his head turned towards the camera. What is so interesting is that, instead of just standing quietly, as other horses tended to do when they were having their pictures taken, St Simon appears to be staring *at* the camera, fascinated, and with a very set and concentrated look on his face.[48]

Portland travelled to Newmarket just a few days before the Goodwood meeting in order to watch St Simon who was to be given a gallop against other runners. Fred kept him well in check, so that he won by a short head rather than 50 yards which he might have gone for had Fred let him.[49]

'I well remember that two of my friends went into the ready money ring at Goodwood,' he later wrote, 'and backed St Simon for all the ready money they could possibly raise. They returned with sovereigns and bank notes bulging out of their pockets, and I believe after that good win, they were again able to bet on what was known as "the nod".'[50]

In early 1884 St Simon became very skittish and unmanageable again. What was worse, he kept falling over and then went to the opposite extreme and seemed lethargic – not his normal hyperactive, ready-for-the-attack self at all. Dawson, Portland and Archer were concerned by this and Fred was told to ride the horse to see how he fared. So, near Newmarket town, with Dawson and Portland nearby on their hacks, Fred mounted St Simon and, perhaps expecting to have to coax a strong gallop out of him, wore his spurs. St Simon's lad, the long-suffering Charlie Fordham, noticed this and, knowing his charge's changeable moods, warned Fred to be careful. Archer, showing all the confidence of a master horseman, told the lad not to worry and, convinced that he knew St Simon well enough by now, happily went on his way. He found, however, that St Simon did not want to co-operate, so he applied the spurs, which did the trick and the horse took off and galloped away – but at such speed that Dawson and Portland could only do their best to follow on their hacks. When they did finally catch up with Archer, not far from town, St Simon did not seem too put out by his run, but Fred was amazed and humbled, declaring that he would never go near the horse with spurs again and that St Simon's speed was such that it was like riding a steam engine.[51]

Fred was still maintaining an almost inflexible pace throughout 1883 and as the year progressed, so did the wins. Once back from France in June, hardly a day went by when he did not have at least two or three to add to his credit. The high success rate which had dominated the early part of the season seemed to be a reflection of the extreme optimism in his life at that point,[52] but, as summer rolled into autumn, he sometimes allowed his nerves to get the better of him, possibly because 1883 had not been the most smooth-running of years. On top of everything else, he came up against George Fordham again and was, once more, 'kidded' into relinquishing yet another race. Being beaten by old George was just too much and, in a fit of temper, Fred, not for the first time, threw his saddle across the weighing-in room.

Despite all of this, his record, at 631 rides, was the highest since 1878 and seemed to reflect a confidence about him which had been inspired, in part, by his new-found happiness and contentment as a married man. If, however, 1883 had been unsettling at times, 1884 was to prove a definitive turning point in his life, both in the short term and the long term.

It began with the most terrible personal tragedy since the death of his brother Billy in 1878. In January 1884, Helen Rose, after a difficult pregnancy, gave birth to a son who was named William after his grandfather and late uncle.[53] Several hours later the baby died and for weeks afterwards Helen Rose was quite ill. Fred was still grieving for his son, but in a pattern that would be repeated later, channelled what positive energy he had after the baby's death into preparing for the new season.

To add to this, also in January 1884, Viscount Falmouth made good his intention to retire. As a memento of his years attached to Heath House, Dawson and Archer presented him with a silver salver, holding the names and dates of fourteen Classic winners; and a portrait of Falmouth, Dawson and Archer together, surrounded by their most successful horses.[54]

The first sale of the Viscount's horses was held on 28 April. There was a huge gathering at the paddock of Heath House on the Monday afternoon, with the lots being brought under the hammer by Edmund Tattersall.[55]

Fred always regretted the sale of two horses, in particular. The first was Busybody, a bay by Petrarch out of Spinaway whom Fred had ridden to victory in the Rous Memorial Stakes on 28 September, the Middle Park Plate on 10 October and the Dewhurst Plate on 24 October 1883. She was sold to one George Alexander Baird, a young multimillionaire, known in turn as 'The Squire' and 'Mr Abington'. He was an amateur jockey, but wandered through life with heavyweight wrestlers as his companions and bodyguards, and had an additional penchant for vandalism. He was, at first, welcomed into society before his true, disagreeable nature came to the surface and he was promptly expelled from society's ranks as most members of the aristocracy refused to have anything to do with him. He cared little for society anyway and looked down on the Derby and Ascot in general, preferring the lesser races.

Being immensely rich, but lacking the sense to use his wealth wisely, he owned horses, houses and a yacht. He also lavished jewellery on women on whom he was just as likely to lavish bruises and rampaged through life, caring for nothing and no-one. He did however have a genuine regard for Archer and wanted, above all else, to be like him and to be as successful as he was as a jockey. In this respect Baird was serious and often went for two or three days without food to keep his weight down. This did not help his temper and his regular intake of alcohol made it worse until his behaviour so disgusted society and the National Hunt Committee that he was warned off the Turf for two years in 1882 for foul riding.[56] In 1884 he was back and bought Busybody for 8,800 guineas which was not far off Archer's prediction of between 8,000 and 10,000 guineas.

Fred was very well aware of Busybody's potential, but missed the chance of riding her in the One Thousand Guineas and the Oaks – two wins (both with Tom Cannon up) which, despite Baird's contempt for the Classics, must have pleased the multimillionaire greatly, particularly if it rankled the aristocracy which snubbed him.

Also sold in the first of Falmouth's sales was a brown colt called Harvester who, like Busybody, had shown great promise in 1883. Fred had ridden him to victory in the Triennial Produce Stakes on 27 September and the Clearwell Stakes on 8 October.[57] As with Busybody, he regretted Harvester's purchase, but at least he would have the chance to ride him once he was transferred to his new owner.

Harvester was bought by Sir John Willoughby for 8,600 guineas. Archer had predicted over 5,000 sovereigns. On 29 July 1884 they won the Gratwicke Stakes before coming second in the Drawing Room Stakes the next day. Interestingly enough Fred had ridden him to third place in the Hardwicke Stakes back in June only to ride another horse straight after called Farewell.[58]

The second part of the sale, the Mereworth Sale, took place on 30 June with the disposal of Falmouth's finest and best remembered horses: Spinaway went for 5,500 guineas; Wheel of Fortune for 5,000 guineas; Jannette for 4,200 guineas; and Galliard for 3,600 guineas which was the top price for his stallions. The overall total was 111,880 guineas.[59]

1884 was a good year for Fred, as far as success on the turf was concerned. March to June had shown him at his absolute best, achieving some 45 wins in June. After that there was a kind of rollercoaster effect. Helen Rose was pregnant again, she was not having an easy time of it and Fred's concern for her was reflected in his work. He had successfully maintained his level of wins throughout July, but in August they were reduced by half.[60] By October he had once more achieved the level he had secured in June, but, given that this year had promised to be his finest yet, he was in danger of relinquishing his title of Champion Jockey to Charlie Wood who was gaining on him in the jockeys' table of wins.[61]

Fred was still very much in demand, was nationally and internationally acclaimed and had a good relationship with the press and public alike, but he had developed a rather clinical view of his efforts to lose weight. These had not become easier over the years, but increasingly, almost dangerously, difficult. One of his doctors later told an associate of Edith M Humphris that Fred was nothing more than skin and bone and that he was in fact wasting muscle because there was no fat to waste, but

Fred, with almost cool detachment, told a friend that he could ride at 8st 10lb and still be able to lose the extra pounds to reach 8st 5lb – as if it were the most natural thing in the world. He still had the energy to travel to and take part in race meetings, then return home. In all probability he was relying on sheer adrenalin to keep him going. Unfortunately the stresses and strains of his work did not necessarily come only from his efforts to meet the weights as he found himself subject once again to public scrutiny and criticism.

Sometime in the year 1884 rumours started over a 'jockey ring' led by Fred Archer and Charlie Wood – a process whereby, in the interests of gambling, horses were pulled up in races in favour of others. 'I heard rumours,' wrote Chetwynd, 'of a supposed arrangement amongst a certain lot of jockeys, of which Archer and Wood were supposed to be the head, that races were to be won by horses selected by the Ring.'[62]

Not believing a word of these rumours, he told Archer and Wood that he was going to bring the matter to the attention of the Stewards and both jockeys were happy to assist in any way to clear their names. Chetwynd then published a notice:

> To ask the Stewards whether they are aware that it is openly stated that a conspiracy exists between certain jockeys and so called 'professional backers' of horses to arrange the result of races for their own benefit, and, if they have heard of such statements, and believe it possible such a plot exists, what steps they propose taking to deal with the matter at once.[63]

The members of the Jockey Club were not appreciative of this and made it clear to Chetwynd that he had put them in an awkward position. 'I fail even now to see how . . .' Chetwynd wrote.

The Earl of March (the Senior Steward) told Chetwynd that the Jockey Club was aware of such rumours and of the fact that such a practice went on and that it would be dealt with should evidence be presented. Chetwynd was not impressed. Who, he asked, was going to bring forward evidence of a jockey ring?[64] 'The jockeys were their servants, their names were freely discussed, and the Stewards could have had them called up and made them produce their betting and bankers' books to prove their innocence.'[65]

In conclusion, Chetwynd decided that such a ring or the conspiracy of one did not exist. It seems that Fred's acting as betting adviser in the past, his telling people on what horse to place their money, had been taken out of context,[66] but the suspicion still attached itself to him. Not everyone is convinced that Chetwynd acted with the best of motives. Perhaps, as John Welcome, Fred's second biographer, thinks he may have used Archer to protect Wood.[67] Either way it was an incident which would not be forgotten as the next few months would show. It is a measure of how things had changed over the years that the mere hint of corruption was being questioned in racing, but in Fred's case everything he did was now open to question. An argument with an owner over a horse led one newspaper to add its four penn'orth and word got about that Fred was suing the newspaper for libel. This proved to be untrue, but reveals the kind of atmosphere which was prevailing just then.

To add insult to injury, Portland, in the autumn of 1884, took offence at Baird asking Archer to go into business with him and it is possible that it was this that caused the split between Portland and Archer, although no-one knows for sure if this was the case. If it was, then Archer may have been annoyed at Portland's attitude, at the Duke's insistence that he should do as he was told and stay away from Baird.[68] It is believed that Archer did indeed take offence and threw his retainer back. What is certain is that he never rode for Portland again and also lost out on riding the irrepressible St Simon – the honour of which went to Charles Wood. Lord Hastings became his principal retainer (despite Portland advising Hastings to dismiss the jockeys – Hastings knew a good opportunity when he saw it). Despite ending their professional relationship on such bad terms, Portland does not mention the split in his 1935 autobiography. Given what happened to Fred later, the Duke probably felt it was pointless to do so and instead praised the jockey and his work.

Fred ended a rather tumultuous year still Champion Jockey with over two hundred wins to his credit and nothing came of the supposed 'business arrangement' between Baird and Fred. He later squandered his millions and, while in America arranging a boxing match for one of his heavyweight companions, he died of pneumonia.[69]

Fred finished the 1884 season winning the Liverpool Autumn Cup on Thebais on 6 November. The day was made perfect when he was then presented with a telegram from Newmarket, informing him that his wife had given birth to a daughter. Elated by this news he prepared to leave Liverpool at once and return to Falmouth House,[70] safe in the knowledge that he could overcome his problems and look forward to a wonderful future with his little family.

Notes

1.   Weatherby, J E & J P, *The Racing Calendar for the Year 1883*
2.   Portland, 6th Duke of, *Memories of Racing and Hunting*, p.16
3.   Ibid. p.209
4.   Weatherby, J E & J P, *The Racing Calendar for the Year 1883*
5.   Mortimer, Roger, Onslow, Richard & Willet, Peter; *The Biographical Encyclopaedia of British Flat Racing*, pp.391–2, 590
6.   Weatherby, J E & J P, *The Racing Calendar for the Year 1883*
7.   Mortimer, Onslow & Willet, p.178
8–9.   Welcome, John, *Fred Archer: A Complete Study*, p.33
10–11.   Portland, p.150
12–13.   Welcome, John, *Fred Archer: A Complete Study*, p.109
14.   Portland, p.146
15.   Lambton, The Honourable George, *Men and Horses I Have Known*, p.45
16.   Weatherby, J E & J P, *The Racing Calendar for the Year 1882*
17.   Lambton, p.45
18.   Welcome, John, *Fred Archer: A Complete Study*, pp.104–7

19. Portland, p.46
20. Lambton, p.45
21–3. *Manchester Guardian*, 24 May 1883
24. Chetwynd, Sir George, *Racing Reminiscences and Experience of the Turf*, p.210
25. *Manchester Guardian*, 24 May 1883
26. *The Sporting Life*, 24 May 1883
27. Mortimer, Onslow & Willet, p.20
28. Chetwynd, p.210
29. Welcome, John, *Fred Archer: A Complete Study*, p.106
30. Lambton, p.45
31. Tanner, Michael & Cranham, Gerry, *Great Jockeys of the Flat: A Celebration of Two Centuries of Jockeyship*, p.86
32. Portland, p.9
33. Weatherby, J E & J P, *The Racing Calendar for the Year 1883*
34. Mortimer, Onslow & Willet, p.533
35. Ibid, pp.536–7
36. Wilson, Julian, *The Great Racehorses*, pp.130–1
37–8. Chetwynd, p.212
39. Portland, p.29
40. Chetwynd, p.212
41. Portland, pp.29–30
42–3. Ibid. p.30
44. Weatherby, J E & J P, *The Racing Calendar for the Year 1883*
45. Humphris, Edith M, *The Life of Fred Archer*, p.130
46. Mortimer, Onslow & Willet, pp.536–7
47. Portland, p.35
48. Wilson, p.131
49–50. Portland, p.31
51. Welcome, John, *Fred Archer: A Complete Study*, p.116
52. Weatherby, J E & J P, *The Racing Calendar for the Year 1883*
53. Details courtesy of Alex Tosetti
54. Mortimer, Onslow & Willet, pp.206–7
55. *Newmarket Journal*, 29 April 1884
56. Onslow, Richard, *The Squire: George Alexander Baird, Gentleman Rider 1861–1893*, pp.23 & 118–19
57–8. Weatherby, J E & J P, *The Racing Calendar for the Year 1883*
59. Welcome, John, *Fred Archer: A Complete Study*, pp.117–21
60–1. Weatherby, J E & J P, *The Racing Calendar for the Year 1884*
62–6. Chetwynd, p.217
67–8. Welcome, John, *Fred Archer: A Complete Study*, p.119
69. Onslow, Richard, *The Squire: George Alexander Baird, Gentleman Rider 1861–1893*, pp.26–32
70. Humphris, *The Life of Fred Archer*, p.222

The Progress of a Champion Jockey

Travelling back from Liverpool to Newmarket by train, Fred took time to muse, confessing to an associate how proud he was to have ended the season so brilliantly. He had fame, fortune, a loving home, a devoted wife and so much to look forward to and yet there was always the tiniest element of doubt – or disbelief – that good fortune was going his way, even wondering why he should be so blessed.[1]

There was an equilibrium in his life – a perfect balance between his home life and his career; he never allowed the latter to take precedence over the former. Speaking of his success, he expressed gratitude at his good fortune, but made it clear that it was only due to the fact that he had been luckier than others who might have done just as well – that he had been in the right place at the right time and he was content with that.[2]

Helen Rose made his life complete, made all the effort to succeed worthwhile and now his motivation came from a need to succeed for them both, for their life together.[3] Arriving at Newmarket, Fred made his way to Falmouth House and was greeted by his sister Emily, who was there to help look after Helen Rose during her confinement. Fred did not go in to see his wife immediately, he later said, as he wanted to look his best for her, and went to change into his hunting 'togs' because she liked them. Unfortunately, Helen Rose would never see him again. Fred recalled that Emily rushed into his room and told

160

him that his Nellie was dying. When Fred went to his wife he found her gripped by convulsions from which she never recovered, and she died without knowing that her husband was there with her.[4]

She was 23 years old.

In the space of a few hours all Fred's dreams were shattered and with Nellie went the Fred Archer who might have been – one supremely happy man with a confident future ahead of him. Without her he was lost and it was clear that if he ever did get over her death, it would take him a very long time. Her funeral took place a few days later and she was buried with her infant son, William, who had been dead for less than twelve months. Her infant daughter was named Nellie Rose.

Helen Rose had meant more to Fred than money and success. When he was asked later if he would ever marry again, he replied that he could not love a woman half so much as he had loved her.

Facing a future without her seemed almost impossible. What was the effort worth now if she was not there to share it? Despair gave way to depression and the future suddenly seemed very dark and hostile. Fred confided to his sister Emily and friend, Captain Bowling,[5] that he had contemplated suicide – a confidence which they both took very seriously, with Bowling even staying in the same room as him. Fred's state of mind was such that the entire family was on the alert.

Winter was closing in and the prospect of dark, gloomy days and nights ahead, particularly now that the flat season was over, was bound to have a negative effect on his mood, so his family, worried about him, thought he needed a complete change of scene and time to recover. It was suggested that he should go to America, accompanied by his valet, William Bartholomew (known as Solomon), and Captain Bowling. If anyone could keep Fred on an even keel it was Bowling, and Fred readily accepted the opportunity to travel abroad. It was arranged that they would sail on 15 November, just days after Nellie's burial.

On the day before they were due to leave, Fred went to his solicitor and drew up his Last Will and Testament, to ensure that his daughter, Nellie Rose Archer, who from now on would live with her Dawson grandparents, was well provided for financially. The solicitor, Mr Jessop, later expressed the view that the will had been drawn up too hastily and he had suggested to Fred that, on his return, he revise it. Despite promising to do so, Fred never did. The bulk of his estate went to his daughter, but he made provisions for his executors, his widowed sister Emily and other family friends.

Of particular interest is the provision he made for his nephew Frederick Pratt.[6] The boy had become like a son to him and, of all his nieces and nephews, he wanted to ensure that this particular one succeeded in life. He was a gifted horseman and would soon become apprenticed. Making provision for the boy in his will, by providing for his education and seeing that money was kept in trust, meant also that the burden was taken off Fred's sister Alice and her husband who had other children, with two more destined to be born later. Fred wanted to make sure that none of his family would have to struggle financially. Security was his priority for them.

The speed of all this – the arrangements for the trip in particular, quite literally leaving in the next available boat – suggests an impulsive need for action, either, on Fred's part, to escape or on the part of his family to get him away from Falmouth House, the centre of all his dreams and ambitions and a constant reminder of his wife. As for the will, just getting it drafted would have been priority enough, bearing in mind that exactly one week before, the prospect of drawing one up had not even entered his head. Once done, however, Fred could rest easy and look forward more to the trip. He and his companions sailed from Queenstown in Ireland on the *Bothnia* and they arrived in New York on 20 November.

It was just meant to be an ordinary sightseeing tour as far as Fred was concerned, but a celebrity as well known as Fred does not arrive on the quay of New York unannounced, particularly one who had ridden the first American winner of the British Derby. He was treated almost like a national hero and the moment the ship docked, reporters were waiting to board and to question Fred about his plans in America.[7]

He was not the first to be treated so. The Americans were fascinated by English culture which added to the prestige of many English actors, writers, poets and sportsmen, so Fred was one of the latest in a long line of famous Englishmen who had left England to sample the United States. In Fred's case, however, it was not to extend his fame or his fortune that he went abroad, but to try to find peace to get through the grief of losing his wife.

Seeking respite from Newmarket and his life as a jockey (he said he would not ride a horse for 5,000 sovereigns) he nevertheless had every intention of seeing as much as he could during his stay. Attending race meetings was not part of his itinerary and he hardly went to any, although he did express a desire to visit Pierre Lorillard's stud. This, however, did not happen as he missed the train to Kentucky, and the opportunity of the owner and jockey meeting on the ground where Iroquois and Parole were trained was lost. It seemed that Fred wanted to do anything that was not associated with horseracing and during the course of his travels across America he visited factories, tobogganed, saw the sights, went to the theatre and went shooting, always staying in the best hotels and accepting invitations from the social elite as an honoured guest. It was a whirlwind tour, he was constantly on the move and the press continually watched his progress with interest.[8]

As in England he was public property and he was adept at handling the occasional interviewer, particularly since some papers could be tongue in cheek about his visit and his popularity. Fred's sister Emily kept a newspaper clipping of her brother's American tour which noted that Fred earned twice as much as an ambassador.[9] The paper then went on to express how much of a favourite Fred currently was with the press, being written about constantly – more so than many learned gentlemen who perhaps deserved more credit. His progress through America had been a triumph, the paper added – particularly for one whose reputation depended on an ability to ride a horse – and it was critical of any comments he may have made about American society and culture.[10]

He had been, at the very least, appreciative of the hospitality he had received and had shown a genuine interest in the country, its people, its architecture. He had also been asked his opinion of Iroquois, Parole and Foxhall, a trio he could not praise hard enough.[11] The newspaper felt that his presence in America was a sign of things to come – that he was helping to establish a new kind of craze in place of the English actors and actresses who had so fascinated the American public for so long.[12]

What Fred himself thought of the articles written about him is not known. Perhaps he sent the newspaper cuttings to his sister to amuse her. One thing is certain – from November 1884 to March 1885 he was never still and may not have had the time to take more than a passing interest in what the papers were writing about him. He had been followed around by reporters most of his life – they came with the job.

Fred, Captain Bowling and Solomon prepared to leave America and they docked in England on 9 March 1885. Fred seemed in much better spirits and was anxious to return to racing even though this meant having to waste especially hard since his weight had gone up to over nine stone. He would continue to remain in mourning for his late wife and wore a black armband out of respect, but the grief showed, compounding the air of melancholy which had gradually developed over the years. The eyes especially held a perpetual sadness about them, as if his mind were always somewhere else and in whatever pictures remain of him today, whether photographs or portraits, he always has a distant look about him which speaks volumes, as though his whole life is captured in a single glance. But if Fred Archer the widower was emotionally elsewhere, Fred Archer the jockey was still alive and kicking.

He had lost none of his dedication to his sport – in fact it had taken on a new dimension. His first race after getting back to England was on 23 March on Laceman in the Batthyany Stakes. He finished third. It was his only race of the day, but on the following day he rode three, coming second in the first race and third in the other two. The standard seemed to slip further on the day after when he ran unplaced in two races – one of them being the Lincolnshire Handicap on St Blaise. He seemed to be back on form again on 26 March when he won two of his four races – Round Shot in the Prince Park Plate and The Bard in the Molyneux Stakes. He was opening the season in fits and starts,[13] but what is significant is not how many races he won, but how many he actually took part in. He was throwing himself into his work and by the end of April it was as if he had never been away.[14]

Even so there were indications that he was not the Fred Archer of old and the ratio between winning and losing was erratic, as if, having found the energy to race, he was still trying to channel it effectively. As time went on, he began to regain the level of consistency which had marked previous years. By May he was more like his old self, but the recollections of others hint that Fred's performance on the racecourse was betraying a state of mind which was still recovering from Helen Rose's death. This appears to have been the case when he rode Paradox in the Two Thousand Guineas on 6 May.

On 7 May the correspondent for *The Sporting Life* wrote:

A sensation of the most decided order was within an ace of being supplied by the Two Thousand Guineas . . . as it was only by a head after all that the 'screaming hot' favourite got home from the unnamed and comparatively speaking despised colt by Kisber and Chopette, on whom Tom

Cannon stuck so closely to Fred Archer on Paradox, that layers of odds trembled in their shoes, and fielders shouted with wild glee in anticipation of the hoped for 'turn up'.[15]

Fred had felt that he had ridden a bad race, particularly since Paradox was not the most obliging of horses and had a tendency to slow down whenever he had the lead. Fred had very nearly lost the race because Tom Cannon, who came second, knew of this particular quirk of Paradox and had tried to use it to his own advantage – unsuccessfully as it had turned out – but since no-one else was aware, it was quite easy to say that Fred had not ridden his best. The odds on Paradox were extended: 'so paramount,' continued *The Sporting Life*, 'was the desire to be on the "moral" at any price, and so little was thought of his opponents . . .'[16]

The Two Thousand Guineas had been a very close finish and, although Paradox had met with expectation to a certain degree, *The Sporting Life*, nevertheless, felt that the coming Derby would be that much more of a struggle. The correspondent noted that Paradox would 'hardly hold his own for the wearing on the great Epsom race . . . Melton . . . may be expected on last year's calculations to give him as much trouble as anything will.'[17]

The Times was effusive but Sir George Chetwynd, who was also at Epsom, thought differently, believing that Grafton, who came second, was 'marvellously ridden by Cannon' and that Fred had not been on his very best form.[18] 'Paradox,' he wrote, 'only got home by a head . . . Archer, who had to make his own running on the favourite, got a little bit flurried and did not ride as well as usual.'[19]

Fred had ridden this race many times and knew the measure of it backwards. Although Paradox was known for being a difficult horse to run and was stubborn in temperament, it did not stop Charlie Wood from adding his weight to the opinion that Fred could have ridden better, telling Chetwynd that Fred had ridden a bad race.[20]

While anxious to work, Fred seemed distracted by it, but then he moved to the opposite extreme and as the season progressed into the summer, the pace began to pick up momentum and racing became the only motivation in his life. In fact work kept him sane. It was no longer a career which provided satisfaction in itself as well as financial security. In America Fred had confided to a friend who had known Helen Rose as a child, that, although he was totally wrapped up in his work, it could never compensate for the loss of his wife. She had been the love of his life, as he said, she had been his 'glory'.[21] He no longer rode with his heart – his work was now governed by his head and he went from race to race, seeking one win after the other.

The public loved it. He was now a legend in his own time and was in the saddle virtually every day without a break. In fact what breaks there were usually fell on weekends. Going from one course to the next, he was constantly on the move. As an example, he rode on 28, 29 and 30 April, followed by no less than seventeen days in May.[22] Epsom, at the beginning of June, found Fred with unbelievable energy which was now focused entirely on his work, but there were times when his concentration lapsed. He rode in no less than six races on 2 June, but won none of them, coming either second or unplaced. Then came the Derby on the following day, a bright, breezy day, proof that the midsummer favoured the Derby, although it seems that the Derby did not favour Paradox.[23]

Paradox, on the morning of the Derby, disappointed the correspondent of *The Sporting Life* when he watched him during the morning gallops, justifying earlier assessments that he would find the Derby a struggle. Being sent on a mile and a quarter gallop he came back 'distressed'.[24] 'In fact he was blowing hard,' *The Sporting Life* noted, 'with his head down, as he was led away.'[25] After evaluating all the other runners for the Derby, the correspondent concluded, 'To be concise and, at the same time, consistent, I stick to Melton.'[26]

Indeed Melton was the overall favourite. By Master Kildare[27] out of Violet Melrose, he was trained by Mathew Dawson and owned by Lord Hastings of Melton Constable, Leicestershire, who also owned Master Kildare. Hastings and his wife were a very popular couple who had no pretensions whatever. Fred was a particular favourite of theirs and they were delighted when it was announced that he would ride Melton in the Derby. This time he was competing against Paradox and succeeded where Tom Cannon failed in the Two Thousand Guineas, using Paradox's habit of slowing down when in the lead, to time his own run, only to reach the finish almost head to head, so that no-one was entirely sure who had won. When it was announced that Archer had the Derby, the rider of Paradox, Fred Webb, Archer's oldest friend, was devastated. This was the fifth Derby he had lost. Lord and Lady Hastings however were ecstatic and offered Fred a substantial reward. Even years later the Derby of 1885 remained one of his most popular races.

He was a 'gallant hero' and, having once placed him on a pedestal, the public kept him there, but, as usual, there is another side to the tale. In remembering Melton's win in the 1885 Derby, regarding the horse's health Chetwynd wrote, 'Doubt about his soundness still lingered, in spite of his victory, and a few days before the race there were all sorts of silly rumours afloat about him – that he would be got at, and that an attempt would be made to knock him over in the race.'[28]

One of the reasons for this apparent nervousness was that interest in the Derby had been more frenetic than it had been for years and people were ready to exaggerate and believe anything, but Chetwynd believed that the fault lay with Archer himself. 'The sole origin of these fairy tales,' he continued, 'was that Archer believed implicitly that Crafton [Melton's rival] would beat him, and told all his friends so, men who were accustomed to go almost entirely by his judgement.'[29]

Admitting that the race was spectacular, on a par with that between Bend Or and Robert the Devil in 1880, Chetwynd also hints at the fact that Archer was not his usual scientific self. 'Archer . . . for some inexplicable reason in this case . . . had laid rather far out of his ground, got to his girths, the issue was in doubt to within the last stride, Melton getting up and winning by a head.'[30]

Still, Lady Hastings, who was a racing fanatic, insisted upon Fred making a personal visit to give a minute-by-minute account of the race so that she could visualise it. Lady Hastings always remained fond of Fred. She found him unassuming on the surface but complex beneath it; a genius in his own right, generous, but reserved – he hated being idolised and did not feel comfortable with his fame, refusing to lunch with Lord and Lady Hastings when they invited him.

After the Derby he won the Oaks on Lonely on 5 June and several days later he was in France, riding Paradox again in the Grand Prix de Paris.[31] Obviously Paradox's form had improved since the spring and the race was now considered by the English press to be all but his, although this had little effect upon the confidence of the French who besieged Longchamps on one of the hottest days of the year. His only contender seemed to be Reluisant who inspired confidence enough to be backed at 4 to 1 and indeed he took the lead, maintained the running and was only overtaken by Paradox, with Archer up, just a hundred yards from the finish. Here Reluisant fell back and Paradox took the race by a length.[32] Even the French, who were wary of and even hostile towards Archer since this was his second Grand Prix win were impressed. In three other Grands Prix he had been placed second.

His level of wins for June matched May and the peak was reached in July. On 28 July alone he secured six wins out of nine races. Earlier, on 17 July, he won five out of eight and, on 21 July, five out of six. There was a drop in August, but the pace resumed in September.[33] Archer was set to ride Melton again, this time in the St Leger on 15 September, when a number of horses were pulled out, either through injury or, inexplicably, lack of preparation. Confidence in those horses that were left rose and, since the weather promised to be fine, the race also promised to be an interesting one.[34]

'To my mind,' Chetwynd wrote, 'Melton was the beau ideal of a racehorse, a whole-coloured bay on the small side with wonderful back and perfect shoulders and action.'[35]

The horse could do no wrong and won by six lengths. Melton took advantage of Farewell falling back, increasing his lead at a steady pace and maintaining it in a fashion described as 'gallant' by *The Times*. *The Sporting Life*, in assessing Melton's performance, recorded, 'All this time Melton, after having jumped away on the first flight, had been holding a rearmost position, and the Red House had been reached and passed without alteration in his position . . . Melton, without ever being called upon for an effort, came up . . . on the rail side . . . Melton raced past the post and added to the laurels of his Derby victory.'[36]

Once again Melton had secured another extremely popular win which served to make him one of the best horses of the season. It crowned Dawson's career as a top-class trainer, particularly since on 3 October 1885 he announced his decision to retire from training altogether and leave Heath House, his home since the late 1860s.[37] The stables would be run by his nephew George Dawson, a brewer in Burton, but the tenancy of Heath House was assigned to Portland, Lord Crewe, Lord Hastings and Lord Londonderry.[38]

People found the idea of a brewer training for the aristocracy rather ludicrous, no matter which family he came from, but Portland, himself, never regretted employing George Dawson as he went on to secure many Classics for him. The Duke took great pleasure in reminding people of this fact years later in his memoirs and adding that the brewer was so good that had he stuck to his original occupation, his beer would have been of the very best! It was one in the eye for the critics.[39]

Mathew Dawson's time at Heath House is marked by a plaque inserted in the entrance wall, with plaques commemorating his brother Joseph and nephew George on either side of it. Between all three of them, the Dawson family had trained at Heath House stables for 38 years from 1861 to 1899.[40]

After vacating Heath House in 1885, Mathew Dawson moved to Manor House – a much more modest residence than his former home – in the neighbouring district of Exning. But he would not be left in retirement long, later training horses for Lord Rosebery.[41] He also kept up his partnership with Fred, although the jockey's association with Heath House would eventually peter out. Dawson's retirement, although not entirely unexpected, must still have been something of a shock to Fred – the sense that this was the end of an era, particularly as it followed fast on the heels of Falmouth's retirement in 1884. The partnership was at an end and that special combination that characterised Falmouth, Dawson and Archer as owner, trainer and jockey would not be seen again until the beginning of the next century, when Lord William Beresford teamed up with the American trainer John Hutton (based at Heath House no less) and the American jockey Tod Sloan.[42] An era had, most definitely, finished – at least publicly.

Dawson still referred to Fred whenever he needed a second opinion on a horse but at the same time tended to act as if they were still trainer and apprentice, as George Lambton discovered when he paid Dawson a visit towards the end of the 1885 season.

Fred had ridden Minting, a particular favourite of Dawson, to victory in the Middle Park Plate on 14 October. Two weeks after the race, George Lambton turned up at Exning to take tea with Mat – or rather he had the tea, while Mat partook of whisky.[43] Fred joined them and eventually the conversation turned to the Middle Park Plate. Mat told Fred that he had been in danger of losing the race. According to Lambton, Fred agreed with him stating that he had underestimated Brass Law and had been too complacent about the other horses, believing that his only real contender was Saraband. He also commented that he had expected too much of Minting at the Dip which threw the horse completely off balance, so that too much energy was expended trying to get him back on track. Fred concluded that the horse was no good downhill and that Epsom – or rather the following year's Derby – would be too much for him. Dawson, however, was in two minds about it – perhaps having a bit more faith in Minting's staying power than Fred.

'I asked Mat what he thought about this with reference to the following year's Derby,' Lambton wrote. By this time Fred had left him and Dawson to their chatter. 'The old man scratched his head,' he continued, 'and said, in his usual broad Scotch, "I'm no saying he's not right; I've hae doubts meself, and the young divil when he's ridden a horse, seems to know more about him than I do." '[44]

This last seemed indicative of Dawson's attitude towards and respect for Fred's professionalism. While the young jockey always remained the 'young divil' or 'that tin-scraping young divil', by the same token it was also 'ask Fred' if anyone asked Dawson his opinion on a particular horse or race. Fred was his own authority now and one which his old trainer was quite happy to acknowledge even if he did not always let him know it, but in the case of Minting he held his ground over the horse's potential.

The 1885 season closed with an unbeaten record of 246 wins out of an incredible 667 rides, the highest since 1876 – almost ten years earlier.[45] Anyone meeting Fred Archer for the first time would not have guessed, by his performance, that there was any hint of tragedy in his life. 1885 saw his professionalism at its very highest with the first six months escalating to the point where he secured over 40 wins in May. His progress through June and July was gradual and the pace secured between March and July was reduced by half in August when he secured some twenty wins only. He recovered sufficiently to gain between 30 and 40 in October and twelve months to the day since he became a father to Nellie Rose, he won three races: the first on Songstress; the second on Chartreuse; and the third on Lyddington. He still continued working throughout the first anniversary of his wife's death and had his final win on Snowden in a Maiden Plate on 27 November.[46]

Within months, the 1886 season had begun but it did not do so on an auspicious note, with Fred finishing unplaced more times than winning.[47] Compared to other years, his progress between March and August seemed slower. It was not as erratic and the drive and motivation which had marked most of his career appeared to have been replaced by a rather more sedate pace, as if, mentally, he had decided that he no longer needed to push himself. Not that he was losing interest; 1886 would still prove to be one of his most successful years, not least because of his association with a massive, powerfully built, but placid bay colt called Ormonde, by Bend Or out of Lily Agnes.

It is a curious fact about Fred's career that of all the horses he ever rode, it would be this horse that he would be identified with the most even though their acquaintance was short. Fred knew no two horses were ever the same – they were all individual, with their own traits, quirks, eccentricities and personalities; and most possessed more charisma than the people who owned, trained or rode them. Fred had ridden donkeys, ponies and horses, and had been bitten, kicked and even kneeled on by one horse. He had ridden the beautiful, the ugly, the fast, the slow, the calm, the skittish, the predictable and the unpredictable. He had had to contend with the bad-tempered and the temperamental to the downright devious and the uncontrollable; and then he had ridden the most pleasant, the most consistent and the most straightforward. Some were fickle, some were docile, some were lazy and others were eccentric.

Fred had ridden horses that were not expected to run well and did and others that were expected to run well and refused to do so, preferring instead to return to the paddock. Some horses won by a nose, a neck, a length or a furlong in front and others just kept on running. He had ridden the short and the tall and he had ridden the extended, the non-extended, the roarers and the worn out. He had had them all. Now he had Ormonde.

Ormonde had bad legs.

When Ormonde was foaled he was very much over at the knee, awkward and backward.[48] He had not improved by the time he was a two-year-old and was suffering from splints. In short he was a considerable disappointment to his owner, the Duke of Westminster, but his trainer, John Porter, did not give up on him and, with training, felt that Ormonde would improve, even though initially he feared that the colt would never grow straight. Ormonde, however, did and in addition reached a height of 16 hands. His performance also improved and he began to attract notice in 1885.[49]

Fred was aware of his potential when he rode him to victory in the Post Sweepstakes on 14 October, the same day he rode Minting to victory in the Middle Park Plate,[50] and in the Criterion Stakes on 26 October. Fred warned Dawson that Ormonde could be a force to be reckoned with, particularly when he was entered for the 1886 Two Thousand Guineas (with G Barrett up), but Dawson was convinced that Minting (with J Watts up) would win: 'All Newmarket swore by Minting when the numbers went up for the Two Thousand,' remembered Chetwynd, 'but he could not live the last two furlongs with Ormonde, who won very easily.'[51]

Minting came second, justifying Fred's belief that he lacked staying power and Fred, himself riding Saraband, came in fourth. Despite Ormonde's victory Chetwynd was critical, acknowledging that the horse was unique, but not especially 'well made'. However, he was 'a splendid goer when extended'[52] – being possessed of a very strong neck and powerful legs which seemed to propel him forward at a formidable rate and which added to his power. This, however, was no consolation to

Dawson who, devastated by Minting's defeat, shut himself up for a week and refused to discuss the race, although he now felt obliged to withdraw him from the Derby and all efforts were made to prepare him for the Grand Prix de Paris. Saraband too was withdrawn, so Fred was snapped up by John Porter to ride Ormonde in the Derby on 26 May 1886.

Ormonde was now classed as unbeatable, particularly with Minting and Saraband out of the way. *The Times* reiterated popular belief that all obstacles were now removed, commenting that where The Bard excelled, Ormonde was even greater and public confidence was absolute, particularly since there were only nine runners, the smallest turn out for years.[53]

He started favourite at 9 to 4 on and he and The Bard had the race between them by the time they reached Tattenham Corner. Giving him a run for his money, The Bard, however, was unable to overreach Ormonde, who cantered home and secured the race by a length and a half. It was an immeasurably popular win, both for the public and Ormonde's owner, the Duke of Westminster.[54]

Ormonde and Archer were greeted with cheers as they made their way back – as was the Duke – but not everyone was convinced that Ormonde was the best of mounts. Even Fred himself expressed the view that St Simon, that veritable steam engine, was the superior horse, although Harry Custance was adamant that there was no better horse in existence at that time than Ormonde.[55] The horse provoked all manner of argument and debate and through it all remained as composed and as impassive as his sire Bend Or would have been.

At least Dawson was eventually justified in his faith in Minting. On a particularly miserable, wet day at Longchamps where the course was described as a quagmire by *The Times*, Fred brought Minting out to take part in the Grand Prix de Paris on 6 June. He still had doubts about the horse's stamina and, even though there were only nine runners, his confidence remained low. His morale was not improved much by the fact that the bookmakers thought the same with offers being increased against Minting.[56] The going was now so heavy that many wondered if he would be able to walk it, never mind run it. Overall attendance at Longchamps too was not as good as in previous years. Rain had never put people off before, but this year only a small number appeared.

In order to reserve as much of Minting's energy as possible, Fred kept him well back until within half a mile of the finish where he overtook the favourite Polyceute and went on to win the race, much to the delight of the small groups of English who had made the journey across the Channel. The French, however, remained silent and this, *The Times* noted, seemed louder than the cheers Fred received from his own country-men.[57] This was Archer's sixth appearance and the French were becoming increasingly bitter and hostile in their attitude, particularly since he seemed to negotiate the course with very little effort. Lambton was in France for the week and had attended the race. He recalled how the atmosphere was so tense there was an overriding fear that there would be a riot.[58] The English were of course ecstatic and the victory was made more sweet by the fact that Minting's half brother, Lambkin, with Archer again taking the reins, had lost the Grand Prix de Paris in 1884, finishing second. *The Times* paid tribute to Minting's training and then went on to criticise the French horses.

On his return to England Fred secured both the Gold Vase on Bird of Freedom and the Trial Stakes on Toastmaster on 8 June. The following day he won the Biennial Stakes on Saraband and on 10 June the St James' Palace Stakes on Ormonde, the All-Aged Stakes on Whitefriar and the New Biennial Stakes on St Mirin.[59] He certainly seemed to be having a good Ascot that year, also securing the Ascot High Weight Plate on Kinsky on 11 June. That same day he came second in the Hardwicke Stakes on Melton[60] – his St Leger winner of 1885.[61]

Fred had ridden for the Prince of Wales, for the first time, earlier in the season on Counterpane in the Maiden Plate at Sandown. 'A very pleasant and quiet meeting took place at Sandown on the Friday and Saturday, between Epsom and Ascot,' Chetwynd wrote and then, in rather cynical tones added, 'When Archer was seen to be winning very easily in the royal colours, a mighty shout was raised from the stands and rings. Sycophants vied with those who were genuinely pleased at the result of the race, to howl their loudest.'[62]

The Prince of Wales, however, was delighted with the win and wrote to his son, Prince George (later George V), 'You will be pleased to hear that my two-year-old "Counterpane" won a Maiden Plate! She was ridden by Archer and won easy and I got quite an ovation from the public afterwards.'[63] In appreciation the Prince rewarded the jockey, and Fred later rode another of the Prince's horses, Lady Peggy, to victory on 26 October.[64]

The weeks progressed and after a successful summer Archer prepared for his ride on Ormonde in the St Leger which was due to take place on 15 September. Despite the fact that Ormonde was one of the most popular horses of the season, only a small crowd attended the St Leger – 'tame' was how *The Sporting Life* described it,[65] but at least Ormonde was on top form. The race got underway and he held a prime position throughout. Referring to the Duke of Westminster's colours, the newspaper reported that, 'The yellow jacket of Ormonde could be seen in a good place all the way round the course and when the little band of competitors swept round the final turn Archer at once sent him to the front. It seemed that as he began to gallop the others stood still.'[66]

In noting that the St Leger had, for a long time, been regarded as 'a one-horse race', *The Sporting Life* felt that opinion was fully justified as far as this particular Leger was concerned. There may have been seven competitors, the newspaper added, but it was a foregone conclusion that Ormonde would win. The newspaper also believed that Ormonde looked better racing than 'on parade',[67] inadvertently hinting at the fact that the horse had not been foaled perfect: 'his fore fetlocks being generally voted round, more especially the off one, whilst on the outsides of his hocks there are some slight disfigurements. When seen in action Ormonde [looked] undoubtedly better . . . he simply kept on terms with his field until Archer let him sail away and won in a hack canter.'[68]

Ormonde was unbeatable and, before parting company for good, Fred rode him in three more races. Successively they came first in the 8th Great Foal Stakes on 28 September, the Champion Stakes on 13 October and the Free Handicap Stakes on 28 October.[69] Though Fred had ridden thousands of horses in his time, Ormonde would be the one he would be associated with fifty years later when *The Times* compared his record with that of other leading jockeys. So impressed were members of the Archer family with the horse that Fred's sister, Alice, named one of her sons after him – Harry Ormonde Pratt.[70]

Ormonde, even today, is classed as one of England's finest racehorses and he kept his celebrity status for years, becoming a legend in his own lifetime. In 1887 he was a focal point during Queen Victoria's Jubilee, when the Duke of Westminster, at his London residence, Grosvenor House, brought him out on show for his guests, among them the Prince and Princess of Wales, the Queen of Belgium and Indian princes.[71] He was sold in 1894 and spent his last years in America where he was put down ten years later. His skeleton was then returned to England and was displayed in the National History Museum; his bones remain in the Museum's collection today.

Back in October 1886 Fred crossed over to Ireland for the Irish Curragh. He was to ride Cambusmore for the Lord Lieutenant, Lord Londonderry. Harry Custance went with him.

'I went over to act as starter,' Custance wrote. 'We arrived in Dublin on Tuesday morning, 19 October, by the mail train, and after breakfasting and looking round the city, we journeyed off to the Curragh.'[72]

Fred's fame had preceded him and he found himself mobbed by admirers. He also received an invitation to attend the theatre and arrived to find that the Royal box had been reserved for him. 'After the performance,' wrote Custance, 'We walked out of the theatre, and were met by a most demonstrative crowd of over three hundred, who followed us all the way to the Shelbourne Hotel, shouting and "Whoo-roo-ing" for the "Great Mr Archer".'[73]

The next day preparations began for Fred's ride on Cambusmore – by way of a Turkish bath since he was 9st 4lb on the Tuesday and had to reduce it by the Thursday. He had also brought the 'Mixture' with him and, finding himself in the company of a Mr G Haughton, who was trying to recover from a sea voyage, had the temerity to recommend a dose of 'Archer's Mixture' as a remedy. No doubt thanking Archer profusely for his kindness and generosity, Mr Haughton accepted a tablespoon of the stuff and never knew what hit him.[74]

As Custance, who found the whole thing rather amusing, explained Mr Haughton 'did "walking exercise" all night and couldn't go to the races the next day.'[75]

As for Fred, he partook of a sherry glassful and achieved his objective. 'As mentioned earlier,' continued Custance, 'he couldn't ride an ounce under 9st 4lb on the Tuesday afternoon, and on the Thursday he rode 8st 12lb.'[76] He believed his friend's stomach to be in a very poor state and his method of wasting dangerous, but Fred was ready to ride Cambusmore and received an ovation when he came on the course.

Custance decided to be blunt. 'Well, Fred,' he said to him, 'I don't know if it is the excitement from the ovation they gave you, or the wasting you have done, but I never saw you look half so bad as you do now.'[77] Fred just laughed and joked about how he would look for the Cambridgeshire the following Wednesday, 26 October. He won his race on Cambusmore and received another ovation as he left the course.

The Dowager Duchess of Montrose had been pushing for Fred to ride her horse St Mirin in the Cambridgeshire before his trip to Ireland. Despite Custance's concerns over his friend's health, she got her man, although she was not aware of how ill he was until he got back. By this time Fred, ignoring the state of his health and Harry's protestations that he should not ride, was convinced that St Mirin would win. He was also trying to persuade others that this was the case, but some felt that his judgement was at fault and that another contender, Carlton, would win. Archer explained, however, that St Mirin had been ridden by an inexperienced lad in the trial and that another inexperienced lad was going to ride Carlton, not the easiest of horses, in the Cambridgeshire itself. Despite this, Carlton was classed as favourite – at 425 to 100.

At first it seemed that Archer's predictions had been correct, but then Sailor Prince caught up and he and St Mirin almost passed the post together, so that it was impossible to tell who had won. Fred thought that he had until Sir George Chetwynd told him otherwise – Sailor Prince had won by a head. Perhaps the facts that he was not in good health and had wasted almost to the extreme cost Archer the race – certainly it would come up as an issue in later weeks, but some spectators had different theories.

Impaired judgement also cost Fred his friendship with Captain Machell.[78] The first signs that all was not well with Fred himself came when he approached Lambton some time after the Cambridgeshire. Riding up to him on Newmarket Heath, Archer said, 'I suppose you have had a very bad week.' Lambton confirmed he had. 'Well,' Archer said, 'you can get out on Queen Bee . . . she can't be beat, but I have only told you and the Captain.' Queen Bee, owned by Robert Peck, was due to race in a 100 Guinea Plate at a Newmarket meeting on 27 October.

Archer went away, later rode the race on Queen Bee and lost it, being beaten by a head. To Captain Machell, it was not so much the losing of the race he found so offensive, but a perceived notion that Fred had deliberately deceived him. He had discovered that a Mrs Chaine had been advised, by Fred, not to back Queen Bee. As Fred later explained, he had done this in an effort to put off 'touting people' as he called them, but despite his great faith in Queen Bee, the horse had still lost and Machell, feeling that he had been duped by Fred and not giving him a chance to explain, completely ignored him when they met in the paddock. He was incensed by Fred's apparent betrayal and was not about to forgive him for it. In fact he never spoke to him again, much to his own cost as it turned out.

Fred sought out Lambton and appeared both physically and mentally exhausted – upset over the fact that he had lost, but even more upset that he had lost Machell's goodwill. He may also have been confused and overwrought – unable to explain to Lambton why he had lost the race despite literally riding the mare into the ground and being so determined to win. In addition he felt the need to justify himself. 'I had to put all those touting people off,' he said, 'and the Captain thinks I put him wrong.'[79]

Considerably depressed, Fred returned to Falmouth House.

Notes

1–4.	Humphris, Edith M, *The Life of Fred Archer*, p.224
5.	Lambton, The Honourable George, *Men and Horses I Have Known*, p.45
6.	The Family Records Office, London: The Last Will and Testament of Frederick James Archer
7.	Humphris, *The Life of Fred Archer*, pp.233–6
8.	Welcome, John, *Fred Archer: A Complete Study*, p.129
9.	Humphris, *The Life of Fred Archer*, p.235
10–12.	Ibid, p.236
13–14.	Weatherby, J E & J P, *The Racing Calendar for the Year 1885*
15–17.	*The Sporting Life*, 7 May 1885
18–20.	Chetwynd, Sir George, *Racing Reminiscences and Experience of the Turf*, p.224
21.	Humphris, *The Life of Fred Archer*, p.223
22–3.	Weatherby, J E & J P, *The Racing Calendar for the Year 1885*
24–6.	*The Sporting Life*, 3 June 1885

27. Mortimer, Roger, Onslow, Richard & Willet, Peter, *The Biographical Encyclopaedia of British Flat Racing*, p.204
28–30. Chetwynd, pp.225–6
31. Weatherby, J E & J P, *The Racing Calendar for the Year 1885*
32. *The Times*, 15 June 1885
33. Weatherby, J E & J P, *The Racing Calendar for the Year 1885*
34. *The Sporting Life*, 17 September 1885
35. Chetwynd, pp.225–6
36. *The Sporting Life*, 17 September 1885
37. *Newmarket Journal*, 3 October 1885
38–9. Portland, 6th Duke of, *Memories of Racing and Hunting*, p.46
40. Details courtesy of Eric Dunning of the Local Historical Society, Newmarket
41. Humphris, *The Life of Mathew Dawson*, p.160
42. Tanner, Michael & Cranham, Gerry, *Great Jockeys of the Flat: A Celebration of Two Centuries of Jockeyship*, pp.106–10
43–4. Lambton, p.113
45–6. Weatherby, J E & J P, *The Racing Calendar for the Year 1885*
47. Weatherby, J E & J P, *The Racing Calendar for the Year 1886*
48. Mortimer, Onslow & Willet, pp.429–30
49. Wilson, Julian, *The Great Racehorses*, p.105
50. Weatherby, J E & J P, *The Racing Calendar for the Year 1885*
51–2. Chetwynd, pp.229–30
53–4. *The Times*, 27 May 1886
55. Custance, Henry, *Riding Recollections and Turf Stories*, p.207
56–7. *The Times*, 8/9 June 1886
58. Lambton, p.117
59–61. Weatherby, J E & J P, *The Racing Calendar for the Year 1886*
62. Chetwynd, pp.231–2
63. Correspondence from Albert Edward, Prince of Wales, to his son, Prince George. Reproduced by the Gracious Permission of Her Majesty the Queen.
64. Weatherby, J E & J P, *The Racing Calendar for the Year 1886*
65–8. *The Sporting Life*, 16 September 1886
69. Weatherby, J E & J P, *The Racing Calendar for the Year 1886*
70. Corporal Ormonde Pratt, J33 Royal Buckinghamshire Hussars (courtesy of defence records, Ministry of Defence)
71. Mortimer, Onslow & Willet, pp.429–30
72. Custance, p.128
73. Ibid, p.130
74–6. Ibid, p.131
77. Ibid, p.132
78–9. Lambton, p.131

The Final Furlong

The last time Harry Custance saw Fred was on the day of the Cambridgeshire, one week after the Irish Curragh. Fred had asked him to meet him at Newmarket, so Custance duly travelled over to Falmouth House, only to be told by Fred's widowed sister, Mrs Emily Coleman (now living at Falmouth House as Fred's housekeeper), that he was in his Turkish bath, so Custance left and later on met his friend at the course. As in Ireland he was shocked by Fred's appearance which had visibly worsened.[1] 'I thought I had never seen him looking so bad before,' he wrote, but Fred was anxious to give the impression that all was well and, in cheerful spirits, talked and laughed about their recent trip to Ireland – perhaps trying to downplay just how ill he looked and, at the same time, dodge Harry's concerned questions.[2]

It came as no surprise to Harry, however, to hear later that Fred was ill before setting off for a meeting at Lewes after he had ridden in Brighton. Since it had been a particularly gruelling season and there was only so much his friend could take, Harry felt that it was the last straw and recalled saying to his wife, 'Fred Archer will never get over this.'[3]

Harry was predicting his friend's death, but in truth the warning signs of impending collapse had been there for months. The wasting that he had endured for years had certainly contributed to the undermining of his health and constitution, but his willpower had always seen him through. Now he was struggling to convince others that he was not as bad as he looked, but people like Custance who had known him for years knew better.

Until 1886 Fred had never suffered any serious illness. The savaging of his arm in 1880, even the shock of being attacked by his own horse, had not deterred him from preparing for the upcoming Derby, and it is a measure of his strength that he went out and won that race. Even his physician of fourteen years, Dr John Rowland Wright, expressed the opinion that although Fred did not have a robust constitution, he was never prone to illness. Somehow he had managed to keep at bay many of the ailments which had felled stronger jockeys than him – in particular tuberculosis which had killed Tom French. Now, he could not summon enough strength to see the end of the 1886 season out.

Both Sir George Chetwynd and George Lambton, perhaps the very last of Fred's friends to see him alive before his final trip to Falmouth House, remembered the race meeting at Lewes. It was also the first time that Fred admitted to being ill, confessing as much to Chetwynd,[4] but assuring him that he was determined to ride, which he did, in the first two races. When Lambton thought back to that meeting, he was pretty certain that his friend was dangerously ill – even though he was still riding.[5]

Having met Lambton at Lewes on the Thursday, Fred is reported to have said to him that his horse would probably win, but that he himself was not one hundred per cent.[6] His will-power was failing him.

This was on 4 November and, riding Tommy Tittlemouse in the Castle Plate, the second race of the day, he ran unplaced. By that time he was feeling worse and it was obvious that he could not carry on. Where Chetwynd stated that he was persuaded to go home,[7] Lambton wrote that Fred himself made the decision to leave.[8] He was perhaps the most dedicated jockey of his generation, but even he knew when he had had enough and subsequently prepared to leave for Newmarket in the company of a trainer and associate, Mr Gurry. Though he was drained physically and unable to continue, mentally he was as astute as ever. To the end his mind was still on racing.[9]

'Just before he left,' wrote Lambton, 'he said "Good-bye" to me. He was walking away when he turned back and said, "If you see a two-year-old called Eunuch in a mile selling race tomorrow, you ought to back him; I got beat on him in a five-furlong race, but he is a certain stayer."'[10]

The friendship ended as it had begun – with a race tip. 'Sure enough,' Lambton remembered, 'Eunuch, the property of the American sportsman, Mr Tom Broeck, was entered, and won easily at 5 to 1.'[11]

Fred telegraphed Falmouth House before leaving Lewes, to inform his sister and the staff there that he was on his way; and then he left, as quietly and as unobtrusively as his career had been both brilliant and turbulent. On arriving at Liverpool Street he had some arrowroot and brandy which had a calming effect upon him and he slept on the train to Cambridge, feeling quite refreshed when he awoke later. In fact he looked so well that, when he finally arrived at Falmouth House, everybody thought he was in good spirits.[12]

'I did not think he was very ill,' his sister, Mrs Emily Coleman, later told the coroner at the inquest into her brother's death, 'and he went to bed at about 11.30 p.m.'[13] But his condition became worse through the night and, unable to get up the following morning, he agreed to see his doctor, whom Emily sent for.[14]

Dr Wright had never had to treat him for any serious illness before. He therefore arrived at Falmouth House not expecting to have to do so now, but he found Fred in a state of rest-lessness. Prescribing some medication, Dr Wright then took his leave, came back at about 2 p.m. and found him no better. In fact he seemed worse and the doctor was greatly concerned.[15] 'His temperature was so high,' he later said at the inquest, 'that I suggested another medical man be sent for.'[16]

Archer did not see the need for this and said no, but Dr Wright thought otherwise and contacted a Cambridge physician called Dr Latham. Wright requested that he attend his patient immediately which Latham agreed to do, duly arriving at Falmouth House where there followed another consultation. Dr Wright returned to Falmouth House at 7 a.m. on 6 November, and by this time delirium had set in. 'He had a delusion,' said Wright, 'that a dinner he had eaten three days before was still in his stomach, although he had suffered from diarrhoea all night.'[17]

Despite everyone's protestations, Fred remained convinced that he was right and they were wrong to the point where he suggested taking his notorious 'Mixture' as a remedy. Wright dissuaded him from taking such a drastic course of action (as far as he could dissuade someone who was delirious) and had the backing of Dr Latham when he made another visit later in the day.[18]

The delirium was still evident when Captain Bowling visited Fred. He stated that, although Fred was able to converse, his mind did wander and he was worried about recovering – a point with which, in light of future events, Mrs Emily Coleman readily agreed. 'During a long conversation I had with him [Fred],' she said at the inquest, 'he occasionally forgot the subject and frequently expressed himself anxious about his recovery.'

Wright and Latham reached their conclusions and that evening Dr Wright issued a bulletin: 'Falmouth House, 6 November 1886, 6.00 p.m. Mr F Archer has returned home suffering from the effects of a severe chill, followed by high fever.'[19]

The diagnosis had been made and Fred was informed by Dr Latham that he had typhoid fever. Still delirious, Fred remained convinced that he had food in his stomach and had to be persuaded once again that this was a delusion. He was also told that he had to rest and remain quiet, at which point he seemed to come to himself and Dr Wright noted that Fred became 'composed'. The two doctors then left him in the care of his sister.

On Sunday, 7 November, Dr Wright returned and discovered that the delirious state had given way to depression with Fred now convinced that he was going to die, but by the afternoon this mood seemed to lift and he was in a better frame of mind. On the following morning, his mind was still wandering, but his condition on the whole seemed better and he was quite happy to talk to his sister, who was so confident that he was improving that during the course of the morning she telegraphed Viscount Falmouth to inform him that her brother was brighter.

Just after 9 a.m., Dr Wright issued the following bulletin: 'Mr Fred Archer is suffering from an attack of typhoid fever. There is an improvement in his symptoms to day.'[20]

But he was, as Wright said later, 'low spirited' and still preoccupied with thoughts of dying, although it has to be remembered that this was also the second anniversary of his wife's death. Fred had never fully recovered from losing both her and their son. Other events had also contributed – Falmouth's retirement, the break with Portland, the Highland Chief incident, the rumours of corruption, the concern that he would lose his status as Champion Jockey. These and a double bereavement in the space of twelve months had prompted him to push harder to overcome worry and depression. He had been mentally and physically exhausted and after his wife's death, harboured suicidal thoughts, so he pushed himself again to defeat the pain of bereavement and loss.[21] He travelled extensively and, on his return to England, resumed the harsh regime of wasting which had been so much a part of his life. If he could not waste, he could no longer race and horseracing had been his security. It was all he knew. So he went on to ride more races, to have more winners until finally he could no longer keep the control he had always had – he could no longer sustain the motivation and his system collapsed.

When Dr Wright left his patient just after 9.30 a.m. on 8 November, in the care of Emily and a Nurse Dennington, Fred was still in a depressed state.[22] At 11.30 a.m. Nurse Charlotte Hornidge of the Cambridge Nursery Institution arrived and she was followed, around midday, by Captain Bowling. But once again, the depression seemed to lift and Bowling found Fred quite cheerful. When he left him, he seemed optimistic that his friend would get well.

Nurse Hornidge then sat with Fred and stayed with him until 2.17 p.m. when Emily, coming in to relieve her, told her to go downstairs and get something to eat. 'During the three hours I was there,' Nurse Hornidge later recalled, '[he] was frequently left alone for several minutes together whilst I went for refreshments for him. Just before Mrs Coleman told me to go out I heard [him] speaking to her, but did not catch what he said. I left the room but came back in about a minute and asked the patient if he was comfortable, he answered "Yes!" '[23]

After opening a bottle of eau de Cologne for Emily, the nurse then went downstairs, leaving the bedroom door ajar. Fred had asked for the nurse to leave them, his sister said later, so that he could speak to her alone. She also added that there was nothing unusual about this, as he had done likewise on previous occasions.

Emily recalled she was looking out of the window when, out of the blue, Fred asked, 'Are they coming?'[24] No-one was able, later, to figure out what he meant. However, 'Almost immediately after,' Emily continued, 'I heard a noise and looking round saw that my brother was out of bed and [had] something in his hand. I ran to him and when I saw it was a revolver tried to push it away.'

A struggle ensued as Emily literally fought with her brother to stop him from harming himself. 'The revolver was in his left hand,' she said, 'and I hurt my hand in trying to push it away.'

Despite the fact that the effects of his illness had left him very weak he was still able to summon enough strength to resist his sister. 'He then threw his right arm around my neck,' she continued, 'and fired the revolver with his left hand. I saw him doing it but could not stop him, he seemed awfully strong.'

Placing the gun in his mouth, he had pulled the trigger and the bullet, passing through the spinal column, severed the spinal cord and killed him outright before exiting through the back of his head and, with a piece of bone still attached to it, landing on the floor nearby. He fell to the floor and lay on the hearthrug. His sister screamed, but no-one came because during the struggle Fred had pushed her against the bedroom door and it had slammed shut. 'Doubtless that is the reason why my screams were not heard,' she said.[25]

In fact no-one downstairs had heard anything, so when her calls for help went unanswered, Emily pulled the bell cord and Nurse Hornidge remembered the housemaid going upstairs to answer it. The nurse did not think there was any emergency until the ringing became 'violent' and, as the nurse herself went up, she heard cries for help. By the time she reached the bedroom, which, she told the inquest, smelt of gunpowder, Fred's valet, Harry Sargent, was already there and as he lifted his late employer's body, the revolver fell to the floor.

Very few had known that the gun was in the room, making his death all the more terrible. It had in fact been there for some three years – from the very first weeks of Fred and Nellie's marriage. It was the gift from Mr Thomas Roughton, the owner of Sterling who won the Liverpool Cup, and the only people who had access to the weapon were Fred and his valet. A month before his death Fred had instructed Sargent to have the gun repaired since more burglaries had been reported in the area.[26] 'My master . . . ordered me to always place it in the pedestal in his room when he was at home,' Sargent said later, 'but to take it into my own bedroom when he was away.'

This was for safety reasons because Sargent was the only male in the house when Fred was away. When Fred had telegraphed from Lewes to say that he was on his way home,

Sargent duly put the revolver back in the pedestal. When Nurse Hornidge looked there after Fred's death, she found a tin box containing 44 of the original 50 cartridges. It seemed to be one of the great ironies of his life, therefore, that he had brought a weapon into the house for his own protection, only to use it to destroy himself in a fit of delirium, brought on by typhoid fever – an illness brought about by overwork, personal tragedy and the need to prove himself and be the absolute best in one of the world's most gruelling sports.

The race against himself was over.

Notes

1–3.   Custance, Henry, *Riding Recollections and Turf Stories*, p.133
4.   Chetwynd, Sir George, *Racing Reminiscences and Experience of the Turf*, p.240
5–6.   Lambton, The Honourable George, *Men and Horses I Have Known*, p.132
7.   Chetwynd, pp.240–1
8.   Lambton, p.132
9.   Welcome, John, *Fred Archer: A Complete Study*, p.155
10–11.   Lambton, p.132
12.   Welcome, John, *Fred Archer: A Complete Study*, p.155
13–20.   *Newmarket Journal*, 13 November 1886
21.   Gross, Richard, *Psychology: The Science of Mind and Behaviour*, p.597
22–6.   *Newmarket Journal*, 13 November 1886

Epilogue

The question of what to do with Falmouth House was resolved the following year and a notice duly appeared in the *Newmarket Journal* on 8 October 1887 to the effect that the contents of the estate were to be put up for auction by George Blencowe of Biddell and Blencowe.[1] The solicitors conducting the sale were the ones who had dealt with Fred's will – W and C H Jessop Solicitors of Cheltenham. The auction was to take place at the Rutland Arms Hotel on Wednesday 12 October at 6 p.m. and, if a good price could not be met on the place being sold as one lot, it was to be sold as two: Lot One comprising the house and grounds, with stabling, lodge and stud; Lot Two comprising a cottage, stud premises and paddock.[2]

Despite a good turnout – this was after all something of an historic event – Falmouth House was not snapped up as one lot. The bidding began at 5,000 sovereigns, but once it had reached 5,200 sovereigns there were no more offers. The auctioneer compared this with the reserve price which remained undisclosed, and announced that this was too low and that no sale could be achieved. So the whole estate was to be sold in two lots and the bidding began once again for Lot One – starting at 1,000 sovereigns. There were no more offers after 2,000 sovereigns and, once again, the reserve price was not met. The offers for Lot Two began at 3,000 sovereigns, rose to 4,050 and became the property of Mr W Gardner of Exning.[3]

The auctioneer returned to Lot One, when he stated, according to the *Newmarket Journal*,[4] that the moment he left the room, he could not accept any more offers, no matter how good they were. A bid of 3,000 sovereigns was made and continued on to 3,750 sovereigns when it was knocked down to a Reverend Edward Ramsden. The whole estate was sold at last, at the best price possible, and one which had exceeded the reserve price.

Falmouth House continued to be a part of the racing scene for many decades after, as the Reverend Edward Ramsden was a well-known racing figure, although more so in Yorkshire than Newmarket. It also became the stuff of legend as people who stayed there became convinced that Fred haunted its rooms – that is of course when he was not being seen galloping across the Heath. By 1919 the grounds of the estate were being used to train the horses of Lord Glanely who would eventually employ another Fred Archer (Charlie's son, Fred's nephew) to act as his private trainer. An engraving, owned by the BBC Hulton Picture Library, shows Falmouth House to be a sturdy-looking residence, but it no longer exists today. The residence which had once housed one of the nineteenth century's greatest jockeys, and in itself could have become a significant training establishment in Newmarket, was demolished less than a hundred years after it was built – with the loss of many features which had helped the place to look so full of character.

Another event, one which can only be described as an incredible coincidence, took place on the very day that Falmouth House was being sold – 12 October 1887[5] – and that was the death of Fred Archer's arch rival, George Fordham, who had died after a long illness. He had been a heavy drinker, and his wasting over the years had affected his lungs and further undermined his health. *The Times* newspaper, which may not have been aware of such a coincidence, noted that the demise of this 51-year-old jockey could not create the same element of sensationalism which Fred's had, almost twelve months before, but it did pay lengthy homage to a man who had, on and off, dominated the racing world for over thirty years, acknowledging what many at the time already believed – that Fordham was the better horseman.

Noted for his knowledge of pace and distance on the turf, he was seen as a genius in his own right and, once again, comparisons were drawn with the late Archer who had not lived long enough to bring his talent to the effortless perfection which seemed to characterise Fordham's skill.

Fordham's funeral took place on 18 October and he was buried in Upton Old Churchyard, Slough. Many distinguished mourners were present at the service, among them Mr Leopold de Rothschild, for whom he had ridden on occasion, his close friend Harry Custance and Tom Cannon, as well as family and friends. The flowers chosen to be placed on the coffin were tied with his light blue and yellow racing colours and there was a brass nameplate on the lid which, in addition to his name and the day upon which he died, 12 October, also bore this message: 'Tis the pace that kills'[6] – a message curiously reminiscent of the one given at Fred Archer's funeral.

Even in death the two could not avoid one another.

As if to reiterate the fact that the Falmouth–Dawson–Archer partnership was indeed dead, fate played another hand. Viscount Falmouth, having suffered general ill health for some time, died just after 9.30 p.m. on 6 November 1889 at Mereworth Castle in Kent.[7] He was surrounded by his family and physician. His had been a very charmed and successful life and *The Times* devoted a column and a half to his racing achievements, in particular his association with Fred Archer, who had died just three years before, almost to the day. *The Times* then detailed Falmouth's financial gains during the Falmouth–Dawson–Archer years. He was a true sportsman and beyond reproach, the paper said. *The Sporting Life*, on 7 November, noted the one characteristic which had separated him from his contemporaries, that he was not influenced by the market value of his horses and ran them independent of what the paper called 'other interests and considerations'.

His funeral took place on 11 November, in Mereworth, and Sir John Astley was among the many mourners who attended. The coffin was placed in the family vault of Le Despencers, his wife's family, but was later transferred to the churchyard itself. A brief notice to this effect appeared in *The Times* the following day.

The survivor of the partnership was Dawson; still alive and kicking, although anxious to retire completely after many decades spent training men and horses. He had thought, once his nephew had taken over Heath House, that he would be allowed to grow old quietly, but his skill, expertise and professionalism were such that he would continue for many years yet.

In fact, once brought back out of retirement, he continued training for some fourteen years, although not on the same level as in previous years. Taking on Lord Rosebery's horses, he trained Ladas to win the Middle Park Plate in 1893 and Sir Vistos to win the Derby and St Leger in 1895. He was so well respected that he was one of the few personages distinguished enough to ride in his brougham at Epsom, instead of walking to the stands.[8]

It was at a race meeting in August 1898 that he contracted his final illness. Deep in conversation with the Prince of Wales, he caught a chill – a consequence of standing with his back towards an open window. The chill developed, became worse and at 8 p.m. on 18 August he died, aged 78.

The Sporting Life, on 19 August, acknowledged how Dawson had discovered Fred Archer and noted that he was the best of masters and an excellent judge of horsemanship.[9] On the following day the *Newmarket Journal* referred to him as a 'veteran trainer'[10] and *The Times* reported on his honesty as well as his success.

His burial took place at Newmarket and he is one of many Dawsons who now surround Fred Archer's grave in the cemetery. Heath House Stables still exist and are owned and run by the trainer Sir Mark Prescott.[11]

The Archer family was only just beginning to come to terms with Fred's death when his father, William Archer, died on 7 December 1889, almost four weeks after Lord Falmouth's funeral. A small obituary appeared in *The Times* four days later.[12] He had died at Cheltenham, the place of his birth, just a few weeks short of his 64th birthday. *The Times*, more so than the *Newmarket Journal*, detailed his life and career, from his apprenticeship in Birmingham, to his success in Russia, to his family. Three days later, a brief notice appeared in the *Newmarket Journal*, observing that William Archer's funeral in Prestbury had been strictly private, suggesting that any news attached to the Archer family was still of great interest to the public and that the Archers were anxious to keep this latest loss very much to themselves.

Fred's mother, Emma Archer, would outlive her husband by almost twenty years and after his death went to live with her daughter Alice. On 27 August 1908, at her daughter's home in Withington, near Cheltenham, she suffered a stroke and remained unconscious until the morning of 7 September when she died.[13] Hers had been a varied and long life. She had seen her sons achieve success, only to see two of them die through accident and suicide respectively; and she had since seen many changes. Her funeral, a quiet affair like that of her husband, took place in Prestbury.

Charlie Archer outlived his brother Fred by 36 years, dying in his 64th year, after developing double pneumonia. He had actually been on the verge of recovery, but then he suffered a relapse and, quite unexpectedly, died in his armchair at Fashion Cottage, Newmarket, on 11 September 1922.[14] He had had many notable successes as a trainer in the years after his brother's death, particularly Wolf's Crag's victory in the Lincolnshire in March 1893. He trained at Ellesmere House, Newmarket and at his death his son, Fred C Archer, came down from the Malton Stables in Yorkshire to take over. Charlie's funeral, at Newmarket Cemetery, was scheduled to take place on the following Friday morning at 11 a.m. and the family requested that no flowers be given, but they were sent anyway – lilies and pink carnations. There were other wreaths and messages from his son (and Fred's namesake), Frederick Charles Archer; Charlie's daughter Ethel and son-in-law Willie Pratt; Fred Archer's daughter, Nellie Rose Archer, now Nellie Rose Tosetti and her husband Alex; and three of Charlie's granddaughters – Lola, Yvonne and Gladys. The large gathering of mourners was a clear indication of how well known and respected Charlie Archer had been by the racing fraternity.

The Times had, on 12 September 1922, detailed his life and career, giving the briefest of mentions to the Highland Chief incident in 1883, which, back then, had been the source of so much controversy.[15]

The account of Charlie's death, being reported in *The Sporting Life* on 12 September, was placed alongside that of John Osborne – one of Fred Archer's contemporaries and opponents – who, born on 7 January 1833, died of heart failure at his home on 10 September 1922 aged 89.[16]

Alice survived most of the family, including her youngest brother Charlie, and some of the next generation, becoming Edith M Humphris's chief source for her biography of Fred's life.

Many of Fred's contemporaries survived him into the next century – among them Captain Machell, who had taken Fred's death very badly and, in the years following his death, had kept up a correspondence with Fred's sister Emily. On 12 May 1889, a portrait and frame was presented to him in memory of Fred, containing a piece of wood for every winner that he had achieved.[17] The separate pieces of wood – each coloured – represented the racing colours of Lord Falmouth, the Duke of Portland, Lord Hastings and the Duke of Westminster. It was certainly a gift to cherish, but one which Machell may have taken little comfort from. He was still in a state of shock over Fred and, unable to forgive himself for snubbing his friend just days before his death, was convinced that the jockey was haunting him and lived in a torment of guilt until his own death in 1902.[18]

Harry Custance died in 1908. Having retired from racing due to poor health in 1879, he had become a starter to the Jockey Club and National Hunt Committees before publishing his autobiography in 1894. In 1905 he suffered a seizure, which he recovered from, but on 19 April 1908 he suffered a second fit and died at the age of 64.[19]

Tom Cannon, who Fred thought was one of the most accomplished jockeys he had ever come across, died in 1917 aged 71.[20] His two sons, Mornington and Thomas, became jockeys and his daughter, Margaret, married Ernest Piggott, a steeplechase jockey. They had a son called Keith who, in his turn, became the father (and trainer) of Lester Piggott.[21]

Also to die in 1917 was Fred Webb, Archer's close friend. He had retired as a jockey and become a trainer, succeeding fellow trainer Sam Pickering to the job of training the horses of Lillie Langtry (now Lady de Bathe).[22]

Webb's death on 27 March had come just days after that of the Jockey Club Steward Sir George Chetwynd, who died in Monte Carlo on 10 March. A great sportsman (hunting, shooting, cricket), he was, of course, chiefly remembered for his association with horseracing, but at his death the papers picked up on an incident which had happened in 1887, known as the Chetwynd and Durham Turf Case and which also involved another of Fred's contemporaries, Charlie Wood. Lord Durham alleged that Charlie had been guilty of pulling up a horse in a race and Chetwynd demanded that his Lordship provide proof of that and of other allegations he had made against a particular stable which was not named in the papers. Durham refused and found himself challenged to a duel. He ignored it and the whole case came before the Jockey Club itself. Wood, for his part, sued the Licensed Victuallers' Gazette for 5,000 sovereigns, but only got a farthing in damages. Sir George Chetwynd had sued for libel and, suing for 2,000 sovereigns, also got one farthing courtesy of the Jockey Club.[23] Chetwynd hardly referred to this as success and was deeply disappointed by his treatment.

Wood, who succeeded Fred Archer as Champion Jockey in 1887, outlived everybody – surviving the above inconvenience, change within racing itself and not one, but two World Wars. Aged 90 when he died on 2 June 1945, he was remembered as one of those who had made the 1880s and '90s world of horseracing the golden age of sport. Placed alongside Archer, Cannon, Goater, Custance, Webb, Watts, Maidment and John Osborne, all of whom were long since dead, his obituary seemed almost like a celebration of excellence and achievement, coming at a time when England, having just gone through six years of war, was seeking heroes to cheer.[24]

The Honourable George Lambton carried on working almost until his death, which came within weeks of Charles Wood's. On 22 July 1945, just four months short of his 85th birthday, Lambton announced his retirement from training after some fifty years. He had trained the winners of thirteen Classics, including four St Legers. His son, Edward George Lambton, took over. Despite giving the reason for his retirement as ill health, the newspapers could not have imagined what would follow so quickly. Just three days after the announcement George Lambton died at his home in Newmarket. *The Times*, in recalling his association with the riders and trainers of the 1880s and '90s, reminded readers that he had laid the foundations of two studs and trained horses for the House of Stanley. For a nation hoping for a better future it seemed a pleasure to write of someone who had had his heyday when British confidence was at its ultimate height.

Lambton's funeral took place at 3.30 p.m. on Thursday 26 July 1945 at All Saints', Newmarket.[25]

The Duke of Portland had died two years earlier on 26 April 1943. He did not enjoy the same kind of success in the new century that he had before 1900 and, after creating a split in the Jockey Club over whether or not racing should be continued during the First World War, gradually retired from the racing scene altogether.[26] In 1935 he published *Memories of Racing and Hunting*, to be followed two years later, by *Men, Women and Things*.

When he died a friend wrote to *The Times*, saying that Portland's demise was like the end of a great era. When he first became Duke, he said, the world was a completely different place with different ideals, but Portland never lost sight of what he considered to be his duty. His funeral took place on Thursday 29 April and on 1 May a memorial service was held at St Mary's Church, Nottingham.

Fred Archer's greatest impact was on his family – in particular the nephews who followed him in his profession after his death. His sister Alice had had nine children – seven of them boys – but only three of them would go on to fulfil long-standing careers in horseracing as jockeys and trainers. The other three died before any promise could be fully distinguished. Two were killed during the First World War[27] – Ernest Hayward Pratt and Harry Ormonde Pratt (named after the racehorse Ormonde). A third, Arthur Wyndham Pratt, became a trainer, but died of cerebrospinal fever, contracted while on active service in the 1914–18 War. A fourth brother, John Francis Pratt, also became a trainer and, although very little else is known about him, it is known that he went to live in India.

The three who went on to have long and distinguished careers in racing and training were Frederick Charles Pratt, born at Tewkesbury on 4 March 1876, William Archer Pratt, born in 1878, and the youngest of Alice's children – Charles Hazel, born at Worcester on 17 January 1894. It was these three, along with their cousin, Charlie's son, Frederick Charles Archer, who carried the family tradition into the new century – through to the 1920s, 1930s, 1940s, 1950s and 1960s – both in England and abroad.[28] Freddy Pratt, the nephew who had lived with his uncle Fred and his aunt Helen Rose, would, after a short career as a jockey in England and Austria, go on to act as a trainer for James 'Jimmy' de Rothschild for over forty years, finally retiring in 1945. A portrait of him now hangs at James Rothschild's former home, Waddesdon Manor, in Buckinghamshire.[29]

His brother William broke his uncle Fred's record of wins of the Grand Prix at Longchamps by securing four in 1898, 1900, 1902 and 1903. After this final win he decided to retire as a jockey and became a trainer, dividing his time between England and France.[30] He worked at the Chantilly stables near Paris until June 1940 when he was forced to leave as France came under German occupation. He later assisted in the final preparations surrounding Alycidon who secured the Triple Crown in the late 1940s – the first to do so since Isonomy. By this time however tragedy had dealt yet another cruel blow – this time on Fred Archer's namesake.

Fred C Archer was Charlie Archer's second son born at a time when the elder Fred's career was at its height. After surviving Gallipoli in 1915 he worked at the Malton stable in Yorkshire, but returned to Newmarket in 1922 when his father died. He brought with him an unprepossessing hack called Double Chance and trained and hunted him laboriously before entering him for the 1925 Grand National at Aintree which the horse won. It was a win made more significant by the fact that the last Archer to secure the Grand National was Fred's grandfather, William Archer, in 1858 – the year Fred's father, Charlie, was born. It was not however the start of a glittering training career. Double Chance drifted into obscurity. His owner kept him at Newmarket and the horse was later handed over to a friend when Fred died unexpectedly on 21 October

1928. He had been returning from a wedding in London and, driving through a small town called Woodford in Essex, fell asleep at the wheel of his car which then drifted on to the wrong side of the road, slamming into the front of a stationary bus, killing Fred instantly. He was 46.[31]

His cousin, Charles H Pratt, the youngest of Alice's children, fared no better. His career only really got off the ground in the years after the First World War and, like his brother William, he divided his time between England and France before settling at Lambourn in Berkshire where he joined the local council. His successes as a trainer were modest and then in August 1962 he secured the William Hill Gold Cup at Redcar with Songedor. He was presented with the cup and, later in the day, boarded a light aircraft with his wife and one or two others. Unfortunately the plane crashed, killing all on board. When the accident was reported in the papers the next day, it was noted that the William Hill Gold Cup was found among the wreckage.[32]

But what of Fred and Helen Rose's daughter, Nellie Rose, left orphaned in 1886 at the age of two?

When her mother died, she was taken to Warren House, the home of her grandparents, Mr and Mrs John Dawson, who accepted the responsibility of bringing her up.[33] Many of Fred's associates enquired after her after his death, but while she was growing up she was kept very much out of the limelight. The home where she was born, Falmouth House, was sold on her behalf in October 1887, for an undisclosed price and it continued as a training establishment for many decades. In the 1960s, however, due to that era's trend for redevelopment it was demolished, with many of its priceless features lost forever, and today a small housing estate stands on the plot of land where Falmouth House once stood.

On 1 June 1911, Nellie Rose married Max Alex Tosetti of Swaffham Prior Hall, Cambridge, at St George's, Hanover Square, London. Max, along with his brothers, had played cricket for Essex between 1898 and 1905. He had also bobsleighed for England, but family duty called and he joined his father's wine trading firm, known as Coverley, Westray, Walbaum and Tosetti Co. Max and Nellie had four children: Helen, born in 1915; Elizabeth, in 1917; John Douglas Alex, in 1920; and Susan, in 1924.[34] Unfortunately Nellie Rose did not live long enough to see any of her children reach maturity. She died on 5 January 1931, just two months after her 46th birthday. She is not buried in Newmarket, where her father, mother and baby brother are buried, but at Nutley Church in Kent where many of her Tosetti in-laws are also buried. Her son, Max Alex, in his eleventh year when his mother died, was left Stamford Hall, Gullane, in Scotland, which had originally been the property of his grandmother, Helen Rose Archer.

Nellie Rose's husband never married again and their son John Douglas Alex would later follow him into the wine merchant business.[35] After schooling, John Douglas Alex Tosetti spent eighteen months at Roberts and Sons, Wine Merchants, Worthing. He was later conscripted into the army and was a captain in the Royal Artillery Militia (frontier surveillance planes). He was also a pilot for Field Marshal Montgomery and a major with the Military Government in Hamburg. Two years after the Second World War ended, he joined his father at Coverley, Westray, Walbaum and Tosetti Co. Cotrali took it over in 1970, but Pickfords took over Cotrali in the late 1970s. John Tosetti married three times (to Penny, then Paula-Ann and finally Pamela) and had four children: Prue, Gail, Max and Alexander Birkin Tosetti.

John's eldest son, Max, was born in 1961 and is married to Karen Michelle Vandenburg. They have two sons – Jake Eliot Otto, born in 1994, and Christian Louis Oscar, born in 1996. These are the great-great-grandchildren of Fred and Helen Rose Archer. Max's brother, Alexander, known as Alex, was born in 1965 and is married to Jane.[36] They live in London.

John Tosetti retired from the wine business in August 1983 and divided his time between Chelsea, Suffolk and Buckinghamshire. He died in 1998.

His younger son, Alex, is a close associate of Graham Snelling, curator of the Newmarket Horseracing Museum in Suffolk, which houses one of the best collections on Fred Archer. York also houses a comprehensive collection, including the Archer photograph album and some memorabilia, such as the colours he wore for the Duke of Westminster and a ring.

People are anxious to preserve Fred Archer's memory. As well as the Fred Archer Stakes being created at Newmarket, he has also found his way on to the Internet alongside twentieth-century greats such as Donoghue, Richards, Piggott, Carson, Shoemaker, Dunwoody and Dettori – a search for his name results in links to numerous web pages about Fred. Fred Archer's memory is kept alive because his achievements on the racecourse were attained not just through incredible skill, but through sheer will and determination to succeed – attributes which enabled him to withstand the physical privations of wasting (which alone killed or damaged other jockeys) and to accomplish what he did in the short time that he did.

In September 2000 Newmarket's town councillors and the Jockey Club decided to take steps to preserve Fred's grave after a thief tried to remove a written tribute from it and was only prevented from doing so by the cemetery custodian, Jim McBride. In order to make the grave a protected site, a plaque was affixed to it in February 2001 detailing Fred's very varied, but very short life and career.[37]

Notes

1.   *Newmarket Journal*, 8 October 1887
2.   Falmouth House Advertisement 1887
3–4.   *Newmarket Journal*, 15 October 1887
5.   *The Times*, 15 October 1887
6.   *The Times*, 19 October 1887
7.   *The Sporting Life*, 7 November 1889

8.   Humphris, Edith M, *The Life of Mathew Dawson*, pp.160–1
9.   *The Sporting Life*, 19 August 1898
10.   *Newmarket Journal*, 20 August 1898
11.   Sir Mark Prescott
12.   *The Times*, 11 December 1898
13.   *The Times*, 8/9 September 1908
14–15. *The Times*, 12 September 1922
16.   *The Sporting Life*, 12 September 1922
17–18. Mortimer, Roger, Onslow, Richard & Willet, Peter, *The Biographical Encyclopaedia of British Flat Racing*, pp.326–7
19.   *The Times*, 20 August 1908
20–21. Mortimer, Onslow & Willet, pp.102 & 103
22.   *The Times*, 13 March 1917
23.   *The Times*, 28 March 1917
24.   *The Times*, 4 June 1945
25.   *The Times*, 22 July 1945
26.   *The Times*, 27 April 1943
27.   Soldiers of the First World War Microfiche based at Liverpool Central Libraries
28.   *The Times*, 5 October 1957
29.   Details courtesy of Archivist at Waddesdon Manor, Buckinghamshire
30.   *The Times*, 5 October 1957; 16 June 1949
31.   *Woodford Times*, 22 October 1928; *The Sporting Life*, 28 October 1928; *Daily Telegraph*, 26 October 1928
32.   *The Sporting Life*, 19 August 1962
33.   Humphris, *The Life of Fred Archer*, pp.230–1
34–6. Details courtesy of Alex Tosetti
37.   Details courtesy of Eric Dunning

Fred Archer's Winners, 1869–86

The following is a list of all the races Fred Archer won between 1869 and 1886 in England, France and Ireland. The bulk of the information was compiled from various newspaper reports and then checked against the entries in Weatherby's Racing Calendars. Because of the sheer number of races, details have been kept to a minimum: the name of the horse, the name and date of the race and the location of the meeting. Please note that 'DH' refers to a 'Dead Heat', and 'WO' refers to a 'Walk Over' (when a jockey walks his horse over the finishing line when there is only one runner).

1869   MAID OF TRENT (Bangor Steeplechase) 1869 Exact date unknown
            (Bangor)

1870   ATHOL DAISY (Nursery Handicap) 28.09.1870 (Chesterfield)
            LINCOLN LASS (Tay Handicap) 14.10.1870 (Royal Caledonian Hunt &
            Perth)

1871   MR RC NAYLOR'S BC (Handicap Plate) 13.04.1871 (Newmarket)
            SKIFF (Kelston Claiming Plate) 16.05.1871 (Bath & Somerset)
            GRAVELTHORPE (Selling Race) 14.08.1871 (Rugby Hunt)

1872   CLASSIC (Wakefield Lawn Stakes) 09.04.1872 Dead heat (Northampton)
            LIVERPOOL (Handicap Sweepstakes/15 Sovereign) 16.04.1872
            (Newmarket)
            SYDMONTON (May Stakes) 30.04.1872 (Newmarket)
            INVADER (Handicap Plate/50 Sovereign) 01.05.1872 (Newmarket)
            INVADER (Handicap Plate) 02.05.1872 (Newmarket)
            TRAITOR (Handicap Plate) 03.05.1872 (Newmarket)
            ST WULFRITH (Handicap Plate) 16.05.1872 (Newmarket)

SUDELEY (Handicap Plate) 24.05.1872 (Harpenden)
CHORISTER (Windham Handicap) 19.06.1872 (Windsor)
NUDEL (Handicap Plate/50 Sovereign) 19.06.1872 (Windsor)
PRESIDENT (Wolsey Plate) 21.06.1872 (Hampton)
DERWENT (Newcastle Handicap) 27.06.1872 (Newcastle Upon Tyne)
BR F (Westmoreland Plate) 26.07.1872 (Stamford)
PERISTERA (Milton Stakes) 26.07.1872 (Stamford)
PELERIN (Berkshire Stakes) 29.08.1872 (Reading)
FANFARON (Thames Valley) 30.08.1872 (Reading)
MOSS ROSE (Berkshire Stakes) 05.09.1872 (Abingdon)
ALARIC (Ayr Gold Cup) 20.09.1872 (Ayr)
BLACK STOCKING (Free Handicap) 07.10.1872 (Newmarket)
SALVANOS (Cesarewitch) 08.10.1872 (Newmarket)
STRATHTAY (Handicap Sweepstakes) 10.10.1872 (Newmarket)
NIGHT STAR (Houghton Handicap) 26.10.1872 (Newmarket)
SIOUX (Liverpool Nursery Stakes) 06.11.1872 (Liverpool)
CINGALINA (Palatine Nursery) 07.11.1872 (Liverpool)
L'ORIENT (Innkeeper Plate) 16.11.1872 (Shrewsbury)
ANNIE BLAND (Donnington Handicap) 19.11.1872 (Warwickshire)
MEREVALE (Great Midlands Counties Handicap) 21.11.1872 (Warwickshire)

1873   WOODCUT (Aintree Handicap) 26.03.1873 (Liverpool)
WOODCUT (Handicap Plate/50 Sovereign) 27.03.1873 (Liverpool)
SYBARITE (Nottingham Spring Handicap) 31.03.1873 (Nottingham)
MR G NICHOLAS BC (Delapre Free Handicap) 01.04.1873 (Northampton)
MR RICHMOND'S BC (Sulby Plate) 01.04.1873 (Northampton)
SACKBUT (Handicap Plate) 05.04.1873 (Warwick)
MANNINGTON (Plate of 50 Sovereign) 18.04.1873 (Newmarket)
COBHAM (2000 Stakes Trial) 29.04.1873 (Newmarket)
BASSOON (Chesterfield Flying Stakes) 07.05.1873 (Chester)
JULIET (May Stakes) 08.05.1873 (Chester)
WEDMORE (Lewes Spring Handicap) 10.05.1873 (Lewes)
PHI (Craven Stakes) 20.05.1873 (York)
INGLEWOOD RANGER (Stamford Stakes) 21.05.1873 (York)
BOHEMIAN (Londesborough Cup) 21.05.1873 (York)
SIR JOHN (Salisbury Cup) 23.05.1873 (Salisbury)
MR BRUTON'S BF (South West Railway) 23.05.1873 (Salisbury)
LORD DARNLEY (Trial Stakes) 27.05.1873 (Epsom)
BLACKSTONE (Bentinck Plate) 28.05.1873 (Epsom)
CINGALINA (Trial Handicap Stakes) 03.06.1873 (Manchester)
BLUE BOY (50 Sovereign Plate) 03.06.1873 (Manchester)
WOODCUT (City Handicap Plate) 04.06.1873 (Manchester)
MERODACH (1st Class of Wokingham Stakes) 13.06.1873 (Ascot)
LIZ (Bushby Park Selling Handicap) 20.06.1873 (Hampton)
COURONNE DE FER (Stockbridge Cup) 26.06.1873 (Stockbridge)
ARCESILAUS (Sweepstakes/10 Sovereign) 02.07.1873 (Newmarket)
LA JEUNESSE (Sweepstakes/20 Sovereign) 02.07.1873 (Newmarket)
PRINCESS CHRISTIAN (Handicap Sweepstakes/10 Sovereign) 03.07.1873
   (Newmarket)

MYSTERY (Sweepstakes/10 Sovereign) 05.07.1873 (Newmarket)
CLARA (Stand Plate) 09.07.1873 (Liverpool)
TANGIBLE (Croxteth Handicap) 10.07.1873 (Liverpool)
FLORIST (Maghull Plate) 11.07.1873 (Liverpool)
GAMEHEN (Flying Stakes) 15.07.1873 (Sutton Park)
GENEVIEVE (2-Year-Old Stakes) 15.07.1873 (Sutton Park)
CHLORIS (Selling Handicap/5 Sovereign) 16.07.1873 (Sutton Park)
GAMEHEN (Sutton Handicap) 16.07.1873 (Sutton Park)
CHLORIS (Stewards Handicap) 17.07.1873 (Worcester)
BASSOON (Worcestershire Stakes) 17.07.1873 (Worcester)
MYSTERY (Severn Stakes) 17.07.1873 (Worcester)
GENEVIEVE (Croome Nursery) 17.07.1873 (Worcester)
MYSTERY (Ladies Plate) 18.07.1873 (Worcester)
COEUR DE LION (Peel Handicap) 22.07.187 (Huntingdon)
PEACOCK (Borough Members Handicap) 24.07.1873 (Stamford)
LILLIE BRIDGE (Wella Selling Plate/Handicap) 24.07.1873 (Stamford)
BLUE BEARD (Westmoreland Plate) 25.07.1873 (Stamford)
EAST ACTON (Handicap Plate) 30.07.1873 (Goodwood)
MILITADES (Marine Plate) 05.08.1873 (Brighton)
SIMON (Ovingdean Plate) 06.08.1873 (Brighton)
HERTFORD (Cleveland Cup) 13.08.1873 (Wolverhampton)
CARMELITE (Borough Members Handicap) 13.08.1873 (Wolverhampton)
MYSTERY (Town Selling Stakes) 14.08.1873 (Windsor)
MEDIATOR (Forest Handicap) 14.08.1873 (Windsor)
LOUISE (Windsor August Handicap) 15.08.1873 (Windsor)
WOODCOTE (Londesborough Cup) 20.08.1873 (York)
NON COMPOS (A Plate/50 Sovereign) 22.08.1873 (Croydon)
MAUD (Stand Plate) 23.08.1873 (Croydon)
STAMFORD (Godstow Selling Plate) 26.08.1873 (Oxford)
TINTERN (Port Meadow Plate) 26.08.1873 (Oxford)
EARLY MORN (Innkeeper Stakes) 27.08.1873 (Oxford)
MAUD (Innkeeper Plate) 29.08.1873 (Reading)
DECORATION (Whitley Stakes) 29.08.1873 (Reading)
EARLY MORN (Thames Valley) 29.08.1873 (Reading)
LOUISE (Leamington Stakes) 02.09.1873 (Warwick)
KING WILLIAM (Shorts Handicap) 02.09.1873 (Warwick)
LOUISE (Her Majesty's Plate) 02.09.1873 (Warwick)
GLOW WORM (County Handicap) 03.09.1873 (Warwick)
THE TESTER (Gloucestershire Stakes) 04.09.1873 (Gloucester)
BIGNONIA (Freemen's Selling Stakes) 05.09.1873 (Gloucester)
LA JEUNESSE (Fitzwilliam Stakes) 09.09.1873 (Doncaster)
TAPIOCA (Stand Stakes) 09.09.1873 (Doncaster)
THUNDERER (Rufford Abbey Stakes) 10.09.1873 (Doncaster)
THE TESTER (Cleveland Handicap) 11.09.1873 (Doncaster)
TYNE (Scurry Stakes) 12.09.1873 (Doncaster)
HONEYSUCKLE (Flying Handicap) 16.09.1873 (Sutton Park)
THERESA (Trial Stakes/5 Sovereign) 16.09.1873 (Sutton Park)
CARMELITE (Birmingham Handicap) 16.09.1873 (Sutton Park)
THERESA (Oscott Selling Stakes) 17.09.1873 (Sutton Park)

QUEENSBERRY (2-Year-Old Plate) 17.09.1873 (Sutton Park)
HONEYSUCKLE (Sutton Park Plate Handicap) 17.09.1873 (Sutton Park)
WILD AGGIE (Stamford Plate) 20.09.1873 (Manchester)
PIROUETTE (Stand Stakes) 20.09.1873 (Manchester)
ATLANTIC (Buckenham Post Produce Stakes) 23.09.1873 WO (Newmarket)
BEDFORD LODGE (Musselburgh Stakes) 03.10.1873 (Edinburgh)
JUVENIS (October Produce Stakes) 06.10.1873 (Newmarket)
MOROCCO (2 Horse Race) 06.10.1873 (Newmarket)
VANISH (Selling Handicap) 07.10.1873 (Newmarket)
DELAY (Heath Stakes) 07.10.1873 (Newmarket)
PERIWIG (Bedford Stakes) 08.10.1873 (Newmarket)
QUEENS HUNTSMAN (Sweepstakes/15 Sovereign) 10.10.1873
    (Newmarket)
TRENT (Juvenile Handicap) 10.10.1873 (Newmarket)
BONNIE LAD (Croydon Nursery Stakes) 15.10.1873 (Croydon)
CORAL (Nursery Selling Handicap) 16.10.1873 (Hereford)
STELLA (Newcourt Selling Handicap) 17.10.1873 (Hereford)
BIGNONIA (Juvenile Stakes) 17.10.1873 (Hereford)
ANTEROS (Ancaster Welter) 23.10.1873 (Newmarket)
SAGESSE (3rd Welter Handicap) 24.10.1873 (Newmarket)
EVERGREEN (2nd Cambridgeshire Handicap) 25.10.1873 (Newmarket)
WHITEBAIT (Nursery Plate) 28.10.1873 (Worcester)
NON COMPOS (Rous Selling Plate) 28.10.1873 (Worcester)
ANDRED (Great Tom Stakes) 29.10.1873 (Lincoln)
DART (Burton Stakes) 29.10.1873 (Lincoln)
ROGER (Haintain Plate) 31.10.1873 (Lincoln)
KINGCRAFT (Great Lancashire Handicap) 05.11.1873 (Liverpool)
SNOWDROP (Handicap Plate/50 Sovereign) 07.11.1873 (Liverpool)
BEECHNUT (County Members Plate) 12.11.1873 (Shrewsbury)
LUNAR ECLIPSE (Handicap Sweepstakes/5 Sovereign) 20.11.1873
    (Warwickshire Hunt)
SWEETNOTE (4th Nursery Handicap) 21.11.1873 (Warwickshire Hunt)
GLAUCUS (Bradgate Cup) 21.11.1873 (Warwickshire Hunt)

1874   NIGHTSTAR (Brocklesby Trial Plate) 24.04.1874 (Lincoln)
TOMAHAWK (Lincoln Handicap) 25.03.1874 (Lincoln)
PRECENTOR (Nottinghamshire Spring) 06.04.1874 (Nottingham)
LITTLE ROVER (Innkeeper Plate) 10.04.1874 (Croydon)
MYSTERY (Short Selling Stakes) 17.04.1874 (Windsor)
LORD ANNESLEY'S BC (Bretby Plate) 21.04.1874 (Newmarket)
ATLANTIC (Sweepstake/100 Sovereign) 21.04.1874 WO (Newmarket)
PEEPING TOM (Sweepstakes/100 Sovereign) 23.04.1874 (Newmarket)
LADY ROSEBERY (Westminster Stakes) 28.04.1874 DH (Epsom)
MILITADES (Heathcote Plate) 29.04.1874 (Epsom)
FLOWER OF DORSET (Prince of Wales Stakes) 29.04.1874 (Epsom)
DELAY (Prince of Wales Handicap) 05.05.1874 (Newmarket)
LADYLOVE (Batthyany Post Sweepstakes) 05.05.1874 (Newmarket)
MR CHAPLIN'S BLF (Welter Selling Stakes) 06.05.1874 (Newmarket)
ATLANTIC (2000 Guineas) 06.05.1874 (Newmarket)

LORD LONSDALE'S BF (City Stakes) 13.05.1874 (Chester)
ANDRED (Great Cheshire Stakes) 15.05.1874 (Chester)
BLACK KNIGHT (Earl of Chester's Stakes) 15.05.1874 (Chester)
HAREWOOD (Spring 2-Year-Old Selling Stakes) 19.05.1874 (Newmarket)
MR CHAPLIN'S BC (Selling Stakes) 20.05.1874 (Newmarket)
NASTURTIUM (Selling Stakes/10 Sovereign) 21.05.1874 (Newmarket)
CLARION (A Plate of 50 Sovereign) 26.05.1874 (Manchester)
CHRISTIANE (Trafford Park Selling Handicap) 27.05.1874 (Manchester)
INSTANTLY (City Handicap) 27.05.1874 (Manchester)
LADYLOVE (Woodcote Stakes) 02.06.1874 (Epsom)
QUEEN OF THE CHASE (Epsom Town Plate) 03.06.1874 (Epsom)
THUNDER (Epsom Cup) 05.06.1874 (Epsom)
ANCHORITE (Plate/50 Sovereign) 10.06.1874 (Newton)
BLUE RIBBON (Grand Stakes) 12.06.1874 (Newton)
CARPET SLIPPER (Lyme Park Stakes) 12.06.1874 (Newton)
MAYORESS (Warrington Handicap) 12.06.1874 (Newton)
LADYLOVE (1st Year 22nd Triennial Stakes) 17.06.1874 (Ascot)
GALOPIN (Fern Hill Stakes) 17.06.1874 (Ascot)
CAMBYSES (2nd Year 11th New Biennial Stakes) 18.06.1874 (Ascot)
LADYLOVE (1st Year of 12th New Biennial Stakes) 18.06.1874 (Ascot)
MYSTERY (Racing Stakes) 23.06.1874 (Windsor)
WHITEBAIT (Eton Handicap) 23.06.1874 (Windsor)
DARLINGTON (Manor 2 Year Stakes) 23.06.1874 (Windsor)
INDEPENDENCE (Thames Handicap) 23.06.1874 (Windsor)
TRANQUILLITY (Cardinal Wolsey Handicap) 26.06.1874 (Hampton)
MOATLANDS (Selling Plate/50 Sovereign) 03.07.1874 (Stockbridge)
LADYLOVE (Filly Stakes) 07.07.1874 (Newmarket)
DREADNOUGHT (Gladiateur Stakes) 07.07.1874 (Newmarket)
LA JEUNESSE (2nd Welter Handicap) 08.07.1874 (Newmarket)
TANKERVILLE (Selling Stakes/10 Sovereign) 09.07.1874 (Newmarket)
MR H BRUCE'S BC (Stetchworth Selling Stakes) 10.07.1874 (Newmarket)
YORKSHIRE BRIDE (Stetchworth Stakes) 10.07.1874 (Newmarket)
MAYORESS (Bentinck Handicap) 16.07.1874 (Liverpool)
BIRBECK (Kimbolton Cup) 21.07.1874 (Huntingdon)
GLADIOLA (Corporation Stakes) 22.07.1874 (Huntingdon)
ROYALIST (Kingsbury and Middlesex Handicap) 24.07.1874 (Kingsbury)
MODENA (Stewards Cup) 28.07.1874 (Goodwood)
ST AGATHA (Maiden Stakes) 29.07.1874 (Goodwood)
YORKSHIRE BRIDE (Sweepstakes/200 Sovereign) 30.07.1874 (Goodwood)
DREADNOUGHT (1st Year Bentinck Members Stakes) 30.07.1874
    (Goodwood)
BANSHEE (Selling Handicap Plate) 07.08.1874 (Lewes)
TRAPPIST (Priory Stakes) 07.08.1874 (Lewes)
LITTLE JIM (Town Plate) 08.08.1874 (Lewes)
THE KNIGHT (Helter Skelter Welter Stakes) 08.08.1874 (Lewes)
HIPPIAS (Wolverhampton Stakes) 11.08.1874 (Wolverhampton)
SIR E BUCKLEY'S CHF (Royal Stakes) 12.08.1874 (Wolverhampton)
MISS CLUMBER (Holyoake Stakes) 12.08.1874 (Wolverhampton)
FLOWER OF THE VALE (Selling Stakes/5 Sovereign) 14.08.1874 (Windsor)

SILURIA (Ladies Handicap) 19.08.1874 (Oxford)
SANS SOUCI (Muswell Hill) 20.08.1874 (Croydon)
LA JEUNESSE (Lonsdale Plate Handicap) 25.08.1874 DH (York)
CATACLYSM (Convivial Stakes) 25.08.1874 (York)
EARLY MORN (Thames Valley) 28.08.1874 (Reading)
OCEANIA (Forbury Stakes) 28.08.1874 (Reading)
ETHEL BLAIR (2-Year-Old Plate) 02.09.1874 (Sutton Park)
NON COMPOS (Selling Handicap Plate) 02.09.1874 (Sutton Park)
RHAPSODY (Sutton Park Handicap Plate) 02.09.1874 (Sutton Park)
BLUE RIBBON (Handicap Plate/50 Sovereign) 02.09.1874 (Sutton Park)
OCEANIA (Irwell Stakes) 03.09.1874 (Manchester)
MAYORESS (Scurry Stakes) 04.09.1874 (Manchester)
VISCOUNTESS (Juvenile Stakes) 04.09.1874 (Manchester)
ROUEN (Chetwynd Welter Cup) 05.09.1874 (Manchester)
MAYORESS (Stamford Handicap Plate) 05.09.1874 (Manchester)
CELIBACY (Woodcote Handicap Plate) 08.09.1874 (Warwick)
ANINA (Maiden Plate) 09.09.1874 (Warwick)
HIPPIAS (County Handicap) 09.09.1874 (Warwick)
ENGLISHMAN (Hereford Stakes) 10.09.1874 (Hereford)
RHAPSODIST (Juvenile Stakes) 11.09.1874 (Hereford)
YORKSHIRE BRIDE (Post Match 200 Sovereign) 15.09.1874 (Doncaster)
DUKEDOM (Doncaster Plate) 15.09.1874 (Doncaster)
LITTLE BILL (Stand Stakes) 15.09.1874 (Doncaster)
MAYORESS (Rufford Abbey Stakes) 16.09.1874 (Doncaster)
INEZ (Milton Stakes) 16.09.1874 (Doncaster)
CARNELLON (Eglinton Stakes) 17.09.1874 (Doncaster)
SELBORNE (Scurry Stakes) 18.09.1874 (Doncaster)
TRAPPIST (Fitzhardinge Stakes) 22.09.1874 (Bristol)
NUTBROWN (Selling Stakes) 22.09.1874 (Bristol)
TECOMA (Ashton Stakes) 22.09.1874 (Bristol)
MODENA (West of England Handicap) 22.09.1874 (Bristol)
ST AGATHA (Somerset Stakes) 23.09.1874 (Bristol)
LAURIER (Totterdown Stakes) 23.09.1874 (Bristol)
DULWICH (Kilburn Handicap Plate) 25.09.1874 (Hendon)
COCETTE (Anglesey Cup) 25.09.1874 (Hendon)
STROLLER (Selling Stakes) 30.09.1874 (Newmarket)
BLUE RIBBON (City Member Plate) 06.10.1874 (Lichfield)
POSTHUMA (County Members Plate Handicap) 06.10.1874 (Lichfield)
JACK O LANTERN (All Aged Selling Plate) 07.10.1874 (Lichfield)
INSTANTLY (Lichfield Cup) 07.10.1874 (Lichfield)
BLOOMFIELD (County Cup) 08.10.1874 (Leicester)
DUKEDOM (Leicestershire Handicap) 08.10.1874 (Leicester)
AGAR (Nursery Plate) 08.10.1874 (Leicester)
SELBORNE (Curzon Nursery Handicap) 09.10.1874 (Leicester)
DUKEDOM (County Members Handicap 10 Sovereign) 09.10.1874
    (Leicester)
AGAR (Selling Race) 09.10.1874 (Leicester)
MIMULUS (Ladies Selling Stakes) 09.10.1874 (Leicester)
PRINCE ARTHUR (A Plate 100 Sovereign) 12.10.1874 (Newmarket)

LORD FALMOUTH'S BC (Clearwell Stakes) 13.10.1874 (Newmarket)
PRINCE ARTHUR (Bedford Stakes) 14.10.1874 WO (Newmarket)
BEACON (Selling Nursery) 15.10.1874 (Newmarket)
ANINA (Packington Nursery Plate) 20.10.1874 (Coventry)
AGAR (Craven 2-Year-Old Selling Stakes) 21.10.1874 (Coventry)
BIGNONIA (City Handicap) 23.10.1874 (Gloucester)
JACK O LANTERN (Freeman's Selling Stakes) 23.10.1874 DH (Gloucester)
THUNDER (Trial Stakes) 26.10.1874 (Newmarket)
LADY ROSEBERY (All Aged Trial Stakes) 27.10.1874 (Newmarket)
CATACLYSM (Home Bred Produce Stakes) 27.10.1874 (Newmarket)
GALOPIN (Sweepstake) 28.10.1874 WO (Newmarket)
SELBORNE (Selling Stakes) 28.10.1874 (Newmarket)
DREADNOUGHT (Glasgow Stakes) 28.10.1874 (Newmarket)
SPINAWAY (Home Bred Sweepstakes) 29.10.1874 (Newmarket)
GATERLEY BELL (Post Match/2-Year-Old colts) 30.10.1874 (Newmarket)
ESMERELDA (Selling Nursery) 30.10.1874 (Newmarket)
SELBORNE (Selling Stakes) 31.10.1874 (Newmarket)
CAPELLA (Rous Selling) 03.11.1874 (Worcester)
ANINA (Nursery Plate) 03.11.1874 (Worcester)
DAY DREAM (Stewards Cup) 10.11.1874 (Liverpool)
GRAND DUCHESS (Selling Nursery Stakes Handicap) 10.11.1874
    (Liverpool)
TRAPPIST (Knowsley Nursery Stakes) 10.11.1874 (Liverpool)
SELBORNE (2 Horse Race) 10.11.1874 (Liverpool)
SELBORNE (Juvenile Plate) 11.11.1874 (Liverpool)
POSTHUMA (Croxteth Cup Handicap) 11.11.1874 (Liverpool)
BLUE BULL (Downe Nursery Handicap) 12.11.1874 (Liverpool)
SPECTATOR (Great Lancashire Handicap) 12.11.1874 (Liverpool)
MACADAM (Groby Cup) 17.11.1874 (Shrewsbury)
MODENA (Shobdon Cup) 19.11.1874 (Shrewsbury)
BENEDICTINE (Forester Plate/Handicap) 20.11.1874 (Shrewsbury)
ASTRAFIAMMANTE (Wrekin Stakes) 20.11.1874 (Shrewsbury)
DAY DREAM (Donnington Handicap) 24.11.1874 (Warwick)
FLEURANGE (Selling Nursery) 24.11.1874 (Warwick)
SILURIA (Handicap Sweepstakes) 26.11.1874 (Warwick)
DAY DREAM (Bradgate Cup) 27.11.1874 (Warwick)

1875   BELLA (Thathwell Stakes) 15.03.1875 (Lincoln)
PATRICIA (Seaforth Plate) 19.03.1875 (Lincoln)
ROUEN (Newcastle Handicap) 24.03.1875 (Nottingham)
NOVAR (Wakefield Lawn Plate) 30.03.1875 (Northampton)
FRAULEIN (St Liz Handicap) 30.03.1875 (Northampton)
BELLA (Althorp Park Stakes) 30.03.1875 (Northampton)
TEACHER (Delapre Welter Handicap) 31.03.1875 (Northampton)
PEEPING TOM (Great Northamptonshire Stakes) 31.03.1875 (Northampton)
PATTY (Racing Stakes) 06.04.1875 (Warwick)
THUNDER (Great Warwickshire Handicap) 07.04.1875 (Warwick)
MEAD (The St George's Stakes) 09.04.1875 (Windsor)
FLINTLOCK (Welter Handicap Plate) 10.04.1875 (Windsor)

GARTERLEY BELL (40th Riddlesworth Post Stakes) 13.04.1875
  (Newmarket)
LITTLE BOY BLUE (Selling Stakes) 14.04.1875 WO (Newmarket)
DELAY (Trial Handicap) 15.04.1875 (Newmarket)
PRINCE ARTHUR (Sweepstakes) 15.04.1875 (Newmarket)
DUKE OF RUTLAND (Bennington Stakes) 16.04.1875 (Newmarket)
PACHA (Handicap Plate) 16.04.1875 (Newmarket)
PEEPING TOM (Newmarket International Free Handicap) 16.04.1875
  (Newmarket)
MR DAWSON'S BC (Selling Stakes) 27.04.1875 (Newmarket)
LAIRD OF GLENORCHY (Welter Selling Stakes) 28.04.1875 (Newmarket)
LORD FALMOUTH'S BC (Newmarket Stakes) 30.04.1875 (Newmarket)
SPINAWAY (1000 Guineas) 30.04.1875 (Newmarket)
SPECTATOR (Grosvenor Stakes) 04.05.1875 (Chester)
BELLA (Mostyn Stakes) 04.05.1875 (Chester)
OUTLAW (Belgrave Cup) 04.05.1875 (Chester)
DUKE OF RUTLAND (Her Majesty's Plate) 06.05.1875 (Chester)
BELLA (Badminton Stakes) 06.05.1875 (Chester)
THUNDER (Great Cheshire Stakes Handicap) 07.05.1875 (Chester)
MAYORESS (Wilton Handicap) 07.05.1875 (Chester)
HARMONIDES (Ditch Mile Handicap) 11.05.1875 (Newmarket)
TRIPAWAY (2 Horse Race) 12.05.1875 (Newmarket)
LORD AYLESBURY'S C (Selling Stakes) 12.05.1875 (Newmarket)
LORD CALTHORPE'S CF (Selling Stakes) 13.05.1875 (Newmarket)
TRIPAWAY (4-Year-Olds Race) 13.05.1875 (Newmarket)
TORPEDO (2-Year-Old Stakes) 14.05.1875 (Lewes)
BEANSTALK (Welter Handicap Plate) 15.05.1875 (Lewes)
WATER LILY (Copeland Stakes) 18.05.1875 (Manchester)
HARRY BLUFF (Palantine Welter Handicap) 18.05.1875 (Manchester)
THE SHAH (Derby Welter Handicap Plate) 19.05.1875 (Manchester)
TEARS (Trafford Park Stakes Selling Handicap) 19.05.1875 (Manchester)
MR E ETCHE'S BG (Maiden Plate) 20.05.1875 (Manchester)
HESPER (Maiden Plate) 25.05.1875 (Epsom)
CROSSBOW (Mickelham Stakes) 27.05.1875 (Epsom)
SPINAWAY (Oaks) 28.05.1875 (Epsom)
MODENA (Epsom Cup Handicap) 28.05.1875 (Epsom)
SPEEDWELL (Muswell Hill Handicap) 02.06.1875 (Alexandra Park)
DUKEDOM (Alexandra Handicap) 02.06.1875 (Alexandra Park)
ANCHORITE (Great Newton Cup Handicap) 03.06.1875 (Newton)
TROJAN (St Helen's Purse) 03.06.1875 (Newton)
MR BEADMAN'S BLC (Juvenile Plate) 04.06.1875 (Croydon)
PARADOXE (Prix Des Pavillons) 06.06.1875 (Paris)
LADYLOVE (22nd Triennial Stakes) 11.06.1875 (Ascot)
BELLA (Royal Stakes) 15.06.1875 (Windsor)
WHITEBAIT (Eton Handicap) 15.06.1875 (Windsor)
BULL'S EYE (Surrey and Middlesex Stakes Handicap) 17.06.1875
  (Hampton)
BANSHEE (Bushy Park Selling Handicap) 18.06.1875 (Hampton)
VASCO DI GAMBA (Railway Stakes) 18.06.1875 (Hampton)

MAID OF THE MILL (Hurstbourne Welter Plate) 22.06.1875 (Odiham)
CAPT PIGOTT'S BRF (Dogmersfield Park Stakes) 22.06.1875 (Odiham)
BLOOMFIELD (Odiham Handicap) 22.06.1875 (Odiham)
LADY MOLLY (Grand Stand Selling Stakes) 01.07.1875 (Odiham)
OWTON (Newcastle Handicap) 01.07.1875 (Newcastle Upon Tyne)
LYTTON (Selling High Welter Plate) 03.07.1875 (Sandown Park)
SKYLARK (Gladiateur Stakes) 06.07.1875 (Newmarket)
PRINCE ARTHUR (1st Welter Handicap) 06.07.1875 (Newmarket)
WORTHLESS (Town Plate) 07.07.1875 (Newmarket)
MOUSQUETAIRE (Maiden Plate) 07.07.1875 (Newmarket)
SKYLARK (Chesterfield Stakes) 08.07.1875 (Newmarket)
FARNESE (Stetchford Stakes) 09.07.1875 (Newmarket)
EUONYMA (Selling Stakes) 09.07.1875 (Newmarket)
BROTHER TO RYSHWORTH (Selling Stakes) 09.07.1875 (Newmarket)
BELLA (Trial Stakes) 13.07.1875 (Nottingham)
QUAIL (Nottinghamshire Handicap) 13.07.1875 (Nottingham)
FAIRY (Selling Stakes) 13.07.1875 (Nottingham)
JULIA PEACHAM (1st year 7th Biennial Stakes) 14.07.1875 (Nottingham)
VERDANT GREEN (Maghull Stakes) 16.07.1875 (Liverpool)
PIER LIGHT (Stanley Stakes) 16.07.1875 (Liverpool)
DAISY (Juvenile Plate) 22.07.1875 (Kingsbury)
FARNESE (Ham Stakes) 27.07.1875 (Goodwood)
TRAPPIST (The Steward's Cup) 27.07.1875 (Goodwood)
SPINAWAY (Gratwicke Stakes) 27.07.1875 WO (Goodwood)
DREADNOUGHT (2nd Year 24th Bentinck Members Stakes) 29.07.1875
　　(Goodwood)
FARNESE (Prince of Wales Stakes) 29.07.1875 (Goodwood)
SPINAWAY (Nassau Stakes) 30.07.1875 (Goodwood)
GLENDINNING (2 Horse Race) 30.07.1875 (Goodwood)
WOODCOCK (Bristol Plate) 03.08.1875 (Brighton)
MODENA (Marine Stakes) 03.08.1875 (Brighton)
ROUGE BONNET (Preston Stakes) 04.08.1875 (Brighton)
MODENA (Sussex Welter Handicap) 04.08.1875 (Brighton)
BASHFUL (Selling Handicap) 06.08.1875 (Lewes)
WORCESTER (Nevill Stakes) 07.08.1875 (Lewes)
MRS GAMP (Juvenile Stakes) 17.08.1875 (Alexandra Park)
BONNYBROOK (100 Sovereign Plate) 17.08.1875 (Alexandra Park)
BANSHEE (Campsbourne Plate) 17.08.1875 (Alexandra Park)
MARTINI (Alexandra Plate) 18.08.1875 (Alexandra Park)
MR WF WOOD'S CHF (Crouch Hill Stakes) 18.08.1875 (Alexandra Park)
TANKERVILLE (Highgate Welter Handicap) 18.08.1875 (Alexandra Park)
SEAMAN (County Members Welter Handicap) 19.08.1875 (Oxford)
PEINE DE COEUR (Stand Selling Plate) 20.08.1875 (Oxford)
SPINAWAY (Yorkshire Oaks) 24.08.1875 (York)
SPINAWAY (York Cup) 26.08.1875 (York)
BELLA (Yare 2-Year-Old Stakes) 01.09.1875 (York)
MEMORY (Innkeeper's Handicap Plate) 01.09.1875 (York)
MABEL (2-Year-Old Stakes) 02.09.1875 (Canterbury)
OAT CAKE (Welter Selling Plate) 08.09.1875 (Warwick)

HIPPIAS (Wolverhampton Stakes Handicap) 09.09.1875 (Wolverhampton)
PRINCE IMPERIAL (The Royal Stakes) 09.09.1875 (Wolverhampton)
BLUE BULL (Wrottesley Stakes) 10.09.1875 (Wolverhampton)
BELLA (Chillington Stakes) 10.09.1875 (Wolverhampton)
EQUANIMITY (Doncaster Plate) 14.09.1875 (Doncaster)
FARNESE (Champagne Stakes) 14.09.1875 (Doncaster)
FETTERLOCK (Match for 200 Sovereign) 14.09.1875 (Doncaster)
TRAPPIST (Ellington Stakes) 16.09.1875 (Doncaster)
PLAYTHING (Juvenile Stakes) 16.09.1875 (Doncaster)
FARNESE (Sweepstakes/10 Sovereign) 16.09.1875 (Doncaster)
SPINAWAY (Doncaster Stakes) 17.09.1875 (Doncaster)
ARQUES (Prix De Sablonville/Selling Race) 19.09.1875 (France)
HIPPIAS (Tradesmen's Plate Handicap) 21.09.1875 (Derby)
PILGRIM (Chatsworth Welter Handicap) 21.09.1875 (Derby)
BERRYFIELD (Rawdon Handicap) 22.09.1875 (Derby)
ENGLISHMAN (Monmouthshire Stakes) 24.09.1875 (Monmouth)
THE FLIRT (Hopeful Stakes) 28.09.1875 (Newmarket)
FARNESE (Buckingham Stakes) 28.09.1875 WO (Newmarket)
SPINAWAY (2nd Year 27th Triennial Produce Stakes) 29.09.1875
    (Newmarket)
CAMBYSES (2nd Welter Handicap) 30.09.1875 (Newmarket)
SKYLARK (Rutland Stakes) 30.09.1875 (Newmarket)
MR WINKLE (Handicap Sweepstakes/10 Sovereign) 01.10.1875
    (Newmarket)
PRINCE ARTHUR (St Leger) 01.10.1875 (Newmarket)
BLACK PRINCE (Anglesey Welter Plate) 05.10.1875 (Lichfield)
CREAM CHEESE (Grendon Nusery Plate) 06.10.1875 (Lichfield)
INSTANTLY (Lichfield Cup) 06.10.1875 (Lichfield)
BARDOLPH (Nursery Plate Handicap) 07.10.1875 (Leicester)
MR WINKLE (Licensed Victuallers Welter Handicap) 08.10.1875
    (Leicester)
JULIAN (1st Welter Handicap) 11.10.1875 (Newmarket)
TRAPPIST (Burwell Stakes) 11.10.1875 (Newmarket)
FARNESE (October Produce Stakes) 11.10.1875 WO (Newmarket)
ELEUSIS (Match/3-Year-Olds) 12.10.1875 (Newmarket)
FARNESE (Clearwell Stakes) 12.10.1875 (Newmarket)
SPINAWAY (Royal Stakes) 12.10.1875 (Newmarket)
SPINAWAY (Newmarket Oaks) 14.10.1875 (Newmarket)
SKYLARK (Post Sweepstakes) 14.10.1875 (Newmarket)
MODENA (Autumn Handicap) 14.10.1875 (Newmarket)
PASQUIN (Match 200 Sovereign) 15.10.1875 (Newmarket)
BULLY (County Welter Handicap Plate) 19.10.1875 (Coventry)
ANCHORITE (Coventry Handicap) 19.10.1875 (Coventry)
PEINE DE COEUR (City Selling Stakes) 19.10.1875 (Coventry)
PATRICIA (2-Year-Old Selling Race) 21.10.1875 (Cheltenham)
SHIPMATE (Cotswold Cup Handicap) 21.10.1875 (Cheltenham)
ENGLISHMAN (Cheltenham Handicap) 22.10.1875 (Cheltenham)
OXONION (All Aged Trial Stakes) 26.10.1875 (Newmarket)
FETTERLOCK (Home Bred Foal Stakes) 27.10.1875 (Newmarket)

LADY OF THE LAKE (Ancaster Welter Handicap Plate) 28.10.1875
   (Newmarket)
GLYN (Selling Stakes) 29.10.1875 (Newmarket)
PASQUIN (Gautby Nursery Plate Handicap) 03.11.1875 (Lincoln)
HARRY BLUFF (Welter Plate Handicap) 04.11.1875 (Lincoln)
MEMORY (Westmoreland Welter Plate) 09.11.1875 (Liverpool)
FOOTSTEP (Knowsley Nursery Stakes) 09.11.1875 (Liverpool)
MODENA (Stewards Cup) 09.11.1875 (Liverpool)
TETRARCH (Gerard Stakes) 10.11.1875 (Liverpool)
INSTANTLY (Croxteth Cup) 10.11.1875 (Liverpool)
ACTIVITY (Liverpool Autumn Cup) 11.11.1875 (Liverpool)
TETRARCH (Fazakerley Stakes) 11.11.1875 (Liverpool)
PACHA (Thursday Stakes) 11.11.1875 (Liverpool)
BLUE BELLE (Jolliffe 2-Year-Old Stakes) 12.11.1875 (Liverpool)
INSTANTLY (Cleveland Handicap) 16.11.1875 (Shrewsbury)
PILGRIM (Welter Handicap) 23.11.1875 (Warwick)
SUZETTE (Racing Stakes) 23.11.1875 (Warwick)
SIR ARTHUR (Selling Welter Plate/50 Sovereign) 23.11.1875 (Warwick)
SIR ARTHUR (Handicap/5 Sovereign) 23.11.1875 (Warwick)
PROFESSOR (100 Sovereign Plate) 25.11.1875 (Warwick)
SIR ARTHUR (Selling Race) 26.11.1875 (Warwick)

1876   LADY OF THE LEA (Molyneux 2-Year-Old Stakes) 23.03.1876 (Liverpool)
CAT'S EYE (Litherland Handicap Plate) 23.03.1876 (Liverpool)
SEGURA (March Sale Stakes) 24.03.1876 (Liverpool)
LADY PATRICIA (Liverpool Spring Cup Handicap) 25.03.1876 (Liverpool)
STROUD (Auction Stakes) 29.03.1876 (Northampton)
LORD LYON (Racing Stakes) 30.03.1876 (Warwick)
MISS CROFT (Selling Race) 01.04.1876 (Warwick)
CHANCE (Trial Stakes) 03.04.1876 (Wolverhampton)
QUIETUDE (Wrottesley Plate) 03.04.1876 (Wolverhampton)
MISS CROFT (Scurry Stakes/10 Sovereign) 03.04.1876 (Wolverhampton)
MR T STEVENS' BF (The Weston Plate) 04.04.1876 (Wolverhampton)
CHANCE (Stamford Handicap) 04.04.1876 (Wolverhampton)
INSTEP (The Cup Handicap) 05.04.1876 (Croxton Park)
ARISTOCRAT (Surly Hall Welter Handicap) 07.04.1876 (Windsor)
BERRYFIELD (Nottingham Spring Handicap) 11.04.1876 (Nottingham)
COLLIER (Thurgarton Priory Selling Stakes) 11.04.1876 (Nottingham)
COLLIER (Bulwell Hall Plate Handicap) 12.04.1876 (Nottingham)
SKYLARK (1st Year of 18th New Biennial Stakes) 18.04.1876 (Newmarket)
CAESARION (Maiden Plate) 19.04.1876 (Newmarket)
BRIGG BOY (2 Horse Race) 20.04.1876 (Newmarket)
MR WINKLE (Handicap Plate) 20.04.1876 (Newmarket)
THUNDER (City and Suburban Handicap) 25.04.1876 (Epsom)
VANGUARD (One Mile Race) 28.04.1876 (Epsom)
THUNDER (2000 Guineas) 02.05.1876 (Newmarket)
SKYLARK (Coffee Room Stakes) 02.05.1876 WO (Newmarket)
DOMIDUCA (Selling Stakes) 02.05.1876 (Newmarket)
MR WINKLE (Handicap Plate/100 Sovereign) 04.05.1876 (Newmarket)

SKYLARK (Newmarket Stakes) 05.05.1876 (Newmarket)
PROFESSOR (Wynnstay Welter Handicap) 09.05.1876 (Chester)
LADY PATRICIA (Belgrave Cup) 09.05.1876 (Chester)
EUTERPE (Dee Stand Cup) 10.05.1876 (Chester)
PILGRIM (Combermere Stakes/Handicap) 11.05.1876 WO (Chester)
MR WINKLE (Cestrian Handicap) 11.05.1876 (Chester)
CRADLE (8th Beaufort Biennial Stakes) 12.05.1876 (Chester)
HIPPIAS (Wirral Welter Plate) 12.05.1876 (Chester)
BEAUTY BRIGHT (Wynnstay 2-Year-Old Stakes) 12.05.1876 (Chester)
THUNDER (Great Cheshire Stakes) 12.05.1876 (Chester)
REREDOS (Ladies Purse) 12.05.1876 (Chester)
LADY OF THE LEA (Spring 2-Year-Old Stakes) 16.05.1876 (Newmarket)
PALM FLOWER (Maiden Plate) 16.05.1876 (Newmarket)
MAVIS (2nd Spring 2-Year-Old Stakes) 18.05.1876 (Newmarket)
DIANA (Selling Stakes) 18.05.1876 (Newmarket)
MARIOSCH (The Tyro Stakes) 20.05.1876 (Lewes)
BLOOMFIELD (Harpenden Handicap) 26.05.1876 (Harpenden)
KITTY SPRIGHTLY (Harpenden 2-Year-Old Stakes) 26.05.1876 (Harpenden)
THUNDER (Craven Stakes) 30.05.1876 (Epsom)
DIANA (Epsom Manor Stakes) 31.05.1876 (Epsom)
TRAPPIST (Paddock Stakes) 01.06.1876 (Epsom)
LADY PATRICIA (De Trafford Cup) 06.06.1876 (Manchester)
MYSTERY (Pendleton Stakes) 06.06.1876 (Manchester)
BURGOMASTER (Buckley Plate) 07.06.1876 (Manchester)
INSTANTLY (Stewards Handicap Plate) 08.06.1876 (Manchester)
LADY RONALD (Beaufort Stakes) 08.06.1876 (Manchester)
MR WINKLE (Wilton Handicap) 08.06.1876 (Manchester)
EUXINE (Grand Stakes Welter Handicap Plate) 08.06.1876 (Manchester)
SWEETNOTE (Consolation Welter Handicap) 09.06.1876 (Manchester)
SIESTA (Winchcombe Hill Stakes) 10.06.1876 (Alexandra Park)
BLUE RIBAND (Maiden Plate) 13.06.1876 (Ascot)
THUNDER (Gold Vase) 13.06.1876 (Epsom)
JESTER (Visitors Plate) 14.06.1876 (Epsom)
GREAT TOM (St James' Palace Stakes) 15.06.1876 DH (Epsom)
QUIETUDE (Manor 2-Year-Old) 20.06.1876 (Windsor)
MOUSQUETAIRE (Thames Handicap) 20.06.1876 (Windsor)
ROSY CROSS (Royal Stakes) 20.06.1876 (Windsor)
PILGRIM (Manor Cup/Handicap) 21.06.1876 (Newton)
CHESTER (Alexandra Plate) 23.06.1876 (Hampton)
XANTHUS (Corporation Plate Handicap) 28.06.1876 DH (Newcastle Upon
    Tyne)
MR WINKLE (Johnstone Plate) 29.06.1876 (Stockbridge)
SPARTACUS (Andover Stakes) 29.06.1876 (Stockbridge)
TOWN CRIER (Anglesey Plate Handicap) 30.06.1876 (Stockbridge)
KITTY SPRIGHTLY (Exeter Stakes) 05.07.1876 DH (Newmarket)
SKYLARK (Midsummer Stakes) 05.07.1876 WO (Newmarket)
CRANN TAIR (Maiden Plate) 05.07.1876 (Newmarket)
MAVIS (Match/2-Year-Olds) 06.07.1876 (Newmarket)
CONJUROR (Selling Plate) 07.07.1876 (Newmarket)

LADY GOLIGHTLY (Stetchworth Stakes) 07.07.1876 (Newmarket)
BLUE RIBAND (Mersey Stakes) 12.07.1876 DH (Newmarket)
BURGOMASTER (Liver Stakes) 12.07.1876 (Newmarket)
SINECURE (Bentinck Plate) 13.07.1876 (Newmarket)
BARONET (Sefton Stakes) 13.07.1876 (Newmarket)
SPARTACUS (Skelmersdale Plate) 13.07.1876 (Newmarket)
LADY PATRICIA (Aintree Cup) 14.07.1876 WO (Newmarket)
CINDERELLA (Warren Nursery Stakes) 15.07.1876 (Sandown Park)
MAYFAIR (Selling High Weight Plate) 15.07.1876 (Sandown Park)
LADY HONEY (Surrey Juvenile Stakes) 15.07.1876 (Sandown Park)
MYSTERY (Fitzwilliam Stakes) 18.07.1876 (Huntingdon)
DIANA (Cambridge 2-Year-Old Stakes) 18.07.1876 (Huntingdon)
STROLLER (Selling Stakes) 18.07.1876 (Huntingdon)
FAIRY KING (Huntingdonshire Stakes) 19.07.1876 (Sheffield)
CAT'S EYE (Great West Riding Handicap) 20.07.1876 (Pontefract)
SILVIO (Ham Stakes) 25.07.1876 (Goodwood)
ORLEANS (Maiden Stakes) 26.07.1876 (Goodwood)
MONARCHUS (Prince of Wales Stakes) 27.07.1876 (Goodwood)
MOUSQUETAIRE (Chichester Stakes) 27.07.1876 (Goodwood)
YOUNG ROSCIUS (1st Year/26th Bentinck Members Stakes) 27.07.1876
    (Goodwood)
SKYLARK (2nd/25th Bentinck Members Stakes) 27.07.1876 (Goodwood)
LADY GOLIGHTLY (Sweepstakes/200 Sovereign) 27.07.1876 (Goodwood)
RED CROSS KNIGHT (Sweepstakes 50 Sovereign) 27.07.1876
ORLEANS (Strafford Stakes) 28.07.1876 (Goodwood)
CRANN TAIR (Nursery Stakes) 28.07.1876 (Goodwood)
CHARON (March Stakes) 28.07.1876 (Goodwood)
MYSTERY (Pavilion Stakes) 02.08.1876 (Brighton)
POLLY PERKINS (Sweepstakes 10 Sovereign) 03.08.1876 (Brighton)
SIR HUGH (Shirley Plate) 07.08.1876 (Croydon)
LORD COLNEY (Selling Handicap Plate/50 Sovereign) 07.08.1876 (Croydon)
SABRINA (Russley Stakes) 08.08.1876 (Lambourn)
MISS CROFT (Visitors Stakes) 08.08.1876 (Lambourn)
ROSY CROSS (Clewer Stakes) 10.08.1876 (Windsor)
STROLLER (Scurry Stakes) 11.08.1876 (Windsor)
ROSY CROSS (Park Stakes) 11.08.1876 (Windsor)
SIESTA (Selling Stakes) 11.08.1876 (Windsor)
DIANA (Harewood Stakes) 16.08.1876 (Stockton)
DECEIT (County Members Welter Plate) 17.08.1876 (Oxford)
ST ANTHONY (Stand Selling Plate) 18.08.1876 (Oxford)
SUNRAY (Convivial Produce Stakes) 22.08.1876 (York)
LILIAN (Great Ebor Handicap Stakes) 23.08.1876 (York)
STROLLER (Member Stakes) 23.08.1876 (York)
WOOD ANEMONE (1st Year of the 21st North of England Biennial Stakes)
    23.08.1876 (York)
THUNDER (Her Majesty's Plate) 23.08.1876 (York)
MALTA (Match/2-Year-Olds) 24.08.1876 (York)
STROLLER (Rufford Abbey Stakes) 24.08.1876 (York)
COPEL (Bracebridge Plate) 30.08.1876 (Sutton Park)

DELIA (2-Year-Old Plate) 30.08.1876 (Sutton Park)
ESMERELDA (Oscott Welter Handicap Plate) 30.08.1876 (Sutton Park)
COL. FOREST BC (Staffordshire Nursery Stakes) 31.08.1876
    (Wolverhampton)
MAID OF SARAGOSA (Royal Stakes) 31.08.1876 (Wolverhampton)
DECEIT (Borough Members Welter Plate) 01.09.1876 (Wolverhampton)
EUXINE (Enville Welter Handicap) 01.09.1876 (Wolverhampton)
RIVULET (Racing Stakes) 05.09.1876 (Wolverhampton)
STYX (Trial Stakes) 07.09.1876 DH (Edinburgh)
BASHFUL (Stewards Handicap) 07.09.1876 (Edinburgh)
BASHFUL (Innkeeper Selling Handicap) 08.09.1876 (Edinburgh)
LADY GOLIGHTLY (Champagne Stakes) 12.09.1876 (Doncaster)
TRAPPIST (Clumber Plate) 12.09.1876 WO (Doncaster)
KALEIDOSCOPE (Corporation Stakes Handicap) 13.09.1876 (Doncaster)
TRAPPIST (Westmoreland Stakes) 15.09.1876 (Doncaster)
LADY GOLIGHTLY (Wentworth Stakes) 15.09.1876 (Doncaster)
GREAT TOM (Doncaster Stakes) 15.09.1876 (Doncaster)
LADY ATHOLSTONE (County Members Plate Handicap) 19.09.1876
    (Lichfield)
PAGEANT (Staffordshire Stakes Handicap) 19.09.1876 (Lichfield)
SCOTCH REEL (Grendon Juvenile Plate) 20.09.1876 (Lichfield)
BURLINGTON (Highgate Welter Handicap) 22.09.1876 (Alexandra Park)
CRANN TAIR (1st October 2-Year-Olds Plate) 27.09.1876 (Newmarket)
GLADIATORE (Sweepstake 10 Sovereign) 27.09.1876 (Newmarket)
LADY GOLIGHTLY (1st Year/29th Triennial Produce Stakes) 28.09.1876
    (Newmarket)
CRANN TAIR (Bestwood Nursery Plate Handicap) 03.10.1876 (Nottingham)
ROCKINGHAM (2 Horse Race) 03.10.1876 (Nottingham)
MR E ETCHE'S BG (Welbeck Welter Plate) 04.10.1876 (Nottingham)
MALPLAQUET (Edwinstowe Plate Handicap) 04.10.1876 (Nottingham)
COSEY (Friar Tuck Stakes) 04.10.1876 (Nottingham)
ROSSINI (Nursery Plate Handicap) 05.10.1876 (Leicester)
SWEETHEART (Selling Stakes) 06.10.1876 (Leicester)
ROSSINI (Curzon Nursery Handicap Stakes) 06.10.1876 (Leicester)
MORGIANA (October Post Produce Stakes) 09.10.1876 (Newmarket)
KITTY SPRIGHTLY (Scurry Nursery) 09.10.1876 (Newmarket)
SUNRAY (Post Sweepstake) 09.10.1876 (Newmarket)
OXONIAN (Sweepstakes/5 Sovereign) 09.10.1876 (Newmarket)
ROSEBERY (Cesarewitch Stakes) 10.10.1876 (Newmarket)
SILVIO (Clearwell Stakes) 10.10.1876 (Newmarket)
OXONIAN (Selling Welter Stakes) 11.10.1876 (Newmarket)
FARNESE (Sweepstakes/10 Sovereign) 11.10.1876 (Newmarket)
FARNESE (Sweepstakes/15 Sovereign) 13.10.1876 (Newmarket)
SKYLARK (Newmarket Derby) 13.10.1876 (Newmarket)
MALTA (Maiden Race) 17.10.1876 (Croydon)
GOOD THING (Croydon Nursery Stakes) 18.10.1876 (Croydon)
OXONIAN (All Aged Stakes) 24.10.1876 (Newmarket)
SILVIO (Post Sweepstakes) 24.10.1876 (Newmarket)
KING CLOVIS (Home Bred Produce Stakes) 24.10.1876 WO (Newmarket)

ZUCCHERO (Home Bred Foal Produce Stakes) 25.10.1876 (Newmarket)
SPRINGFIELD (Free Handicap) 26.10.1876 (Newmarket)
SILVIO (Glasgow Stakes) 27.10.1876 WO (Newmarket)
TRAPPIST (All Aged Stakes) 27.10.1876 (Newmarket)
SLUMBER (A Selling Stakes/10 Sovereign) 28.10.1876 (Newmarket)
PALM FLOWER (2-Year-Old Stakes) 28.10.1876 (Newmarket)
MISS PATRICK (Corporation Stakes) 31.10.1876 (Brighton)
STROLLER (Witham Selling Stakes) 01.11.1876 (Lincoln)
GLADIATORE (Gautby Nursery Plate) 01.11.1876 (Lincoln)
MONARCH (Elsham Welter Handicap) 02.11.1876 (Lincoln)
ALLERTON (Fossdyke Selling Handicap) 02.11.1876 (Lincoln)
PLAISANTE (Blankney Nursery Handicap) 02.11.1876 (Lincoln)
PLAISANTE (Brownlow Nursery Plate) 03.11.1876 (Lincoln)
ALLERTON (Pelham Selling Stakes) 03.11.1876 (Lincoln)
MRS WILLIN'S F (Waterloo Welter Handicap) 07.11.1876 (Liverpool)
POLENA (Selling Nursery Handicap) 07.11.1876 (Liverpool)
OXONIAN (Stewards Cup) 07.11.1876 (Liverpool)
KING DEATH (Tuesday Plate) 07.11.1876 (Liverpool)
INSTANTLY (Croxteth Cup) 08.11.1876 (Liverpool)
BONNIE DUNDEE (Liverpool Nursery Stakes) 08.11.1876 DH (Liverpool)
CELOSIA (Alt Welter Handicap) 08.11.1876 (Liverpool)
OXONIAN (Wavertree Handicap) 09.11.1876 (Liverpool)
CRANN TAIR (Downe Nursery Handicap) 09.11.1876 (Liverpool)
FAREHAM (Abbey Stakes) 14.11.1876 (Shrewsbury)
BALDACCHINO (2-Year-Old Stakes) 14.11.1876 (Shrewsbury)
JOLLIFICATION (Maiden Plate) 15.11.1876 (Shrewsbury)
FAREHAM (Welter Selling Stakes) 15.11.1876 (Shrewsbury)
BRIDGET (Forester Plate Handicap) 17.11.1876 (Shrewsbury)
HIPPIAS (Hawkestone Welter Cup) 17.11.1876 (Shrewsbury)
CAT'S EYE (Selling Welter Plate) 21.11.1876 (Warwick)
ARBITRATOR (Nursery Handicap) 21.11.1876 (Warwick)
LE PROMENEUR (Selling Stakes) 22.11.1876 (Warwick)
LADY OF THE LEA (2nd Nursery Handicap) 22.11.1876 (Warwick)
INSTANTLY (Guy Welter Handicap) 22.11.1876 (Warwick)
INSTANTLY (Welter Handicap) 23.11.1876 (Warwick)
CLAREMONT (Great Autumn Welter Cup Handicap) 23.11.1876 DH
    (Warwick)
TELESCOPE (Selling Race) 24.11.1876 (Warwick)
LE PROMENEUR (Shorts Handicap) 24.11.1876 (Warwick)
PIBROCH (Selling Stakes) 25.11.1876 (Warwick)

1877   BRIGG BOY (Trial Plate) 19.03.1877 (Lincoln)
       INSTANTLY (Hylton Stakes) 23.03.1877 (Liverpool)
       TELEGRAM (Starkle Stakes) 23.03.1877 (Liverpool)
       ROSINANTE (Stand Cup) 03.04.1877 (Northampton)
       COERULEUS (Earl Spencer Plate) 03.04.1877 (Northampton)
       BERZELIUS (2-Year-Old Stakes) 10.04.1877 (Croydon)
       CARADOC (West Wickham Plate) 10.04.1877 (Croydon)
       RED ROSE (Innkeepers Plate) 11.04.1877 (Croydon)

ANCIENT MUSIC (Selling Plate) 11.04.1877 (Croydon)
SAMARIA (Juvenile Selling Plate) 13.04.1877 (Windsor)
KING CLOVIS (Post Sweepstake) 17.04.1877 (Newmarket)
FARNESE (A Plate/100 Sovereign) 18.04.1877 (Newmarket)
LADY GOLIGHTLY (Column Stakes) 18.04.1877 WO (Newmarket)
SKYLARK (2nd Year/18th Newmarket Biennial Stakes) 19.04.1877
    (Newmarket)
LITTLE FIF (Refuse 2-Year-Olds) 19.04.1877 (Newmarket)
EUXINE (Welter Handicap Sweepstake) 19.04.1877 (Newmarket)
BELLE OF SUTHERLAND (Maiden Plate) 19.04.1877 (Newmarket)
FARNESE (Sweepstake/10 Sovereign) 19.04.1877 (Newmarket)
SKYLARK (Claret Stakes) 19.04.1877 (Newmarket)
JOACHIM (A Plate/100 Sovereign) 20.04.1877 (Newmarket)
JULIA PEACHAM (Selling Stakes) 20.04.1877 (Newmarket)
BIRDIE (Maiden Plate) 24.04.1877 (Epsom)
JULIUS CAESAR (City and Suburban) 24.04.1877 (Epsom)
CREATURE (Beaufort Stakes) 25.04.1877 (Epsom)
LYCEUM (Princess of Wales Stakes) 26.04.1877 (Sandown Park)
BONNIE LASSIE (Selling Plate) 01.05.1877 (Newmarket)
SKYLARK (Prince of Wales Stakes) 02.05.1877 (Newmarket)
DALGARNO (Maiden Plate) 03.05.1877 (Newmarket)
CARTHUSIAN (3rd Welter Handicap) 04.05.1877 (Newmarket)
KING CLOVIS (Newmarket Stakes) 04.05.1877 WO (Newmarket)
HIPPIAS (Wynnstay Welter Handicap) 08.05.1877 (Chester)
GABERLUNZIE (Badminton Stakes) 10.05.1877 (Chester)
BONNIE ROBIN (65th Dee Stakes) 10.05.1877 (Chester)
HAWTHORN (Selling Handicap) 12.05.1877 (Alexandra Park)
OXONIAN (Selling Stakes/10 Sovereign) 15.05.1877 (Newmarket)
WIDEAWAKE (3rd Class 2-Year-Old Plate) 16.05.1877 (Newmarket)
CALEDONIA (2-Year-Old Stakes) 18.05.1877 (Lewes)
BRIGG BOY (Trial Plate) 19.05.1877 (Lewes)
CALEDONIA (Landport Stakes) 19.05.1877 (Lewes)
LORD BYRON (Welter Race) 21.05.1877 (Streatham)
VICTOIRE (Lancaster Welter Handicap Plate) 23.05.1877 (Manchester)
UNICORN (Stamford Stakes) 24.05.1877 (Manchester)
LORD STAMFORD'S F (John O'Gaunt Plate) 25.05.1877 (Manchester)
MISS GERTRUDE (Consolation Welter Handicap) 25.05.1877 (Manchester)
TRAPPIST (Egmont Plate) 29.05.1877 (Epsom)
ROEHAMPTON (Rous Stakes) 29.05.1877 (Epsom)
PARAMATTA (Ashtead Stakes) 29.05.1877 (Epsom)
LADY LUMLEY (Stanley Stakes) 30.05.1877 (Epsom)
SILVIO (Derby Stakes) 30.05.1877 (Epsom)
INSTANTLY (Paddock Stakes) 31.05.1877 (Epsom)
GRANADA (Ebbisham Stakes) 31.05.1877 (Epsom)
HESPER (Epsom Cup) 01.06.1877 (Epsom)
AMBUSCADE (Epsom 2-Year-Old Plate) 01.06.1877 (Epsom)
MISS MANSFIELD (Shirley Plate) 05.06.1877 (Croydon)
IRONSTONE (Croydon Summer Handicap) 05.06.1877 (Croydon)
MISS MANSFIELD (Coombe Manor Plate) 06.06.1877 (Croydon)

KISMET (Corinthian Handicap) 06.06.1877 (Croydon)
SKYLARK (Gold Vase) 12.06.1877 (Ascot)
POLESTAR (Maiden Plate) 12.06.1877 (Ascot)
JANNETTE (1st Year Triennial of 25th Ascot Biennial Stakes) 13.06.1877 (Ascot)
ROB ROY (2nd of 19th Ascot Biennial Stakes) 13.06.1877 (Ascot)
SILVIO (Ascot Derby Stakes) 13.06.1877 (Ascot)
TRAPPIST (Windsor Ltd Handicap) 14.06.1877 (Ascot)
GADFLY (Manor 2-Year-Olds) 19.06.1877 (Windsor)
HELENA (Eton Welter Cup) 19.06.1877 (Windsor)
GRANDEE (Shorts Selling Stakes) 19.06.1877 (Windsor)
TRIBUTE (Thames Handicap) 19.06.1877 (Windsor)
GORSE (West Molesey Stakes) 21.06.1877 (Hampton)
WIDEAWAKE (Hurst Stakes) 21.06.1877 (Hampton)
AMBUSCADE (Claremont Stakes) 21.06.1877 (Hampton)
MAY DAY (Prince of Orange Stakes) 21.06.1877 (Hampton)
KING DEATH (Manor Stakes) 21.06.1877 (Hampton)
GORSE (Cardinal Wolsey Stakes) 22.06.1877 (Hampton)
ROSINANTE (Trial Stakes) 26.06.1877 (Newcastle Upon Tyne)
FARNESE (Gibside Stakes) 27.06.1877 (Newcastle Upon Tyne)
TRAPPIST (Stockbridge Cup) 28.06.1877 (Stockbridge)
DOVEDALE (Johnstone Plate) 28.06.1877 (Stockbridge)
REDWING (Hurstbourn Plate) 29.06.1877 (Stockbridge)
EQUINOX (2-Year-Old Stakes) 03.07.1877 (Newmarket)
VRIL (1st Welter Handicap) 03.07.1877 (Newmarket)
REDWING (Exeter Stakes) 04.07.1877 (Newmarket)
CHILDERIC (Chesterfield Stakes) 05.07.1877 (Newmarket)
CORREGIO (Summer Handicap) 05.07.1877 (Newmarket)
JOLLIFICATION II (Selling Stakes) 06.07.1877 (Newmarket)
TRAPPIST (Molyneux Cup Handicap) 10.07.1877 (Liverpool)
GADABOUT (Liver Stakes) 11.07.1877 (Liverpool)
CORONA (Gerard Stakes) 11.07.1877 (Liverpool)
BAYARD (Bentinck Handicap) 11.07.1877 (Liverpool)
TRIBUTE (Surbiton Handicap) 17.07.1877 (Sandown Park)
LADY PALMER (Great King Stakes) 17.07.1877 (Sandown Park)
KING DEATH (High Welter Stakes) 17.07.1877 (Sandown Park)
KING DEATH (Members Welter Handicap) 18.07.1877 (Sandown Park)
KILLIECRANKIE (Handicap Plate/100 Sovereign) 18.07.1877 (Sandown Park)
FLORRY YORK (Visitors Plate) 19.07.1877 (Lambourn)
FULSHAW (Haringey Plate) 21.07.1877 (Alexandra Park)
GADABOUT (Ramsey Plate) 24.07.1877 (Huntingdon)
CHESTERTON (Her Majesty's Plate) 24.07.1877 (Huntingdon)
CHESTERTON (Huntingdon Stakes) 25.07.1877 (Huntingdon)
BRAVISSIMA (Cambridgeshire 2-Year-Old Stakes) 25.07.1877 (Huntingdon)
ASTEROIDAL (Corporation Selling Stakes) 25.07.1877 (Huntingdon)
ROEHAMPTON (Sweepstakes 10 Sovereign) 31.07.1877 (Goodwood)
JANNETTE (Richmond Stakes) 31.07.1877 (Goodwood)
MANOEUVRE (Gratwicke Produce Stakes) 31.07.1877 (Goodwood)

BONNIE LASSIE (Match 200 Sovereign) 31.07.1877 (Goodwood)
LADY GOLIGHTLY (Sweepstake 300 Sovereign) 01.08.1877 WO
    (Goodwood)
DALGARNO (Lavant Stakes) 01.08.1877 (Goodwood)
MOUSQUETAIRE (Chichester Stakes Handicap) 02.08.1877 (Goodwood)
RED HAZARD (Molecombe Stakes) 02.08.1877 (Goodwood)
CHILDERIC (Prince of Wales Stakes) 02.08.1877 (Goodwood)
BRIOCHE (Nursery Stakes) 03.08.1877 (Goodwood)
PARAMATTA (Duke of Richmond's Plate Handicap) 03.08.1877
    (Goodwood)
CANNON BALL (March Stakes) 03.08.1877 (Goodwood)
LADY GOLIGHTLY (Nassau Stakes) 03.08.1877 (Goodwood)
PRECEDENCE (Bevendean Stakes) 07.08.1877 (Brighton)
RED GAUNTLET (Selling Welter Handicap/5 Sovereign) 09.08.1877
    (Brighton)
MOUSQUETAIRE (De Warrenne Handicap) 10.08.1877 (Lewes)
REDWING (Astley Stakes) 10.08.1877 (Lewes)
RED GAUNTLET (Castle Plate) 10.08.1877 (Lewes)
SALTIER (Windmill Welter Stakes) 11.08.1877 (Lewes)
CHESTERTON (Her Majesty's Plate 200 Guinea) 14.08.1877 (Egham)
MR VYNER'S BRC (Lambton Plate) 15.08.1877 (Stockton)
THE REEVE (Castle Welter) 16.08.1877 (Windsor)
BRAVISSIMA (Osterley Park) 16.08.1877 (Windsor)
SAILOR (Hamilton Welter) 17.08.1877 (Windsor)
REDWING (Convivial Stakes) 21.08.1877 DH (York)
LADY GOLIGHTLY (Yorkshire Oaks) 21.08.1877 (York)
GOOD THING (Bradgate Park Stakes) 21.08.1877 (York)
SUNRAY (Ebor St Leger) 22.08.1877 (York)
SKYLARK (York Cup) 23.08.1877 (York)
KING OLAF (Gimcrack Stakes) 23.08.1877 (York)
CHESTERTON (Her Majesty's Plate) 23.08.1877 (York)
MR M DAWSON'S BRF (2-Year-Old Stakes) 28.08.1877 (Sutton Park)
BONNIE ROBIN (Sutton Park Welter Plate) 29.08.1877 (Sutton Park)
MR M DAWSON'S BRF (Erdington Plate) 29.08.1877 (Sutton Park)
ARROWROOT (Stratton Audley Stakes) 31.08.1877 (Oxford)
SAILOR (County Welter Handicap) 05.09.1877 (Warwick)
LYCEUM (Patshull Handicap) 06.09.1877 (Wolverhampton)
HOME MADE (Cleveland Cup) 07.09.1877 (Wolverhampton)
HIPPIAS (Holyoake Stakes) 07.09.1877 (Wolverhampton)
MOUSQUETAIRE (Fitzwilliam Stakes) 11.09.1877 (Doncaster)
SILVIO (St Leger) 12.09.1877 (Doncaster)
CHESTERTON (Her Majesty's Plate 200 Guinea) 12.09.1877 (Doncaster)
GWENDOLINE (Selling Handicap Stakes) 13.09.1877 (Doncaster)
CHILDERIC (Sweepstakes 10 Sovereign) 13.09.1877 (Doncaster)
LADY GOLIGHTLY (Park Hill Stakes) 14.09.1877 (Doncaster)
LADY GOLIGHTLY (Doncaster Stakes) 14.09.1877 (Doncaster)
JANNETTE (Wentworth Stakes) 14.09.1877 WO (Doncaster)
SALTIER (Anglesey Welter Plate) 18.09.1877 (Lichfield)
KING DEATH (Welter Cup) 19.09.1877 (Lichfield)

GRANDEE (Free Handicap) 20.09.1877 (Lichfield)
POLICY (Selling Stakes) 20.09.1877 (Lichfield)
MR W WALKER'S BF (2-Year-Old Selling Handicap Plate) 21.09.1877
(Lichfield)
KISMET (Land of Burns Cup) 21.09.1877 (Lichfield)
THE MANDARIN (Great Eastern Railway Handicap) 25.09.1877
(Newmarket)
HYDROMEL (Hopeful Stakes) 25.09.1877 (Newmarket)
REDWING (Boscawen Stakes) 25.09.1877 (Newmarket)
JANNETTE (Buckenham Stakes) 25.09.1877 WO (Newmarket)
SWEET WILLIAM (Selling Stakes) 28.09.1877 (Newmarket)
MAID OF THE VALLEY (Friar Tuck Selling Plate) 03.10.1877 (Nottingham)
TELEGRAM (Rufford Abbey Nursery Plate) 03.10.1877 (Nottingham)
NIGER (Bradgate Park Welter Handicap Plate) 03.10.1877 (Nottingham)
KINO (Grand Stakes Handicap) 04.10.1877 (Leicester)
PALPITO (Nursery Plate) 04.10.1877 (Leicester)
CHOPIN (Licensed Victuallers' Welter Handicap) 05.10.1877 (Leicester)
STRATHFLEET (Post Sweepstake/200 Sovereign) 08.10.1877 (Newmarket)
LADY GOLIGHTLY (Royal Stakes) 09.10.1877 (Newmarket)
JANNETTE (Clearwell Stakes) 09.10.1877 (Newmarket)
GREAT TOM (Cesarewitch Stakes) 09.10.1877 (Newmarket)
CINCINNATUS (Selling Stakes) 10.10.1877 (Newmarket)
KING DEATH (Selling Welter Stakes) 10.10.1877 (Newmarket)
POLLY PERKINS (Sweepstakes/10 Sovereign) 10.10.1877 (Newmarket)
MOODY (Selling Nursery Handicap) 11.10.1877 (Newmarket)
TRAPPIST (Autumn Handicap) 11.10.1877 (Newmarket)
JANNETTE (Bretby Stakes) 11.10.1877 WO (Newmarket)
LADY GOLIGHTLY (Newmarket Oaks) 11.10.1877 (Newmarket)
LA GITANA (Sweepstake 10 Sovereign) 12.10.1877 (Newmarket)
CHILDERIC (Prendergast Stakes) 12.10.1877 (Newmarket)
LADY GOLIGHTLY (Newmarket Derby) 12.10.1877 (Newmarket)
MEMORANDUM (Shirley Plate) 16.10.1877 (Croydon) (Newmarket)
MAID OF THE VALLEY (West Wickham Plate) 17.10.1877 (Newmarket)
MADGE GORDON (Selling 2-Year-Old Plate) 19.10.1877 (Sandown Park)
MIREBOLANTE (All Aged Stakes) 22.10.1877 (Newmarket)
MOODY (2-Year-Old Race) 22.10.1877 (Newmarket)
KATHERINE (Nursery Handicap) 22.10.1877 (Newmarket)
JANNETTE (Criterion Stakes) 22.10.1877 (Newmarket)
TRAPPIST (All Aged Stakes) 23.10.1877 (Newmarket)
HYDROMEL (Home Bred/Foal Stakes) 24.10.1877 (Newmarket)
CINCINNATUS (Sweepstakes) 24.10.1877 (Newmarket)
TRAPPIST (Stand Handicap) 24.10.1877 (Newmarket)
HYDROMEL (Home Bred Sweepstakes) 25.10.1877 (Newmarket)
KISMET (Match 500 Sovereign) 25.10.1877 (Newmarket)
ROSY CROSS (Limited Free Handicap) 25.10.1877 (Newmarket)
RED HAZARD (Troy Stakes) 25.10.1877 (Newmarket)
HACKTHORPE (2 Horse Race, 2-Year-Olds) 25.10.1877 (Newmarket)
LORD CLIVE (Houghton Plate) 26.10.1877 (Newmarket)
MIREBOLANTE (Selling Welter Sweepstakes) 27.10.1877 (Newmarket)

GREAT TOM (Winding Up Handicap) 27.10.1877 (Newmarket)
FIDDLESTRING (2-Year-Old Stakes) 27.10.1877 (Newmarket)
CINCINNATUS (Chaplin Stakes) 31.10.1877 (Lincoln)
OASIS (Brown Nursery Plate) 02.11.1877 (Lincoln)
KING DEATH (Mersey Trial Plate) 06.11.1877 (Liverpool)
HACKTHORPE (Knowsley Nursery Stakes) 06.11.1877 (Liverpool)
TEMPLAR (Alt Welter Handicap) 07.11.1877 (Liverpool)
BONNIE LASSIE (Downe Nursery) 08.11.1877 (Liverpool)
DEACON (Bentinck Welter Handicap) 08.11.1877 (Liverpool)
ARBITRATOR (Great Lancashire Handicap) 09.11.1877 (Liverpool)
MERRY THOUGHT (Abbey Stakes) 13.11.1877 (Shrewsbury)
LORD CLIFDEN (Innkeeper Welter Handicap) 13.11.1877 (Shrewsbury)
TEMPLAR (Wrekin Cup) 13.11.1877 (Shrewsbury)
LORD WILTON'S BC (Innkeepers Welter Plate) 14.11.1877 (Shrewsbury)
ROBIN (Acton Burn) 14.11.1877 (Shrewsbury)
VIC (Racing Stakes) 20.11.1877 (Warwick)
EUXINE (Innkeepers Stakes) 22.11.1877 (Warwick)
EUXINE (Welter Handicap) 22.11.1877 (Warwick)
BRENTA (100 Sovereign Plate) 23.11.1877 (Warwick)
TEMPLAR (Welter Handicap) 23.11.1877 (Warwick)
BAYARD (Selling Race) 24.11.1877 (Warwick)
QUEENSLAND (Welter Handicap) 24.11.1877 (Warwick)
SAILOR (Winding Up Welter Handicap) 24.11.1877 (Warwick)

1878   HESPER (Liverpool Spring Cup Handicap) 28.03.1878 (Liverpool)
HESPER (Prince of Wales Cup Free Handicap) 29.03.1878 (Liverpool)
TOMMY UP A PEAR TREE (Starkie Stakes) 29.03.1878 (Liverpool)
PICCALILLI (Lancastrian Plate) 29.03.1878 (Liverpool)
PRINCE (Scurry Stakes) 02.04.1878 (Windsor)
TITUS FLAVIUS (Shorts Selling Stakes) 02.04.1878 (Windsor)
REDOUBT (The Cup Handicap) 05.04.1878 WO (Croxton Park)
HAMPTON (Her Majesty's Plate) 09.04.1878 (Northampton)
PRESTO (Town Selling Stakes) 10.04.1878 (Northampton)
VRIL (St Liz Handicap) 10.04.1878 (Northampton)
NIGHTINGALE (Stoneleigh 2-Year-Old Plate) 11.04.1878 (Warwick)
CAREW (Juvenile Flying Plate) 11.04.1878 (Warwick)
ZAZEL (All Aged Selling Plate) 11.04.1878 (Warwick)
ADVANCE (Warwickshire Handicap) 12.04.1878 (Warwick)
THE ARAB (Colwick Hall Selling Stakes) 16.04.1878 (Nottingham)
CHILDERIC (Post Sweepstakes) 23.04.1878 (Newmarket)
ADVANCE (Bushes Handicap) 23.04.1878 (Newmarket)
ADVANCE (100 Guinea Plate) 24.04.1878 (Newmarket)
SILVIO (2nd Year/19th Newmarket Biennial Stakes) 25.04.1878
     (Newmarket)
BONCHURCH (Selling Stakes) 26.04.1878 (Newmarket)
HYDROMEL (Bennington Stakes) 26.04.1878 (Newmarket)
VEGETARIAN (Westminster Stakes) 30.04.1878 (Epsom)
MEDORA (Pall Mall Stakes) 01.05.1878 (Epsom)
PLACIDA (Great Surrey Handicap) 01.05.1878 (Epsom)

BRITISH BEAUTY (Railway Plate) 01.05.1878 (Epsom)
OXONION (Selling Stakes) 07.05.1878 (Newmarket)
FLORENTINE (Selling Plate) 07.05.1878 (Newmarket)
BERZENEZE (2-Year-Old Sweepstakes) 07.05.1878 (Newmarket)
SILVIO (Prince of Wales Stakes) 08.05.1878 (Newmarket)
BUMPKIN (2-Year-Old Selling Stakes) 10.05.1878 (Newmarket)
LYCEUM (Curzon Plate) 14.05.1878 (Chester)
WILD LYON (Badminton Stakes) 15.05.1878 (Chester)
PARAMETTA (Combermere Handicap Stakes) 15.05.1878 (Chester)
WOODLANDS (Great Cheshire Handicap Stakes) 16.05.1878 (Chester)
NONSENSE (Welter Handicap) 17.05.1878 (Alexandra Park)
HELOISE (Strafford 2-Year-Old Stakes) 18.05.1878 (Alexandra Park)
ALTYRE (Ditch Mile Handicap) 21.05.1878 (Newmarket)
ELSHAM LAD (Selling Stakes) 21.05.1878 (Newmarket)
MOWERINA (Sweepstakes) 21.05.1878 (Newmarket)
ASCANIUS (Handicap Sweepstake) 22.05.1878 (Newmarket)
OASIS (Pilgrimage) 22.05.1878 (Newmarket)
STRATHERN (2nd Spring 2-Year-Old Stakes) 23.05.1878 (Newmarket)
COLLINGBOURNE (Welter Handicap) 23.05.1878 (Newmarket)
MEDIATOR (Tradesmen's Selling Plate) 28.05.1878 (Bath & Somerset)
LANSDOWN (Weston Stakes) 29.05.1878 (Bath & Somerset)
LANSDOWN (Salisbury Stakes) 30.05.1878 (Salisbury)
XANTHO (Wheathampstead Stakes) 31.05.1878 (Harpenden)
GLADIATORE (Harpenden Handicap Stakes) 31.05.1878 (Harpenden)
HESPER (Craven Stakes) 04.06.1878 (Epsom)
COLLINGBOURNE (Ashtead Stakes) 04.06.1878 (Epsom)
WOODLANDS (High Level Handicap) 04.06.1878 (Epsom)
INSTANTLY (Epsom Town Plate) 05.06.1878 (Epsom)
LORD CLIVE (Welter Handicap) 06.06.1878 (Epsom)
WEATHERWISE (Mickleham Stakes) 06.06.1878 (Epsom)
PARDON (Handicap Plate) 06.06.1878 (Epsom)
JANNETTE (Oaks Stakes) 07.06.1878 (Epsom)
OXONION (Durdan's Stakes) 07.06.1878 (Epsom)
HAMPTON (Epsom Gold Cup) 07.06.1878 (Epsom)
IL GLADIATORE (Her Majesty's Plate 200 Guinea) 13.06.1878 (Manchester)
NUGGET (Stand Plate) 14.06.1878 (Manchester)
GARSWOOD (Post Sweepstakes/500 Sovereign) 18.06.1878 (Ascot)
LADY LUMLEY (Fern Hill Stakes) 19.06.1878 (Ascot)
JULIUS CAESAR (Royal Hunt Cup) 19.06.1878 (Ascot)
REDWING (Coronation Stakes) 19.06.1878 (Ascot)
MULEY EDRIS (1st Year/26th Triennial Stakes) 19.06.1878 (Ascot)
SONSIE QUEEN (2nd Year/20th Ascot Biennial Stakes) 19.06.1878 (Ascot)
LORD CLIVE (1st Year/16th Newmarket Biennial Stakes) 20.06.1878 (Ascot)
TRAPPIST (All Aged Stakes) 20.06.1878 (Ascot)
PETRARCH (Rous Memorial Stakes) 20.06.1878 (Ascot)
OUT OF BOUNDS (Maiden Plate) 21.06.1878 (Ascot)
TRAPPIST (Wokingham Stakes) 21.06.1878 (Ascot)
JANNETTE (25th Triennial Stakes) 21.06.1878 (Ascot)
LANSDOWN (Royal Stakes) 25.06.1878 (Windsor)

Bibury Club (Selling Welter Plate) 25.06.1878 (Windsor)
IRONSTONE (Eton Welter Cup) 25.06.1878 (Windsor)
LARCENY (Chetwynd Plate) 25.06.1878 (Windsor)
RUSK (Stand Plate 100 Guinea) 26.06.1878 (Windsor)
KING DEATH (Trial Welter Plate) 27.06.1878 (Hampton)
COLLINGBOURNE (Manor Plate Handicap) 27.06.1878 (Hampton)
JULIUS CAESAR (Surrey and Middlesex Stakes Handicap) 27.06.1878
    (Hampton)
JULIUS CAESAR (Her Majesty's Plate 200 Guinea) 28.06.1878 (Hampton)
ADMIRAL NELSON (Dogmersfield Park Plate) 02.07.1878 (Odiham)
DAISY WREATH (South Western Railway Plate) 02.07.1878 (Odiham)
SHOESTRING (Maiden Stakes) 03.07.1878 (Bibury Club) (Odiham)
ELF KING (Champagne Stakes) 03.07.1878 (Odiham)
MEXICO (Maiden 2-Year-Old Plate) 06.07.1878 (Alexandra Park)
JULIUS CAESAR (Plate) 09.07.1878 (Newmarket)
JANNETTE (Midsummer Stakes) 10.07.1878 (Newmarket)
VRIL (Selling Plate) 10.07.1878 (Newmarket)
TEMPLAR (Sweepstakes 10 Sovereign) 11.07.1878 (Newmarket)
LORD CLIVE (Summer Cup) 11.07.1878 (Newmarket)
LEAP YEAR (Chesterfield Stakes) 11.07.1878 (Newmarket)
BONIFACE (Match 300 Sovereign) 12.07.1878 (Newmarket)
WHIRLWIND (Stetchworth Stakes) 12.07.1878 (Newmarket)
CHEVRON (Newcastle Stakes Handicap) 12.07.1878 (Newmarket)
SHOESTRING (Liver 2-Year-Old Stakes) 16.07.1878 (Liverpool)
VENTNOR (Woolton Stakes) 16.07.1878 (Liverpool)
HESPER (Windermere Plate) 16.07.1878 (Liverpool)
BIRDIE (Sefton Stakes) 17.07.1878 (Liverpool)
HESPER (Liverpool Plate Handicap) 18.07.1878 (Liverpool)
SALAMIS (Queen Elizabeth Stakes) 19.07.1878 (Kempton Park)
VENTNOR (Apethorpe Selling Stakes) 23.07.1878 (Huntingdon)
JULIUS CAESAR (Portholme Cup) 23.07.1878 (Huntingdon)
ADMIRAL NELSON (Cumberland 2-Year-Old Stakes) 24.07.1878
    (Huntingdon)
LE PROMENEUR (Oakley Selling Stakes) 24.07.1878 (Huntingdon)
JULIUS CAESAR (Huntingdonshire Stakes Handicap) 24.07.1878
    (Huntingdon)
LE PROMENEUR (Corporation Selling Stakes) 24.07.1878 (Huntingdon)
WHEEL OF FORTUNE (Richmond Stakes) 30.07.1878 (Goodwood)
VENTNOR (Sweepstakes 10 Sovereign) 30.07.1878 (Goodwood)
PACIFIC (Gratwicke Stakes) 30.07.1878 (Goodwood)
LORD CLIVE (Goodwood Derby) 31.07.1878 (Goodwood)
TRAPPIST (Lennox Stakes) 31.07.1878 (Goodwood)
MULEY EDRIS (1st Year/Last Bentinck Memorial Stakes) 01.08.1878 DH
    (Goodwood)
CHARIBERT (Prince of Wales Stakes) 01.08.1878 (Goodwood)
TRAPPIST (Singleton Stakes) 01.08.1878 (Goodwood)
BLONDE (Selling Stakes) 01.08.1878 (Goodwood)
COUNT FESTETIC'S C (Molecomb Stakes) 01.08.1878 (Goodwood)
DEACON (Goodwood Corinthian Plate Handicap) 02.08.1878 (Goodwood)

MIRIAM (Selling Stakes) 02.08.1878 (Goodwood)
DUNMOW (Marine Stakes) 06.08.1878 (Brighton)
VENTNOR (Patcham Stakes) 06.08.1878 (Brighton)
WHITE POPPY (Corporation Stakes) 06.08.1878 (Brighton)
VENTNOR (Pavilion Stakes) 07.08.1878 (Brighton)
KING DAVID (Rottingdean Handicap) 08.08.1878 (Brighton)
FIDDLESTRING (Welter Handicap/5 Sovereign) 08.08.1878 (Brighton)
JULIUS CAESAR (Her Majesty's Plate) 09.08.1878 (Lewes)
BONIFACE (Southdown Club Welter Handicap) 09.08.1878 (Lewes)
TRAPPIST (The County Cup) 10.08.1878 (Lewes)
BORGIA (Ankerwycke Plate) 13.08.1878 (Egham)
LE PROMENEUR (Magna Carta Selling Plate) 13.08.1878 (Egham)
BERTRAM (Runnymeade Plate) 14.08.1878 (Egham)
ALPHA (Park Plate) 15.08.1878 (Windsor)
SIR HUGH (Castle Welter Plate) 15.08.1878 (Windsor)
BRAVISSIMA (A Race) 20.08.1878 (Sutton Park)
MISS CROFT (Aston Selling Plate 100 Guinea) 20.08.1878 (Sutton Park)
CUCKOO (Sandwell Welter Handicap Plate) 21.08.1878 (Sutton Park)
LADY RONALD (Port Meadow Plate) 22.08.1878 (Oxford)
TRIBUTE (County Members Plate) 22.08.1878 (Oxford)
ST AUGUSTINE (Middleton 2-Year-Old) 22.08.1878 (Oxford)
ST AUGUSTINE (Stratton Audley's 2-Year-Old) 22.08.1878 (Oxford)
NUGGET (Ladies' Plate Welter Handicap) 23.08.1878 (Oxford)
ALPHA (Badminton Plate) 27.08.1878 (Oxford)
JANNETTE (Yorkshire Oaks) 27.08.1878 (Oxford)
ROWLSTON (Lonsdale Plate) 27.08.1878 (Oxford)
WHEEL OF FORTUNE (Prince of Wales Stakes) 28.08.1878 (Oxford)
CLAUDIUS (1st Year/23rd North England Biennial Stakes) 28.08.1878
    (Oxford)
HAMPTON (Her Majesty's Plate 200 Guinea) 29.08.1878 (Oxford)
LADY GOLIGHTLY (York Cup) 29.08.1878 (Oxford)
CHARIBERT (Champagne Stakes) 10.09.1878 (Doncaster)
CARTHUSIAN (Stand Stakes) 10.09.1878 (Doncaster)
ECOSSAIS (Fitzwilliam Stakes) 10.09.1878 WO (Doncaster)
WHITE POPPY (Corporation Stakes) 11.09.1878 (Doncaster)
JANNETTE (St Leger) 11.09.1878 (Doncaster)
DALHAM (Alexandra Plate) 12.09.1878 (Doncaster)
WHEEL OF FORTUNE (Wentworth Post Produce Stakes) 13.09.1878 WO
    (Doncaster)
CHILDERIC (Doncaster Stakes) 13.09.1878 (Doncaster)
JANNETTE (Park Hill Stakes) 13.09.1878 (Doncaster)
HAMPTON (Her Majesty's Plate) 18.09.1878 WO (Lichfield)
DUNKENNY (Lichfield Cup Handicap) 18.09.1878 (Lichfield)
DAISY WREATH (Irwell Selling Stakes) 19.09.1878 (Manchester)
DAISY WREATH (Buckley Selling Stakes) 20.09.1878 (Manchester)
ROWLSTON (Stamford Handicap) 20.09.1878 (Manchester)
MISENUS (Oldham Welter Handicap) 20.09.1878(Manchester)
PRIMESAULTIER (Pendleton Selling Handicap Plate) 21.09.1878
    (Manchester)

HELENA (De Trafford Handicap) 21.09.1878 (Manchester)
SALAMIS (Eglinton Nursery Handicap Plate) 21.09.1878 (Manchester)
LADY GOLIGHTLY (3rd Year 29th Triennial Produce Stakes) 24.09.1878
    (Newmarket)
WHEEL OF FORTUNE (Buckenham Stakes) 24.09.1878 (Newmarket)
HACKTHORPE (Great Eastern Railway Handicap) 24.09.1878 (Newmarket)
LEAP YEAR (Boscawen Stakes) 24.09.1878 (Newmarket)
LORD CLIVE (Grand Duke Michael Stakes) 24.09.1878 (Newmarket)
WHEEL OF FORTUNE (1st Year/31st Triennial Produce Stakes) 26.09.1878
    (Newmarket)
ANDRELLA (Selling Stakes) 26.09.1878 (Newmarket)
FIDDLESTRING (Soham Stakes) 26.09.1878 (Newmarket)
IRONSTONE (Annesley Park Plate) 02.10.1878 (Nottingham)
LORD CLIVE (Her Majesty's Plate) 02.10.1878 (Nottingham)
JULIUS CAESAR (Lothians Handicap) 03.10.1878 (Edinburgh)
MAID OF WYE (Halliford Welter Handicap) 05.10.1878 (Kempton Park)
CHILDERIC (Royal Stakes) 07.10.1878 (Newmarket)
BOWNESS (Post Sweepstakes) 07.10.1878 (Newmarket)
LORD CALTHORPE'S C (100 Guinea Plate) 08.10.1878 (Newmarket)
ROWLSTON (100 Sovereign Plate) 08.10.1878 (Newmarket)
FIDDLESTRING (Sweepstakes/10 Sovereign) 08.10.1878 (Newmarket)
SATIRA (Flying Welter Handicap) 09.10.1878 (Newmarket)
LORD CLIVE (Select Stakes) 09.10.1878 (Newmarket)
KING COB (2-Year-Old Selling Plate) 09.10.1878 (Newmarket)
DUKE OF BEAUFORT'S BC (Maiden Plate) 10.10.1878 (Newmarket)
JANNETTE (Champion Stakes) 10.10.1878 (Newmarket)
BOWNESS (Bretby Stakes) 10.10.1878 (Newmarket)
JANNETTE (Newmarket Oaks) 10.10.1878 (Newmarket)
LEAP YEAR (Prendergast Stakes) 11.10.1878 (Newmarket)
HAMPTON (Her Majesty's Plate) 11.10.1878 (Newmarket)
CARNETHY (Juvenile Handicap) 11.10.1878 WO (Newmarket)
BERZELIUS (Welter Handicap/5 Sovereign) 15.10.1878 (Croydon)
MONACHUS (West Wickham Plate) 16.10.1878 (Croydon)
PLEVNA (Corinthian Welter Handicap) 16.10.1878 (Croydon)
HIGH AND MIGHTY (Monday Nursery Handicap/10 Sovereign) 21.10.1878
    (Newmarket)
CHARIBERT (Home Bred Post Produce Stakes) 22.10.1878 (Newmarket)
PLACENTIA (Home Bred Foal Post Stakes) 23.10.1878 (Newmarket)
WHEEL OF FORTUNE (Dewhurst Plate) 23.10.1878 (Newmarket)
KALEIDOSCOPE (Subscription Stakes) 24.10.1878 (Newmarket)
LORD CLIVE (Free Handicap Sweepstake) 24.10.1878 (Newmarket)
LORD WILTON'S F (Match 300 Sovereign) 24.10.1878 (Newmarket)
BREADFINDER (Bretby Nursery Plate) 24.10.1878 (Newmarket)
SILVIO (Jockey Club Cup) 25.10.1878 (Newmarket)
NYDIA (Selling Plate/100 Guinea) 26.10.1878 (Newmarket)
PARAMATTA (Selling Plate/200 Guinea) 26.10.1878 (Newmarket)
NYDIA (Ovingdean Plate) 29.10.1878 (Brighton)
BONDSMAN (Sussex Welter Handicap) 29.10.1878 (Brighton)
PLACIDA (Brighton Autumn Cup) 29.10.1878 (Brighton)

EVA (Maiden Plate) 31.10.1878 (Brighton)
EVA (Rottingdean Handicap) 31.10.1878 (Brighton)
PARAMATTA (Tuesday Plate) 05.11.1878 (Liverpool)
HACKTHORPE (Liverpool Stewards Cup) 05.11.1878 (Liverpool)
INSTANTLY (Mersey Trial Plate) 05.11.1878 WO (Liverpool)
MONARCHUS (Wednesday Plate) 06.11.1878 (Liverpool)
SHOESTRING (Fazakerley Plate) 07.11.1878 (Liverpool)
BRIGG BOY (Thursday Plate 100 Guinea) 07.11.1878 (Liverpool)
BRIGG BOY (Friday Plate) 08.11.1878 (Liverpool)
CENSER (Innkeeper's Welter Plate) 13.11.1878 (Shrewsbury)
TRIBUTE (Wrekin Cup) 13.11.1878 (Shrewsbury)
EREMITE (Acton Burnell Stakes) 14.11.1878 (Shrewsbury)
STAR AND GARTER (Whitehall Handicap) 15.11.1878 (Shrewsbury)
THE CELLARER (Selling Nursery Handicap Plate) 19.11.1878 (Warwick)
BRIGG BOY (Innkeeper Selling Welter Plate) 20.11.1878 (Warwick)
AVONTES (Great Autumn Welter Cup) 20.11.1878 (Warwick)
LADY RONALD (Halliford Welter Handicap Plate) 21.11.1878 (Kempton Park)
AVONTES (Kempton Park Handicap) 23.11.1878 (Kempton Park)
BREADFINDER (Richmond Nursery Handicap Plate) 23.11.1878 (Kempton
    Park)

1879 FIDDLESTRING (Brocklesby Trial Plate/Welter 100 Guinea Handicap)
          25.03.1879 (Lincoln)
      FIDDLESTRING (Stonebow Plate High Weight Handicap) 26.03.1879
          (Lincoln)
      RESTORE (Castle Selling Plate) 26.03.1879 (Lincoln)
      PARAMATTA (Netherton Plate/100 Guinea) 27.03.1879 (Liverpool)
      PARAMATTA (Buccleugh Cup) 01.04.1879 (Northampton)
      VANDERBILT (Selling Stakes) 01.04.1879 (Northampton)
      FIDDLESTRING (Welter Cup Handicap) 02.04.1879 (Northampton)
      MIDDLE TEMPLE (All Aged Selling Plate/100 Guinea) 03.04.1879 (Warwick)
      HYPATIA (Stoneleigh 2-Year-Old Plate) 03.04.1879 (Warwick)
      PARDON (Rufford Abbey Plate/Welter Handicap) 09.04.1879 (Nottingham)
      HUDIBRAS (Halliford Welter Handicap Plate 100 Guinea) 14.04.1879
          (Kempton Park)
      CAPT. MACHELL'S BF (Weeds Plate) 15.04.1879 (Newmarket)
      ALCHEMIST (1st Year/21st Newmarket Biennial Stakes) 15.04.1879
          (Newmarket)
      LANDRAIL (Double Trial Plate) 15.04.1879 (Newmarket)
      OXONIAN (All Aged Selling Plate) 16.04.1879 (Newmarket)
      NIGHTCAP (Maiden Plate) 16.04.1879 (Newmarket)
      PARDON (Rous Course Handicap Plate) 16.04.1879 (Newmarket)
      RETURNS (Refuse 2-Year-Old Plate) 17.04.1879 (Newmarket)
      LOUNGER (Selling Plate 100 Guinea) 17.04.1879 (Newmarket)
      TOWER AND SWORD (Sweepstakes) 17.04.1879 (Newmarket)
      SIGN MANUAL (Welter Handicap Sweepstakes) 17.04.1879 (Newmarket)
      ADJUTANT (Bennington Stakes) 18.04.1879 (Newmarket)
      THE ABBOT OF ST MARY'S (Sweepstake 15 Sovereign) 18.04.1879
          (Newmarket)

PAROLE (City and Suburban) 22.04.1879 (Epsom)
WOODQUEST (Durdan's Stakes) 22.04.1879 (Epsom)
MARASCHINO (Westminster Stakes) 22.04.1879 (Epsom)
PAROLE (Great Metropolitan Stakes Handicap) 23.04.1879 (Epsom)
THE MANDARIN (Esher Stakes Handicap) 24.04.1879 (Sandown)
RINGLEADER (Post Sweepstake) 29.04.1879 DH (Newmarket)
PARDON (2000 Guineas) 29.04.1879 (Newmarket)
KING DUNCAN (Coffee Room Stakes) 29.04.1879 (Newmarket)
OXONIAN (Selling Plate 100 Guinea) 30.04.1879 (Newmarket)
CHARIBERT (2000 Guinea Stakes) 30.04.1879 (Newmarket)
THE MANDARIN (Sweepstakes) 01.05.1879 (Newmarket)
WHEEL OF FORTUNE (1000 Guinea Stakes) 02.05.1879 (Newmarket)
MULEY EDRIS (Newmarket Stakes) 02.05.1879 (Newmarket)
QUEEN'S COUNTY (Shorts Selling Plate 100 Guinea) 05.05.1879
    (Newmarket)
FIDDLESTRING (Crown Welter Handicap) 05.05.1879 (Newmarket)
CLAYMORE (Grosvenor Trial Stakes) 06.05.1879 (Chester)
MAXIMILIAN (Belgrave Welter Cup Handicap) 06.05.1879 (Chester)
DOURANEE (Mostyn Stakes) 06.05.1879 (Chester)
LORD STAMFORD'S CHF (Maiden Plate) 06.05.1879 (Chester)
MORIER (Dee Stand Cup) 07.05.1879 (Chester)
PAROLE (Great Cheshire Handicap Stakes) 08.05.1879 (Chester)
MY JESSIE (Roodee Selling Welter Handicap Plate 100 Guinea) 08.05.1879
    (Chester)
SALTIER (Alexandra Plate/Handicap 100 Guinea) 09.05.1879 (Alexandra
    Park)
OUSE (Welter Cup Handicap 100 Guinea) 09.05.1879 (Alexandra Park)
FRIAR TUCK (Maiden Plate) 13.05.1879 (Newmarket)
MULEY EDRIS (Burwell Stakes) 13.05.1879 (Newmarket)
STRATHAVON (Rous Course Race) 13.05.1879 (Newmarket)
MANGOSTAN (2 Horse Race) 13.05.1879 (Newmarket)
AVENTURIER (Selling Stakes) 13.05.1879 (Newmarket)
PARAMATTA (Selling Plate 100 Guinea) 14.05.1879 (Newmarket)
MR HE BEDDINGTON'S BC (Exning 2-Year-Old Plate) 15.05.1879
    (Newmarket)
MR H OWEN'S BC (Plumpton Plate 100 Guinea) 17.05.1879 (Lewes)
SPITZBERG (Maiden Plate 100 Guinea) 27.05.1879 (Epsom)
HACKTHORPE (Egmont Plate Handicap) 27.05.1879 (Epsom)
SIGN MANUAL (Bentinck Welter Handicap) 28.05.1879 (Epsom)
TOWER AND SWORD (Welter Handicap) 29.05.1879 (Epsom)
WHEEL OF FORTUNE (Oaks) 30.05.1879 (Epsom)
DOURANEE (Acorn Stakes) 30.05.1879 (Epsom)
WOODLARK (Philip's Handicap Plate) 03.06.1879 (Manchester)
MAXIMILIAN (De Trafford Welter Cup/Handicap) 03.06.1879 (Manchester)
BLONDE (Derby All Aged Stakes) 04.06.1879 (Manchester)
STRATHAVON (City Welter Handicap Plate100 Guinea) 05.06.1879
    (Manchester)
MAXIMILIAN (Eglinton Welter Handicap) 05.06.1879 (Manchester)
ALFRED THE GOOD (Cobham Stakes) 06.06.1879 (Sandown)

FANFARE (Sandown Welter Handicap) 06.06.1879 (Sandown)
BONNIE BELL (Maiden 2-Year-Old Plate) 06.06.1879 (Sandown)
HACKTHORPE (Queen's Stakes Plate) 10.06.1879 (Ascot)
WHEEL OF FORTUNE (Prince of Wales Stakes) 10.06.1879 (Ascot)
SABELLA (1st Year/22nd Ascot Biennial Stakes) 10.06.1879 (Ascot)
JANNETTE (3rd Year/25th Triennial Stakes) 10.06.1879 (Ascot)
SPRING CAPTAIN (1st Year/27th Triennial Stakes) 11.06.1879 (Ascot)
LORD CLIVE (2nd Year/16th New Biennial Stakes) 12.06.1879 (Ascot)
HACKTHORPE (All Aged Stakes) 12.06.1879 (Ascot)
DOURANEE (Royal Plate) 17.06.1879 (Windsor)
QUEEN'S COUNTY (Selling Plate/100 Guinea) 18.06.1879 DH (Windsor)
ZAZEL (Trial Welter Plate 100 Guinea) 20.06.1879 (Hampton)
POLICY (Prince of Orange Stakes) 20.06.1879 (Hampton)
ROBIN HOOD (Maiden Plate 100 Guinea) 21.06.1879 (Hampton)
WHITEBINE (King Hal Stakes) 21.06.1879 (Hampton)
VON DER TANN (Champagne Stakes) 25.06.1879 (Bibury Club)
ST CUTHBERT (Andover Stakes Handicap) 26.06.1879 (Stockbridge)
MORIER (Selling Plate 100 Guinea) 01.07.1879 (Newmarket)
DOURANEE (Exeter Stakes) 02.07.1879 (Newmarket)
THE SHAKER (Maiden Plate) 02.07.1879 (Newmarket)
HOPBLOOM (4th Welter Handicap) 04.07.1879 (Newmarket)
PETAL (Stetchworth Stakes) 04.07.1879 (Newmarket)
EVASION (Mersey Stakes) 08.07.1879 (Liverpool)
RADIATOR (Liverpool Plate) 08.07.1879 WO (Liverpool)
TOWER AND SWORD (Croxteth Handicap) 09.07.1879 (Liverpool)
TITANIA II (Newsham Handicap 100 Guinea) 09.07.1879 (Liverpool)
BOWNESS (Sefton Stakes) 09.07.1879 (Liverpool)
SHELDRAKE (Shepperton Handicap) 10.07.1879 (Kempton Park)
CONFETTI (2-Year-Old Selling Plate) 10.07.1879 (Kempton Park)
PROTECTION (Fulwell Selling Plate) 11.07.1879 (Kempton Park)
MASTER KILDARE (Kempton Park Cup/Handicap) 12.07.1879 (Kempton
    Park)
GOVERNOR (Victoria Cup) 24.07.1879 (Sandown Park)
SHILLELAGH (Welter Handicap) 25.07.1879 (Sandown Park)
MP (Mile Selling High Weight Plate) 25.07.1879 (Sandown Park)
BEND OR (Richmond Stakes) 29.07.1879 (Goodwood)
BOWNESS (Sweepstakes 10 Sovereign) 29.07.1879 (Goodwood)
CRADLE (Drayton High Weight Handicap) 30.07.1879 (Goodwood)
DOURANEE (Findon Stakes) 30.07.1879 (Goodwood)
DREAMLAND (Selling Stakes Handicap) 31.07.1879 (Goodwood)
MULEY EDRIS (2nd Year Last Bentinck Members Stakes/Triennial Stakes)
    31.07.1879 (Goodwood)
BROTHERHOOD (Molecomb Stakes) 01.08.1879 (Goodwood)
DOURANEE (Corporation Stakes) 05.08.1879 (Brighton)
TITANIA II (Pavilion Stakes) 06.08.1879 (Brighton)
MAY QUEEN (Brookside Plate) 06.08.1879 (Brighton)
ADVANCE (Stewards Cup Handicap) 07.08.1879 (Brighton)
DOURANEE (Cliftonville Plate) 07.08.1879 (Brighton)
MANGOSTAN (Windmill Welter Plate) 08.08.1879 (Lewes)

MAYFIELD (Town Plate Handicap) 09.08.1879 (Lewes)
COUNT FESTETIC'S BC (Osterley Park Stakes) 14.08.1879 (Windsor)
BISHOP BURTON (Trial Stakes) 19.08.1879 (Stockton)
EIRENE (Hardwicke Stakes) 20.08.1879 (Stockton)
MELTON (Stockton Stewards Cup/Handicap) 21.08.1879 (Stockton)
BELFRY (1st Year/23rd Zetland Biennial Stakes) 21.08.1879 (Stockton)
LITTLE DUCK (Grand Selling Stakes) 21.08.1879 (Stockton)
MYCENAE (2nd Year 22nd Zetland Biennial Stakes) 26.08.1879 (York)
ALFRED THE GOOD (Bradgate Park Stakes) 26.08.1879 (York)
WHEEL OF FORTUNE (Yorkshire Oaks) 26.08.1879 (York)
STRATHARDLE (Badminton Plate) 26.08.1879 (York)
BEND OR (Prince of Wales Stakes) 27.08.1879 (York)
ALFRED THE GOOD (Falmouth Plate) 27.08.1879 (York)
BISHOP BURTON (Consolation Scramble Handicap) 28.08.1879 (York)
DUKE OF CUMBERLAND (Gimcrack Stakes) 28.08.1879 (York)
MYCENAE (Her Majesty's Plate) 28.08.1879 (York)
PLAISANTE (Warwick Welter Cup Handicap) 03.09.1879 (Warwick)
HELLESPONT (Borough Members Welter Plate Handicap) 03.09.1879
    (Warwick)
ECHO II (Milton Stakes) 10.09.1879 (Doncaster)
TADCASTER (Municipal Stakes) 10.09.1879 (Doncaster)
MASTER KILDARE (Alexandra Plate/Handicap) 11.09.1879 (Doncaster)
TOASTMASTER (Rous Plate) 11.09.1879 (Doncaster)
HACKTHORPE (Portland Plate Handicap) 11.09.1879 (Doncaster)
RETURNS (2 Horse Race) 12.09.1879 (Doncaster)
RED CROSS KNIGHT (Anglesey Welter Plate) 16.09.1879 (Lichfield)
MONK (Beaudesert Welter Plate Handicap) 16.09.1879 (Lichfield)
HOWDIE (Boreham Welter Stakes) 17.09.1879 (Chelmsford)
HAZELNUT (Selling Welter Handicap Plate) 19.09.1879 (Western Meeting)
HAZELNUT (Consolation Welter Plate) 19.09.1879 (Western Meetin
SWORD DANCE (September Plate) 20.09.1879 (Manchester)
WHIRLWIND (2nd Year/31st Triennial Produce Stakes) 24.09.1879
    (Newmarket)
MERRY GO ROUND (1st Foal Stakes) 24.09.1879 (Newmarket)
VALENTINO (2nd Nursery Stakes/Handicap) 25.09.1879 (Newmarket)
BELFRY (Rutland Stakes) 25.09.1879 (Newmarket)
BEND OR (1st Year/32nd Triennial Produce Stakes) 25.09.1879
    (Newmarket)
TYPHOON (Selling Stakes) 25.09.1879 (Newmarket)
LANDRAIL (Double Trial Plate) 25.09.1879 (Newmarket)
HACKTHORPE (Handicap Sweepstake) 26.09.1879 (Newmarket)
SUSQUEHANA (Selling Sweepstake) 26.09.1879 (Newmarket)
BEND OR (Rous Memorial Stakes) 26.09.1879 (Newmarket)
BISHOP BURTON (Billesdon Coplow Selling Plate) 02.10.1879 (Leicester)
TOASTMASTER (Melton Stakes) 03.10.1879 (Leicester)
OXONIAN (Thames Selling Plate) 04.10.1879 (Kempton Park)
MASTER KILDARE (Kempton Park October Handicap) 04.10.1879 (Kempton
    Park)
TITANIA II (A Plate/100 Sovereign) 07.10.1879 (Newmarket)

FIDDLESTRING (Cambridgeshire Welter Stakes Handicap) 08.10.1879
    (Newmarket)
WHIRLWIND (Newmarket Oaks) 09.10.1879 (Newmarket)
TITANIA II (Sweepstakes) 09.10.1879 (Newmarket)
FIRE KING (Rous Course) 10.10.1879 (Newmarket)
ECHO II (Woodside Plate Handicap) 14.10.1879 (Croydon)
DALMATIC (Maiden Stakes) 14.10.1879 (Croydon)
NIGHTINGALE (West Wickham Plate) 15.10.1879 (Croydon)
ANTYCERA (Juvenile Stakes) 16.10.1879 (Sandown Park)
FIRE KING (Great Saplings Plate) 17.10.1879 (Sandown Park)
STRATHAVON (Flying Plate Handicap) 17.10.1879 (Sandown Park)
PARAMATTA (All Aged Selling Plate) 20.10.1879 (Newmarket)
BISHOP BURTON (Selling Stakes) 20.10.1879 (Newmarket)
TITANIA II (Sweepstakes/5 Sovereign) 21.10.1879 (Newmarket)
TRIERMAIN (Selling Stakes) 23.10.1879 (Newmarket)
CHARIBERT (Sweepstakes/10 Sovereign) 24.10.1879 (Newmarket)
JANNETTE (Jockey Club Cup) 24.10.1879 (Newmarket)
PLAISANTE (Mile Selling Plate 29.10.1879 (Brighton)
ECHO II (Sussex Welter Handicap) 29.10.1879 (Brighton)
MY DELIGHT (Southdown Gold Cup) 31.10.1879 (Lewes)
BOUNCING BESSIE (Westmoreland Welter Plate Handicap) 04.11.1879
    (Liverpool)
TOASTMASTER (Knowsley Nursery Stakes Handicap) 04.11.1879
    (Liverpool)
CAPT MACHELL'S CHF (Juvenile Plate) 04.11.1879 (Liverpool)
        BISHOP BURTON (New Stand Plate) 04.11.1879 (Liverpool)
CRADLE (Croxteth Cup Welter Handicap) 04.11.1879 (Liverpool)
INSTANTLY (Autumn Welter Handicap) 05.11.1879 (Liverpool)
BOUNCING BESSIE (Aintree Feather Plate) 06.11.1879 (Liverpool)
MASTER KILDARE (Liverpool Autumn Cup Handicap) 06.11.1879
    (Liverpool)
RAMSBURY (Thursday Plate) 06.11.1879 (Liverpool)
BISHOP BURTON (Toxteth Welter Handicap) 07.11.1879 (Liverpool)
SPARKENHOE (Bootle Nursery Plate Handicap) 07.11.1879 (Liverpool)
DON JUAN (Friday Plate) 07.11.1879 (Liverpool)
QUICKSTEP (Acton Burnell Stakes) 12.11.1879 (Shrewsbury)
BISHOP BURTON (Selling Stakes) 12.11.1879 (Shrewsbury)
CAIRNGORM (Rous Selling Stakes) 18.11.1879 (Manchester)
HYPATIA (Garrick 2-Year-Old Plate) 20.11.1879 (Kempton Park)
CHARLES I (Wolsey Selling Welter Handicap) 21.11.1879 (Kempton Park)
QUICKSTEP (Winding Up Welter Handicap) 22.11.1879 (Kempton Park)
RED HAZARD (Shepperton Selling Plate) 22.11.1879 (Kempton Park)

1880   ACCOLADE (Castle Selling Plate) 17.03.1880 (Lincoln)
    ROULETTE (Union Jack Stakes) 18.03.1880 (Liverpool)
    ADVANCE (Liverpool Spring Cup/Handicap) 19.03.1880 (Liverpool)
    ALONE (Sefton Park Plate) 19.03.1880 (Liverpool)
    TEMPLAR (Welbeck Selling Cup) 23.03.1880 (Nottingham)
    ESSAYEZ (Sunbury Welter Handicap Plate) 29.03.1880 (Kempton Park)

ESSAYEZ (Halliford Welter Handicap Plate) 30.03.1880 (Kempton Park)
KILCORRAN (Wickham Plate) 01.04.1880 (Kempton Park)
VERSIGNY (Prix De Longchamps) 04.04.1880 (Longchamps)
ALPHA (Buccleugh Cup) 06.04.1880 (Northampton)
PLAISANTE (St Liz Handicap Welter Plate) 06.04.1880 (Northampton)
ULTIMATUM (Selling Welter Plate) 09.04.1880 (Warwick)
BEAUMINET (1st Year/23rd Biennial Stakes) 10.04.1880 (Warwick)
APOLLO (1st Year/22nd Newmarket Biennial Stakes) 13.04.1880
    (Newmarket)
MERRY GO ROUND (Column Produce Stakes) 14.04.1880 (Newmarket)
QUICKSTEP (Sweepstakes) 15.04.1880 (Newmarket)
LORD CALTHORPE'S F (Maiden Plate) 16.04.1880 (Newmarket)
APOLLO (Bennington Stakes) 16.04.1880 (Newmarket)
VERSIGNY (Prix De St James) 18.04.1880 (France)
PLACIDA (Trial Stakes) 20.04.1880 (Epsom)
CRADLE (Prince of Wales Stakes Handicap) 20.04.1880 (Epsom)
LORD CALTHORPE'S F (Juvenile Selling Stakes) 21.04.1880 (Epsom)
ANGELINA (Hyde Park Plate) 21.04.1880 (Epsom)
KUHLEBORN (Nork Plate) 22.04.1880 (Epsom)
MASTER KILDARE (City and Suburban Handicap) 22.04.1880 (Epsom)
FANFARE (Welter Handicap) 24.04.1880 (Sandown Park)
THECKLA (2-Year-Old Sweepstakes) 27.04.1880 (Newmarket)
MERRY GO ROUND (Newmarket Stakes) 30.04.1880 (Newmarket)
REGRETTEE (2-Year-Old Stakes) 30.04.1880 (Newmarket)
HAVOC (2-Year-Old Stakes) 19.05.1880 (Manchester)
HELLESPONT (Duchy Welter Handicap Plate) 19.05.1880 (Manchester)
TULARCHARD (Selling Handicap Plate) 20.05.1880 (Manchester)
MYCENAE (Her Majesty's Plate) 21.05.1880 (Manchester)
BEAUMINET (Prix Du Jockey Club) 23.05.1880 (France)
FLODDEN (Maiden Plate) 25.05.1880 (Epsom)
CHARIBERT (Egmont Plate Handicap) 25.05.1880 (Epsom)
ANGELINA (Woodcote Stakes) 25.05.1880 (Epsom)
ADVANCE (Epsom Stakes Handicap) 25.05.1880 (Epsom)
BEND OR (Derby Stakes) 26.05.1880 (Epsom)
DREAMLAND (Match 200 Sovereign) 26.05.1880 (Epsom)
DISCOURSE (Mickleham Stakes) 27.05.1880 (Epsom)
ANGELINA (Acorn Stakes) 28.05.1880 (Epsom)
BAL GAL (Richmond Stakes) 27.07.1880 (Goodwood)
CRADLE (Visitors Plate/Handicap) 28.07.1880 (Goodwood)
BAL GAL (Rous Memorial Stakes) 29.07.1880 (Goodwood)
MURIEL (Nassau Stakes) 30.07.1880 (Goodwood)
PRIORY (Juvenile Stakes) 03.08.1880 (Brighton)
LORD WILTON'S BF (Maiden Plate) 03.08.1880 DH (Brighton)
TRIERMAIN (Pavilion Stakes) 04.08.1880 (Brighton)
FORTISSIMO (Rottingdean Plate) 04.08.1880 (Brighton)
CHARIBERT (Rous Stakes) 05.08.1880 (Brighton)
LADY OF LYONS (Hampton Court Plate) 10.08.1880 (Kempton Park)
BATTLEMENT (Teddington 2-Year-Old Selling Plate) 10.08.1880 (Kempton
    Park)

ZAZEL (Welter Selling Plate) 12.08.1880 (Windsor)
BATTLEMENT (Magna Carta 2-Year-Old Stakes) 17.08.1880 (Egham)
ZAZEL (Ankerwycke Plate) 17.08.1880 (Egham)
BATTLEMENT (Milton Plate) 17.08.1880 (Egham)
MOUNT PLEASANT (Egham Welter Handicap) 18.08.1880 (Egham)
NAPSBURY (2nd Year/24th North England Biennial Stakes) 24.08.1880
    (York)
TOWER AND SWORD (Lonsdale Plate Welter) 24.08.1880 (York)
THECKLA (Convivial Stakes) 24.08.1880 (York)
METEORA (Filly Sapling Stakes) 25.08.1880 (York)
BAL GAL (Prince of Wales Stakes) 25.08.1880 (York)
LAURIER (Kimbolton Welter Handicap) 27.08.1880 (Huntingdon)
MAYFIELD (Selling Welter Handicap Plate) 28.08.1880 (Huntingdon)
UNICORN (Oakley Selling Plate) 28.08.1880 (Huntingdon)
KNIGHT OF MALTA (All Aged Selling Plate) 31.08.1880 (Warwick)
KNIGHT OF MALTA (County Selling Welter Plate) 01.09.1880 (Warwick)
TEA GOWN (Grendon Nursery Handicap Plate) 01.09.1880 (Warwick)
SKEDADDLE (Juvenile Selling Handicap Plate) 01.09.1880 (Warwick)
TEMPLAR (Elvaston Castle Selling Plate) 03.09.1880 (Derby)
ROSALIND (Chaddesdon Plate/Welter Handicap) 03.09.1880 (Derby)
KNIGHT OF MALTA (Shirley Plate) 09.09.1880 (Croydon)
TOWER AND SWORD (Fitzwilliam Stakes) 14.09.1880 (Doncaster)
BAL GAL (Champagne Stakes) 14.09.1880 (Doncaster)
QUEEN'S MESSAGE (Maiden Plate) 14.09.1880 (Doncaster)
GREAT CARLE (200 Sovereign Match) 15.09.1880 (Doncaster)
FORTISSIMO (Tattersall Sale Stakes) 17.09.1880 (Doncaster)
APOLLO (Doncaster Stakes) 17.09.1880 (Doncaster)
EARL GODWIN (Wentworth Stakes) 17.09.1880 (Doncaster)
BEAUMINET (Prix Royal Oak) 19.09.1880 (France)
TRESSILIAN (Anglesey Welter Plate) 21.09.1880 (Lichfield)
LORD WILTON'S BF (County Selling Welter Plate) 22.09.1880 (Lichfield)
THE ABBOT (Grand Duke Michael Stakes) 28.09.1880 (Newmarket)
LENNOXLOVE (Boscawen Stakes) 28.09.1880 WO (Newmarket)
LAMPREY (1st Nursery Stakes Handicap) 28.09.1880 (Newmarket)
ORANGE LILLY (Maiden Plate) 30.09.1880 (Newmarket)
BAL GAL (Rous Memorial Stakes) 01.10.1880 (Newmarket)
LA PAUME (Selling Plate) 01.10.1880 (Newmarket)
SUNNYBRAE (Billesdon Coplow Selling Plate) 07.10.1880 (Leicester)
LITTLE DUCK (Walton Selling Plate) 09.10.1880 (Kempton Park)
RHIDORROCH (Kempton Park 2 Miles October Handicap) 09.10.1880
    (Kempton Park)
BAL GAL (Clearwell Stakes) 11.10.1880 (Newmarket)
FLAVIUS (A Plate/100 Sovereign) 12.10.1880 (Newmarket)
APOLLO (Royal Stakes Post Sweepstakes) 12.10.1880 (Newmarket)
TOASTMASTER (Select Stakes) 13.10.1880 (Newmarket)
QUEEN'S MESSAGE (A Maiden Plate/100 Sovereign) 14.10.1880
    (Newmarket)
DONATO (Rous Course) 14.10.1880 (Newmarket)
MURIEL (Newmarket Oaks Sweepstakes) 14.10.1880 (Newmarket)

TOWER AND SWORD (Sweepstakes 15 Sovereign) 15.10.1880
   (Newmarket)
LADY OF LYONS (Sweepstakes 10 Sovereign) 15.10.1880 (Newmarket)
ATHOL LAD (Shirley Plate) 19.10.1880 (Croydon)
CRADLE (Trial Stakes) 25.10.1880 (Newmarket)
GREAT CARLE (Home Bred Produce Stakes) 26.10.1880 (Newmarket)
BAL GAL (Dewhurst Plate) 27.10.1880 (Newmarket)
DOURANEE (Subscription Stakes) 28.10.1880 (Newmarket)
THORA (Troy Stakes) 28.10.1880 (Newmarket)
DOURANEE (3rd Welter Handicap) 28.10.1880 (Newmarket)
ATALANTA (Rous Course) 29.10.1880 (Newmarket)
TYPHOON (Ovingdean Plate) 02.11.1880 (Brighton)
WAR PAINT (Bristol Mile Nursery Handicap) 03.11.1880 (Brighton)
REEFER (Lewes Autumn Handicap) 04.11.1880 (Lewes)
ATHOL LAD (Houndean Plate/Handicap) 05.11.1880 (Lewes)
ROWLSTON (New Stand Plate) 09.11.1880 (Liverpool)
PRIORY (Tuesday Plate) 09.11.1880 (Liverpool)
INES DE CASTRO (Selling Nursery Handicap) 10.11.1880 (Liverpool)
ATHOL LAD (Wednesday Plate) 10.11.1880 (Liverpool)
ATHOL LAD (Thursday Plate) 11.11.1880 (Liverpool)
CARNETHY (Westmoreland Welter Plate) 11.11.1880 (Liverpool)
STREET ARAB (Palatine Nursery Handicap) 11.11.1880 (Liverpool)
ATHOL LAD (Friday Plate) 12.11.1880 (Liverpool)
ATHOL LAD (Abbey Stakes) 16.11.1880 (Shrewsbury)
BISHOP BURTON (Battlefield Welter Plate) 16.11.1880 (Shrewsbury)
FLY BY NIGHT (Newport Selling Handicap) 18.11.1880 (Shrewsbury)

1881   TOWER AND SWORD (Batthyany Stakes Handicap) 21.03.1881 (Lincoln)
BELLE LURETTE (Brocklesby Stakes) 22.03.1881 (Lincoln)
ROWLSTON (Prince Park Plate) 24.03.1881 (Liverpool)
MY JESSIE (Northern Selling Handicap) 25.03.1881 (Liverpool)
TOWER AND SWORD (Crosby Plate Handicap) 25.03.1881 (Liverpool)
VERSIGNY (La Bourse) 03.04.1881 (France)
LE DESTRIER (Prix De Lutece) 03.04.1881 (France)
ELSHAM LAD (Castle Ashby Stakes) 05.04.1881 (Northampton)
CHAMPAGNE (Juvenile Flying Plate) 07.04.1881 (Northampton)
MISS BETTY (Selling Welter Plate) 08.04.1881 (Warwick)
CRADLE (Trial Stakes) 19.04.1881 (Newmarket)
SEE SAW (Trial Stakes) 19.04.1881 (Newmarket)
BEST AND BRAVEST (44th Riddlesworth Post Stakes) 19.04.1881 WO
      (Newmarket)
GREAT CARLE (Columns Produce Stakes) 20.04.1881 (Newmarket)
QUEEN OF THE TYC (Selling Plate) 21.04.1881 (Newmarket)
HENRY II (Bennington Stakes) 22.04.1881 (Newmarket)
TOWER AND SWORD (Handicap) 22.04.1881 DH (Newmarket)
NIMBLE (Maiden Plate) 26.04.1881 (Epsom)
JUBILEE (Westminster Stakes) 26.04.1881 (Epsom)
BEND OR (City and Suburban) 27.04.1881 (Epsom)
CHEVRONEL (Stamford Plate High Welter Handicap) 27.04.1881 (Epsom)

LEGHORN (Welter Handicap Plate) 27.04.1881 (Epsom)
LILLIPUTIAN (Welter Handicap) 29.04.1881 (Sandown Park)
TOWER AND SWORD (Claygate Plate) 29.04.1881 (Sandown Park)
LAST BORN (2-Year-Old Sweepstakes) 03.05.1881 (Newmarket)
TOWER AND SWORD (Visitors Plate Handicap) 03.05.1881 DH
   (Newmarket)
MERRY GO ROUND (1st Welter Handicap) 03.05.1881 (Newmarket)
VALOUR (Sweepstake 10 Sovereign) 05.05.1881 (Newmarket)
SPURS (Selling Stakes) 05.05.1881 (Newmarket)
SILVER BELL (Maiden Plate) 05.05.1881 (Newmarket)
CRADLE (Selling Stakes) 05.05.1881 (Newmarket)
LEGHORN (Selling Stakes) 06.05.1881 (Newmarket)
NETHERTON (2-Year-Old Selling Stakes) 06.05.1881 (Newmarket)
ROSEBUD (2-Year-Old Stakes) 06.05.1881 (Newmarket)
FIRE KING (Grosvenor Trial Stakes) 10.05.1881 (Chester)
DUNMORE (Mostyn Stakes) 10.05.1881 (Chester)
AU REVOIR (Members Selling Welter Handicap Plate) 10.05.1881 (Chester)
GROBY (Stamford 2-Year-Old Plate) 11.05.1881 (Chester)
FIRE KING (Dee Stand Cup Welter Handicap) 11.05.1881 (Chester)
DREAMLAND (Earl of Chester Welter Handicap) 11.05.1881 (Chester)
CHARIBERT (Prince of Wales' Cup) 12.05.1881 WO (Chester)
BRONZE HORSE (Wynn Stakes) 12.05.1881 (Chester)
POST ORBIT (Great Cheshire Handicap Stakes) 12.05.1881 (Chester)
LEITH (Shepperton Selling Welter Handicap) 13.05.1881 (Chester)
LILLIPUTIAN (Halliford Maiden Plate) 13.05.1881 (Chester)
JOCKO (Selling All Aged Welter Stakes) 17.05.1881 (Newmarket)
BROSELEY (Sweepstakes 25 Sovereign) 17.05.1881 (Newmarket)
DOWNPOUR (2-Year-Old Stakes) 18.05.1881 (Newmarket)
MARQUESA (2nd Spring 2-Year-Old Stakes) 19.05.1881 (Newmarket)
AGNETA (Selling Stakes) 19.05.1881 (Newmarket)
LADY EMILY (Exning 2-Year-Old Plate) 19.05.1881 (Newmarket)
DUNMORE (Woodcote Stakes) 31.05.1881 (Epsom)
PETRONEL (Epsom Stakes) 31.05.1881 (Epsom)
FOXGLOVE (Maiden Plate) 31.05.1881 (Epsom)
VALOUR (Craven Stakes) 31.05.1881 (Epsom)
NEWHAVEN (Epsom Manor Stakes) 01.06.1881 (Epsom)
IROQUOIS (Derby Stakes) 01.06.1881 (Epsom)
NEWHAVEN (Mickleham Stakes) 02.06.1881 (Epsom)
BEND OR (Epsom Gold Cup) 03.06.1881 (Epsom)
SIDROPAEL (Juvenile Selling Plate) 06.06.1881 WO (Epsom)
MAIRI (Maiden Stakes) 07.06.1881 (Epsom)
ULSTER QUEEN (John O'Gaunt Plate) 08.06.1881 (Epsom)
GLADSTONE (Mile Selling Handicap Plate) 08.06.1881 DH (Epsom)
VALOUR (Manchester Cup) 09.06.1881 (Manchester)
CHARIBERT (Stewards Cup) 10.06.1881 (Manchester)
IROQUOIS (Prince of Wales Stakes) 14.06.1881 (Ascot)
CRADLE (Trial Stakes) 14.06.1881 (Ascot)
MISS MADCAP (Match/100 Sovereign) 14.06.1881 DH (Ascot)
PETER (Royal Hunt Cup) 15.06.1881 (Ascot)

GOLDEN EYE (Fern Hill Stakes) 15.06.1881 (Ascot)
VOLUPTUARY (2nd Year 23rd Ascot Biennial Stakes) 15.06.1881 (Ascot)
IROQUOIS (St James' Palace Stakes) 16.06.1881 (Ascot)
CHARIBERT (All Aged Stakes) 16.06.1881 (Ascot)
PETER (Hardwicke Stakes) 17.06.1881 (Ascot)
SWORD DANCE (Ascot High Welter Plate) 17.06.1881 (Ascot)
MISENUS (Eton Welter Cup handicap) 21.06.1881 (Windsor)
GRUACH (2-Year-Old Plate) 24.06.1881 (Hampton)
BEDDINGTON (Cardinal Wolsey Stakes) 24.06.1881 (Hampton)
SWORD DANCE (Grendon Welter Handicap) 28.06.1881 (Four Oaks Park)
RED CROSS KNIGHT (All Aged Selling Plate) 28.06.1881 (Four Oaks Park)
MR JARDINE'S CHC (Four Oaks 2-Year-Old Plate) 28.06.1881 (Four Oaks
    Park)
ROMANY KING (Aston Selling Welter Plate) 28.06.1881 (Four Oaks Park)
ROSCIUS (Town Handicap Plate) 28.06.188 (Four Oaks Park)1
TOWER AND SWORD (Park Plate) 29.06.1881 (Four Oaks Park)
THE ROMANY KING (Manor Selling Welter Handicap) 29.06.1881 (Four
    Oaks Park)
RED CROSS KNIGHT (Walmsley Plate) 29.06.1881 (Four Oaks Park)
CHARIBERT (Stockbridge Cup) 30.06.1881 (Stockbridge)
AMBERLEY (Houghton Plate) 30.06.1881 (Stockbridge)
PETRONEL (Her Majesty's Plate) 01.07.1881 (Newmarket)
SWEET LEMON (Selling Stakes) 05.07.1881 (Newmarket)
DUNMORE (Match 200 Guinea) 06.07.1881 (Newmarket)
CHARIBERT (July Cup) 06.07.1881 (Newmarket)
TRISTAN (Horseheath Stakes) 07.07.1881 (Newmarket)
PETER (Banbury Stakes) 07.07.1881 (Newmarket)
FROLICSOME (Princess of Wales Cup) 08.07.1881 (Newcastle)
MOWERINA (Newcastle Stakes) 08.07.1881 (Newcastle)
VOLUPTUARY (St George Stakes) 12.07.1881 (Liverpool)
ROSARIO (Mersey Stakes) 12.07.1881 (Liverpool)
MISS EDWARDS (All Aged Plate) 13.07.1881 (Liverpool)
CRADLE (Sefton Plate) 13.07.1881 (Liverpool)
BEDDINGTON (Shepperton Welter Handicap Plate) 14.07.1881 (Kempton
    Park)
MISENUS (Kempton Trial Stakes) 14.07.1881 (Kempton Park)
LEGHORN (Richmond Midweight Handicap Plate) 14.07.1881 (Kempton
    Park)
BORDER QUEEN (Halliford Welter Handicap Plate) 15.07.1881 (Kempton
    Park)
BORDER QUEEN (Thames Maiden Plate) 16.07.1881 (Kempton Park)
THE SHAKER (Wolsey Selling Plate) 16.07.1881 (Kempton Park)
MISS EDWARDS (Fitzwilliam Stakes) 19.07.1881 (Huntingdon)
RHIDORROCH (Queens Plate) 19.07.1881 (Huntingdon)
BEDDINGTON (Cromwell Welter Handicap) 20.07.1881 (Huntingdon)
PIERA (Selling Welter Handicap Plate) 20.07.1881 (Huntingdon)
MARY GUY (Oakley Selling Plate) 20.07.1881 (Huntingdon)
ISABEAU (Warren Nursery Plate) 22.07.1881 (Huntingdon)
WOOD REEVE (Surrey Juvenile Stakes) 22.07.1881 (Huntingdon)

CHARIBERT (Gold Cup) 22.07.1881 (Huntingdon)
DUTCH OVEN (Richmond Stakes) 26.07.1881 (Goodwood)
MARASCHINO (Sweepstakes/10 Sovereign) 26.07.1881 (Goodwood)
CHARIBERT (Lennox Stakes) 27.07.1881 (Goodwood)
LIMESTONE (Sussex Stakes) 27.07.1881 (Goodwood)
BALIOL (Levant Stakes) 27.07.1881 (Goodwood)
DUTCH OVEN (Rous Memorial Stakes) 28.07.1881 (Goodwood)
SWORD DANCE (Goodwood Corinthian Plate) 28.07.1881 (Goodwood)
MATLOCK (Selling Stakes) 28.07.1881 (Goodwood)
WOLSEY (Nursery Stakes) 29.07.1881 (Goodwood)
THE ROMANY KING (Thames Selling Welter Handicap Plate) 10.08.1881
    (Kempton Park)
NIMBLE (Garrick 2-Year-Old Plate) 10.08.1881 (Kempton Park)
MAGICIAN (A Plate) 11.08.1881 (Kempton Park)
ELDERBERRY (Mile Selling Welter Handicap Plate) 11.08.1881 (Kempton
    Park)
FIRST CHOICE (Town Selling Stakes) 11.08.1881 (Kempton Park)
BLONDE (Datchett Welter Handicap Plate) 12.08.1881 (Kempton Park)
ADVANCE (Trial Stakes) 16.08.1881 (Stockton)
DOWNPOUR (Cleveland Stakes) 16.08.1881 (Stockton)
CAPRI (South Stockton Selling Stakes) 16.08.1881 (Stockton)
DOWNPOUR (Lambton Plate) 17.08.1881 (Stockton)
LADY STUART (Harewood Stakes) 17.08.1881 (Stockton)
SILVER BELL (Hardwicke Stakes) 17.08.1881 (Stockton)
SIWARD (Thornaby Stakes) 17.08.1881 (Stockton)
GEHEIMNISS (Convivial Stakes) 23.08.1881 (Stockton)
AMALFI (1st Year/26th North England Biennial Stakes) 24.08.1881 (York)
THE SHAKER (Savile Stakes) 25.08.1881 (York)
SWEET LEMON (Flying 2-Year-Old Plate) 30.08.1881 (Warwick)
CAPT. PRIME'S BF (Juvenile Plate) 31.08.1881 (Warwick)
DUTCH OVEN (Champion Breeders Foal Stakes) 01.09.1881 (Warwick)
WAR HORN (County Members Welter Handicap) 08.09.1881 (Sandown
    Park)
NIMBLE (Gopsal Nursery Handicap Plate) 08.09.1881 (Sandown Park)
PETRONEL (Great Yorkshire Handicap) 13.09.1881 (York)
IROQUOIS (St Leger) 14.09.1881 (Doncaster)
LITTLE SISTER (Tattersall Sale Stakes) 14.09.1881 (Doncaster)
MOWERINA (Portland Plate) 15.09.1881 (Doncaster)
SWORD DANCE (Alexandra Plate) 15.09.1881 (Doncaster)
BAL GAL (Park Hill Stakes) 16.09.1881 (Doncaster)
PETRONEL (Doncaster Cup) 16.09.1881 (Doncaster)
LITTLE SISTER (Wentworth Stakes) 16.09.1881 (Doncaster)
VAN DYKE (150 Sovereign Cup) 22.09.1881 (Newmarket)
MISENUS (De Trafford Plate) 23.09.1881 (Newmarket)
STRATHAVON (Selling Welter Stakes) 23.09.1881 (Newmarket)
ACME (Selling Stakes) 23.09.1881 (Newmarket)
DUTCH OVEN (Buckenham Post Produce Stakes) 27.09.1881 (Newmarket)
GOODNESS (Selling Plate) 27.09.1881 (Newmarket)
MURIEL (3rd Year 32nd Triennial Stakes) 27.09.1881 (Newmarket)

DUTCH OVEN (1st Year 34th Triennial Produce Stakes) 29.09.1881
(Newmarket)
DUTCH OVEN (Rous Memorial Stakes) 30.09.1881 (Newmarket)
MARITORNES (1st October 2-Year-Old Produce Stakes) 30.09.1881
(Newmarket)
WARRIOR (Moulton Handicap) 30.09.1881 (Newmarket)
SILVER BELL (Bestwood Nursery Plate Handicap) 04.10.1881 (Nottingham)
METEORA (Welbeck Welter Plate Handicap) 04.10.1881 (Nottingham)
TELESCOPE (Mapperley Selling Plate) 04.10.1881 (Nottingham)
CAPRI (Castle Selling Plate) 05.10.1881 (Nottingham)
ATALANTA (Annesley Park Plate Welter Handicap) 05.10.1881
(Nottingham)
STRATHAVON (Shepperton Selling Stakes) 06.10.1881 (Nottingham)
KNIGHT OF BURGHLEY (Thames Selling Handicap Plate) 06.10.1881
(Nottingham)
FIRST FLIGHT (Hanworth Park Nursery Handicap) 07.10.1881 (Kempton
Park)
DUTCH OVEN (Clearwell Stakes) 10.10.1881 (Newmarket)
DARNAWAY (October Post Produce Stakes) 10.10.1881 (Newmarket)
MARITORNES (100 Sovereign Plate) 10.10.1881 (Newmarket)
ANGELINA (Heath Stakes) 11.10.1881 (Newmarket)
GOLDEN EYE (Burwell Stakes) 11.10.1881 (Newmarket)
CRADLE (100 Sovereign Plate) 11.10.1881 (Newmarket)
HEMLOCK (Scurry Nursery Handicap) 11.10.1881 (Newmarket)
CYLINDER (Cambridgeshire Welter Stakes) 12.10.1881 (Newmarket)
COMELY (Ditch Mile Nursery) 12.10.1881 (Newmarket)
FOXHALL (Select Stakes) 12.10.1881 (Newmarket)
MOWERINA (Flying Welter Handicap) 12.10.1881 (Newmarket)
BEND OR (Champion Stakes) 13.10.1881 (Kempton Park)
PETRONEL (Her Majesty's Plate) 13.10.1881 (Kempton Park)
NIMBLE (Sweepstake) 14.10.1881 (Kempton Park)
CAPRI (Juvenile Plate) 18.10.1881 (Four Oaks Park)
THE SHAKER (Edgbaston Selling Plate) 18.10.1881 (Four Oaks Park)
MAY QUEEN (Four Oaks Welter Plate) 18.10.1881 (Four Oaks Park)
METEORA (Craven Handicap Plate) 18.10.1881 (Four Oaks Park)
CAPRI (Selling Nursery Handicap Plate) 19.10.1881 (Newmarket)
TWINKLING ARROW (100 Guinea Match) 20.10.1881 (Newmarket)
STRATHAVON (Park Selling Stakes) 20.10.1881 (Newmarket)
PASSAIC (Cambridgeshire Trial Plate) 20.10.1881 (Newmarket)
DUTCH OVEN (Dewhurst Plate) 26.10.1881 (Newmarket)
MILLICENT (Selling Stakes) 27.10.1881 (Newmarket)
BROTHERHOOD (Selling Plate) 28.10.1881 (Newmarket)
COMUS (Houghton Stakes) 28.10.1881 (Newmarket)
TELESCOPE (Selling Welter Handicap Plate) 02.11.1881 (Brighton)
PELERINE (Chaplin Stakes) 03.11.1881 (Lewes)
STRATHAVON (Witham Selling Plate) 03.11.1881 (Lewes)
MAZURKA (Croxteth Cup) 08.11.1881 (Liverpool)
TOWER AND SWORD (New Stand Plate) 08.11.1881 (Liverpool)
RUBICON (Wednesday Plate) 09.11.1881 (Liverpool)

SPRINGTIDE (City Cup Welter Handicap) 09.11.1881 (Liverpool)
SIR THEOBALD (Palatine Nursery Handicap) 10.11.1881 (Liverpool)
TARTARY (Thursday Plate) 10.11.1881 (Liverpool)
STRATHAVON (Friday Plate) 11.11.1881 (Shrewsbury)
PETRONEL (Her Majesty's Plate) 11.11.1881 (Shrewsbury)
STRATHAVON (Abbey Stakes) 16.11.1881 (Shrewsbury)
HAUTBOY (Maiden Plate) 16.11.1881 (Shrewsbury)
PETRONEL (Her Majesty's Plate) 16.11.1881 (Shrewsbury)
PASSAIC (Haughmond Plate) 17.11.1881 (Shrewsbury)
BEATUS (Grendon Welter Handicap Plate) 17.11.1881 (Shrewsbury)
RUBICON (Acton Burnell Stakes) 17.11.1881 (Shrewsbury)
COQ DU VILLAGE (Newport Selling Handicap) 18.11.1881 (Shrewsbury)
WINSOME (Town Plate) 22.11.1881 (Warwick)
ORTYX (Selling 2-Year-Old Plate) 22.11.1881 (Warwick)
RUBICON (Selling Welter Plate) 22.11.1881 (Warwick)
REGENT (Guy Welter Handicap Plate) 22.11.1881 (Warwick)
VALOUR (November Cup) 23.11.1881 (Manchester)
ISABEL (Lancaster Nursery Handicap) 23.11.1881 (Manchester)
SCARAMOUGH (Cup 200 Sovereign) 26.11.1881 (Manchester)
KING OF SCOTLAND (Welter Handicap Plate) 26.11.1881 (Manchester)

1882 TOWER AND SWORD (Prince Park Plate) 23.03.1882 (Liverpool)
ALFONSO (Althorp Park Stakes) 28.03.1882 (Northampton)
SPECIALITE (Wakefield Lawn Stakes) 28.03.1882 (Northampton)
TRISTAN (Queens Plate) 28.03.1882 (Northampton)
VAGRANT (St Liz Welter Handicap) 28.03.1882 (Northampton)
ALFONSO (Croxton Park Stakes) 30.03.1882 (Croydon)
STAR AND GARTER (Thurgarton Priory Welter Selling Plate) 05.04.1882
    (Nottingham)
KNIGHT OF BURGHLEY (Kempton Park Easter Plate Handicap) 10.04.1882
    (Kempton Park)
RED SPECTRE (1st Year/2nd Biennial Plate) 12.04.1882 (Newmarket)
DAISY (Refuse 2-Year-Old Plate) 13.04.1882 (Newmarket)
MYRA (2nd Year 1st Biennial Plate) 14.04.1882 (Newmarket)
DAISY (Refuse 2-Year-Old) 15.04.1882 (Newmarket)
CHEVRONEL (Stamford Plate) 19.04.1882 (Epsom)
FAUGH A BALLAGH (Riddles Plate) 19.04.1882 (Epsom)
MISS WARDLE (Juvenile Selling Plate) 19.04.1882 (Epsom)
TOWER AND SWORD (Selling Handicap/5 Sovereign) 19.04.1882 (Epsom)
KATE CRAIG (Sandown Park Stakes) 21.04.1882 (Sandown Park)
STRATHAVON (Selling Plate/100 Guinea) 25.04.1882 (Sandown Park)
SPEEDWELL (1st Year 2nd Cambridge Biennial Stakes) 25.04.1882
    (Sandown Park)
EASTERN EMPRESS (Stand Stakes) 26.04.1882 (Sandown Park)
CAMILLA (Mostyn Plate) 02.05.1882 (Chester)
COLUMBINE (Cestrian Sweepstake Handicap Plate) 02.05.1882 (Chester)
DUVAL (Belgrave Welter Cup Handicap) 02.05.1882 (Chester)
PETTICOAT (Stamford Plate) 02.05.1882 (Chester)
CAMILLA (Badminton Plate) 03.05.1882 (Chester)

BROTHERHOOD (Wilton Stakes) 03.05.1882 (Chester)
GAYDENE (Earl of Chester Welter Plate) 03.05.1882 (Chester)
WHIPPER INN (Dee Stakes) 04.05.1882 (Chester)
CHANOINE (Wynn Handicap Plate) 04.05.1882 (Chester)
LOTUS EATER (May Stakes) 04.05.1882 (Chester)
TRISTAN (Her Majesty's Plate) 04.05.1882 (Chester)
HESPER (Kempton Park May Handicap) 05.05.1882 (Kempton Park)
SULPHUR (Halliford Plate) 05.05.1882 (Kempton Park)
LOWLAND CHIEF (Welter Handicap/10 Sovereign) 10.05.1882 (Newmarket)
LITTLE SISTER (Selling Plate) 10.05.1882 DH (Newmarket)
BRF (Selling Stakes) 11.05.1882 (Newmarket)
EASTERN EMPRESS (Fly Handicap) 11.05.1882 (Newmarket)
KEEL ROW (Hopeful Stakes) 18.05.1882 (Doncaster)
LADY VESTA (Weatham Stakes) 19.05.1882 (Harpenden)
BEAU BRUMMEL (Woodcote Stakes) 23.05.1882 (Epsom)
LIMESTONE (Royal Stakes Handicap) 25.05.1882 (Epsom)
DISTEL (Ebbisham Stakes) 25.05.1882 (Epsom)
MISS WARDLE (Mickleham Stakes) 25.05.1882 (Epsom)
TRISTAN (Epsom Gold Cup) 26.05.1882 (Epsom)
SULPHUR (Hampton Midweight Handicap Plate) 29.05.1882 (Kempton
     Park)
CENTENARY (Selling Stakes) 30.05.1882 (Manchester)
LIZZIE (A Plate/100 Guinea) 30.05.1882 (Manchester)
ATALANTA (Stewards Welter Handicap) 31.05.1882 (Manchester)
HOTSPUR (Duchy Welter Handicap) 31.05.1882 (Manchester)
CHANOINE (Selling Handicap Plate) 01.06.1882 (Manchester)
LOTTIE (Selling Plate/2-Year-Old) 01.06.1882 (Manchester)
RAMSBURY (City Welter Handicap Plate) 01.06.1882 (Manchester)
MOONSTONE (Wilton Welter Handicap Plate) 02.06.1882 (Manchester)
STRATHAVON (Summer Plate) 02.06.1882 (Manchester)
HAPPY BOY (Selling Handicap Plate) 02.06.1882 (Manchester)
FRIAR RUSH (Isonomy Plate) 02.06.1882 (Manchester)
FORTISSIMO (Queens Plate) 02.06.1882 WO (Manchester)
TYNDRUM (Maiden 2-Year-Old Plate) 03.06.1882 (Sandown Park)
HERALD (St James' Stakes) 03.06.1882 (Sandown Park)
BRUCE (Grand Prix De Paris) 04.06.1882 (Paris)
RETREAT (Ascot Stakes Handicap) 06.06.1882 (Ascot)
SYMPHONY (1st Year 30th Triennial Stakes) 07.06.1882 (Ascot)
BATTLEFIELD (St James' Palace Stakes) 08.06.1882 (Ascot)
RETREAT (Rous Memorial Stakes) 08.06.1882 (Ascot)
ROOKERY (Windsor Castle Stakes) 09.06.1882 (Ascot)
EASTERN EMPRESS (Queen Stakes Plate) 09.06.1882 (Ascot)
MOLDA (Selling Welter Plate) 13.06.1882 (Windsor)
STRATHAVON (Salt Hill Plate) 13.06.1882 WO (Windsor)
CAUCASUS (Prince of Orange Stakes) 15.06.1882 (Hampton)
SIMNEL (Railway Stakes) 16.06.1882 (Hampton)
REMEMBER (Surrey Welter Handicap) 21.06.1882 (Bibury Club)
BRITOMARTIS (Champagne Stakes) 21.06.1882 (Bibury Club)
PETRONEL (Her Majesty's Plate) 23.06.1882 (Stockbridge)

LEPUS (All Aged Welter Plate) 23.06.1882 (Stockbridge)
ROOKERY (Great Midland Plate) 27.06.1882 (Four Oaks Park)
DISTEL (Great Welter Handicap) 27.06.1882 (Four Oaks Park)
TOWER AND SWORD (Park Plate) 28.06.1882 (Four Oaks Park)
HAPPY BOY (Walmsley Plate) 28.06.1882 (Four Oaks Park)
PETRONEL (Her Majesty's Plate) 29.06.1882 (Newcastle)
GISELLA (Selling Stakes/10 Sovereign) 04.07.1882 (Newmarket)
TOWER AND SWORD (Selling Plate/100 Guinea) 04.07.1882 (Newmarket)
MOWERINA (Visitors Plate) 04.07.1882 (Newmarket)
TRISTAN (July Cup) 05.07.1882 (Newmarket)
TOWER AND SWORD (Selling Plate/100 Guinea) 05.07.1882 (Newmarket)
GALLIARD (Chesterfield Stakes) 06.07.1882 (Newmarket)
STRATHAVON (Sweepstakes/10 Sovereign) 06.07.1882 (Newmarket)
VANDUARA (Selling Stakes/10 Sovereign) 06.07.1882 (Newmarket)
EDENSOR (July Handicap) 06.07.1882 (Newmarket)
BRITOMARTIS (Stetchworth Stakes) 07.07.1882 (Newmarket))
VANDUARA (Bentinck Plate) 11.07.1882 (Liverpool)
MOWERINA (Molyneux Cup Handicap) 11.07.1882 (Liverpool)
TOWER AND SWORD (Lancaster Welter Handicap) 11.07.1882 (Liverpool)
KEEL ROW (Mersey Stakes) 11.07.1882 (Liverpool)
TOWER AND SWORD (Windermere Plate) 11.07.1882 WO (Liverpool)
RAMSBURY (Rays Welter Handicap) 12.07.1882 (Windsor)
CENTENARY (Town Plate) 12.07.1882 (Windsor)
SIMNEL (Sunsbury Welter Handicap) 13.07.1882 (Kempton Park)
SULPHUR (Prince of Wales Cup) 13.07.1882 (Kempton Park)
COSTA (Teddington Selling Stakes) 13.07.1882 (Kempton Park)
ROOKERY (International 2-Year-Old Plate) 14.07.1882 (Kempton Park)
KING HUMBERT (Hanworth Park Welter Handicap) 15.07.1882 (Kempton Park)
SUTLER (Royal Stakes Handicap) 21.07.1882 (Kempton Park)
REPUTATION (Midweight Handicap) 21.07.1882 (Sandown Park)
REMEMBER (Mile Selling Handicap) 21.07.1882 (Sandown Park)
KATE CRAIG (Nursery Warren Welter Plate) 21.07.1882 (Sandown Park)
KNIGHT OF BURGHLEY (Sweepstakes/10 Sovereign) 25.07.1882 (Goodwood)
RANELAGH II (Maiden Stakes) 26.07.1882 (Goodwood)
ELZEVIR (Molecomb Stakes) 28.07.1882 DH (Goodwood)
CANON (Maiden Plate) 01.08.1882 (Brighton)
SKIPETAR (Patcham Stakes) 01.08.1882 (Brighton)
KATE CRAIG (Rottingdean Plate) 02.08.1882 (Brighton)
RAMSBURY (Preston Handicap) 03.08.1882 (Brighton)
RANELAGH II (Kempton Town Plate) 03.08.1882 (Brighton)
ALCADE (Mile Selling Plate) 03.08.1882 (Brighton)
KATE CRAIG (Cliftonville Plate) 03.08.1882 (Brighton)
FORTISSIMO (Her Majesty's Plate) 04.08.1882 (Lewes)
POLARIS (Priory Stakes) 05.08.1882 (Lewes)
FORTISSIMO (Lewes Handicap) 05.08.1882 (Lewes)
SUNSHINE (Town Plate) 05.08.1882 (Lewes)
LA FIANCEE (Castle Plate) 05.08.1882 (Lewes)

ALFONSO (Mount Harry Plate) 05.08.1882 (Lewes)
RAMSBURY (Hamsey Welter Handicap) 05.08.1882 (Lewes)
CANON (Richmond Plate) 08.08.1882 (Kempton Park)
KNIGHT OF BURGHLEY (Kempton Park Midweight Handicap Plate)
    08.08.1882 (Kempton Park)
COSTA (Thames Selling Plate) 09.08.1882 (Kempton Park)
FRIAR RUSH (Sunbury Midweight Handicap Plate) 09.08.1882 (Kempton
    Park)
MR J GRETTON'S BF (Garrick Selling Plate 2-Year-Old) 10.08.1882
    (Windsor)
F (Bray Stakes) 10.08.1882 (Windsor)
BRAYLEY (Park Plate) 10.08.1882 (Windsor)
LONGFELLOW (Welter Selling Plate/100 Guinea) 10.08.1882 (Windsor)
LONGFELLOW (Boveney Plate) 11.08.1882 (Windsor)
FLASH (Frogmore Selling Plate) 11.08.1882 (Windsor)
SIMNEL (Datchett Cup) 11.08.1882 (Windsor)
THE SHAKER (Zetland Stakes) 22.08.1882 (York)
MATILDA (Badminton Plate) 22.08.1882 (York)
DUTCH OVEN (Yorkshire Oaks) 22.08.1882 (York)
GALLIARD (Prince of Wales Stakes) 23.08.1882 (York)
FRIAR RUSH (Londesborough Cup) 23.08.1882 (York)
KNIGHT OF BURGHLEY (Harewood Plate) 24.08.1882 (York)
COSTA (Fitzwilliam Selling Stakes) 29.08.1882 (Huntingdon)
POLARIS (Hinchingbrook Plate) 29.08.1882 (Huntingdon)
POLARIS (Milton Plate) 30.08.1882 (Huntingdon)
TOWER AND SWORD (Shipley Handicap) 31.08.1882 (Derby)
TYNDRUM (Devonshire Nursery) 01.09.1882 (Derby)
LENNOXLOVE (Elvaston Castle) 01.09.1882 (Derby)
BOSWELL (Clumber Plate) 12.09.1882 (Doncaster)
MOB ORATOR (2 Horse Race) 12.09.1882 (Doncaster)
DUTCH OVEN (St Leger Stakes) 13.09.1882 (Doncaster)
BEATUS (Milton Stakes) 13.09.1882 (Doncaster)
SUTLER (Alexandra Plate Handicap) 14.09.1882 (Doncaster)
DUCHESS OF CORNWALL (Wentworth Post Produce Stakes) 15.09.1882
    (Doncaster)
RESERVE (City Member Plate) 19.09.1882 (Doncaster)
ELIACIN (Beaudesert Welter Plate) 19.09.1882 (Lichfield)
CENSER (Anglesey Welter Plate) 19.09.1882 (Lichfield)
INCENDIARY (Lichfield Welter Handicap Plate) 20.09.1882 (Lichfield)
TOWER AND SWORD (A Cup of 150 Sovereign) 21.09.1882 (Manchester)
TOWER AND SWORD (Selling Welter Stakes) 21.09.1882 (Manchester)
SPRING GUN (Selling Stakes) 22.09.1882 (Manchester)
CANON (A Plate/2-Year-Old) 22.09.1882 (Manchester)
RAMSBURY (Oldham Welter Plate) 22.09.1882 (Manchester)
FRIAR RUSH (Manchester Autumn Handicap) 23.09.1882 (Manchester)
LA FIANCEE (Selling Handicap Plate) 23.09.1882 (Manchester)
LYRIC (September Cup) 23.09.1882 (Manchester)
BEAU BRUMMEL (Hopeful Stakes) 26.09.1882 (Newmarket)
DUTCH OVEN (4th Great Foal Stakes) 26.09.1882 (Newmarket)

BOSWELL (All Aged Trial) 26.09.1882 (Newmarket)
DUCHESS OF CORNWALL (Buckenham Post Produce Stakes) 26.09.1882 (Newmarket)
DUTCH OVEN (2nd Year/34th Triennial Produce Stakes) 27.09.1882 (Newmarket)
LADISLAS (1st October 2-Year-Old Stakes) 29.09.1882 DH (Newmarket)
ADDY (Scurry Nursery) 29.09.1882 (Newmarket)
LENNOX LOVE (Mapperley Selling Plate) 03.10.1882 (Nottingham)
CENSER (Friar Tuck Selling Plate) 04.10.1882 (Nottingham)
DREAMLAND (Richmond Stakes) 05.10.1882 (Kempton Park)
ROYAL GEORGE (2-Year-Old Auction Plate) 05.10.1882 WO (Kempton Park)
CHEVALIER (Walton Selling Welter Handicap) 06.10.1882 (Kempton Park)
ROYAL GEORGE (Teddington 2-Year-Old) 06.10.1882 (Kempton Park)
TOASTMASTER (Kempton Park Cambridgeshire Triennial Handicap) 06.10.1882 (Kempton Park)
DILETTO (Maiden Plate) 10.10.1882 (Newmarket)
TRISTAN (Champion Stakes) 12.10.1882 DH (Newmarket)
BRITOMARTIS (Bretby Stakes) 12.10.1882 (Newmarket)
ROYAL GEORGE (Sweepstakes/10 Sovereign) 13.10.1882 (Newmarket)
KEEL ROW (Portland Nursery Plate) 17.10.1882 (Four Oaks Park)
LA FIANCEE (Edgbaston Selling Plate) 17.10.1882 (Four Oaks Park)
JUBILEE (Oscott Midweight Handicap Plate) 17.10.1882 (Four Oaks Park)
LA FIANCEE (Tamworth Plate) 18.10.1882 (Four Oaks Park)
FLEUR D'ORANGE (Orleans Nursery Handicap Plate) 19.10.1882 (Sandown Park)
SIMNEL (Park Selling Stakes) 20.10.1882 (Sandown Park)
ELIACIN (All Aged Selling Plate) 23.10.1882 (Newmarket)
GISELA (Sweepstakes/10 Sovereign) 23.10.1882 (Newmarket)
WITCHCRAFT (Last Six Furlongs) 24.10.1882 (Newmarket)
HIGHLAND CHIEF (Home Bred Sweepstakes) 25.10.1882 (Newmarket)
NIMBLE (Ovingdean Stakes) 31.10.1882 (Brighton)
BRAG (Sussex Welter Handicap) 31.10.1882 (Brighton)
LANDROST (Selling Welter Handicap Plate) 01.11.1882 (Brighton)
DUNMORE (Witham Selling Stakes) 02.11.1882 (Lincoln)
TORPEDO (Chaplin Stakes) 02.11.1882 (Lincoln)
LITTLE CHARLIE (Tuesday Plate) 07.11.1882 (Liverpool)
LENNOX LOVE (Alt Welter Handicap) 08.11.1882 (Liverpool)
KNIGHT OF BURGHLEY (Liverpool Stewards Cup) 08.11.1882 (Liverpool)
ANEMORE (Palatine Nursery Handicap) 09.11.1882 (Liverpool)
LENNOXLOVE (Wavertree Welter Handicap) 09.11.1882 (Liverpool)
ERCILDOUNE (Toxteth Welter Handicap) 10.11.1882 (Liverpool)
LEGHORN (Haughmond Plate) 14.11.1882 (Shrewsbury)
MARIA (Borough Members Plate) 14.11.1882 (Shrewsbury)
SUNSHINE (County Member Plate) 15.11.1882 (Shrewsbury)
LEGHORN (Beaudesert Selling Plate) 16.11.1882 (Derby)
RED KING (Allestree Plate) 17.11.1882 (Derby)
LITTLE CHARLIE (2-Year-Old Selling Stakes) 22.11.1882 (Manchester)

ADDY (Stamford Nursery Handicap) 23.11.1882(Manchester)
SIREN (Cuerdon Cup) 23.11.1882 (Manchester)
SUNSHINE (Irwell Stakes) 24.11.1882 (Manchester)

1883   WHITEBINE (Kempton Park Eastern Cup/Handicap Plate) 26.03.1883
            (Kempton Park)
        ELIACIN (Prince of Wales Cup Handicap) 29.03.1883 (Liverpool)
        LANDDROST (County Welter Handicap) 29.03.1883 (Liverpool)
        PEBBLE (Spring Nursery Stakes Handicap) 30.03.1883 (Liverpool)
        LANDDROST (Lancastrian Plate Handicap) 31.03.1883 (Liverpool)
        THE MATE (St Liz Welter Handicap) 03.04.1883 (Northampton)
        BACCARAT (Selling Stakes) 04.04.1883 (Northampton)
        LIMOSA (Croydon Spring 2-Year-Old Race) 05.04.1883 (Croydon)
        GRANDMASTER (Craven Stakes) 12.04.1883 (Newmarket)
        DUTCH OVEN (2nd Year/24th New Biennial Stakes) 12.04.1883 WO
            (Newmarket)
        FAUGH A BALLAGH (2nd Year 2nd Biennial Plate) 13.04.1883 (Newmarket)
        KINCALDINE (Westminster Stakes) 17.04.1883 (Epsom)
        LACEMAN (Great Surrey Handicap) 17.04.1883 DH (Epsom)
        CAMLET (Sandown Park 2-Year-Old Stakes) 20.04.1883 (Sandown Park)
        PELERINE (Hampton Selling Handicap) 21.04.1883 (Sandown Park)
        GALLIARD (2000 Guineas) 25.04.1883 (Newmarket)
        PIRAEUS (3rd Welter Handicap Plate) 26.04.1883 (Newmarket)
        MERRIMAC (Newmarket Stakes) 27.04.1883 (Newmarket)
        PAN (Mostyn 2-Year-Old Plate) 01.05.1883 (Chester)
        CENSER (Wilton Stakes) 02.05.1883 WO (Chester)
        SILVER SEA (Badminton 2-Year-Old Plate) 02.05.1883 (Chester)
        INCENDIARY (Combermere Handicap) 02.05.1883 (Chester)
        PELERINE (Dee Stand Cup Handicap) 02.05.1883 (Chester)
        RHINELAND (Earl of Chester's Welter Plate Handicap) 02.05.1883 (Chester)
        CENSER (City Selling Plate) 03.05.1883 (Chester)
        INCENDIARY (Wynn Handicap Plate) 03.05.1883 (Chester)
        REPRIEVE (Kempton Park International Breeders 2-Year-Old Stakes)
            05.05.1883 (Kempton Park)
        CAMLET (Spring 2-Year-Old Stakes) 08.05.1883 (Newmarket)
        ERCILDOUNE (Selling Plate) 09.05.1883 (Newmarket)
        TOURIST (Selling Plate) 09.05.1883 (Newmarket)
        CAMLET (Exning 2-Year-Old Plate) 10.05.1883 (Newmarket)
        QUEEN'S COUNSEL (Hampton 2-Year-Old Plate) 14.05.1883 (Kempton Park)
        PRINCESS Charlotte (May 2-Year-Old Selling Plate) 14.05.1883 (Kempton
            Park)
        REPRIEVE (Hartington Plate) 15.05.1883 (Manchester)
        CENSER (Selling Stakes) 15.05.1883 (Manchester)
        ERCILDOUNE (May Cup) 15.05.1883 (Manchester)
        SOUTHAMPTON (Stewards Welter Handicap) 16.05.1883 (Manchester)
        PRESIDENT (Mile Selling Handicap Plate) 16.05.1883 (Manchester)
        STUMP ORATOR (Derby All Aged Plate) 16.05.1883 (Manchester)
        CENSER (Selling Stakes) 16.05.1883 WO (Manchester)
        YORKIST (Duchy Welter Handicap) 16.05.1883 (Manchester)

SPONDEE (Selling 2-Year-Old Plate) 17.05.1883 (Manchester)
STUMP ORATOR (Derby All Aged) 18.05.1883 (Manchester)
MOCCOLO (Summer Plate) 18.05.1883 (Manchester)
BELINDA (Whitsuntide Plate) 18.05.1883 (Manchester)
CENSER (Selling Handicap Plate) 18.05.1883 (Manchester)
FRONTIN (Prix Du Jockey Club) 20.05.1883 (France)
KNIGHT ERRANT (Maiden Plate) 22.05.1883 (Epsom)
REPUTATION (Egmont Plate Handicap) 22.05.1883 (Epsom)
BARCALDINE (Epsom Stakes Free Handicap) 22.05.1883 (Epsom)
HERALD (Headley Stakes) 23.05.1883 (Epsom)
LONGFELLOW (Selling Welter Handicap) 24.05.1883 (Epsom)
SANDIWAY (Acorn Stakes) 25.05.1883 (Epsom)
LORD BYRON (Epsom 2-Year-Old Plate) 25.05.1883 (Epsom)
CAMLET (Hopeful Stakes) 30.05.1883 (Doncaster)
WHIRLPOOL (Municipal Stakes) 30.05.1883 (Doncaster)
ELIACIN (Londesborough Plate Handicap) 30.05.1883 (Doncaster)
HENLEY (Sandown Welter Handicap) 02.06.1883 (Sandown Park)
GALLIARD (Prince of Wales Stakes) 05.06.1883 (Ascot)
GEHEIMNISS (Trial Stakes) 05.06.1883 (Ascot)
BARCALDINE (Orange Cup) 06.06.1883 (Ascot)
SWEETBREAD (Visitor's Plate Handicap) 06.06.1883 (Ascot)
GALLIARD (St James Stakes) 07.06.1883 (Ascot)
TYNDRUM (2nd Year 20th New Biennial Stakes) 07.06.1883 (Ascot)
DESPAIR (All Aged Stakes) 07.06.1883 (Ascot)
FAUGH A BALLAGH (Alexandra Plate) 08.06.1883 (Ascot)
DESPAIR (Wokingham Stakes) 08.06.1883 (Ascot)
GALLIARD (2nd Year 30th Triennial Stakes) 08.06.1883 (Ascot)
ANTLER (Manor Plate Handicap) 14.06.1883 (Hampton)
MRS MALAPROP (Prince of Orange Stakes) 14.06.1883 (Hampton)
PEBBLE (Wolsey Midweight Handicap Plate) 19.06.1883 (Kempton Park)
THE RAKER (Hampton 2-Year-Old Plate) 19.06.1883 (Kempton Park)
ISHAH (Home Bred Sweepstakes) 20.06.1883 WO (Bibury Club)
CENSER (A Plate/100 Sovereign) 20.06.1883 (Bibury Club)
SANDIWAY (Mottisfont Stakes) 21.06.1883 (Stockbridge)
SANDIWAY (Troy Stakes) 22.06.1883 (Stockbridge)
CLATFORD (Penton All Aged Welter Plate) 22.06.1883 (Stockbridge)
DUTCH OVEN (Her Majesty's Plate) 22.06.1883 (Stockbridge)
ST BLAISE (2nd Year 24th Biennial Stakes) 22.06.1883 WO (Stockbridge)
ROUT (Park Plate) 26.06.1883 (Four Oaks Park)
BARCALDINE (Northumberland Plate) 27.06.1883 (Newcastle)
WHITEBINE (Ravensworth Handicap Plate) 27.06.1883 (Newcastle)
KNIGHT ERRANT (Seaton Delaval Stakes) 28.06.1883 (Newcastle)
SILVER BELL (Bunbury Mile) 03.07.1883 (Newmarket)
WHITEBINE (Sweepstakes 10 Sovereign) 03.07.1883 (Newmarket)
GEHEIMNISS (Bunbury Handicap Plate) 03.07.1883 (Newmarket)
FLETA (2 Horse Race) 04.07.1883 (Newmarket)
PATRIARCH (Selling Stakes) 05.07.1883 (Newmarket)
GLEN ALBYN (Sweepstakes) 05.07.1883 (Newmarket)
ALCALDE (County Welter Handicap) 10.07.1883 (Windsor)

HENTLAND (Upton 2-Year-Old Stakes) 10.07.1883 (Windsor)
COMET (Mile Selling Stakes) 10.07.1883 (Windsor)
MR G LISTER'S BRF (Paddock Stakes) 11.07.1883 (Windsor)
SUPERBA (Midsummer Plate) 11.07.1883 (Windsor)
MR TE WALKER'S CHF (Walton Selling Welter Handicap) 12.07.1883
    (Kempton Park)
ATHOL MAID (Halliford Welter Handicap Plate) 13.07.1883 (Kempton Park)
LINARIA (1st Year/19th Winchester Biennial Stakes) 18.07.1883
    (Winchester)
ST BLAISE (2nd Year/18th Winchester Biennial Stakes) 18.07.1883 WO
    (Winchester)
CHESTERFIELD (Speculation Plate) 19.07.1883 (Pontefract)
CANON (Oadby Selling Plate) 24.07.1883 (Leicester)
PIRAEUS (Bradgate Park Plate Handicap) 25.07.1883 (Leicester)
    MINIATURE (Billesdon Selling Plate) 25.07.1883 (Leicester)
LEEDS (Curzon Plate Handicap) 25.07.1883 (Leicester)
REPRIEVE (National Breeders Produce Stakes) 27.07.1883 (Sandown Park)
MR G LISTER'S BRF (Surrey Juvenile Stakes) 27.07.1883 (Sandown Park)
ST SIMON (Halnaker Stakes) 31.07.1883 (Goodwood)
AVIGNON (Ham Produce Stakes) 31.07.1883 (Goodwood)
SANDIWAY (Findon Stakes) 01.08.1883 (Goodwood)
ST SIMON (Maiden Stakes) 01.08.1883 (Goodwood)
EASTERN EMPRESS (Lennox Stakes) 01.08.1883 (Goodwood)
SWEETBREAD (Visitor's Plate Handicap) 01.08.1883 (Goodwood)
PERDITA II (Selling Stakes) 02.08.1883 (Goodwood)
SANDIWAY (Nursery Stakes) 03.08.1883 (Goodwood)
LA TRAPPE (Molecomb Stakes) 03.08.1883 (Goodwood)
MACALPINE (Patcham Stakes) 07.08.1883 (Brighton)
KINCARDINE (Rottingdean Plate) 08.08.1883 (Brighton)
MACALPINE (Pavilion Stakes) 08.08.1883 (Brighton)
GARETH (Preston Handicap) 09.08.1883 (Brighton)
MR R PECK'S BRG (Selling Welter Plate) 09.08.1883 (Brighton)
SUPERBA (Astley Stakes) 10.08.1883 (Lewes)
SIRIUS (Southdown Club Open Welter Plate) 10.08.1883 (Lewes)
MR S SAVAGE'S BF (Windmill Welter Plate) 10.08.1883 (Lewes)
REPRIEVE (Great South of England Breeders 2-Year-Old Stakes) 10.08.1883
    (Lewes)
FAILLIE (Town Plate Handicap) 11.08.1883 (Lewes)
BREST (Priory Stakes) 11.08.1883 (Lewes)
BELLE LURETTE (Kingston Welter Handicap Plate) 14.08.1883 (Kempton
    Park)
ALBAN (August Handicap) 14.08.1883 (Kempton Park)
GALVANIC (Kempton Park Midweight Handicap Plate) 14.08.1883
    (Kempton Park)
LORD SIDMOUTH (Hampton Selling Welter Handicap Plate) 15.08.1883
    (Kempton Park)
ALCALDE (Sunbury Midweight Handicap Plate) 15.08.1883 (Kempton Park)
BEDOUIN (Park Plate) 16.08.1883 (Windsor)
THE DUKE (Castle Weight Handicap) 16.08.1883 (Windsor)

FANTAIL (Round Tower Plate) 17.08.1883 (Windsor)
CYLINDER (Bray Cup) 17.08.1883 (Windsor)
SAUCY (Windsor August Handicap) 17.08.1883 (Windsor)
RAMSBURY (Zetland Stakes) 21.08.1883 (York)
CLOCHETTE (Badminton Plate) 21.08.1883 (York)
BRITOMARTIS (Yorkshire Oaks) 21.08.1883 (York)
FLEMINGTON (Rous Stakes) 22.08.1883 (York)
JUVENTUS (Gimcrack Stakes) 23.08.1883 (York)
HEDGEHOG (Flying 2-Year-Old Plate) 28.08.1883 (Warwick)
PLAY ACTOR (Warwick Welter Cup Handicap) 29.08.1883 (Warwick)
BARFLEUR (Alcester 2-Year-Old Plate) 29.08.1883 (Warwick)
GARETH (Her Majesty's Plate) 29.08.1883 (Warwick)
ORACLE (Elvaston Castle Selling Plate) 31.08.1883 (Derby)
LACEMAN (Hartington Plate) 31.08.1883 (Derby)
KINCARDINE (Harrington Plate) 31.08.1883 (Derby)
ALCALDE (Belper Plate) 01.09.1883 (Derby)
ST SIMON (Devonshire Nursery Plate) 01.09.1883 (Derby)
BEDOUIN (Sandown Nursery Stakes Handicap) 04.09.1883 (Sandown Park)
INCENDIARY (St Leger Trial Plate) 05.09.1883 (Sandown Park)
FRENCH GREY (Olympian Welter Handicap) 05.09.1883 (Sandown Park)
MAID OF ORLEANS (Billesdon Coplow Selling Plate) 06.09.1883 (Leicester)
LACEMAN (Quorn Plate Handicap) 07.09.1883 (Leicester)
SUPERBA (Champagne Stakes) 11.09.1883 (Doncaster)
WHITEBINE (Fitzwilliam Stakes) 11.09.1883 (Doncaster)
MAID OF ORLEANS (Stand Stakes) 11.09.1883 (Doncaster)
THE LAMBKIN (Rous Plate) 13.09.1883 (Doncaster)
CHAMELEON (Scurry Stakes) 14.09.1883 (Doncaster)
ST SIMON (Prince of Wales Nursery Plate Handicap) 14.09.1883
  (Doncaster)
BRITOMARTIS (Park Hill Stakes) 14.09.1883 (Doncaster)
TULLIA (Wentworth Post Produce Stakes) 14.09.1883 WO (Doncaster)
MOUNT PLEASANT (Newbold Revil Welter Plate) 18.09.1883 (Lichfield)
LADY JOHN (Harrington Welter Plate) 19.09.1883 (Lichfield)
TOWER AND SWORD (County Selling Welter Plate) 19.09.1883 (Lichfield)
GLEN RONALD (Thursday Selling Stakes) 20.09.1883 (Manchester)
MISS F (Autumn Cup) 20.09.1883 WO (Manchester)
PASSAIL (Selling Welter Plate) 20.09.1883 (Manchester)
LINNAEUS (De Trafford Welter Handicap) 20.09.1883 DH (Manchester)
CYLINDER (Heaton Park Plate) 21.09.1883 (Manchester)
CORMEILLE (Lancaster Nursery Handicap) 21.09.1883 (Manchester)
SOUVENIR (Selling Stakes) 21.09.1883 (Manchester)
WHIPPER IN (Manchester Autumn Handicap) 22.09.1883 (Manchester)
MISS C (Selling Nursery Handicap) 22.09.1883 (Manchester)
DUTCH OVEN (3rd Year 34th Triennial Produce Stakes) 25.09.1883
  (Newmarket)
SANDIWAY (Troy Stakes) 25.09.1883 (Newmarket)
WOODPECKER (Buckenham Stakes) 25.09.1883 (Newmarket)
GRANDMASTER (Puce Stakes) 26.09.1883 (Newmarket)
SAVOUR (Granby Stakes) 26.09.1883 (Newmarket)

HARVESTER (1st Year 36th Triennial Produce Stakes) 27.09.1883
  (Newmarket)
BUSYBODY (Rous Memorial) 28.09.1883 (Newmarket)
MOLYNEUX (Selling Plate) 28.09.1883 (Newmarket)
FANTAIL (Scurry Nursery Stakes Handicap) 28.09.1883 (Newmarket)
KINCARDINE (1st October 2-Year-Old Stakes) 28.09.1883 (Newmarket)
LORD ROSEBERY'S BC (Annesley Park Plate Handicap) 03.10.1883
  (Nottingham)
BLUESKIN (Thames Selling Welter Handicap Plate) 04.10.1883 (Kempton
  Park)
ISABEAU (Middlesex All Aged Selling Plate) 04.10.1883 (Kempton Park)
GEHEIMNISS (Kempton Park Cambridgeshire Trial Handicap) 05.10.1883
  (Kempton Park)
SPECTRUM (Claremont 2-Year-Old Selling Plate) 05.10.1883 (Kempton
  Park)
GREENORE (Walton Welter Handicap) 05.10.1883 (Kempton Park)
HARVESTER (Clearwell Stakes) 08.10.1883 (Newmarket)
FANTAIL (Stand Nursery Handicap) 09.10.1883 (Newmarket)
BUSYBODY (Middle Park Plate) 10.10.1883 (Newmarket)
BALLOON (Renewal of Bretby Stakes) 11.10.1883 WO (Newmarket)
ST MEDARD (Maiden Plate) 11.10.1883 (Newmarket)
SWEETBREAD (Her Majesty's Plate) 11.10.1883 (Newmarket)
FAUGH A BALLAGH (The Whip) 12.10.1883 (Newmarket)
KEEL ROW (3rd Welter Handicap) 12.10.1883 (Newmarket)
LEOVILLE (Watford Welter Plate Handicap) 16.10.1883 (Four Oaks Park)
CHAMELEON (Edgbaston Selling Plate) 16.10.1883 (Four Oaks Park)
LACEMAN (Alexandra Cup Handicap) 17.10.1883 (Four Oaks Park)
INCENDIARY (Park Selling Stakes) 19.10.1883 (Sandown Park)
GEHEIMNISS (Trial Stakes) 22.10.1883 (Newmarket)
NAUTILUS (A Plate/3-Year-Olds) 23.10.1883 WO (Newmarket)
CLOCHETTE (Home Bred Post Produce Stakes) 23.10.1883 (Newmarket)
LORD STRATHNAIRN (Home Bred Sweepstakes) 24.10.1883 (Newmarket)
ST SIMON (Bretby Stakes Course) 24.10.1883 (Newmarket)
SANDIWAY (Coffee Room Handicap) 25.10.1883 (Newmarket)
FAST AND LOOSE (Selling Stakes) 25.10.1883 (Newmarket)
FANTAIL (Bretby Nursery Handicap Plate) 25.10.1883 (Newmarket)
NAUTILUS (Selling Plate) 26.10.1883 (Newmarket)
KELPIE (2-Year-Old Selling Plate) 26.10.1883 (Newmarket)
AILSA CRAIG (Juvenile Selling Stakes) 30.10.1883 (Brighton)
POLARIS (Sussex Welter Handicap Plate) 30.10.1883 (Brighton)
PASSAIC (2 Mile Selling Welter Plate) 30.10.1883 (Brighton)
MADRID (Mile Selling Stakes) 31.10.1883 (Brighton)
RAMSBURY (Selling Welter Handicap) 31.10.1883 (Brighton)
SIMNEL (Ashcombe Handicap) 01.11.1883 (Lewes)
CARMEN (Tuesday Plate) 06.11.1883 (Liverpool)
PIBROCH (Palatine Nursery Handicap) 08.11.1883 (Liverpool)
AILSA CRAIG (Borough Members Plate) 13.11.1883 (Shrewsbury)
KEEL ROW (Grendon Welter Handicap) 14.11.1883 (Shrewsbury)
FORAGER (County Members Plate) 14.11.1883 (Shrewsbury)

FRIAR RUSH (Column Welter Handicap) 14.11.1883 (Shrewsbury)
ROUND SHOT (Doveridge Selling Plate) 15.11.1883 (Derby)
RHINELAND (Town Plate) 19.11.1883 (Warwick)
DIAMOND (Grendon Nursery Handicap Plate) 20.11.1883 (Warwick)
LEOVILLE (Emscote Plate) 20.11.1883 (Warwick)
ROUT (Warwick Autumn Welter Cup) 21.11.1883 (Warwick)
SOUTHAMPTON (Flying Welter Handicap) 22.11.1883 (Manchester)
MAID OF ORLEANS (Thursday Selling Stakes) 22.11.1883 (Manchester)
ROUND SHOT (Cuerden Cup) 23.11.1883 (Manchester)
FRENEY (Stand Selling Handicap Plate) 24.11.1883 (Manchester)

1884   MISS F (Northern Welter Plate Handicap) 24.03.1884 (Lincoln)
FLETA (Castle Selling Plate) 25.03.1884 (Lincoln)
ROUND SHOT (Prince's Park Plate) 27.03.1884 (Liverpool)
CORMEILLE (Union Jack Stakes) 27.03.1884 WO (Liverpool)
DEEPDALE (Crosby Plate Handicap) 28.03.1884 WO (Liverpool)
FLETA (Formby Plate) 29.03.1884 (Liverpool)
MATE (Buccleugh Welter Cup Handicap) 01.04.1884 (Northampton)
RAMSBURY (Whittlebury Cup) 01.04.1884 (Northampton)
CHARTIST (Wakefield Lawn Stakes) 01.04.1884 (Northampton)
LIZZIE (Her Majesty's Plate) 01.04.1884 (Northampton)
FRIAR RUSH (St Liz Welter Handicap) 02.04.1884 (Northampton)
VACILLATION (Ascott Plate) 02.04.1884 DH (Northampton)
LYRIC (Portland Plate Handicap) 08.04.1884 (Nottingham)
LOWLAND DUKE (Welbeck Selling Plate) 08.04.1884 (Nottingham)
LOWLAND DUKE (Sunbury Cup) 14.04.1884 WO (Kempton Park)
WHIPPER IN (Kempton Park Eastern Handicap) 14.04.1884 (Kempton Park)
SIR REGINALD (Selling Plate) 15.04.1884 (Kempton Park)
SPLENDOR (Bretby Plate Handicap) 16.04.1884 (Kempton Park)
WHIPPER IN (Brabaham Stakes) 17.04.1884 (Newmarket)
SIR REGINALD (Selling Plate) 18.04.1884 (Newmarket)
RAMSBURY (Banstead Stakes) 22.04.1884 (Epsom)
NOVITIATE (Maiden Plate) 22.04.1884 (Epsom)
MATE (Welter Handicap Plate) 23.04.1884 (Epsom)
VACILLATION (Hyde Park Plate) 23.04.1884 (Epsom)
SUNSHINE (Selling Welter Handicap) 23.04.1884 (Epsom)
JOVIAL (High Weight Selling Handicap) 24.04.1884 (Thirsk)
LAVEROCK (6th Great Yorkshire Foal Stakes) 24.04.1884 (Thirsk)
SOUTHAMPTON (Princess of Wales Free Handicap) 26.04.1884 (Sandown
    Park)
THE LAMBKIN (Esher Stakes Handicap) 26.04.1884 (Sandown Park)
ARCHIDUC (Poule D'Essai) 27.04.1884 (France)
LOWLAND DUKE (Selling Plate/100 Guinea) 29.04.1884 (France)
GLIMMER (Maiden Plate) 29.04.1884 (France)
WHIPPER IN (Prince of Wales Stakes) 29.04.1884 (France)
RICOCHET (Selling Plate) 30.04.1884 (France)
INSIGNIA (1st Spring 2-Year-Old Stakes) 01.05.1884 (France)
LAVEROCK (Stud Produce Stakes) 01.05.1884 (France)
FAUGH A BALLAGH (2 Horse Race) 01.05.1884 (France)

CLONMEL (2-Year-Old Selling Stakes) 02.05.1884 (France)
GRANDEE (Grosvenor Trial Stakes) 06.05.1884 (Chester)
HERALD (Belgrave Welter Cup Handicap) 06.05.1884 (Chester)
DONATELLO (Stamford 2-Year-Old Plate) 06.05.1884 (Chester)
HEDGEHOG (Wilton Stakes) 07.05.1884 (Chester)
DONATELLO (Badminton 2-Year-Old Plate) 07.05.1884 (Chester)
WHIPPER IN (Combermere Handicap) 07.05.1884 (Chester)
PELERINE (Dee Stand Cup Handicap) 07.05.1884 (Chester)
MARMORA (May Selling Stakes) 08.05.1884 (Kempton Park)
HEDGEHOG (Roodee Selling Welter Handicap Plate) 08.05.1884 (Kempton
     Park)
GEHEIMNISS (Westminster Cup) 09.05.1884 (Kempton Park)
CHERRY (Kempton Park Grand Prize) 09.05.1884 (Kempton Park)
NECROMANCER (Kempton Park Great Breeders Produce Stakes)
     10.05.1884 (Kempton Park)
HENTLAND (Fulwell Stakes) 10.05.1884 (Kempton Park)
DRAKENSBERG (Richmond Midweight Handicap Plate) 10.05.1884
     (Kempton Park)
SIR REGINALD (Selling All Aged Welter Plate) 13.05.1884 (Newmarket)
MEARNS (Sweepstakes) 13.05.1884 (Newmarket)
KEIR (Newmarket Spring Handicap) 13.05.1884 (Newmarket)
HELICON (Selling Plate) 14.05.1884 (Newmarket)
TAME LOWERCINTH (Selling Plate) 14.05.1884 (Newmarket)
INSIGNIA (2-Year-Old Stakes) 14.05.1884 (Newmarket)
MARMORA (Selling Stakes) 15.05.1884 (Newmarket)
HERALD (Beaufort Handicap Plate) 20.05.1884 (Bath)
DUCKLING (Worcester Selling Welter Plate) 21.05.1884 (Bath)
PANIC (Wheathampstead Stakes) 23.05.1884 (Harpenden)
WESTWOOD (St Georges Plate) 24.05.1884 (Windsor)
LOWLAND DUKE (May Cup) 24.05.1884 WO (Windsor)
THE GENERAL (Public Sale Stakes) 24.05.1884 (Windsor)
SHY (Juvenile Selling Stakes) 24.05.1884 (Windsor)
HILDA II (Dorney Selling Stakes) 24.05.1884 (Windsor)
ROSY MORN (Woodcote Stakes) 27.05.1884 (Epsom)
FRENCH GREY (Ashtead Stakes) 27.05.1884 (Epsom)
GRECIAN BRIDE (Stanley Stakes) 28.05.1884 (Epsom)
CHERRY (Epsom Grand Prize) 29.05.1884 (Epsom)
THEBAIS (Royal Stakes) 29.05.1884 (Epsom)
MACALPINE (Glasgow Plate Handicap) 30.05.1884 (Epsom)
SHRIVENHAM (Anglesey 2-Year-Old Plate) 02.06.1884 (Four Oaks Park)
REDCLYFFE (Corinthian Welter Handicap Plate) 02.06.1884 (Four Oaks Park)
LOVELY (Phillips Handicap) 03.06.1884 (Manchester)
LOWLAND DUKE (June Cup) 03.06.1884 (Manchester)
ENERGY (Salford Borough Handicap) 03.06.1884 (Manchester)
RENNY (Hartington Plate) 03.06.1884 (Manchester)
RAMSBURY (Tuesday Selling Stakes) 03.06.1884 (Manchester)
NAUTILUS (Duchy Welter Handicap) 04.06.1884 (Manchester)
SIR REGINALD (Stand Cup) 05.06.1884 WO (Manchester)
POSTE RESTANTE (Stamford Welter Handicap) 05.06.1884 (Manchester)

MR R CREST'S BC (Thursday Selling 2-Year-Old Stakes) 05.06.1884
    (Manchester)
NAUTILUS (Lambton Handicap Plate) 05.06.1884 (Manchester)
SIR REGINALD (Summer Plate) 06.06.1884 (Manchester)
FLORENCE (De Trafford Welter Cup) 06.06.1884 (Manchester)
THEBAIS (County Palatine Stakes) 06.06.1884 (Manchester)
LUMINARY (1st Year/27th Ascot Biennial Stakes) 10.06.1884 (Ascot)
SANDIWAY (Coronation Stakes) 11.06.1884 (Ascot)
CAMBUSMORE (St James' Stakes) 12.06.1884 (Ascot)
GEHEIMNISS (All Aged Stakes) 12.06.1884 (Ascot)
MELTON (New Stakes) 12.06.1884 (Ascot)
GEHEIMNISS (Queens Stakes Plate) 13.06.1884 (Ascot)
FLORENCE (Ascot High Welter Plate) 13.06.1884 (Ascot)
ENERGY (Wokingham Stakes) 13.06.1884 (Ascot)
CORRIE ROY (Alexandra Plate) 13.06.1884 (Ascot)
TAME LOWERCINTH (2-Year-Old Selling Stakes) 17.06.1884 (Windsor)
PELERINE (Manor Stakes) 17.06.1884 (Windsor)
ZADIG (Windsor Handicap) 18.06.1884 (Windsor)
VACILLATION (Athens Plate) 18.06.1884 (Windsor)
JOVIAL (Bretby Selling Plate) 19.06.1884 (Derby)
LONGMYND (Foston Selling Plate) 19.06.1884 (Derby)
DUKE OF ALBANY (Mile Selling Plate Handicap) 20.06.1884 (Derby)
MENEVIA (Rangemore Plate) 20.06.1884 (Derby)
LONGMYND (Glossop Park Selling Plate) 20.06.1884 (Derby)
NAUTILUS (Needwood Plate Handicap) 20.06.1884 (Derby)
COCK ROBIN (Champagne Stakes) 24.06.1884 (Bibury Club)
HURRY (Bibury Club Sale Stakes) 24.06.1884 (Bibury Club)
KING'S BOUNTY (Home Bred Sweepstakes) 24.06.1884 (Bibury Club)
LORD STRATHNAIRN (Scurry Welter Handicap) 24.06.1884 (Bibury Club)
MATCH GIRL (Bibury Club Home Bred Foal Stakes) 24.06.1884 WO (Bibury
    Club)
GEHEIMNISS (Stockbridge Cup) 25.06.1884 (Stockbridge)
FAREWELL (Mottisfont Stakes) 25.06.1884 (Stockbridge)
LORD STRATHNAIRN (Wallop Plate Handicap) 26.06.1884 (Stockbridge)
WHITE NUN (Troy Stakes) 26.06.1884 (Stockbridge)
LORD ROSSMORE'S CHF (Penton All Aged Welter Plate) 26.06.1884
    (Stockbridge)
LUMINARY (Hurstbourne Stakes) 26.06.1884 (Stockbridge)
THE GENERAL (9th 2-Year-Old Sale Stakes) 02.07.1884 (Newmarket)
WHIPPER IN (Beaufort Stakes) 02.07.1884 (Newmarket)
HERITAGE (Midsummer Stakes) 02.07.1884 (Newmarket)
GEHEIMNISS (July Cup) 02.07.1884 WO (Newmarket)
GEHEIMNISS (Bunbury Stakes) 03.07.1884 WO (Newmarket)
EXILE II (Sweepstakes) 03.07.1884 (Newmarket)
THEMISTO (Selling Stakes) 03.07.1884 (Newmarket)
ROSIE (July Handicap) 03.07.1884 (Newmarket)
WOODPECKER (Selling Plate) 04.07.1884 (Newmarket)
MEARNS (Mersey Stakes) 08.07.1884 (Liverpool)
PEBBLE (Lancaster Welter Handicap) 08.07.1884 (Liverpool)

PEBBLE (Preston Welter Handicap) 09.07.1884 (Liverpool)
CHERRY (Knowsley Dinner Stakes) 09.07.1884 WO (Liverpool)
GLIMMER (Southport Plate) 09.07.1884 (Liverpool)
BLACK DIAMOND (All Aged Plate) 09.07.1884 (Liverpool)
TAME LOWERCINTH (Blackpool 2-Year-Old Plate) 10.07.1884 (Liverpool)
MR CHOLMLEY'S BH (Birkenhead Cup) 10.07.1884 (Liverpool)
HAMBLEDON (2-Year-Old Plate) 11.07.1884 (Manchester)
NECROMANCER (Irwell Plate) 11.07.1884 (Manchester)
PRINCESS EULALIE (2-Year-Old Selling Stakes) 12.07.1884 (Manchester)
FRIAR RUSH (July Handicap) 12.07.1884 (Manchester)
NECROMANCER (July Plate) 12.07.1884 (Manchester)
PHRYNE (Stewards Selling Plate) 15.07.1884 (Winchester)
MACALPINE (Summer Cup) 17.07.1884 (Kempton Park)
LADY BEATRICE (Royal 2-Year-Old Plate) 17.07.1884 (Kempton Park)
CRITERION (Halliford Welter Handicap Plate) 18.07.1884 (Kempton Park)
EDITH (Queen Elizabeth Stakes) 18.07.1884 (Kempton Park)
DEAN SWIFT (Oatlands Park Handicap Stakes) 19.07.1884 (Kempton Park)
MR J GRETTON'S BRC (Twickenham 2-Year-Old Selling Stakes) 19.07.1884
	(Kempton Park)
LACEMAN (Surbiton Handicap) 22.07.1884 (Sandown Park)
ASIL (Arabian Stakes) 23.07.1884 (Sandown Park)
HERALD (Royal Stakes Handicap) 23.07.1884 (Sandown Park)
BOULEVARD (Bradgate Park Plate Handicap) 24.07.1884 (Leicester)
TAME LOWERCINTH (Belvoir Castle Plate) 25.07.1884 (Leicester)
HARVESTER (Gratwicke Stakes) 29.07.1884 (Goodwood)
ROSY MORN (Richmond Stakes) 29.07.1884 (Goodwood)
LANGWELL (Maiden Stakes) 30.07.1884 (Goodwood)
GEHEIMNISS (Lennox Stakes) 30.07.1884 (Goodwood)
GEHEIMNISS (Singleton Stakes) 31.07.1884 WO (Goodwood)
DUKE OF RICHMOND (Racing Stakes) 31.07.1884 (Goodwood)
CAN'T (Selling Stakes/5 Sovereign) 31.07.1884 (Goodwood)
SANDIWAY (Nassau Stakes) 01.08.1884 (Goodwood)
ENERGY (Chichester Stakes Handicap) 01.08.1884 (Goodwood)
LUMINARY (Molecomb Stakes) 01.08.1884 (Goodwood)
FAST AND LOOSE (March Stakes) 01.08.1884 (Goodwood)
LOWLAND DUKE (Bristol Plate Handicap) 05.08.1884 (Brighton)
PEARL DIVER (Maiden Plate) 05.08.1884 (Brighton)
GAYTHORN (Juvenile Stakes) 05.08.1884 (Brighton)
GAYTHORN (Brookside Plate) 06.08.1884 (Brighton)
RAMSBURY (Ovingdean Welter Handicap) 06.08.1884 (Brighton)
BRAG (Stewards Cup Handicap) 07.08.1884 (Brighton)
CRASH (Selling Welter Plate) 07.08.1884 (Brighton)
FLORENCE (Her Majesty's Plate) 08.08.1884 (Brighton)
LADY BEATRICE (Kempton Park International Breeders 2-Year-Old Stakes)
	12.08.1884 (Kempton Park)
CYMBAL (Boveney Plate) 14.08.1884 (Windsor)
SIR PLUME (Juvenile Plate) 22.08.1884 (Warwick)
CLOCHETTE (Yorkshire Oaks) 26.08.1884 (York)
MATE (Lonsdale Plate) 26.08.1884 (York)

SEAMORE (One Mile Race) 26.08.1884 (York)
VERONA (Falmouth Plate) 27.08.1884 (York)
NECROMANCER (Harrington Plate) 05.09.1884 (Derby)
PEARL DIVER (Elvaston Nursery Handicap Plate) 06.09.1884 (Derby)
NAUTILUS (Belper Plate) 06.09.1884 DH (Derby)
LANGWELL (Champagne Stakes) 09.09.1884 (Doncaster)
ALBERT MELVILLE (Clumber Plate) 09.09.1884 (Doncaster)
THEBAIS (Cleveland Handicap) 10.09.1884 (Doncaster)
THE WREKIN (Bradgate Park Stakes) 10.09.1884 (Doncaster)
EXILE II (Milton Stakes) 10.09.1884 (Doncaster)
SIREN (Staffordshire Stakes Handicap) 16.09.1884 (Lichfield)
JENNY (Grendon Juvenile Plate) 16.09.1884 (Lichfield)
STOCKHOLM (Her Majesty's Plate) 17.09.1884 (Lichfield)
ROSE NOBLE (Harrington Welter Plate) 17.09.1884 (Lichfield)
RAMSBURY (Autumn Cup) 18.09.1884 (Manchester)
MIDDLETHORPE (Oldham Welter Handicap) 19.09.1884 (Manchester)
MR J GRETTON'S BC (Lancaster Nursery Handicap) 19.09.1884
    (Manchester)
EN JACME (Selling Nursery Handicap) 20.09.1884 (Manchester)
WHIPPER IN (September Handicap) 20.09.1884 (Manchester)
CAMBUSMORE (6th Great Foal Stakes) 23.09.1884 (Manchester)
ENERGY (Great Eastern Railway Handicap) 24.09.1884 (Newmarket)
MACALPINE (Selling Plate) 24.09.1884 (Newmarket)
MEARNS (1st October 2-Year-Old Plate) 24.09.1884 (Newmarket)
CAMBUSMORE (2nd Year 36th Triennial Produce Stakes) 24.09.1884
    (Newmarket)
MACALPINE (10 Sovereign Selling Stakes) 25.09.1884 (Newmarket)
XARIFA (Northern Welter Plate Handicap) 30.09.1884 (Nottingham)
THEBAIS (Her Majesty's Plate) 01.10.1884 (Nottingham)
SCOTCH PEARL (Friar Tuck Selling Plate) 01.10.1884 DH (Nottingham)
FRENCH GREY (Thames Selling Welter Stakes) 02.10.1884 (Kempton Park)
SPEC (Claremont 2-Year-Old Selling Plate) 03.10.1884 (Kempton Park)
LANGWELL (Clearwell Stakes) 06.10.1884 (Newmarket)
BARRISTER (100 Sovereign Plate) 06.10.1884 WO (Newmarket)
GRECIAN BRIDE (Post Sweepstakes) 06.10.1884 (Newmarket)
SOLITUDE (100 Guinea Maiden Plate) 06.10.1884 (Newmarket)
ZAGAZIG (October Post Produce Stakes) 06.10.1884 (Newmarket)
CAMBUSMORE (Royal Stakes) 07.10.1884 (Newmarket)
MELTON (Middle Park Plate) 08.10.1884 (Newmarket)
DUKE OF RICHMOND (Select Stakes) 08.10.1884 (Newmarket)
THEBAIS (Her Majesty's Plate) 09.10.1884 (Newmarket) (Newmarket)
SANDIWAY (Newmarket Oaks) 09.10.1884 (Newmarket)
WHEATSHEAF (Renewal of Bretby Stakes) 09.10.1884 (Newmarket)
ENERGY (7th Great Challenge Stakes) 10.10.1884 (Newmarket)
HERMITAGE (Newmarket Derby) 10.10.1884 (Newmarket)
LEEDS (Alexandra Cup Handicap) 16.10.1884 DH (Four Oaks Park)
TOMBOY (Harrington Welter Handicap) 16.10.1884 (Four Oaks Park)
MELTON (Criterion Stakes) 20.10.1884 (Newmarket)
TOASTMASTER (20 Sovereign Trial Stakes) 20.10.1884 DH (Newmarket)

EXILE II (100 Guinea Plate) 21.10.1884 (Newmarket)
VILLAGE BOY (50 Sovereign Match) 21.10.1884 (Newmarket)
HOUSEWIFE (Home Bred Post Produce Stakes) 21.10.1884 (Newmarket)
PARADOX (Dewhurst Plate) 22.10.1884 (Newmarket)
ALBERT MELVILLE (Ditch Mile Handicap) 22.10.1884 (Newmarket)
EXILE II (Selling Plate) 23.10.1884 (Newmarket)
MEARNS (Cheveley Stakes) 23.10.1884 (Newmarket)
DUKE OF RICHMOND (All Aged Stakes) 24.10.1884 WO (Newmarket)
BEILBY (2-Year-Old Selling Plate) 24.10.1884 (Newmarket)
CANZONI (Selling Plate) 24.10.1884 (Newmarket)
PEARL DIVER (Brighton Nursery Handicap Plate) 28.10.1884 (Brighton)
PIBROCH (Ovingdean Stakes) 28.10.1884 (Brighton)
KIRK O'FIELD (Bevendean Selling Nursery Handicap) 29.10.1884 (Brighton)
MODRED (Brighton Free Welter Handicap Plate) 29.10.1884 (Brighton)
SIMNEL (Ashcombe Handicap) 30.10.1884 (Lewes)
LADY BEATRICE (Liverpool Nursery Plate Handicap) 05.11.1884 (Lewes)
CAN'T (Palatine Nursery Handicap) 06.11.1884 (Liverpool)
THEBAIS (Liverpool Autumn Cup Handicap) 06.11.1884 (Liverpool)

1885   ROUND SHOT (Prince Park Plate) 26.03.1885 (Liverpool)
THE BARD (Molyneux Stakes) 26.03.1885 (Liverpool)
BH (Lancastrian Plate) 28.03.1885 (Liverpool)
SIR BEUBEN (Her Majesty's Plate) 28.03.1885 (Liverpool)
PEBBLE (Crosby Plate/Handicap) 28.03.1885 (Liverpool)
ARBACES (Portland Plate) 31.03.1885 (Nottingham)
ANTLER (Nottingham Spring Handicap) 31.03.1885 (Nottingham)
POSTE RESTANTE (Robin Hood Cup Handicap) 01.04.1885 (Nottingham)
MACALPINE (Sunbury Cup) 06.04.1885 (Kempton Park)
GREENORE (Pytchley Plate)14.04.1885 (Northampton)
MATE (St Liz Welter Handicap) 14.04.1885 (Northampton)
THE BARD (Althorp Park Stakes) 14.04.1885 (Northampton)
MATE (Buccleugh Welter Cup) 15.04.1885 (Northampton)
THE BARD (Ascott Plate) 15.04.1885 (Northampton)
ECLAT (Kelmarsh Plate) 15.04.1885 (Northampton)
CAPITOLINA (Fawsley Park Plate Welter Handicap)15.04.1885
    (Northampton)
CASTRUM (Selling Plate/100 Guinea) 22.04.1885 (Newmarket)
LORD BYRON (Selling Plate/100 Guinea) 22.04.1885 (Newmarket)
ESTERLING (Craven Stakes) 23.04.1885 (Newmarket)
STRATHBLANE (Bretby Plate) 24.04.1885 (Newmarket)
GOGGLES (Riddlesdown Plate) 28.04.1885 (Epsom)
MACALPINE (Banstead Stakes) 28.04.1885 (Epsom)
THE BARD (Westminster Stakes) 29.04.1885 (Epsom)
TITBIT (Juvenile Selling Stakes) 29.04.1885 (Epsom)
THE BARD (Hyde Park Plate) 29.04.1885 (Epsom)
MACALPINE (Tadworth Stakes) 29.04.1885 (Epsom)
NESSCLIFF (Trial Plate) 30.04.1885 (Sandown Park)
THE BARD (Sandown Park Plate) 30.04.1885 (Sandown Park)
FLUCTUATION (Juvenile Selling Stakes) 30.04.1885 (Sandown Park)

LISBON (Walton 2-Year-Old Race) 01.05.1885 (Sandown Park)
EXPLOIT (Selling Plate) 06.05.1885 (Newmarket)
LORGNETTE (2-Year-Old Plate) 06.05.1885 (Newmarket)
PARADOX (2000 Guinea Stakes) 06.05.1885 (Newmarket)
NAUTILUS (2nd Welter Handicap Plate) 06.05.1885 (Newmarket)
ALBERT MELVILLE (Rous Course) 08.05.1885 (Newmarket)
EXPLOIT (2-Year-Old Selling Stakes) 08.05.1885 (Newmarket)
ALBERT VICTOR (Newmarket Stakes) 08.05.1885 WO (Newmarket)
CYMBALARIA (Grosvenor Trial Stakes) 12.05.1885 (Chester)
ELIAS (Cestrian Selling Welter Handicap) 12.05.1885 (Chester)
KENDAL (Mostyn 2-Year-Old Plate) 12.05.1885 (Chester)
BROCKEN (Wynnstay Handicap) 12.05.1885 (Chester)
CANNY SCOTT (Badminton Plate) 13.05.1885 (Chester)
MIZPAH (Dee Stand Cup) 13.05.1885 (Chester)
MIZPAH (Roodee Selling Welter Handicap Plate) 14.05.1885 (Chester)
METAL (Dee Stakes) 14.05.1885 (Chester)
WHIPPER IN (Great Cheshire Handicap Stakes) 14.05.1885 (Chester)
SARABAND (Kempton Park Great Biennial Produce Stakes) 16.05.1885
    (Kempton Park)
THE BARD (Spring 2-Year-Old Stakes) 19.05.1885 (Newmarket)
PHILOSOPHY (Sweepstake Stakes/25 Sovereign) 19.05.1885 (Newmarket)
NAUTILUS (Newmarket Spring Handicap Plate) 19.05.1885 (Newmarket)
DEAN SWIFT (Selling Plate) 20.05.1885 (Newmarket)
MELTON (Payne Stakes) 20.05.1885 (Newmarket)
WEDDING DAY (Selling Plate) 20.05.1885 DH (Newmarket)
EXPLOIT (2-Year-Old Selling Stakes) 22.05.1885 (Royal Windsor)
THE BARD (St George's Plate) 22.05.1885 (Royal Windsor)
ALCADE (May Cup) 22.05.1885 (Royal Windsor)
THE ECHO (Winkfield Welter Handicap) 22.05.1885 (Royal Windsor)
PIBROCH (Oscott Plate) 25.05.1885 (Four Oaks Park)
ARBACES (May Five Furlong Handicap) 25.05.1885 (Four Oaks Park)
TOMBOY (Corinthian Welter Handicap) 25.05.1885 (Four Oaks Park)
BALMORAL (Maiden Plate) 26.05.1885 (Manchester)
MCMAHON (Salford Borough Handicap) 26.05.1885 (Manchester)
HUNGARIAN (Tuesday Selling Plate) 26.05.1885 (Manchester)
THE BARD (Hartington Plate) 26.05.1885 (Manchester)
WEST END (Wednesday Selling 2-Year-Old Plate) 27.05.1885 (Manchester)
ARCHER (May Plate) 27.05.1885 (Manchester)
THE BARD (John O'Gaunt Plate) 27.05.1885 (Manchester)
EREBUS (Friday 2-Year-Old Plate) 29.05.1885 (Manchester)
NESSCLIFF (Worsley Handicap) 29.05.1885 (Manchester)
PHILOSOPHY (Whitsuntide Plate) 29.05.1885 (Manchester)
GAY HERMIT (Woodcote Stakes) 02.06.1885 (Epsom)
MATE (2 Horse Race) 02.06.1885 (Epsom)
MELTON (106 Renewal/Derby Stakes) 03.06.1885 (Epsom)
MISFORTUNE (Epsom Manor Stakes) 03.06.1885 (Epsom)
NESSCLIFF (Headley Stakes) 03.06.1885 (Epsom)
STAFFA (Horton Stakes) 04.06.1885 (Epsom)
MAGLONA (Mickleham Stakes) 04.06.1885 (Epsom)

BIRD OF FREEDOM (Epsom Grand Prize) 04.06.1885 (Epsom)
PHILOSOPHY (Acorn Stakes) 05.06.1885 (Epsom)
LONELY (Oaks) 05.06.1885 (Epsom)
LACEMAN (Glasgow Plate) 05.06.1885 (Epsom)
THEBAIS (Epsom Cup) 05.06.1885 WO Epsom)
MENEVIA (Shorts Plate) 09.06.1885 (Windsor)
EXNING (Berkshire Plate) 09.06.1885 (Windsor)
CLASH (Manor Selling Welter Handicap) 10.06.1885 (Windsor)
PELERINE (Wadham Stakes) 12.06.1885 (Sandown Park)
MCMAHON (Wellington Stakes) 12.06.1885 (Sandown Park)
ENERGY (Craven Stakes) 13.06.1885 (Sandown Park)
PARADOX (Grand Prix De Paris) 14.06.1885 (Paris)
STORM LIGHT (Maiden Plate) 16.06.1885 (Ascot)
THEBAIS (Gold Vase) 16.06.1885 (Ascot)
SARABAND (1st Year/28th Ascot Biennial Stakes) 16.06.1885 (Ascot)
FANTAIL (2nd Year/22nd New Biennial Stakes) 18.06.1885 (Ascot)
ENERGY (All Aged Stakes) 18.06.1885 (Ascot)
CHATTER (4th Oaks 2-Year-Old Plate) 23.06.1885 (Four Oaks Park)
EXPLOIT (Beaudesert 2-Year-Old Plate) 24.06.1885 (Four Oaks Park)
B SHARP (Aston 2-Year-Old Stakes) 24.06.1885 (Four Oaks Park)
WHITE NUN (Ditton Park Plate) 25.06.1885 (Windsor)
PELERINE (Thursday Selling Plate) 25.06.1885 (Windsor)
FORBIDDEN FRUIT (Athens Plate) 26.06.1885 (Windsor)
LEEDS (June Handicap) 26.06.1885 (Windsor)
WHITE NUN (Temple Welter Handicap Plate) 26.06.1885 (Windsor)
PHILOSOPHY (Midsummer Plate) 26.06.1885 (Windsor)
PRETTY FACE (Grosvenor Stakes) 30.06.1885 (Bibury Club)
VOLTA (Champion Stakes) 30.06.1885 (Bibury Club)
GAY HERMIT (1st Year/27th Stockbridge Biennial Stakes) 30.06.1885
     (Bibury Club)
LISBON (Zetland Biennial Post Stakes) 01.07.1885 (Stockbridge)
HERMITAGE (Beaufort Half Plate) 01.07.1885 (Stockbridge)
KENDAL (Stockbridge Post Sweepstake) 02.07.1885 (Stockbridge)
PEPPER AND SALT (2nd Year/26th Biennial) 02.07.1885 (Stockbridge)
SARABAND (Hurstbourne Stakes) 02.07.1885 (Stockbridge)
MR CHOLMLEY'S BH (Old Mile) 02.07.1885 (Stockbridge)
ENERGY (July Cup) 08.07.1885 (Newmarket)
GAY HERMIT (Exeter Stakes) 08.07.1885 (Newmarket)
ROSARY (Selling Stakes) 09.07.1885 (Newmarket)
STORM LIGHT (Princess of Wales Cup) 10.07.1885 (Newmarket)
CANZONI (Selling Plate/100 Guineas) 10.07.1885 (Newmarket)
ORCHID (Knowsley Dinner Stakes) 15.07.1885 (Liverpool)
ARCHER (Lancaster Welter Handicap) 15.07.1885 (Liverpool)
LORGNETTE (Gerald Plate) 15.07.1885 (Liverpool)
THE BARD (Mersey Stakes) 15.07.1885 WO (Liverpool)
CYMBALARIA (Walton Selling Plate) 16.07.1885 (Kempton Park)
EDINBURGH (Teddington 2-Year-Old Selling Plate) 16.07.1885 (Kempton
     Park)
CAPITOLINA (Summer Cup) 16.07.1885 (Kempton Park)

THE BARD (July Plate) 17.07.1885 (Manchester)
STAFFA (Flying Handicap) 17.07.1885 (Manchester)
PHILOSOPHY (Summer 2-Year-Old Plate) 18.07.1885 (Manchester)
CHAPEL ROYAL (Selling Welter Handicap Plate) 18.07.1885 (Manchester)
ALARIC (Irwell Plate) 18.07.1885 (Manchester)
FORNAX (Harborough Selling Plate) 21.07.1885 (Leicester)
FORNAX (Mile Selling Plate) 21.07.1885 (Leicester)
WEDDING DAY (Sutton Juvenile Selling Plate) 21.07.1885 (Leicester)
LACEMAN (Bradgate Park Plate) 21.07.1885 (Leicester)
STE ALVERE (Knighton Plate) 21.07.1885 (Leicester)
ENERGY (Dingley Plate) 22.07.1885 (Leicester)
TOMBOLA (Tapton Welter Plate) 22.07.1885 (Leicester)
PANIC (Braunston Selling Handicap Plate) 23.07.1885 (Leicester)
PELERINE (Cobham All Aged Selling Plate) 24.07.1885 (Sandown Park)
FOOTLIGHT (Ditton Selling Plate) 24.07.1885 (Sandown Park)
THE BARD (Great Kingston 2-Year-Old Race) 24.07.1885 (Sandown Park)
ALBERT MELVILLE (Drayton High Weight) 28.07.1885 (Goodwood)
KENDAL (Ham Produce Stakes) 28.07.1885 (Goodwood)
METAL (Gratwicke Produce Stakes) 28.07.1885 (Goodwood)
ENERGY (Lennox Stakes) 28.07.1885 (Goodwood)
PHILOSOPHY (Lavant Stakes) 28.07.1885 (Goodwood)
PARADOX (Sussex Stakes) 28.07.1885 (Goodwood)
SARABAND (Rous Memorial Stakes) 30.07.1885 (Goodwood)
ARMINDA (Nassau Stakes) 31.07.1885 (Goodwood)
PRETTY FACE (Nursery Stakes) 31.07.1885 (Goodwood)
CRAIG NORTH (Juvenile Stakes) 04.08.1885 (Brighton)
FAIR LILLIAN (Patcham Stakes) 04.08.1885 (Brighton)
PELERINE (Pavilion Stakes) 05.08.1885 (Brighton)
PRINCE IO (Rottingdean Plate) 05.08.1885 (Brighton)
MODRED (Bevendean Handicap) 06.08.1885 (Brighton)
SARABAND (Astley Stakes) 07.08.1885 (Lewes)
SULPHUR (De Warrenne Handicap) 07.08.1885 (Lewes)
CONSIGNE (Priory Stakes) 08.08.1885 (Lewes)
NEWTON (Her Majesty's Plate) 08.08.1885 (Lewes)
VOLTA (Kempton Park International Breeders 2-Year-Old) 11.08.1885
    (Kempton Park)
MYSTIC (Middlesex 2-Year-Old Selling Stakes) 11.08.1885 (Kempton Park)
TIB (Selling 2-Year-Old Stakes) 13.08.1885 (Windsor)
PRETTY FACE (Clewer Plate) 14.08.1885 (Windsor)
STE ALVERE (Round Tower Plate) 14.08.1885 (Windsor)
STE ALVERE (Hardwicke Stakes) 19.08.1885 (Stockton)
KENDAL (Great Breeders Convivial Produce Stakes) 25.08.1885 (York)
YULE TIDE (Badminton Plate) 25.08.1885 (York)
MATE (Great Ebor Handicap) 26.08.1885 (York)
GAY HERMIT (Prince of Wales Stakes) 26.08.1885 (York)
PINK MAY (Shipley Hall Selling Plate) 04.09.1885 (Derby)
AYLESFORD (Northern Plate) 04.09.1885 (Derby)
THE CHILD (Highfield Selling Plate) 04.09.1885 (Derby)
RAMSBURY (Selling High Plate) 05.09.1885 (Derby)

PRINCE IO (Haddon Hall Nursery Handicap) 05.09.1885 (Derby)
DROITWICH (Town Stakes) 08.09.1885 (Warwick)
MYSTIC (Castle Bromwich 2-Year-Old Plate) 10.09.1885 (Four Oaks Park)
TREASON (Flying 2-Year-Old Plate) 12.09.1885 (Sandown Park)
MINTING (Champion Stakes) 15.09.1885 (Doncaster)
MELTON (St Leger Stakes) 16.09.1885 (Doncaster)
THE BARD (Tattersall Sale Stakes) 16.09.1885 (Doncaster)
ALBERT MELVILLE (Milton Stakes) 16.09.1885 (Doncaster)
KENDAL (Municipal Post Stakes) 16.09.1885 WO (Doncaster)
MODRED (Wharncliffe Stakes) 17.09.1885 (Doncaster)
PRINCE IO (Rous Plate) 17.09.1885 (Doncaster)
CAMBUSMORE (Beaudesert Welter Plate) 22.09.1885 (Lichfield)
ETOLIAN (Selling Nursery Plate) 23.09.1885 (Lichfield)
GLASGOW (Thursday Selling Stakes) 24.09.1885 (Manchester)
DROITWICH (Heaton Park Stakes) 25.09.1885 (Manchester)
GLASGOW (Mile Selling Plate) 26.09.1885 (Manchester)
PORTHOS (Selling Nursery Handicap Plate) 26.09.1885 (Manchester)
BLAZON (Selling Plate/100 Guinea) 29.09.1885 (Newmarket)
MELTON (7th Great Foal Stakes) 29.09.1885 (Newmarket)
CAMBUSMORE (3rd Year/36th Triennial Produce Stakes) 29.09.1885
    (Newmarket)
GAY HERMIT (Hopeful Stakes) 29.09.1885 DH (Newmarket)
ARMIDA (2nd Year/37th Triennial Produce Stakes) 30.09.1885 (Newmarket)
ANDRASSY (Sweepstake/10 Sovereign) 30.09.1885 (Newmarket)
FANTAIL (Selling Stakes) 01.10.1885 (Newmarket)
MINTING (1st Year/38th Triennial Produce Stakes) 01.10.1885 (Newmarket)
NAUTILUS (Sweepstake/10 Sovereign) 02.10.1885 (Newmarket)
THE PRINCE (Moulton Handicap Sweepstake) 02.10.1885 (Newmarket)
LITTLE WENLOCK (1st October 2-Year-Old Stakes) 02.10.1885 (Newmarket)
JOYOUS (Selling Plate) 02.10.1885 (Newmarket)
MR J PICKERSGILL'S CG (Gopsal Plate) 08.10.1885 (Leicester)
FAIR LILLIAN (Thursday Selling Plate) 08.10.1885 (Leicester)
ESCAPADE (Village Nursery Handicap) 08.10.1885 (Leicester)
CAPITOLINA (Berkshire Selling Handicap Plate) 09.10.1885 (Leicester)
NAUTILUS (Club Welter Handicap) 09.10.1885 (Leicester)
CYLINDER (Mile Selling Plate) 09.10.1885 (Leicester)
PRINCE IO (Kempton Park Cambridgeshire Nursery) 10.10.1885 (Kempton
    Park)
ENERGY (Trial Plate) 12.10.1885 (Newmarket)
NAUTILUS (1st Welter Handicap) 12.10.1885 (Newmarket)
OBERON (October Post Produce Stakes) 12.10.1885 WO (Newmarket)
ORMONDE (Post Sweepstake/200 Sovereign) 14.10.1885 (Newmarket)
MINTING (Middle Park Plate) 14.10.1885 (Newmarket)
PARADOX (Champion Stakes) 15.10.1885 (Newmarket)
LE CASSIER (Juvenile Handicap) 16.10.1885 (Newmarket)
MERRY DUKE (October Maiden Plate) 20.10.1885 (Four Oaks Park)
DUCHESS OF ALBANY (Juvenile Plate) 20.10.1885 (Four Oaks Park)
TIBICEN (Shenstone Selling Plate) 20.10.1885 (Four Oaks Park)
TIBICEN (Tamworth Plate) 21.10.1885 (Four Oaks Park)

ORMONDE (Criterion Stakes) 26.10.1885 (Newmarket)
CLANDIAN (Maiden Plate/100 Guinea) 27.10.1885 (Newmarket)
LUMINARY (3-Year-Old Handicap Sweepstake) 27.10.1885 (Newmarket)
MODRED (A Plate/3-Year-Olds) 27.10.1885 WO (Newmarket)
THE COB (Home Bred Sweepstake) 28.10.1885 (Newmarket)
SANDPIPER (A Plate/100 Guinea) 28.10.1885 (Newmarket)
ORMONDE (Dewhurst Plate) 28.10.1885 (Newmarket)
TRAVANCORE (Troy Stakes) 29.10.1885 (Newmarket)
PARADOX (Free Handicap) 29.10.1885 (Newmarket)
ENERGY (All Aged Stakes) 30.10.1885 (Newmarket)
LOVED ONE (Home Bred Stakes) 30.10.1885 (Newmarket)
DONALD (2 Mile Selling Welter Plate) 03.11.1885 (Brighton)
SONGSTRESS (Castle Plate) 05.11.1885 (Lewes)
SONGSTRESS (Houndean Plate) 06.11.1885 (Lewes)
CHARTREUSE (Juvenile Plate) 06.11.1885 (Lewes)
LYDDINGTON (Lewes Nursery Handicap) 06.11.1885 (Lewes)
GAIETY (Westmoreland Welter Plate) 10.11.1885 (Liverpool)
COLLEEN BAWN II (Alt Welter Handicap) 11.11.1885 (Liverpool)
DRAKENSBERG (Wavertree Welter Handicap) 12.11.1885 (Liverpool)
ANDRASSY (Osmaston Nursery Handicap) 18.11.1885 (Derby)
PRINCE IO (Free 2-Year-Old Plate) 20.11.1885 (Northampton)
ARNCLIFFE (Hartwell Welter Handicap) 20.11.1885 (Northampton)
ARBACES (Blisworth Plate) 21.11.1885 (Northampton)
KNIGHT OF BURGHLEY (Town Plate) 23.11.1885 (Warwick)
STOURHEAD (Midland County Handicap Plate) 24.11.1885 (Warwick)
MONTE ROSE (Budbrook Stakes) 24.11.1885 (Warwick)
GLYNDON (Banbury Selling Welter Plate) 25.11.1885 (Warwick)
MALLOW (Flying Welter Handicap) 26.11.1885 (Manchester)
SNOWDOUN (Maiden Plate) 27.11.1885 (Manchester)

1886   TIBICEN (Carholme Selling Plate) 22.03.1886 (Lincoln)
SULPHUR (Brocklesby Trial Plate Handicap) 23.03.1886 (Lincoln)
SILVERSMITH (Maiden Plate) 23.03.1886 (Lincoln)
GRANVILLE (Gautby Selling Plate) 24.03.1886 (Lincoln)
LADY'S MAID (Lancastrian Plate) 26.03.1886 WO (Liverpool)
BINDER (Excelsior Breeders Foal Stakes) 02.04.1886 (Leicester)
THE CARDINAL (Midland Selling Plate) 02.04.1886 (Leicester)
THE CARDINAL (Saturday Selling Plate) 03.04.1886 (Leicester)
KILT (Holiday Selling Plate) 03.04.1886 (Leicester)
VERITY (Hyde Park Plate) 07.04.1886 (Leicester)
MONKSHOOD (Juvenile Selling Plate) 08.04.1886 (Sandown Park)
NAUTILUS (Claygate Plate) 09.04.1886 (Sandown Park)
LADY'S MAID (Pall Mall Welter Handicap) 09.04.1886 (Sandown Park)
SEATON (Sweepstakes) 14.04.1886 (Newmarket)
KILT (Selling Plate/100 Guinea) 16.04.1886 (Newmarket)
SULPHUR (Bestwood Park/Plate Handicap) 21.04.1886 (Nottingham)
KILT (Elvaston Castle Selling Plate) 21.04.1886 (Nottingham)
CENTIME (2-Year-Old Selling Stakes) 24.04.1886 (Windsor)
QUICKSAND (2-Year-Old Plate) 28.04.1886 (Newmarket)

CLAUDIAN (A Selling Stakes) 29.04.1886 (Newmarket)
SLEEVE LINK (Stamford 2-Year-Old Plate) 04.05.1886 (Chester)
EN JACME (Cestrian Selling Welter Handicap Plate) 04.05.1886 (Chester)
SULPHUR (Wilton Stakes) 05.05.1886 (Chester)
GREENSHANK (Roodee Selling Welter Handicap Plate) 06.05.1886
    (Chester)
SULPHUR (Wynn Handicap Plate) 06.05.1886 (Chester)
LIBATION (Shepperton Selling Handicap Stakes) 07.05.1886 (Kempton
    Park)
MONKSHOOD (Sunbury 2-Year-Old Selling Plate) 08.05.1886 (Kempton
    Park)
REPPS (Wolsey Welter Handicap Plate) 08.05.1886 (Kempton Park)
EXNING (Visitor's Plate Handicap) 11.05.1886 (Newmarket)
LITTLECOTE (Sweepstakes) 11.05.1886 (Newmarket)
SCHERZO (Burwell Stakes) 11.05.1886 (Newmarket)
NAUTILUS (Selling Plate) 12.05.1886 (Newmarket)
EXNING (Flying Handicap) 12.05.1886 (Newmarket)
WOODLAND (St George's Place) 14.05.1886 (Windsor)
CHEVELEY (Wheathampstead Stakes) 21.05.1886 (Harpenden)
PETULANCE (Alexandra Stakes) 21.05.1886 (Harpenden)
ORMONDE (Derby Stakes) 26.05.1886 (Epsom)
CORINA (Free Handicap) 27.05.1886 (Epsom)
ROSY MORN (Walton Stakes) 28.05.1886 (Epsom)
LORD STRATHNAIRN (Chipstead Stakes) 28.05.1886 (Epsom)
COUNTERPANE (Maiden 2-Year-Old Plate) 04.06.1886 (Sandown Park)
CHEVELEY (Cobham Plate) 05.06.1886 (Sandown Park)
MINTING (Grand Prix De Paris) 06.06.1886 (Paris)
TOASTMASTER (Trial Stakes) 08.06.1886 (Ascot)
BIRD OF FREEDOM (Gold Vase) 08.06.1886 (Ascot)
SARABAND (2nd Year/28th Ascot Biennial Stakes) 09.06.1886 (Ascot)
WHITEFRIAR (All Aged Stakes) 10.06.1886 (Ascot)
ORMONDE (St James' Palace Stakes) 10.06.1886 (Ascot)
ST MIRIN (2nd Year/23rd New Biennial Stakes) 10.06.1886 (Ascot)
KINSKY (Ascot High Weight Plate Handicap) 11.06.1886 (Ascot)
CAMPBELL (Nevill Holt Handicap Plate) 15.06.1886 (Leicester)
BAGPIPE (Hathern Selling Plate) 15.06.1886 (Leicester)
HIPPOCREWE (Friar Welter Plate) 15.06.1886 (Leicester)
SHRIVENHAM (Humberston Welter Handicap Plate) 15.06.1886 (Leicester)
GALLANT (Derby Plate) 16.06.1886 (Manchester)
TOTTENHAM (Thursday Selling Plate) 17.06.1886 (Manchester)
SPOT (Champagne Stakes) 22.06.1886 (Bibury Club)
SHIMMER (The Grosvenor) 22.06.1886 (Bibury Club)
BAGPIPE (100 Sovereign Plate) 22.06.1886 (Bibury Club)
ST PIERRE (Budbury Cup Homebred Foal Stakes) 22.06.1886 (Bibury Club)
TIMOTHY (Stockbridge Post Sweepstake) 23.06.1886 (Stockbridge)
GAY HERMIT (2nd Year/27th Stockbridge Biennial Stakes) 24.06.1886
    (Stockbridge)
FLETA (All Aged Plate) 24.06.1886 (Stockbridge)
BIRD OF FREEDOM (Her Majesty's Plate) 24.06.1886 (Stockbridge)

HAZELWOOD (Chetwynd Plate) 02.07.1886 (Windsor)
NAUTILUS (A Trial) 06.07.1886 (Newmarket)
ENTERPRISE (July Stakes) 06.07.1886 (Newmarket)
ST MICHAEL (Midsummer Stakes) 07.07.1886 (Newmarket)
NAUTILUS (100 Guinea Plate) 07.07.1886 (Newmarket)
BAGPIPE (100 Guinea Selling Plate) 07.07.1886 (Newmarket)
MELTON (July Cup) 07.07.1886 (Newmarket)
MALVERN (Warrington Plate) 13.07.1886 (Liverpool)
THE BARD (St Georges Stakes) 13.07.1886 (Liverpool)
NAUTILUS (Liverpool Plate Handicap) 13.07.1886 (Liverpool)
MALVERN (Jolliffe Stakes) 14.07.1886 (Liverpool)
VERONIA (Blackpool 2-Year-Old Plate) 14.07.1886 (Liverpool)
SATIRIST (Tyro Free 2-Year-Old Plate) 16.07.1886 (Manchester)
STETCHFORD (Flying Handicap) 16.07.1886 (Manchester)
SALISBURY (Zetland Plate) 20.07.1886 (Leicester)
KILT (Birstall Selling Plate) 20.07.1886 (Leicester)
MELTON (Leicestershire Cup) 21.07.1886 (Leicester)
SONG BIRD (Belvoir Castle Plate) 21.07.1886 (Leicester)
NAUTILUS (Prince of Wales Cup) 22.07.1886 (Sandown Park)
WHITEFRIAR (Gratwicke Produce Stakes) 27.07.1886 (Goodwood)
FORBIDDEN FRUIT (March Stakes) 27.07.1886 (Goodwood)
ST MICHAEL (Drawingroom Stakes) 28.07.1886 (Goodwood)
FREEDOM (Molecomb Stakes) 30.07.1886 (Goodwood)
CAVALIER (Charlton Welter Handicap) 30.07.1886 (Goodwood)
CRAFTON (Marine Stakes) 03.08.1886 (Brighton)
THE BARON (Astley Stakes) 06.08.1886 (Lewes)
BAGPIPE (Castle Plate) 06.08.1886 (Lewes)
NAUTILUS (Hamsey Welter Handicap) 07.08.1886 (Lewes)
CAMBUSMORE (August Handicap) 10.08.1886 (Kempton Park)
STEEL (Middlesex 2-Year-Old Selling Stakes) 10.08.1886 (Kempton Park)
CAVALIER (Sunbury Midweight Handicap Stakes) 11.08.1886 (Kempton
    Park)
BF (Selling 2-Year-Old Stakes) 12.08.1886 (Windsor)
PELERINE (Hamilton Plate) 12.08.1886 (Windsor)
KINFAUNS (Castle Welter Handicap) 12.08.1886 (Windsor)
QUEEN BEE (Round Tower Plate) 13.08.1886 (Windsor)
KILWARLINE (Wynhard Plate) 17.08.1886 (Stockton)
HORTON (Harewood Stakes) 18.08.1886 (Stockton)
WHITTINGTON (Great Breeders Convivial Produce Stakes) 24.08.1886
    (York)
PHILOSOPHY (Yorkshire Oaks) 24.08.1886 (York)
LOUGHGLYNN (Badminton Plate) 24.08.1886 (York)
GAY HERMIT (2nd Year/30th North England Biennial Stakes) 24.08.1886
    (York)
ST MICHAEL (Ebor St Leger) 25.08.1886 (York)
HORTON (Rous Stakes) 25.08.1886 (York)
GAY HERMIT (Great Yorkshire Stakes) 26.08.1886 (York)
HEDGE PRIEST (Kimbolton Welter Handicap) 31.08.1886 (Huntingdon)
MIGNON (Cambridge 2-Year-Old Stakes) 31.08.1886 (Huntingdon)

CANNY SCOTT (Fitzwilliam Selling Stakes) 31.08.1886 (Huntingdon)
CRAFTON (Peveril of the Peak Plate) 02.09.1886 (Derby)
KILWARLINE (Harrington Stakes) 03.09.1886 (Derby)
MR J GRETTON'S CHC (Friary Selling Plate) 03.09.1886 (Derby)
OLGA (Selling Nursery Handicap Plate) 04.09.1886 (Derby)
DRAKENSBERG (Moor Hall Plate) 06.09.1886 (Four Oaks Park)
DRAKENSBERG (Boswell Selling Plate) 07.09.1886 (Four Oaks Park)
FELTA (All Aged Selling Plate) 08.09.1886 (Warwick)
BC (Juvenile Plate) 09.09.1886 (Warwick)
JOHN BARLEYCORN (Warwick Welter Cup Handicap) 09.09.1886 (Warwick)
BG (Avon 2-Year-Old Plate) 09.09.1886 (Warwick)
EMSCOTE (Flying 2-Year-Old Plate) 10.09.1886 (Sandown Park)
CAVALIER (Milsbourne Plate) 10.09.1886 (Sandown Park)
DRAKENSBERG (All Aged Selling Plate) 10.09.1886 (Sandown Park)
ORMONDE (St Leger Stakes) 15.09.1886 (Doncaster)
PHIL (Tattersall Sales Stakes) 15.09.1886 (Doncaster)
ORISON (Municipal Post Stakes) 15.09.1886 (Doncaster)
GAY HERMIT (Zetland Stakes) 16.09.1886 (Doncaster)
QUEEN BEE (Juvenile Stakes) 16.09.1886 (Doncaster)
GERVAS (Selling Handicap Stakes/10 Sovereign) 16.09.1886 (Doncaster)
MERRY DUCHESS (Handicap Sweepstakes/10 Sovereign) 17.09.1886
      (Doncaster)
LOURDES (Wentworth Post Produce Stakes) 17.09.1886 (Doncaster)
DEVA (Grendon Juvenile Plate) 21.09.1886 (Lichfield)
KILT (City Plate) 21.09.1886 (Lichfield)
RECLUSE (Beaudesert Welter Plate Handicap) 21.09.1886 (Lichfield)
KILT (Barclay Welter Plate) 22.09.1886 (Lichfield)
FLORENTINE (September Plate) 24.09.1886 (Manchester)
CORUNNA (September Handicap Plate) 25.09.1886 (Manchester)
STOURWICK (Welter Handicap Plate) 25.09.1886 (Manchester)
COBBLER (Selling Plate) 28.09.1886 (Newmarket)
ORMONDE (8th Great Foal Stakes) 28.09.1886 (Newmarket)
TIMOTHY (Buckenham Post Produce Stakes) 28.09.1886 (Newmarket)
ESTEREL (1st Foal Produce Stakes) 29.09.1886 WO (Newmarket)
GAY HERMIT (2nd Year 38th Triennial Produce Stakes) 29.09.1886
      (Newmarket)
BLANCHARD (Sweepstakes/10 Sovereign) 29.09.1886 (Newmarket)
ST MIRIN (Grand Duke Michael Stakes) 30.09.1886 (Newmarket)
CANDLEMAS (2nd Year/1st Zetland Biennial) 30.09.1886 (Newmarket)
ORMONDE (St Leger Stakes) 01.10.1886 WO (Newmarket)
WYMESWOLD (Mapperley Hall Selling) 04.10.1886 (Nottingham)
DEVA (Bookham Plate) 06.10.1886 (Epsom)
WYMESWOLD (Halford Selling Plate) 08.10.1886 (Leicester)
JOHN BARLEYCORN (1st Welter Handicap) 11.10.1886 (Newmarket)
OBERON (Select Plate) 13.10.1886 (Newmarket)
GAY HERMIT (High Welter Handicap) 13.10.1886 (Newmarket)
LUCERNE (Sweepstakes/10 Sovereign) 14.10.1886 (Newmarket)
ORMONDE (Champion Stakes) 14.10.1886 (Newmarket)
EASTERN EMPEROR (Challenge Whip) 15.10.1886 (Newmarket)

ST MIRIN (Newmarket Derby) 15.10.1886 (Newmarket)
MONSIEUR DE PARIS (Sweepstake/15 Sovereign) 15.10.1886 (Newmarket)
CAMBUSMORE (Lord Lieutenant's Plate) 21.10.1886 (The Curragh, Ireland)
ISIDORE (Sweepstakes/5 Sovereign) 21.10.1886 (The Curragh, Ireland)
DAN DANCER (Maiden 2-Year-Old) 22.10.1886 (Sandown Park)
MEZZOTINT (Selling Plate/100 Guinea) 25.10.1886 (Newmarket)
CALLER HERRIN (Criterion Stakes) 25.10.1886 (Newmarket)
LADY PEGGY (Maiden Plate) 26.10.1886 (Newmarket)
LIVINGSTONE (Home Bred Sweepstakes) 27.10.1886 (Newmarket)
ORMONDE (Free Handicap Sweepstakes) 28.10.1886 (Newmarket)
KINGFISHER (Bretby Nursery Handicap) 28.10.1886 (Newmarket)
ORMONDE (Private Sweepstake) 29.10.1886 WO (Newmarket)
CARRASCO (Old Nursery Stakes) 29.10.1886 (Newmarket)
BELISARIUS (Home Bred Foal Stakes) 29.10.1886 (Newmarket)
ST GATIEN (Jockey Club Cup) 29.10.1886 (Newmarket)
BLANCHARD (Houghton Stakes) 29.10.1886 (Newmarket)

Bibliography

Astley, Sir John Dugdale, *Fifty Years of My Life in the World of Sport at Home and Abroad*, Hurst And Blackett Ltd, London, 1893

Batchelor, Denzil, *The Turf of Old*, H F & G Witherby Ltd, London, 1951

Beatty, Laura, *Lillie Langtry: Manners, Masks & Morals*, Chatto & Windus, London, 1999

Bedford, Julian, *The World Atlas of Horseracing*, The Hamlyn Publishing Group Ltd, London, 1989

Bland, Ernest, *Flat Racing Since 1900*, Andrew Dakers Ltd, London, 1950

Browne, T H, *A History of the English Turf*, Virtue & Co Ltd, 1931

Burnet, Alastair (with Tim Neligan), *The Derby: The Official Book of the World's Greatest Race*, Michael O'Mara Books, London, 1993

Chetwynd, Sir George, *Racing Reminiscences and Experience of the Turf*, Longmans, Green & Co, London, 1891

Cowles, Virginia, *The Rothschild Family Fortune*, Weidenfeld & Nicolson, London, 1973

Custance, Henry, *Riding Recollections and Turf Stories*, Edward Arnold, London, 1894

D'Arcy, Fergus A, *Horses, Lords and Racing Men*, The Turf Club, County Kildare, Ireland, 1991

Ennor, George and Mooney, Bill, *The World Encyclopaedia of Horse Racing: An Illustrated Guide to Flat Racing and Steeplechasing*, Carlton Books, London, 2001

Fairfax-Blakeborough, J, *Melton Memories and l'Anson Triumphs*, Truslove & Bray Ltd, London, 1925

Green, Reg, *The Grand National: Aintree's Official Illustrated History*, Virgin, London, 2000

Green, Reg, *The History of the Grand National: A Race Apart*, Hodder & Stoughton, London, 1983

Green, Reg, *National Heroes: The Aintree Legend* (revised and updated), Mainstream Publishing, 1997

Gross, Richard, *Psychology: The Science of Mind and Behaviour*, 3rd edn., Hodder & Stoughton, London, 1996

Harthausen, August Von, ed., *Studies on the Interior of Russia*, University of Chicago Press, London, 1972

Humphris, Edith M, *The Life of Fred Archer*, Hutchinson, London, 1923
Humphris, Edith M, *The Life of Mathew Dawson*, H F & G Witherby, London, 1928
Huxley, Gervais, *Victorian Duke: The Life of Hugh Lupus Grosvenor, First Duke of Westminster*, Oxford University Press, London, 1967
Laird, Dorothy, *Royal Ascot: A History of Royal Ascot From Its Founding By Queen Anne to the Present Time*, Hodder & Stoughton, London, 1976
Lambton, The Honourable George, *Men and Horses I Have Known*, Thornton Butterworth, London, 1924
Lane, Charles, *Harry Hall's Classic Winners*, J A Allen & Co Ltd, London, 1990
Longrigg, Roger, *The History of Horseracing*, Macmillan, London, 1972
March, Russell, *The Jockeys of Vanity Fair*, March Publications, Kent, 1985
Massie, Suzanne, *The Beauty of Old Russia: Land of the Firebird*, Hamish Hamilton, London, 1980
Matthews, Peter and Morrison, Ian, *The Guinness Encyclopaedia of International Sports Records and Results*, 2nd edn., Guinness Publishing Ltd, London, 1990
Mortimer, Roger, *Flat Racing in Britain Since 1939*, George Allen & Unwin Ltd, London, 1979
Mortimer, Roger, *The History of the Derby Stakes*, Cassell & Co Ltd, London, 1962
Mortimer, Roger, *The Jockey Club*, Cassell & Co Ltd, London, 1958
Mortimer, Roger, Onslow, Richard and Willet, Peter, *The Biographical Encyclopaedia of British Flat Racing*, Macdonald & Jane's Publishers Ltd, London, 1978
Mortimer, Roger and Willet, Peter, *More Great Racehorses of the World*, Michael Joseph Ltd, London, 1972
Oaksey, Lord John and Rodney, Bob, *A Racing Companion*, Lennard Books, London, 1992
Onslow, Richard, *Headquarters: A History of Newmarket and Its Racing*, Great Ouse Press, Cambridge, 1983
Onslow, Richard, *Royal Ascot*, The Crowood Press, Wiltshire, 1990
Onslow, Richard, *The Squire: George Alexander Baird, Gentleman Rider 1861–1893*, Harrap, London, 1980
Pakenham, Simon, *Cheltenham*, Macmillan, London, 1971
Plumptre, George, *Back Page Racing: A Century of Newspaper Coverage*, Queen Anne Press: A Division of MacDonald & Co (Publishers) Ltd, London, 1971
Portland, 6th Duke of, *Memories of Racing and Hunting*, Faber and Faber, London, 1935
Richards, Sir Gordon, *My Story*, Hodder & Stoughton, London, 1955
Rothschild, Mrs James de, *The Rothschilds at Waddesdon Manor*, Collins, London, 1979
Rous, Admiral Henry John, *The Laws and Practice of Horseracing*, Baily & Co, London, 1850

Ryder, T A, *A Portrait of Gloucestershire*, 3rd edn., Robert Hale & Co, London, 1972

Smyley, Patricia, *Encyclopaedia of Steeplechasing*, Robert Hale & Co, London, 1979

Tanner, Michael and Cranham, Gerry, *Great Jockeys of the Flat: A Celebration of Two Centuries of Jockeyship*, Guinness Publishing Ltd, London, 1992

Thompson, Laura, *Newmarket: From James I to the Present Day*, Virgin Publishing Ltd, London, 2000

Tyrrel, John, *Running Racing: The Jockey Club Years Since 1750*, Quiller Press Ltd, London, 1997

Waterman, Jack, *The Sporting Life: The Punter's Friend: A Guide to Racing and Betting*, 2nd edn., Queen Anne Press: A Division of Lennard Associates Ltd, Harpenden, Herts., 1996

Weatherby, J E and J P, *The Racing Calendar: Races Past*, London, 1870–1886

Welcome, John, *Fred Archer: A Complete Study*, Lambourn, London, 1990

Welcome, John, *Fred Archer: His Life and Times*, Faber and Faber, London, 1967

White, John, *The Racegoer's Encyclopaedia*, HarperCollins, London, 1996

Who Was Who: A Companion to 'Who's Who' Containing the Biographies of Those Who Died During the Period 1897–1916, A & C Black, 1920

Wilson, Julian, *The Great Racehorses*, Little Brown & Co, London, 1998

Wynn Jones, Michael, *The Derby: A Celebration of the World's Most Famous Horse Race*, Croom Helm Ltd, London, 1979